AWESOME GAME CREATION

NO PROGRAMMING REQUIRED

SECOND EDITION

CD-ROM INCLUDED

i

AWESOME GAME CREATION

NO PROGRAMMING REQUIRED

SECOND EDITION

LUKE AHEARN

CLAYTON CROOKS II

CHARLES RIVER MEDIA, INC.

Hingham, Massachusetts

Publisher: David F. Pallai
Production: Publishers' Design and Production Services, Inc.
Cover Design: The Printed Image

CHARLES RIVER MEDIA, INC.
10 Downer Avenue
Hingham, Massachusetts 02043
781-740-0400
781-740-8816 (FAX)
info@charlesriver.com
www.charlesriver.com

This book is printed on acid-free paper.

Luke Ahearn and Clayton Crooks. *Awesome Game Creation: No Programming Required, Second Edition.*
ISBN: 1-58450-223-1

All brand names and product names mentioned in this book are trademarks or
service marks of their respective companies. Any omission or misuse (of any kind)
of service marks or trademarks should not be regarded as intent to infringe on the
property of others. The publisher recognizes and respects all marks used by companies, manufacturers, and developers as a means to distinguish their products.
Library of Congress Cataloging-in-Publication Data

Ahearn, Luke.
    Awesome game creation : no programming required / Luke Ahearn and
Clayton Crooks.— 2nd ed.
        p. cm.
    ISBN 1-58450-223-1 (pbk. : acid-free paper)
    1. Computer games—Programming.   I. Crooks, Clayton E.   II. Title.
QA76.76.C672 A422 2002

                    2002004543

Printed in the United States of America
03 7 6 5 4 3 2

CONTENTS

PREFACE

Developing games is undoubtedly one of the most rewarding and challenging aspects of computer science. And like most areas of computing, it is constantly evolving. While creating a game is a very attractive concept to aspiring developers, it is often very difficult for them to learn the intricacies of C/C++ and the advanced techniques required specifically for game development. In addition to the programming, there are also other areas that need to be mastered, including 2D graphics, 3D modeling, music, and sound effects.

With all of these requirements, would-be developers can often feel overwhelmed. That's where this book comes in. It introduces a series of tools designed to be used with absolutely no programming. With these tools, developers can focus their attention on putting a game together, instead of on programming. This turns the normally technical concept of game development into a more artistic process, and in doing so, makes game development available to anyone.

ACKNOWLEDGMENTS

There are many people who have been involved with the development of this book, and because of their hard work and dedication, you are now holding it. First, I'd like to thank everyone at Charles River Media, especially Dave Pallai, for the opportunity to write this book. I'd also like to thank all of the developers of the tools that are being used in this book. Their ingenuity has opened the game development door for everyone.

1 INTRODUCTION TO GAME DEVELOPMENT

Developing a computer game is a truly unique production, in which you combine a wide range of elements into what you hope will be an enjoyable experience for the end user. Games consist of a wide variety of components. For a new developer, this can seem overwhelming. In this chapter, we'll look at what you need to set up your own development studio. Later chapters will introduce you to the various components that make up a game project and will walk you through the creation of several complete games.

SETTING UP A GAME STUDIO

Before you can make anything, you need to have the proper equipment. While it may sound expensive, setting up a game development studio doesn't have to be. With Moore's Law continuing to hold true (the law states that the processing power of computers doubles every 18 months), the cost of computers continues to plummet. Everywhere you look, there are great deals for relatively powerful computers.

To go along with inexpensive computers, the variety of software designed for small game developers has greatly increased in the past couple of years. With these tools, you can now develop games without doing any programming.

When you are setting up your game studio, several factors help determine the type of equipment you need to have. Fortunately, you may already have the essentials of a game studio—a computer and this book. However, we will look more closely at how to determine if what you have is enough and the best way to determine what more you may need.

As an aspiring game developer, you have a wide range of computers from which to choose. Trying to determine which system you need can be a daunting task. One way to look at this problem is to compare it to the purchase of other items, such as an automobile. For instance, if you were driving six kids to school, driving in a road race, or driving into combat, what vehicle would you choose? Computers are similar to vehicles in this respect. While a minivan, a race car, and a jeep all have four wheels, they are all designed for very different purposes.

So the big question for you is, what will you be doing with your computer? This book will help you answer this question, by giving you a chance to try the different types of things you will have to do on your computer as a game developer. After you have worked a bit in the various applications and learned their specific requirements, as well as your needs as a developer, you will know what kind of system you need.

The first thing to consider while working on your current system is the system requirements for the applications you will be using or intend to use. These requirements are usually clearly stated on the box, in ads, and on the home pages of the product. The system requirements are usually broken down into Minimum and Recommended.

Warning! Usually, the Minimum System Requirements are just that—the bare minimum to run the application. A minimum system will usually not be the most comfortable or even the most usable system to run the application. Also, the minimum requirements do not take into account other applications that you may be running at the same time.

Let's say that the minimum RAM requirement for your art application is 16 MB. But as a game developer, you also need to run other applications at the same time, such as a level editor, game engine, word processor, and 3D application. Your system will be severely taxed and may run poorly, if at all. And the Minimum System Requirements usually do not take into account the files you will be working with. If you have experience with image editing applications such as Photoshop or Paint Shop Pro, you know that files can range from a few hundred kilobytes to over 50 megabytes, depending on what you're working on. While you can open and close applications that are not in use, this takes time (especially with slow, RAM-deficient machines) and will severely cut into your productivity and work flow.

Another area you should watch is the recommended amount of hard drive space for installing the application. This number includes only the application itself. It does not take into account the files you create with the application. So you also need to ensure that you have room for your files. The processor speed is another variable that you should look at, which again only includes the speed to run the application and does not take into account larger files.

System and Equipment

The equipment you will need to create a computer game depends on the type and scope of your project. The right setup can range from a very minimal investment to tens of thousands of dollars for the latest and most powerful computer and peripheral setup. To get started, you need to own a basic computer setup with a few important peripherals.

Computer

A computer is obviously a necessary item for game development. As previously mentioned, you can get many great deals these days for a minimal investment. Unless the requirements for your software indicate that you need a high-end system, a general-purpose, off-the-shelf system is sufficient.

When purchasing your system, you should take into account the work and applications you will run. The operating system is important (Windows 98 or above for the tools in this book). New systems usually ship with the latest version of the biggest OS on the market at the time. The minimal system today usually has a 17-inch monitor, lots of RAM (RAM stands for *Random Access Memory* and is measured in megabytes or MB—a slang term, *megs*, is also often used), and a fairly large hard drive. You should have no problem with an off-the-shelf system or a mail-order system from a reputable company.

 See the end of this chapter for tips on buying equipment.

Processor

The processor can often be very difficult to upgrade. With this in mind, you should try to buy as fast a system as you can afford. There are two main manufacturers of processors on the Windows side of things: Intel (Pentium®), and AMD (Athlon™). We won't get into a big discussion or try to decide which processor you should buy. You can simply assume that they are basically comparable. At this time, you should look to purchase a processor that is at least 1GHz. If you'd like a more detailed discussion on this topic, you should refer to the Charles River Media book *Building a PC*, which offers advice and a detailed description on these components.

One reason you should buy the fastest processor you can is that it's harder to upgrade the processor than to upgrade other components. Getting the fastest chip possible makes sense if you are purchasing a system for general work. It's even more important for you as a game developer—you'll be pushing your system harder than most other users and will have a need for the speed. But don't worry if your system isn't the latest and greatest. You can still design and develop games with a minimal system, as long as it can run the specific applications you are using.

RAM

Along with the fastest processor you can afford, you should get as much RAM as possible. The computer uses RAM as *temporary* storage for the applications that you run. When the system is turned off or the power goes out, the information that is in RAM is lost. Although RAM is cheap and very easy to upgrade, the prices are so low now that it's often a good idea to purchase a system that has a slightly slower processor, but more RAM. This results in overall better performance at less cost. RAM is definitely the most important thing you can have. You should consider a system with 256MB of RAM or more.

Graphic (Video) Cards and 3D Cards

Having a quality video or graphics card is becoming more important as time goes on. These cards allow images to appear on your monitor. A video card usually controls how big the image is on your screen, how much detail the image can have, and how many colors are displayed (in the next chapter, we will discuss the specific elements of an image).

Recently there has been a trend toward faster video cards that are hardware accelerated. Many applications only display simple pictures, but if you are interested in doing 3D-related games, it will make sense to look at buying one of these cards. Most new systems will have a hardware-accelerated card, but the type of card and the amount of graphics memory that it has will affect your performance. Two manufacturers are head and shoulders above the rest—NVIDIA® with its GeForce™ line of cards, and ATI with the Radeon™ line. Regardless of the type of card you get, a 3D card is specifically designed to take the tasks of 3D rendering away from the processor by handling textures, effects, and geometric calculations.

Other Peripherals

Other peripherals you will need are standard on most computers: a modem, a CD-ROM or DVD-ROM drive, and a sound card. If your system comes with a modem, it will most likely be a 56K modem, the fastest modem available on a standard dial-up connection. Your system will probably have a CD-ROM or DVD-ROM drive—you can simply choose the type that benefits you the most. For instance, you may have a need for an all-around solution for archiving your data or distributing your games. There are many options but the CD-RW (CD Rewriteable) drive, which can also be used as a CD-ROM, is very popular. The sound card allows sound output to be sent to a set of speakers. There are many manufacturers of sound cards, and many options for these cards. Again, you can choose a sound card that meets your requirements.

Last, there are several other peripherals you will want to consider if you have the extra funds.

Scanner

A scanner basically works like a copy machine. It converts your flat document or image into a digital image that can be manipulated in the computer, as described in the next chapter. This can be very useful for creating game art, Web sites, and logos, and for simply getting your picture on a Quake guy's face.

Digital Camera

The next item is a digital camera. Digital cameras work like a standard camera, but instead of using film, they produce digital images, like a scanner does. The major difference is that a scanner requires flat images that have already been created on paper, while you can use a digital camera to take a picture of anything.

Modem

As previously mentioned, most computers will come with a 56K modem. This is adequate for many uses, but if you are serious about downloading information or researching on the Web, you should try to get high-speed Internet access. The Internet is such an invaluable resource, especially to game developers, that paying for high-speed access is a worthwhile investment. Some of the large downloads you will be making are images, game demos, sound files, development tools, and animation files.

Backup Devices

The next item is rapidly becoming an affordable necessity. That's because the prices of recordable CD-ROM drives and media are now very low, and many systems now come with them as a standard item. There are two types of recordable drives: a CD-Recordable (CD-R) drive that can write to a given CD only once, and a CD-Rewriteable (CD-RW) drive that can write (and erase) the media many times. After you start creating content for your games, you will need a way to back them up. A CD-R or CD-RW drive is perfect for this. It is also a perfect way to deliver your materials to potential publishers when you are finished with a project. Instead of putting a project on 10 or 15 floppy disks, you can safely distribute it on a CD-R.

Besides CD-R or CD-RW drives, you have several other options for backing up and storing your content. There are drives like the standard 100 megabyte Zip® drive and the larger capacity 250 megabyte Zip drive. There are also various options for tape backup drives that can hold several gigabytes of data. A standard floppy disk holds only 1.44 MB of data, so you can quickly see the advantages of a high capacity drive.

Digitizers

Another interesting item is a Digitizer, which artists will like. These are pen-like devices that allow you to draw more naturally on the computer. They are far from a necessity, though, and are very expensive. The less expensive digitizers are good for recording signatures and for basic sketching, but they lack the fine control an artist needs.

Network

A network is another very important item. It allows multiple computers to communicate with each other. While this sounds like an expensive proposition and a complex undertaking, it is a very achievable goal. A good SOHO (Small Office Home Office) network system can be had for under $100. It comes in a kit with everything you need, dramatically extending your computing abilities. One benefit of a home network is being able to share peripherals and resources. You can have one scanner, printer, or other device on the network, and have it be available from multiple computers. This can be useful because most computers (especially older PCs) can only be connected to a limited number of devices. Also, having many devices installed on a system tends to slow down the system's boot up and response times. Having a network also lets you easily back up data on multiple PCs. During development of a project, having a network is almost essential, because multiple team members can simultaneously update code and resources.

Ethernet Network

Ethernet is the most common home-networking system and the easiest to hook multiple computers into. A typical system for two computers uses two cards, called Ethernet cards, and a special cable called a crossover cable. If you have three or more computers, you need what is called a hub. You plug all the computers into the hub, and it routes, or directs, the traffic. The software portion of a network can range from simply finding the other computers on the network and accessing the data on their drives, to setting up special software that operates peripherals and adds security, chatting, and other advanced functions.

Wireless Network

Another type of network is a wireless network, which allows you to share information between computers without physically connecting them. Although they have advantages, wireless networks tend to be more expensive, are susceptible to data corruption, and are limited in distance between computers.

Phone Wire Network

Some networks connect through phone wires, rather than through Ethernet cables or wireless connections. These are quickly becoming more prevalent for home users but are also susceptible to problems.

AC Wire Network

The last type of network is an AC wire network. It uses electrical wiring as the network wires. AC wire networks tend to be slower and prone to interference. They also have a security problem, because they use the transformer (the big thing on the telephone pole outside) as the common link for data traveling through your power lines. The transformer may be shared by twenty or more houses on the street, and it is possible for anyone with the same network system to pry into your computers.

A Good Chair and Desk

One last suggestion is to buy a good chair and desk. You will be sitting for long periods of time, so this will prove to be an invaluable investment.

Tips for Buying Equipment

Now that you have some ideas about the type of hardware you'll need to purchase, here are a few common sense ideas to keep in mind:

1. Use a Credit Card: You should use a credit card or find someone to do this for you, especially when buying online. With a credit card, you have the credit card company and the Fair Credit Billing Act behind you. This act allows you sixty days in which to report a billing error or to dispute a charge with a vendor.

2. Don't be Cheap: Avoid the so-called "budget" computers unless you *really* know what you are getting into. In some cases these systems may not include components that meet your needs (such as a larger hard drive and a quality monitor). Expect to pay about $1,500–$2,500 for a computer with all the fixins'. Depending on your experience, it may be a good idea to get an extended warranty, although many new systems have three-year warranties. (After three years, your system will probably be behind the times and need replacing.)

3. Protect Everything: Buy a recordable CD-ROM drive or a Zip drive. Try to back up data daily to a Zip drive (or to another computer on your network), and monthly to a CD-ROM. You can never be too safe. Also, buy a battery-operated surge protector or UPS (Uninterruptible Power Supply). For about a $100 you can get a UPS that will protect several components, including your modem and phone lines. The UPS will also allow you plenty of time to save your work and shut down your computer if the power goes out. You should also get a surge protector. Surge protectors are easy to use—you just plug them in and plug your computer into them. They will protect your computer from power spikes and shutdowns. A surge protector will actually blow a fuse or circuit if it gets hit by a surge of electricity from lightning or bad wiring. This keeps your computer's innards from being damaged. Of course, the best protection is to turn off your computer and unplug it during thunderstorms as a surge protector will not always protect your system. For further protection, you may wish to consider a UPS which is a type of battery that allows you the time to properly shut down your system if the electricity goes out.

4. Research: Above all, learn about computers for yourself. If possible, try the applications you expect to run on a few systems first. See how those systems handle massive graphic files and the huge levels found in many popular games. And remember, most people are very biased about their own systems, so be careful when you ask others for their opinions. No matter how many opinions you get, you'll need to make up your own mind.

CHAPTER REVIEW

In this chapter, we looked at the basic components that you will need to create a development studio. Once you have assembled your game development studio and have it up and running (whether it is an off-the-shelf special or the latest and greatest system money can buy), you will have made a huge step toward becoming a game developer. The next step is to learn the basic building blocks of a game. We'll start looking at those in the next chapter.

2

GRAPHICS: THE BASIC BUILDING BLOCKS OF A GAME

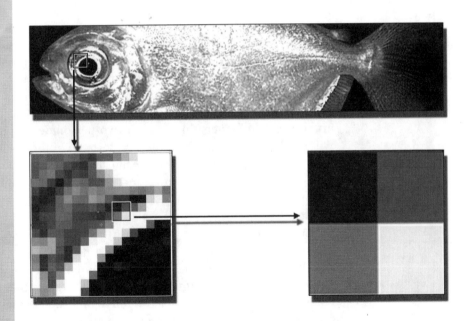

T o create games, you will need to learn, and perhaps even master, the fundamental elements that make up a game—sights, sounds, and interactivity. Although interactivity (the ability to interact with a computer to play a game) is important, the basics of this interactivity depend on the game type and on the application you are using to develop the game. We will learn more about interactivity in the tutorials later in the book, as we make several different types of games, using various tools. In this chapter, we will concern ourselves with the core building blocks that exist in virtually every game—the sights you see. (Chapter 3 will deal with the sounds).

This simple approach will help you break down and understand a game at its most fundamental level. You can apply this knowledge to many areas beyond game development as well, since it is the core of graphic design, Web layout, and almost all of interactive computing.

SIGHTS

When we talk about sights, we are obviously talking about what you see on the screen during gameplay. In any major production, from a Web site to a game, the layout of the screens and of the graphic images that are used to make them is very important. In a large development team, they are usually worked on by a number of people, including a designer, producer, art director, and others. In a one- or two-person development effort, you will need to wear several hats and perform all of these roles. Your 2D art assets (the images you use in your games) need to look good, and they also need to fit in with the audience, technology, and atmosphere for which you are designing. We'll talk about this again later when we look at marketing a game.

Creating the assets that you will use to make interface elements requires the use of many software tools and techniques. These assets are often sketched on paper or mocked up on the computer before they are created. Some of the tools you can use are 2D paint programs that work only with flat images, 3D programs that allow you to build and render objects that realistically recreate a 3D environment or object, and even digital photographs and scans. To create the images, you will need to have an understanding of the concepts of the images, and a grasp of the tools you will be using.

The 2D art assets you will create include, but are not limited to, the following:

- Menu screens. Look at the toolbar in your word processor, browser, or even your favorite game, and you will see art that was created by an artist.

- Credit screens. These screens often contain art such as logos, images, and even fonts or special letters unique to the product, people, and company they represent.
- Logos for companies, products, and services. Logos can be simple letters, 2D masterpieces, or fully rendered 3D scenes. Look around on the Web and you will see logos that range from clip art to actual pieces of art.
- User interfaces. These are broken down into background images, buttons, cursors, and other art objects that a user must click or interact with.
- In-game assets. These include the textures on the walls, the floors, and the characters. Even the 3D models and objects have 2D art applied to them.

Early computers did not display graphics. They were limited to alphanumeric characters, such as letters, punctuation marks, and numbers. Surprisingly, games were still made on these primitive machines. When computers started including graphics cards, games started their move towards the amazing graphics we see today. It can be argued that games have pushed the development of the computer as gamers demanded (and were willing to pay for) faster chips, better graphics cards, and better sound. But even as the technology advanced, it was common for the artist on any given project to primarily be a programmer. This was because it was still very difficult to get decent art into a computer format, and an understanding of technology was necessary to do so. Today, we can almost ignore the technology we are working with.

Let's look at the core technology that a computer artist deals with every day. In computer graphics today, there are two basic types of art: 2D and 3D. All 2D, or two-dimensional, art is a flat image with no depth. On the other hand, 3D art shows depth, as illustrated in Figure 2.1.

The three dimensions in 3D art are described in the Cartesian coordinate system, using X, Y, and Z coordinates. This may be one of the most surprising aspects of game development–you can actually use some of the math topics you learned in school! In fact, algebra, geometry and physics all play a role in game making. Simply stated, in the Cartesian coordinate system, X represents the distance along a horizontal line (or axis), Y represents the distance along a vertical line, and Z represents the distance backward and forward (see Figures 2.2, 2.3, and 2.4).

 Capitals (X,Y,Z) or lower case (x,y,z) are used interchangeably in the text.

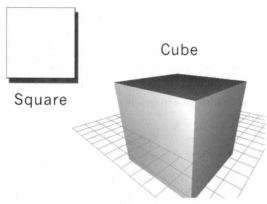

Cube

Square

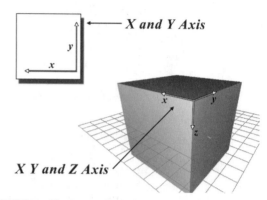

X and Y Axis

X Y and Z Axis

FIGURE 2.1 A square is 2D, while a cube is 3D.

FIGURE 2.2 The Cartesian coordinate system. The X axis, Y axis, and Z axis.

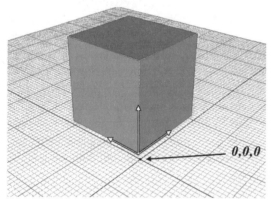

0,0,0

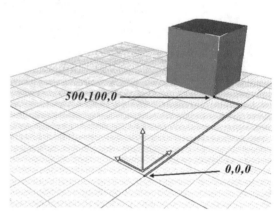

500,100,0

0,0,0

FIGURE 2.3 A cube and the xyz value of its location in space.

FIGURE 2.4 Another cube in a different xyz position.

Basic Elements of an Image

To properly understand 2D images, you must understand a few things about the basic elements that compose those images. These are covered below.

Pixel

We'll start with the most fundamental of fundamentals, the most basic element of an image—the pixel, or picture element. A pixel is a colored dot on the screen. A computer image is made up of these pixels arranged in rows and columns. See Figure 2.5 for an illustration of a pixel. No matter how big and fancy a computer image is or what has been done to it, it's all just a bunch of pixels.

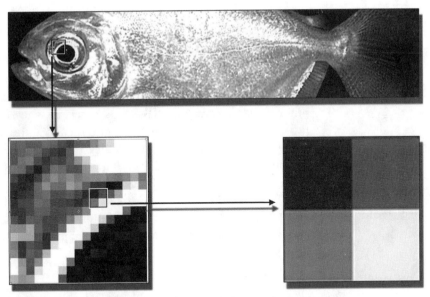

FIGURE 2.5   A pixel is the smallest unit of a computer image—simply colored dots.

Once an image has been created with a particular number of pixels, the maximum detail is set and cannot be increased. The image can be enlarged and the number of pixels can be increased by a mathematical process called interpolation, which is illustrated in Figures 2.6 and 2.7. But this does not increase the detail. It simply adds extra pixels to smooth the transition between the original pixels.

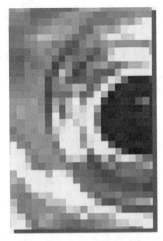

FIGURE 2.6   Here is an area of the fish image before enlarging.

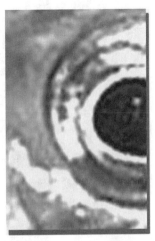

FIGURE 2.7   Here is the same area enlarged with pixels interpolated.

Resolution

Resolution is the number of pixels displayed (width × height) in an image. A typical computer monitor displays 75 to 90 dpi (dots per inch, which refers to the number of pixels per inch in an image). A printed image usually needs to be 300 dpi or more to look good in print. Often, when computer people receive an image from a person who is used to working in print, they are surprised when the one-inch icon they requested takes up a HUGE number of bytes, but the image is still one inch by one inch. The reason for the enormous size is that a print person is used to using, and saving images at a higher dpi. Some of the most common screen resolutions are 320 × 200 pixels, 640 × 480, 800 × 600, 1024 × 768, 1152 × 864, and 1280 × 1024. An 800 × 600 resolution means that the screen is 800 pixels wide (horizontal) and 600 pixels high (vertical). See the examples in Figures 2.8, 2.9, and 2.10.

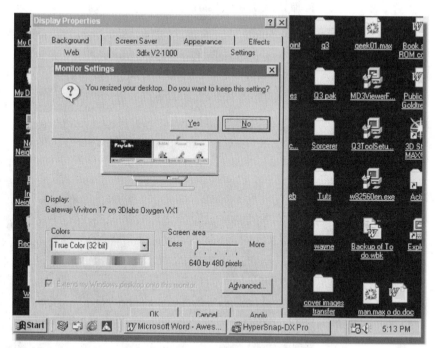

FIGURE 2.8 Here is the Windows Desktop at 640 × 480 dots per inch.

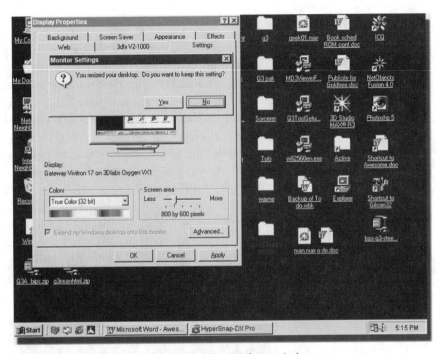

FIGURE 2.9   Here is the Windows Desktop at 800 × 600 dots per inch.

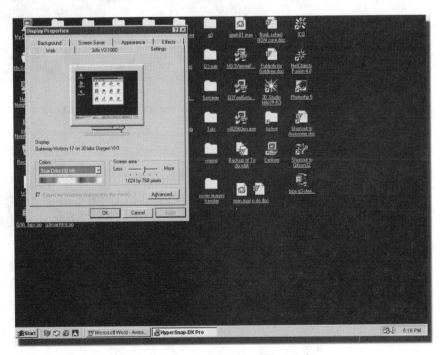

FIGURE 2.10   Here is the Windows Desktop at 1024 × 768 dots per inch.

Aspect Ratio

Another important component of resolution is aspect ratio, or the ratio of the pixel's width to the pixel's height. Not all images are square. In 640 × 480, 800 × 600, and 1024 × 768 mode, the aspect ratio is 1:1 or 1. This means that the pixels are perfectly square.

In 320 × 200 mode, the aspect ratio is 1.21:1 or .82, meaning that the pixels are higher than they are wide. If you create an image in 320 × 200 mode and display it in 640 × 480 mode, it will appear slightly squashed, since the pixels are about 20% shorter. See Figures 2.11 and 2.12 and notice the distortion in the image.

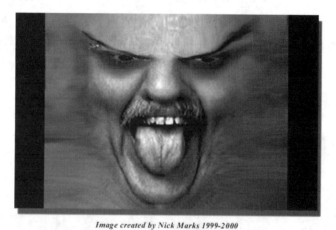

Image created by Nick Marks 1999-2000

FIGURE 2.11 Here is an image created at 320 × 200 dots per inch.

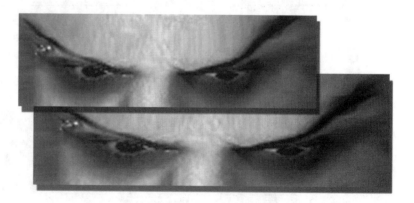

Image created by Nick Marks 1999-2000

FIGURE 2.12 Here is the same image displayed in 640 × 480 mode.

Colors

When working with most interactive content, you need to understand how color works in the computer. In some situations, such as games and Web sites, you will need precise control over your colors to achieve the effects you want. Colors are usually specified as RGB values, and artists may sometimes give you the specific value to use for a color in an image. An RGB value is the mixture of Red, Green, and Blue to make other colors—it's just like in art class when you mixed red and yellow paint to make orange.

The first number represents Red, the second represents Green, and the third represents Blue. These values range from 0 to 255. So 255,0,0 means you have all Red and no Green or Blue. Black would be 0,0,0 (no colors at all) and white would be 255,255,255 (all colors at their highest intensity). In Figures 2.13 through 2.17, you can see the RGB values of the color, and (even though the images are in 0,0,0 and 255,255,255—excuse me, black and white) you can see the position of the marker in the color palette.

Red = 0
Green = 0
Blue = 0

FIGURE 2.13   This is the RGB color palette for black.

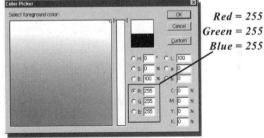

Red = 255
Green = 255
Blue = 255

FIGURE 2.14   This is the RGB color palette for white.

Red = 255
Green = 0
Blue = 0

FIGURE 2.15   This is the RGB color palette for red.

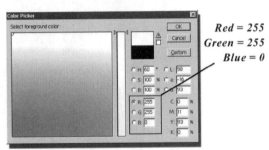

Red = 255
Green = 255
Blue = 0

FIGURE 2.16   This is the RGB color palette for yellow.

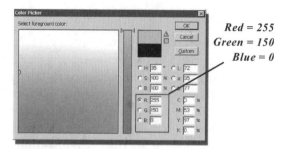

Red = 255
Green = 150
Blue = 0

FIGURE 2.17 This is the RGB color palette for orange.

 You will also hear color referred to as CMYK. CMYK is a mode used by traditional printing processes and stands for Cyan, Magenta, Yellow, and Black. You'll almost certainly never use CMYK color in game and computer content creation—you'll always deal in RGB or indexed color.

Number of Colors

A computer video card can display a certain number of colors at a time— 16 or 256 at the low end, or even thousands, or millions at the high end (see Figures 2.18, 2.19, 2.20, and 2.21). The number of colors is called color depth, which describes how many colors can be displayed on your screen at once. Color depth is described in terms of bits, and refers to the amount of memory used to represent a single pixel. The most common values are 8-bit, 16-bit, 24-bit, and 32-bit color. The more bits, the wider the range of colors that can be displayed.

FIGURE 2.18 This is an image in 16 colors. See the color gallery for the color version of this image.

FIGURE 2.19 This is an image in 256 colors. See the color gallery for the color version of this image.

FIGURE 2.20   This is an image in thousands of colors. See the color gallery for the color version of this image.

FIGURE 2.21   This is an image in millions of colors. See the color gallery for the color version of this image.

True Color (24-bit color) can display about 16.8 million colors for each pixel on the screen. The human eye cannot distinguish the difference between that many colors. High Color (16-bit color) only displays about 32,000, or about 64,000 colors. But this is still a very impressive range of colors, enough for most work. The 256 Color setting is more limited. It stores its color information in a palette. Each palette can be set to contain any of thousands or millions of different color values, but the screen can't show more than 256 different colors at once.

Some games still use this more limited palette because, as with increased resolution, having more colors means that more data must be pumped to the screen. So if you can get away with only 256 colors, you can render (or draw) the game pictures to the screen faster. More recently, games are starting to use thousands of colors, as the hardware permits.

The word render *is used in games, especially Real Time 3D games, because the computer and software literally render or build an image instantly, based on where a user is in the 3D world. Hence the term interactive. In a movie, you watch a series of unchangeable frames, as they were created by the movie maker. But when you play a 3D game, you control how each frame looks by where you choose to go in the world and what you do. Each frame of your gaming experience is made for you "on the fly," or as your experience is happening.*

256 palettes explained   You may never need to know this, but here goes. In a 256-color palette, each pixel can have a numerical value from 0-255

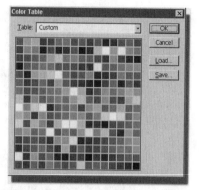

FIGURE 2.22 A 256 color palette. You can only see shades of gray here, but those squares are 256 different colors.

(a total of 256!). However, the 256 colors can be different in one palette than they are in another. The color number tells the graphics card where to get the color from in the palette, but it does not say what the color will be. Figure 2.22 shows the 256 color palette.

Let's say that you have a picture and you open the color palette to have a look. If you note that a certain color is assigned to the number 3 position on the color palette, and you then decide to reassign another color to the number 3 position, your image will now display that new color, rather than the the original color.

After the color is reassigned, even if you have the original color in the palette, it will not be displayed in the number 3 position. This means that a computer can't distinguish color; it sees numbers. You will have to be aware of this for later tutorials. In Figures 2.23 and 2.24, you can see how the changing of one color affects the image.

Now that we've seen the basics of images, let's move on to the basics of manipulating those images.

Manipulating Images

During the development of your project, you will have to manipulate images to get them to fit your needs. The basics of image manipulation are similar to the text editing that you may have done in your word processor. Commands such as Cut, Copy, and Paste are common. We will also look at Skew, Rotate, Resize, Crop, and Flip.

- Cut. If you cut an image, you remove it from the scene, as shown in Figure 2.25. But don't worry—you can paste it back or undo your action.

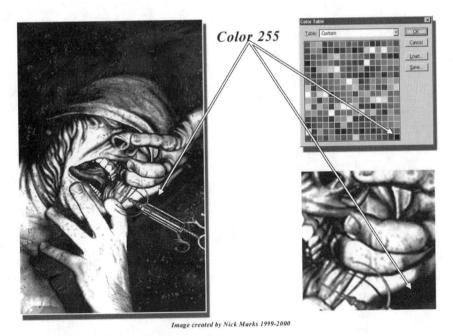

Image created by Nick Marks 1999-2000

FIGURE 2.23   This is a 256-color image.

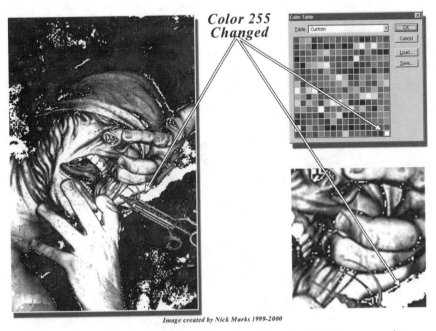

Image created by Nick Marks 1999-2000

FIGURE 2.24   This is the same image after changing the palette colors. The computer sees the number, not the color.

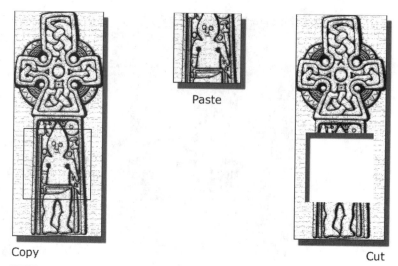

FIGURE 2.25 Cutting and copying sections of an image. Note: Copying does not affect the image.

- Copy. Copy does not alter your image. It creates a copy in the memory of your computer that you can paste somewhere else, as shown in Figure 2.25.
- Paste. As mentioned above, after cutting or copying an image, you can paste it somewhere else, as shown in Figure 2.26.

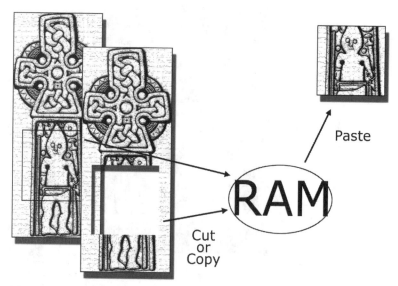

FIGURE 2.26 Pasting a section of an image.

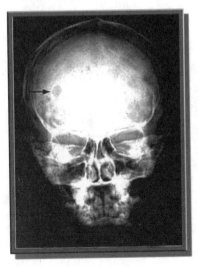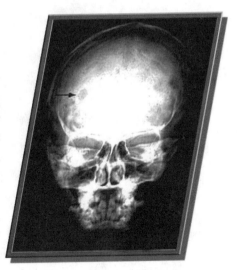

FIGURE 2.27   Skewing an image.

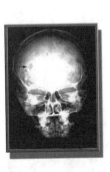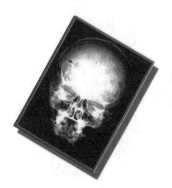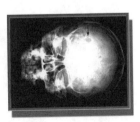

FIGURE 2.28   Rotating an image.

- Skew. Some image manipulation programs allow you to skew (slant, deform, or distort) an image, as shown in Figure 2.27.
- Rotate. Rotating is pretty self explanatory. You can free rotate an image or rotate it precisely a certain amount, as shown in Figure 2.28.
- Resize. Resizing an image is useful, but be careful. Any severe manipulation of an image degrades it, and resizing can do a lot of damage.

 If you reduce an image and then enlarge it again, you will seriously degrade it. This is because, in effect, you are enlarging a small image. The degradation takes place when you reduce an image, as well as when you enlarge it. This is illustrated in Figures 2.29, 2.30, and 2.31.

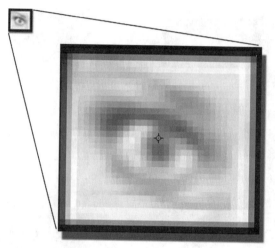

FIGURE 2.29 A smaller image blown up; pixel rip.

FIGURE 2.30 An image reduced.

FIGURE 2.31 The same image enlarged to its original size. Notice what this has done.

- Crop. Cropping cuts an image to a smaller area that you define, as shown in Figures 2.32 and 2.33.
- Flip (horizontal and vertical). Finally, you can flip images horizontally and vertically (see Figures 2.34, 2.35, and 2.36).

Image created by Jennifer Mever 1999-2000

FIGURE 2.32   Cropping an image. The crop outline.

FIGURE 2.33   The image cropped. Everything outside the crop outline is now gone.

FIGURE 2.34   The image.

FIGURE 2.35   The image flipped horizontally.

FIGURE 2.36   The image flipped vertically.

Advanced Image Manipulation

In the last section, we looked at some basic image editing operations. This only scratched the surface of what you'll need to do to create graphics for a game. Here are some more advanced operations.

Sprites

A sprite is a graphic image that can move within a larger image. In your games, these might be characters, buttons, and other items. Notice that the sprite image in Figure 2.37 has a solid border around it, and in Figure 2.38, the solid part is not seen.

Sprite animation is done just like cartoon animation. A series of images is played in sequence to make it appear that a character is walking or a logo is spinning, for instance. Figures 2.39 and 2.40 show examples of sprite frames.

Masking

A mask is a special image that is used to "mask" off portions of another image. A mask works like a stencil—it lets you paste a non-rectangular image into another image. When you paste a mask into another image, it overlays whatever was in the image at the spot where the mask is pasted (see Figures 2.41, 2.42, and 2.43).

FIGURE 2.37 A sprite image. Notice the solid part surrounding the image.

FIGURE 2.38 A sprite image in a game. Notice that the solid part is not displayed. You can see the background.

FIGURE 2.39   A series of sprite images for a game animation.

FIGURE 2.40   A series of sprite images for a spinning logo.

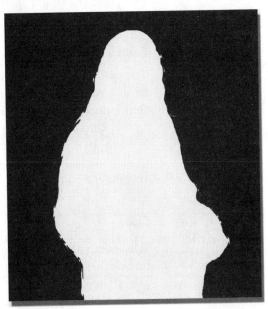

FIGURE 2.41   An image of a ghost.

FIGURE 2.42   The mask for the ghost image.

FIGURE 2.43 The mask and image combined in a scene.

Color Masking

Masking can also be used to specify that a specific color should be rendered as clear or transparent. Game programmers usually choose something like an ugly green or purple that most likely will not be used anywhere else in the game art.

Palette or Positional Masking

The last kind of masking lets you use a specific position on the color palette to determine what color should be rendered as clear or transparent. Remember, the computer sees color numbers, not the colors themselves. In this kind of masking, the computer looks at the position on the palette, not the color, to determine transparency. Usually, the last color place on the palette is used. Whenever the color with that number is called for, the computer will render it as clear, rather than using that color.

Opacity

Images can also be displayed in games as opaque—halfway between solid and clear (like our ghost image). To determine opacity, the computer looks at each pixel in the image and at the pixel directly under it. It then creates a new pixel that is a blended value of the original pixels (see Figures 2.44 and 2.45).

FIGURE 2.44   The masked ghost image with opacity set at 50%.

FIGURE 2.45   A close-up detail of the ghost image.

Anti-Aliasing

Look closely at the computer-generated images in Figures 2.46, 2.47, and 2.48. See those jagged edges on the letters? Those are the pixels we have been talking about. They look jagged if they are all made from a solid color. But by using various shades of a color and gradually blending the edge color with the background color, the computer can make the transition smooth and fool the eye from a distance. Yes, this is similar to opacity.

FIGURES 2.46   This image has no anti-aliasing.

FIGURES 2.47   This image has anti-aliasing.

FIGURES 2.48   Here is a closeup of both of the image's edges.

This technique is called *anti-aliasing*. It's one of the reasons that images with more colors look better. With more colors, you can blend them more gradually. This is also the reason that using a higher resolution (more pixels) makes an image look better—the blending is smoother between pixels.

Graphic Formats

Graphic images are stored in many different formats, for many reasons. In business, this may be for technical support and product design reasons, competitive reasons, and security reasons. But the main reason is image quality and usefulness. Some image formats produce very large files, because they retain a lot of image data, while some formats can compress an image and strip out data for a smaller file size. Still other formats degrade images (in an acceptable way) so they can be very small, for uses such as Web sites. Figures 2.49 and 2.50 show two versions of an image. The degradation is not that bad (see Figure 2.51), considering that the file size of the BMP image is almost 20 times the file size of the JPG image. The specifics you need to know about graphics formats are discussed later in this book and in the documentation of any applications you will be working with.

FIGURE 2.49 This 640 × 480 image is in the BMP format. It is 900K.

FIGURE 2.50 This 640 × 480 image is a compressed JPEG and is only 40K.

FIGURE 2.51 Here is a close-up of the same area of both images.

Chapter Review

In this chapter we looked at the basic elements of images and at how they are created. Now that you are familiar with graphics, you are almost ready to start creating content for a game. In the next chapter, we'll look at how to create music and sound effects.

CHAPTER

3

SOUND AND MUSIC

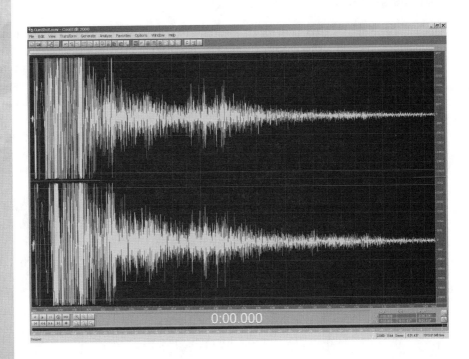

Of the many components that go into making a video game, perhaps none are given less attention than music and sound effects. Adding quality music and sound effects is one of the best ways to add production value to your games. For single developers or small teams, there is now a tremendous array of software and low-cost hardware that aids in this process. Believable sound effects and music will greatly enhance the game player's emotional experience.

WHY SOUND AND MUSIC ARE IMPORTANT

There are many parallels between making a movie and developing a game. Hollywood has long realized the benefits of music and sound effects to the moviegoer. Over the past decade, film makers have spent a tremendous amount of time and resources on improving these aspects of a movie. During that time, we have seen the use of surround sound in both theatrical and home movie releases.

The long and varied history of the movie industry offers us a tremendous amount of guidance. While you will find very little documentation on the creation of music and sound effects for games, there is a great deal of information available for the movie maker, both professional and amateur. Many books have been written over the years, and numerous resources are available at Web sites, not to mention in the movies themselves, which can often provide inspiration and ideas.

As the music and sound of video games improves, the video game industry has started to receive recognition for its work. Beginning with the 42nd Annual Grammy® Awards,the NARAS (National Academy of Recording Arts and Sciences) approved three new award categories, including music written for "Other Visual Media." This is the term they are using to include the music from games.

TYPES OF SOUNDS

What you hear in a game can range from recorded (or sampled) sounds such as voices and music; menu sounds like beeps and button clicks; and other effects, such as explosions, weapons fire, footsteps, and a long list of other in-game sound effects, both subtle and deafening.

Sound and music can be very important to a game, for atmospheric reasons alone. With the lights off and the sound turned up, players can really get immersed in a game. Sound and music can set the mood, as well as change it (think of the *Indiana Jones* score or Darth Vader theme).

Among the many cues that it gives, sound can clue players in about the threat of enemies. It greatly influences the level of satisfaction that they get from the game. And it can deliver a strong message to players about the quality of your game, and even your company.

And sound is more immersive than graphics. Let's say that again. Sound is more immersive than graphics. While graphics will draw players into a scene, the sound going on in the background and all around has a mental effect on a player that can never be achieved with graphics alone. This is probably because real-life sounds can be reproduced on a computer much better than real-life visuals. A dinosaur's roar can sound real on a computer, but a visual of a dinosaur doesn't look nearly as real.

Visually, players are looking into another world through a tiny window, and they can feel safe from that world. But when they hear that world all around them, they really feel that they are in it.

A good example of sound effectiveness is the movie *Jaws*. Who can forget the sound that announces that the shark is coming? In gaming, the sounds in Trespasser are incredible. They make the game a terribly tense and scary experience. One of the authors of this book actually had to turn the sound off, to avoid scaring his dog! But without the sound, the game is laughable. It looks just like that—a game. Puppet-like raptors stumble about and float like balloons. The tension is gone.

What makes playing the game with and without sound such a different experience? If you pull out one by one the various sound effects, ambient noises, and music that make the game scary, you'll find out. The raptors' footfalls top the list. This shows in the "distraction factor." With the sound off, you can actually play better, because you won't be distracted by the footfalls or raptor screams.

Sound can reinforce a physical feeling and create a physical sensation. Did you ever hit a rollover button with your speakers all the way up? You feel it roll, baby! Sound can be important, even for menu buttons. In a menu, sound can convey a solid feeling like steel switches being moved, or a light feeling like paper pages turning with a ruffle. This adds a lot to your production values. This is the same principle that car manufacturers use. The sensation you get when slamming a car door is important. If the door gives a solid *thunk* and doesn't rattle, the car must be safe and really solid, right?

OBTAINING OR CREATING SOUNDS AND MUSIC

Sound is everywhere in our daily life, so it's obvious why it would be so important to a gameplayer. Sound effects often take on meaning in a game. A dark alley with a strange noise coming from behind an overflowing dumpster delivers a message of fear more than the dark alley would by itself. People yelling loudly can draw our attention to an area or make us want to flee in the opposite direction. You can also use sound effects to establish a time and a place. For instance, hearing crickets in the background or waves beating on a shore can add a great deal to a setting, without visually displaying anything.

Sound effects can also convey actions, such as a gun being fired or a car colliding with a wall. It is this part of sound effects, the part that adds emotion or action to a scene, in which game programmers are most interested.

You don't have to come up with all the sounds yourself. Just as musicians buy CDs with loops, you can buy sound effects libraries. These libraries include sounds that will work directly, or can be modified to work with, the vast majority of sound effects.

If you want to create unique sounds, or if you'd just prefer to do sounds yourself, it is often a very simple process. If you have a Personal Digital Assistant (PDA) or a portable recorder of some sort, you can often record the sounds for yourself. For instance, if you have a game with animals, a visit to a pet store or local zoo is often all you would need to add the appropriate noises. If you are creating a sports title, visiting a local sporting event will give you all of the crowd and background noises you would ever need.

A word of caution. If you visit local areas to record sounds, keep in mind that you often need more than you would have imagined. For example, the sounds may not be as good as you had thought, or after editing, you may only have a few usable minutes from a 10-minute segment. Always try to get more material than you think you'll need.

The other basic type of sound effect for a game is the effects that occur when some type of action occurs. These sounds can take a great deal of time to produce and may require a tremendous amount of specialized equipment. Fortunately, as we'll see below, with a little effort and common items, you can use some very simple ideas to record these types of sounds for your games.

Recording Sounds

It doesn't really matter what type of device you use to record sounds. Ultimately, you have to get the data into the computer. For our setup, we'll assume that you are using a tape recorder, a digital recorder, or a PDA. Below, you'll see how to connect these devices to the sound or microphone inputs on the computer's sound card. You'll also see how to change the sounds into a digital form and use Cool Edit, a great shareware tool for game developers, to edit them.

How to Record

The first step in this process is creating the recordings. You'll be creating several games in this book, and with this in mind, you'll need to create effects for a variety of sounds, such as gun shots, footsteps, and perhaps even collision noises. These are actually quite easy to record.

The following table lists several types of actions that you can easily record with common household items. You can use this list, or change it, so that you can come up with sounds for many types of games.

Sound Type	How to Record
Car Crash	Fill a box with scrap metal and chunks of wood. Shake vigorously.
Fire	Take a piece of cellophane and crinkle it with your hands.
Door Slamming	Place the recording device near the door hinges and slam the door. While you're at it, open and close the door slowly, if you also need that type of noise.
Body Collisions	Strike an item such as a pumpkin or watermelon with a piece of wood, or a rubber mallet. Try various methods to get just the right sound. Watch out though—this can be very messy! Another method is to wrap wet towels around wood planks and then strike them together. Or drop the planks a short distance to a concrete or hardwood surface.
Rain	Record the sound of rain on a roof or metal sheet. Or if you don't want to wait for rain, simulate the effect. Cut the bottoms of five plastic cups into different shapes, such as a square, star, or ellipse. Then tape the cups together. Pour uncooked rice into the top of the cups. This will sound like rain falling.
Thunder	As with rain, record a thunderstorm. Or simulate it, as follows. Make a simple "thunder sheet" by getting a piece of sheet metal cut to approximately 18" × 50." Then fit 1" × 2" boards on one end (to use as a handle) and cut

several holes in the other end. Hang the sheet by the holes from a ceiling or beam. To simulate thunder, shake the end with the handle. This can take some practice to master, so be patient if it doesn't sound realistic at first.

Footsteps	The best way is to record the real thing. For outdoor simulations, walk on a gravel area. For indoor simulations, walk on a hardwood floor with a hard-heeled shoe. If you don't have a hardwood floor, build a 3' × 3' wooden box and use it to step in place. You can then flip it over to record stepping noises, or fill it with things like straw or newspaper to vary the noises.
	To simulate walking in snow, press a shoe on an old strawberry container, a sofa cushion, or something similar. If you do this at an approximate stepping rhythm, it will simulate footsteps very well.
	You can also simulate animal footsteps. For a horse, strike together small squares of wood, or the two halves of a coconut with all the pulp removed. Or put sand in the box you made for human footsteps, and strike the box with the coconut halves.
Machines	If possible, record the actual machine noises. For instance, if you are creating a car racing game, go to a race and record the sounds yourself. Additional sounds that work well in games include saws, drills and even hammers.
Gunshots	Hit a leather seat with a thin wooden stick, such as a yardstick or ruler. For different types of sounds, experiment by hitting other materials with the wooden stick.
Gunshots Hitting Wood	Cut plywood into thin strips and then break them. It will sound as if shots are splintering the wood.

For ideas about experimentation, let's consider gunshots. As mentioned in the table, you can hit a leather seat with a thin wooden stick. Strike various objects, and use sticks of varying strengths. Creating sound effects is very much trial and error. Spend time finding several objects that sound good, and record all of them.

Using a PDA

The next step is to connect your recorder to the computer. If you are using a PocketPC or Windows CE-based PDA, you can simply connect it to the computer and transfer the recordings, which will already be in WAV format (refer to your documentation). If you are using this method, skip the next section, "Using a Recording Device."

Depending on the sound quality of your PDA, the sounds may or may not be of value. If they are not good quality, you will probably have to use one of the methods listed below to record your sounds.

Using a Recording Device

If you are using a tape recorder, mini-disc recorder, or other recording device, you will have to attach it to your computer's sound card. Most sound cards have four connectors: Line In, Line Out, Microphone, and a MIDI/Game Port. Figure 3.1 shows the layout of a typical sound card.

Most modern sound cards also use diagrams to label the connections. See Figure 3.2 for a sample.

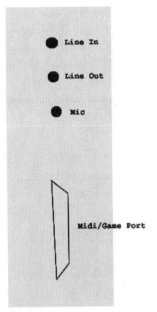

FIGURE 3.1   The layout of a typical sound card.

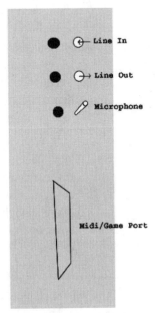

FIGURE 3.2   Sound cards often have labels.

Figures 3.1 and 3.2 use different labels for Microphone (Mic and Microphone). They are both very common and are used as an example of the variations you may find.

The following list explains the various connectors:

- MIDI / Game Port: A port which is most commonly used to connect a game paddle or joystick to the computer. This port also lets you connect a MIDI (Musical Instrument Digital Interface) device, such as a keyboard, to the computer.
- Line In: A connector that lets you connect a sound source to the computer. Examples include CD players, tape recorders, and other recording devices.
- Line Out: A connector that lets you connect the computer to anything that accepts sound input. Used most commonly for speakers or headphones.
- Microphone: A connector that lets you connect a microphone to record your own sound files. If necessary, you can also connect a recording device to this port.

After you have located the Line In or Mic (microphone) connection, attach your device to the computer. Depending on the device, you may need different types of cables and connectors. The vast majority of sound cards use 1/8″ (miniplug) jacks for Mic and Line In.

Using Your Sound Card's Mixer Panel

After connecting the device, open up your sound card's mixer panel. On many systems, you can do this by double-clicking the yellow speaker icon in the system tray. This is usually near the clock on the Windows taskbar. But because Windows system setups can vary, you may need to call it up a different way. A standard sound card mixer panel looks like Figure 3.3 (the panel on your system may look different).

When you first open the mixer, you will see all of the possible playback volumes. Set the volumes as follows.

1. If the Wave Balance (the second slider from the left in Figure 3.3) is checkmarked, click the Mute all box to uncheck it.
2. Make sure that the Wave Balance slider and the Volume Control Balance slider (the leftmost one in Figure 3.3) are both at least halfway up.

Next, set the sound card's recording devices, as follows.

1. Choose Options | Properties.

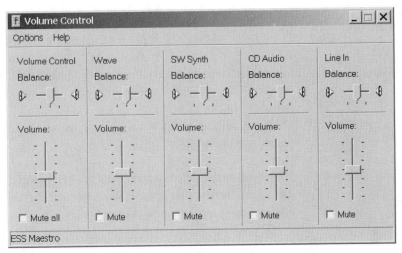

FIGURE 3.3 The mixer panel allows you to choose options related to the sound card.

2. In the box labeled "Adjust volume for," select Recording. Each of the devices from which your sound card can record will be listed in the window.
3. Click the OK button. This will display the Recording Controls window.

Make sure that volume of the category you plan to use is half way up. For instance, if you are using the Line In, you should make sure that Line In is half way up. Figure 3.4 displays the Line Up as it should appear.

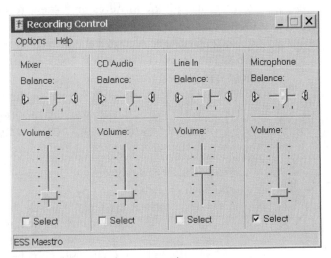

FIGURE 3.4 Line In with the correct settings.

Using Cool Edit to Record a Gunshot

The CD-ROM that accompanies the book includes a trial version of Cool Edit 2000. You should run the Cool Edit installation from the CD-ROM and follow the steps as directed during the installation before continuing this section. This will allow you to follow along as we look at some of the basic features of Cool Edit.

Now, let's record a sound effect, using Cool Edit. In this case, we'll record a gunshot. Here's how:

The procedure that follows assumes that you've recorded a gunshot sound on a device and have connected that device to your computer. For suggestions on how to simulate a gunshot, see the table earlier in this chapter.

1. Start up Cool Edit.
2. Choose Options | Settings.
3. Choose Devices. Make sure that the correct device is selected for both Waveform Playback and Waveform Record. Then click OK.
4. To create a new file, choose File | New.
5. Choose the WAV file type, and click OK.
6. Click the Record button and start the playback from the device you've chosen.
7. When you have finished recording, press the Stop button. Depending on your sample, you should see something like Figure 3.5.

Before going on, be sure to test the playback volume in Cool Edit. If the volume is too low, you can rewind or reset your device, or increase or decrease its volume as necessary. Then, record the sound effect again in Cool Edit, as shown above.

After you have recorded the sound effect in Cool Edit and the volume is OK, you can save and edit it. The save function is in the File menu like most Windows applications.

Let's take a look at Figure 3.5, which shows a recorded gunshot sound. The three waveforms that go from top to bottom show the three times that a stick was used to strike a leather chair in this recording.

Let's change the file to contain just one "shot." Here's what to do.

1. Select the first waveform by clicking with your mouse and dragging and then choose Edit | Copy.
2. Place the mouse at the end of the selection and click. If it appears that you have selected the area directly next to the first sample, choose Edit | Paste. Otherwise continue to move this by a single click until it is directly to the right of the first selection before choosing Edit | Paste. The screen should now look like Figure 3.6.

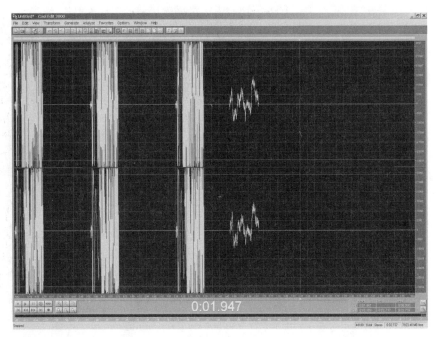

FIGURE 3.5   Cool Edit displaying the recorded sample.

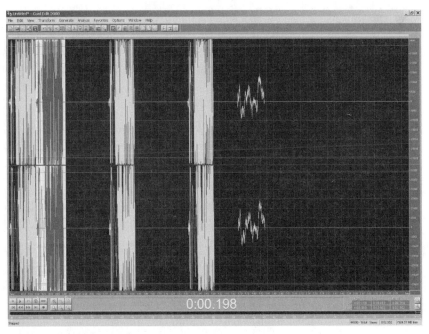

FIGURE 3.6   The newly pasted area.

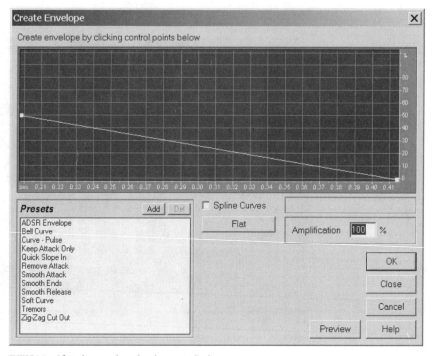

FIGURE 3.7 After the envelope has been applied.

3. Choose Transfer | Amplitude and then Envelope. Drag the line down in the window so that it looks like Figure 3.7. Next, click OK.
This will produce a tapered effect that will add an echo to the gunshot.
4. Highlight the areas to the right of the newly pasted area and then press the Delete key. This will leave only a single gunshot and echo. You can see the final result in Figure 3.8.

In Figure 3.8, you may notice that just before the halfway point, there is an area where the volume increases before falling back down. This adds to the echo effect. You can do this as follows.

1. Select an area. Choose Transfer | Amplitude and then Amplify.
2. From this window, drag the Amplification to create a higher value. (You can also use Amplify to increase or decrease the volume of the entire sample if your volume is too high or low.)

That's all there is to creating our single gunshot. You can follow this same basic process for creating the other sound effects, using the methods we looked at previously in the chapter.

Another way to get sound effects is to buy them or download them from the Web (some sites have sounds for free). This is especially valuable

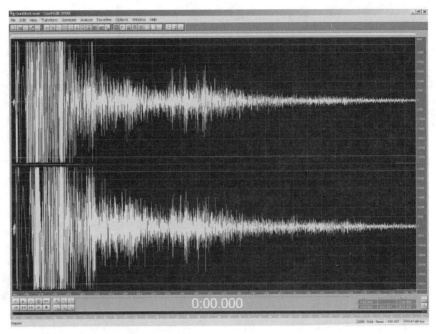

FIGURE 3.8   The final version of the WAV file.

for something that might be hard to record, such as a lion's roar. You can do a search on your favorite search engine for "free sound effects" or "sound effects libraries."

Creating Music

When you start creating music for a game, you usually begin with a basic understanding of the type of music you need. For instance, if you are creating music for a wrestling game, classical music is probably not going to be part of the piece. You may need to do some research. Discuss the requirements with someone, or find a way to listen to existing music that fits your needs. For a wrestling game, you might watch wrestling on television or attend a wrestling match. This would allow you to get a very good understanding of the kind of music that users would expect.

On the other hand, if you are writing music for a game that reenacts the Civil War, you might watch movies about the Civil War or talk with music historians about the types of instruments or music that would have been popular in that time period.

It's important to understand that you're not looking to simply copy the music, but to discover what makes music appropriate for the time or era.

Keep your mind open. You might base your music on what you've seen and heard, or you might come up with completely unique ideas.

As in other parts of this book, we'll try to give you some hands-on experience here. We're going to use ACID™, a program that has several advantages over other similar applications. First, it's easy. Even if you don't have a music background, you can use ACID. Also, it includes samples that you can use in your musical creations. Finally, you can download clips to use in the program from several Web sites.

Using Loops

ACID is based on the ability to create music from loops, much like mainstream music is produced today. In the past fifteen years, the vast majority of the music industry has used loops or samples in one way or another. This has drastically altered the music landscape, changing the way that both amateur and professional producers create their music. A quick glance at many modern albums makes it clear they use loops.

 The terms samples and loops are used in the text to refer to the same type of repeating music.

The use of samples in many forms of music has brought about an entire industry that produces music especially for this purpose. There are thousands of CDs that contain samples that can be used for almost any purpose. Along with the CDs that contain samples in standard CD Audio format, you can get CDs that include samples in the file formats used by many leading music programs, including ACID.

Many of these CDs require that you pay for using their samples. There are two basic methods. The first is a royalty-based system. With this system, the CDs themselves may be free. However, you pay a royalty for every time the sample is used. In the second method, you pay an up-front fee. This gives you a royalty free license that allows you to do almost anything with the loops from that point on. However, with either method, you usually cannot distribute the materials as a new collection of loops.

The Internet offers a third way to obtain samples. Many Web sites offer fee-based downloads, while others allow you to download their loops for free. We'll take a look at ACIDplanet.com, which is run by the Sonic Foundry. Every week, it has a freely available download called an 8Pack. This is an ACID project file that includes eight loops arranged into a song. The 8Packs can help you learn how to combine loops into a final project. They also include tips and tricks that show you how the 8Packs were put together.

Another excellent site is PocketFuel.com. It offers the largest collection of royalty-free files for ACID on the Internet. This book uses many files from this site. If you register at PocketFuel.com, you can download the files that we'll use in the next section.

Creating the Music

Because of licensing issues, the CD for this book does not contain any files downloaded from the Internet. In particular, including downloaded files could violate the licensing agreement for PocketFuel. Before downloading anything from a Web site, you should thoroughly read through the licensing agreement.

To start our project, we'll be finding and downloading several types of loops from the Web. Because files are always being added to and deleted from Web sites, you may not be able to duplicate this project exactly as shown below. But this exercise will still be very useful.

The screen shots in this chapter are from ACID Pro 3. They may look slightly different from the free version of ACID you will download from the Internet. However, because this project only uses features available in the free version, you should be able to follow along.

Creating a Project with ACID Pro

Before creating a project in ACID, you will need to download it from the Sonic Foundry web site at www.sonicfoundry.com. Click on Software and then choose ACID Pro. Next, click on Download and follow the links to download ACID. Once you have downloaded it, follow the directions to install it.

When you open ACID Pro, you'll be presented with a blank project, as shown in Figure 3.9. The area at the bottom that looks like Windows Explorer is the Explorer window. The smaller blank area at the upper left is the Track List. The larger blank area at the upper right is the Track View.

The following procedure shows you how to create your first project.

1. From the File menu, choose Properties. Enter the information for your project, such as the title of the project and the copyright information. The Project Properties window can be seen in Figure 3.10.
   In the next steps, you'll add your first loop to the project.
2. To add a file to your ACID project, double-click it in the Explorer window, or drag it from the Explorer window to the Track List.

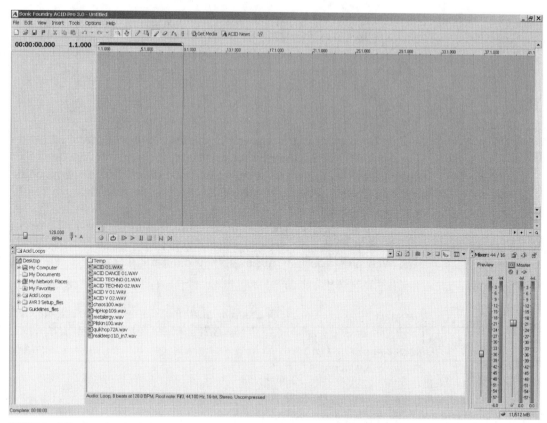

FIGURE 3.9 A blank project in ACID.

 If you add a file that is longer than thirty seconds, ACID's Beatmapper wizard will automatically be displayed. If this happens, right-click and drag the file to the Track View or Track List to specify the type of track that will be created. When you drop the file, a shortcut menu is displayed that allows you to choose whether the file will be treated as a loop, a one-shot, a Beatmapped track, or as an autodetected type. You can just choose autodected type if you run into this (or simply make sure to use something less than 30 seconds).

When you have added a file, it should appear at the top of the Track List, as shown in Figure 3.11.

3. Next, drag the time in the Track View so that it ends at approximately 21 seconds. Your screen should now look like Figure 3.12. If for some reason your ruler has a different measure of time, you can change it by choosing View | Time Ruler and then selecting the appropriate format.

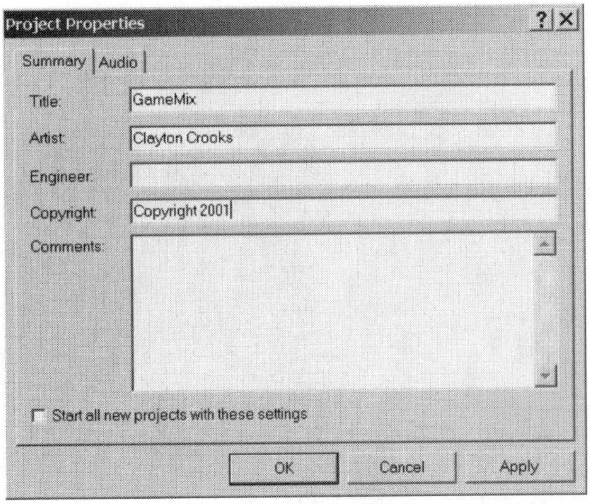

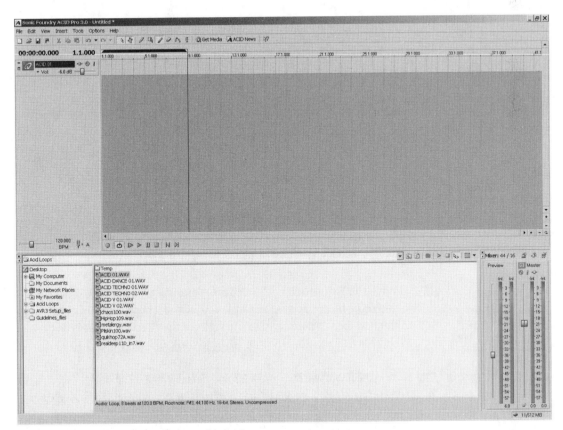

FIGURE 3.10   The Project Properties window.

FIGURE 3.11   The project with a single loop added to it.

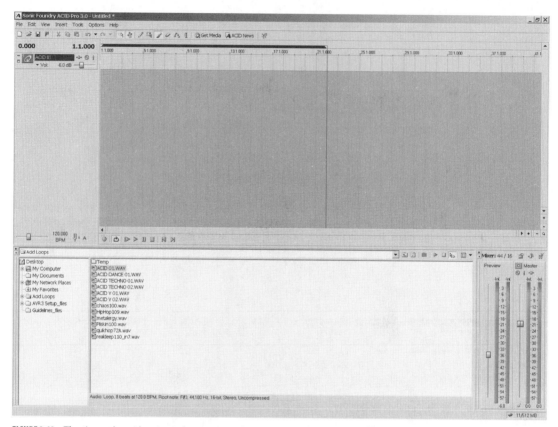

FIGURE 3.12 The time ruler with a time of approximately 21 seconds.

4. In this step, we'll use the Paint tool which lets you "paint" events by clicking and dragging the mouse. An event is simply the loop being played. This tool is also useful for inserting single events evenly along the grid.

   With the Paint tool, click in the are of the Track View that is directly to the right of the filename displayed in the Track List. This will draw in the first location directly to the right of the filename that is displayed in the Track List. Your project should look like Figure 3.13.

The names you'll encounter in the next few figures (3.12, 3.13 and 3.14), such as ACID 01 and ACID V02, might be different in your project. Don't worry about the names—instead concentrate on the processes you'll be using.

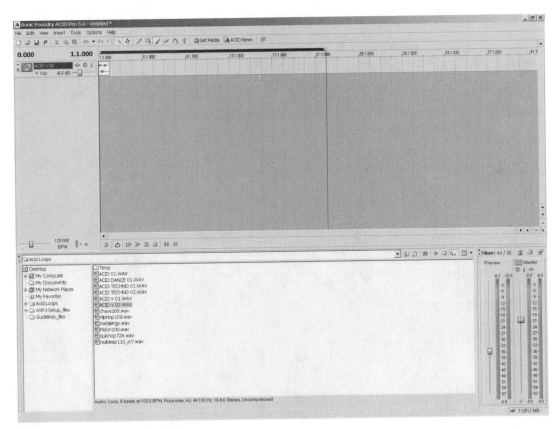

FIGURE 3.13   The first entry in the grid.

5. Click the Play button to test the project before moving on. If it plays correctly, it would be a good time to give your project the name "My-FirstACIDProject." The extension is added automatically for you, so don't worry about it at this time.

6. Now, add the rest of your loops to the project. Follow the steps listed above for each loop that you want to add. When you have finished, you can begin creating your music by drawing with the Paint Tool inside the grid next to the individual tracks. Figure 3.14 shows the finished project.

There are only a few up on the Web site at any given time, so it would be impossible to talk about one of them.

If you have any problems with this project, or wish to get into more advanced work with ACID, you should take the time to download the

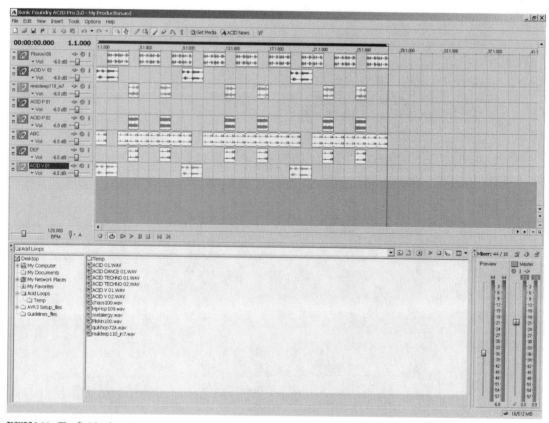

FIGURE 3.14   The finished project.

8Packs available at ACIDPlanet.com. They have pre-constructed projects that will give you an idea of how to better put things together.
7. When you have finished your project, save it in WAV format. The full ACID Pro can save projects in MP3 format, but the free version of ACID cannot.

ON THE CD

The CD-ROM has several project examples, including files in MP3, WAV, and RM (Real Media) format. These projects are in the Music *and* SFX *directory.*

CHAPTER REVIEW

It's easy to see why music and sound effects are so important to the development of a game. They can add so much to the experience of a game player by setting a mood or location. Well thought out music and sound effects go hand in hand with the eye candy that so many developers focus upon. They have become an integral part of the game development process.

In this chapter, we used two of the best tools available for game developers: ACID, with its easy-to-use interface to create a very simple song, and Cool Edit to record and edit sound effects for our final project. In the next chapter, we'll look at the history of game development.

4

THE HISTORY OF GAME DEVELOPMENT

In this chapter, we'll look at the history of computer game development. Understanding the history of something helps you appreciate where you are and what you are working with. We'll look at how the computer gaming industry began and at how the industry has evolved into what it is today.

The game and interactive developer has come a long way from the days when one had to memorize codes and numbers—every bit as opaque and complicated as an alien language—to even work on a game. Basically, you had to be a programmer, and the focus was on the code, and not the art. Currently, anyone can make a game—2D and 3D. The doors have been opened for great artists to contribute to a game, and even for the lowliest newcomers to try their hands at game design and development. Let's take a look at how far we have come.

SOLID-STATE STONE KNIVES AND MICRO BEARSKINS

In 1959, Jack St. Kirby at Texas Instruments, and Robert Noyce and Jean Hoerni at Fairchild Semiconductor Corporation, independently devised a way to shrink much of the redundant and sluggish elements on an electronic circuit board and place them all onto a tiny square of silicon. It was called the integrated circuit; you know it as the microchip.

Remember those names: Kirby, Noyce, Hoerni. They are the folks who really jump-started the computer game revolution. The microchip led to the microprocessor; the microprocessor led to high-level computer languages; high-level computer languages led to death matches and 3D worlds!

The year 1959 laid the path that led to the computer as we know it today, but there were a number of hurdles to jump before there was a PC on every desk. When the microchip appeared, it was hampered by high prices and very small stock, much like when any new technology debuts. For awhile, game programmers would simply have to content themselves with the electric equivalent of stone knives and bearskins. Did this stop the advent and evolution of computer games? Of course not. The computer had already been invented. "How," you may ask, "did they do it?"

Before the microprocessor, everything was "solid-state." This refers to a circuit board full of electrical components that provide a system of computing power and temporary memory. The capacitor played the lead to this troupe. A capacitor could hold electric charges, negative or positive, for a variety of purposes. It was, in a room-sized nutshell, the world's first RAM. Indeed, it was on a "solid-state digital computer" that the first computer game would be written.

SPACEWAR

In November of 1960, Digital Equipment Corporation (DEC) debuted the first of a widely successful computer line, the Programmed Data Processor (PDP). The first PDP, PDP-1, showed up at The Hingham Institute in Cambridge, Massachusetts, where J. Martin Graetz and his colleagues awaited it. Everything the group had read about the PDP-1 told them it would be the world's first useful computer, the world's first "toy computer," as Graetz put it in a 1981 issue of *Creative Computing* magazine.

In Graetz's words, "The PDP-1 would be faster than the Tixo, more compact, and *available*." (The Tixo, a nickname for TX-0, was an earlier computer, also at Hingham.) He adds, "It was the first computer that did not require one to have an E.E. degree and the patience of Buddha to start it up in the morning; you could turn it on any time by flipping one switch, and when you were finished you could turn it off. We had never seen anything like that before." The PDP-1 is shown in Figure 4.1.

It was in the Institute's "kludge room," next to the Tixo, that the PDP-1 resided. Graetz, a published author, along with Stephen R. "Slug" Russell, an artificial intelligence specialist, and Wayne Witanen, a mathematician, had all experimented with coding on the Tixo for months, showing off such things as "Bouncing Ball," which was advanced for the late 1950s. When they sat around the PDP-1, they transferred Tixo code and rewrote it for the PDP to get a feel for the new "toy."

They wrote and rewrote, trying new experiments. They tried various ideas. A particular favorite was lines intersecting one another, or the "Min-

FIGURE 4.1   The Programmed Data Processor (PDP-1) by DEC.

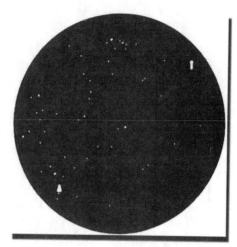

FIGURE 4.2 A screen from the original Spacewar on the PDP-1.

skytron." Soon enough, two spaceships appeared, a sun, then a star field—images fueled by a recent, healthy dose of 1950s pulp science fiction in the form of E.E. "Doc" Smith's Lensman novels. They added features such as a way to rotate the ships, a thrust, and torpedoes. The result was Spacewar. On the PDP's so-called "Precision CRT Type 40" monitor, two spaceships drifted against a backdrop of silent stars. In the middle, a larger star grew and shrank, tugging the ships toward it, as seen in Figure 4.2.

In Spacewar, players flipped console switches to control their spacecraft—one for clockwise rotation, another for counterclockwise, one to shoot "torpedoes," and the last for thrust (see Figure 4.3). The game looked very much like the arcade game Asteroids; white outlines and dots made up the figures against a "black" background (This graphics style would come to be known as "Vector Graphics.") The PDP-1 also allowed two users to operate the computer simultaneously. That's right—the world's first death match!

Immediately, Institute dwellers and students from nearby MIT took a liking to Spacewar. And as more computers showed up on campuses around the country, Spacewar was often copied. You can still find Spacewar on the Internet. It has been ported (or re-coded) to other computer languages, such as Java, and can be played in your Web browser (see Figure 4.4).

Soon after Spacewar, new and different games started to appear. Adventure, the world's first computer text adventure, was created shortly thereafter, as were Lunar Lander, Hammurabi (the first simulated [sim] world), and many others. Spacewar had made a single, clear point: Computer games were fun—and cool.

FIGURE 4.3   The controller for *Spacewar* (a while away from Force Feedback Joysticks!)

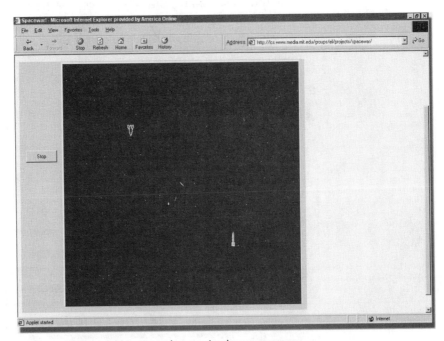

FIGURE 4.4   The same old *Spacewar*, but now in a browser near you.

SPEAKING PROCESSOR-EESE!

But however cool Spacewar was, it was difficult to program—at least by today's standards. The programmers had to write the game in a proprietary code—one that only the PDP-1 could understand. Indeed, this language could be called a form of *assembly language*.

 Machine language *speaks directly to the computer hardware and tells it what to do. Assembly* language *is a level above this in ease of use, and above that is the current crop of high-level languages such as C, C++, Pascal, and FORTRAN (see Figure 4.5).*

At the most basic levels, computers can only process a low-level code called *machine language*. All computers understand machine language, but humans? Forget about it. It consists entirely of numbers.

Assembly language is one step toward what are known as "human-readable" languages. Instead of numbers, it uses labels, or codes, that tell the processor to perform different functions. Assembly language is "readable" in the sense that the different codes have a structure and format that people can understand. Well, at least that's the way the theory goes.

Here is an example of the assembler code:

```
.$13e3   [26 61    ]   rol $61
.$13e5   [26 62    ]   rol $62
.$13e7   [26 63    ]   rol $63
.$13e9   [26 52    ]   rol $52
```

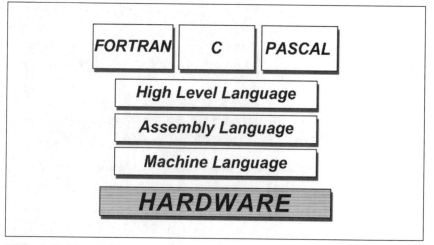

FIGURE 4.5   The hierarchy of computer languages.

```
.$13eb  [26 53   ]  rol $53
.$13ed  [26 54   ]  rol $54
.$13ef  [a5 54   ]  lda $54
```

Assembly language was, and is, difficult to master. It's about the closest a programmer can come to understanding a processor's native tongue. Master it, and you can speak to your processor. But remember: Your processor can only understand one particular dialect. Maybe you've learned the assembly language for an 80×86 or Pentium processor. Now you want to write assembly language for a 6502 processor? You'll have to learn another dialect.

Spacewar was written in assembly language—many early games were—and it remained a staple of game programming for nearly twenty years. If someone wanted to port Spacewar to another processor, they had to rewrite it in that processor's assembly language. This is still true today. But it became especially significant in the early 70s, when another invention changed everything.

Later in this book, we'll cover TGF. Using TGF, you can create a drag-and-drop game in minutes that is technically far beyond Spacewar, with textures, sounds, and a lot more (see Figure 4.6). You'll see that when you can drag and drop to create a game, instead of hand-coding everything, your creativity can really take off.

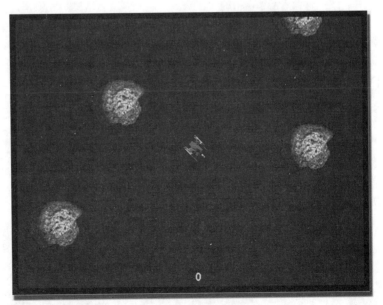

FIGURE 4.6   A TGF game that is similar to Spacewar and technically superior, due to modern tools.

A Computer on a Chip

In the late 60s, science writers in various trade and consumer science magazines theorized about a so-called "computer-on-a-chip." The microchip was still fresh in many scientists' minds, and many wondered about that next step. Everyone concluded that integrated circuits weren't where they needed to be. Certainly, many more experiments would have to be conducted before the "computer on a chip" could become a reality. It would take years! People weren't waiting and holding their breath.

By the late 60s, Intel had invented a so-called "MOS technology" (Metal Oxide Semiconductor), which used the inherent properties of silicon to create gates that insulated conducting channels from nonconducting ones. This, theorized Ted Hoff, Stanley Mazor, and Federico Faggin, would make a single-chip CPU possible.

Suddenly, it wasn't theory any more. In 1971, Intel officially announced the first microprocessor, the Intel 4004, a single chip as powerful as ENIAC, the giant first electronic computer that filled an entire room. The 4004 was more of a technological curiosity than anything. But what it did was spur development of other microprocessors. Rockwell introduced the 6502 microprocessor series in the mid-1970s, which would power the Atari 2600 and the Commodore 64. General Instruments developed the 1610, which Mattel used in the Intellivision. And, of course, Intel developed the 8088, and later, the 80x86 family (80186, 80286, 80386, 80486, and Pentium). Motorola achieved great things with its 68000 and PowerPC® series of chips.

Throughout the life span of each processor, games were developed for it—some simple, some bad, some ingenious. Each one tried to squeeze just a little more out of each processor. That squeezing continues today.

But at some point, the microprocessor itself, while certainly remaining at the forefront of developers' minds, became just a little less important. The speed was there, and it continued to accelerate as new and better processors came out. Then, many developers turned their attention to graphics. The question was: How do we make better pictures?

Advances in Graphics

It's a perpetual battle: Gamers want better graphics. They see the games in the arcade and they want to bring all that color and explosive sound home. Developers want to give consumers all of that and more. Developers like the same graphics that gamers do. In the middle lies the hardware, pulled at from both ends. Developers had to forge a compromise.

The first compromise was vector graphics. These consist of light—stretched into lines or squeezed into points. Remember the original Asteroids? Tempest? Battlezone? All vector. In its earliest days, colored gels were physically placed on the screen to color the light.

But vector graphics didn't appear outside of the arcade very often. The world's only vector video game console, the Vectrex, is now a highly sought after collector's item. But for the millions of people who owned Atari 2600s, Apple IIe's, and Commodore 64s, the developer/processor/gamer compromise was *sprites*.

You will remember from Chapter 2 that the basic definition of a sprite is: A graphic image that can move within a larger image. Remember Pac-Man®? Ol' Pac was a sprite. As were the ghosts and the dots. Even the maze walls were sprites. Each sprite can be animated to move about a game board or "world," or it can stay in one place, acting as a border or barrier. Usually, the character or machine you controlled in a game (ol' Pac!) was a sprite. It could be decoration. It could collide and react to other sprites, as we'll see later when we look at TGF.

By the time the first round of home computer systems debuted, the ability to draw sprites on the screen was available in just about every computer language. Some processors were even created with them in mind. As such, sprites ruled games for more than a decade.

But sprites had one inherent flaw: They were 2D—flat, without depth. You could paint a sprite anyway you wanted, but it was still flat 2D. The advent of 3D would make games so much better.

IT'S A POLYGONAL WORLD

In 1984, a new game made its way to the arcade. It never progressed much beyond it either—a mere few hundred machines were produced—but it paved the way for Quake, Kingpin, and all those death matches you've fragged around in.

The game was I, Robot from Atari. It was somewhat based on the Isaac Asimov story of the same name. In I, Robot, you guide a robot around a "world," looking for and walking onto red squares. Once in contact with the red, the robot lasers a foreboding red eye at the other end of the world. Touch all the red, the eye dies. After a small fly-through-space-shoot-objects game, you reach another world with more red, and another eye. Yeah, it's simple, but fun. What is more important is that I, Robot was the first game to use polygons.

You've probably heard of polygons. They're the latest buzzword in game advertising. "Each world consists of 40 bazillion polygons, all rendered on-the-fly!" Polygons are the key to 3D games and those more "realistic" worlds that developers want to create and gamers want to play in.

In 1984, I, Robot was the impetus to develop 3D worlds. For a long time, such amazing stuff would stay in the arcade in games like Hard Drivin' and Virtua Fighter. The processors in home computers couldn't handle all the necessary computations to draw polygons and what they represented—three-dimensional graphics. But, you know, it was only a matter of time.

Making Programming Languages Easier

In the meantime, many programmers tried hard to get away from the opaque complexity of assembly language. Some programmers used other languages, but by and large, assembly language was the most powerful choice. But for all its power, it was a pain. You couldn't port a game to a different processor easily. And it was a bit of a memory hog. Or, at least, assembly language programming handled precious memory resources inefficiently.

In answer to these and other problems, Dennis Ritchie and Brian Kernighan at Bell Labs introduced a "flexible" programming language, C, in the late 1970s. They called it a "high-level" programming language and it quickly became very popular. It took up less memory, was much easier to learn, and was more "human-readable."

"Human-readable" is not a difficult concept to grasp. Remember our assembly example? Well, some programmers wanted to get beyond those cryptic codes to something humans could "read."

Here's an example of things not being "human readable" from the early days of word processing programs. In WordStar for DOS, if you wanted to boldface or italicize text, you had to insert a marker before and after that text. For bold, you pressed CONTROL-P and then CONTROL-B, typed the text, and then pressed CONTROL-P, CONTROL-B again. For italics, you pressed CONTROL-P, CONTROL-Y (yes, "Y") before and after the text. Here's how it looked onscreen:

```
The last three words here are B^Ybold and italic^Y^B.
```

Here's how it printed out:

```
The last three words here are bold and italic.
```

This is also very similar to HTML, or Hyper Text Markup Language, which is what Web browsers use to display a site's pages.

```
<FONT COLOR="#000000" FACE="Times New Roman,Times,Times NewRoman">
The last three words here are <B><I>bold and italic</I></B></FONT>
```

These commands tell the Web browser what font (style of letter) to use, as well as the color of the font. And you can see the <B> and <I> commands for bold and italic before and after the last three words.

The same point applies to programming languages. Assembly language required programmers to remember and use arcane codes. But with the newest tools for making games, you can "point and click" to get the effects you want.

In a lot of respects, the push toward "human-readable" languages parallels the push toward WYSIWYG (What You See Is What You Get) interfaces. From codes in word processors came buttons that quickly and easily formatted the words in the document and showed text onscreen exactly as it would appear in print.

Home computers were not as plentiful or prevalent as they are now when C first debuted. It found success, but only with tinkerers, hobbyist programmers, and some business folk. It never gained the popularity of its more human-readable second-generation version (called C++), which Bell Labs debuted in the late 1980s.

C++ revolutionized programming and game development in two distinct ways. First, it took advantage of a newly created programming structure called "Object-Oriented Programming," (OOP). OOP, in a nutshell, takes functions, and the data those functions operate on, and places them in separate, independent structures that float inside a larger house program. This structure is the "object." Once an object is created, the main program can call the object to perform its function. The data created is then served up to the main program, or even to other objects, which have their own specific functions. Objects are portable. They can be moved to, and used in, any other C++ program.

By the time C++ came about, computers—especially IBM clones—had become affordable. So, hobbyist and even professional programmers spread C++ objects and code throughout online bulletin boards , and later, the Internet. Any programmer who knew C++ could use these objects. Programmers didn't have to reinvent the wheel every time they wrote a new program. Do you need a routine that creates sounds? If an object for this exists on the Web, it's easy. Download, modify a bit, and presto.

C++'s portability exploded beyond anything that developers imagined. It brought on the second revolution in game programming. Developers created whole 3D engines for games like Doom, Quake, and Unreal; then they'd sell them to other developers to use in other projects. Can't afford to buy a 3D engine? That's cool, because free 3D engines started to appear on the Web—along with code for sound cards, objects for polygon calculation, and so much more, all of it nearly plug-and-play.

The ease of use and the portability of C++ revolutionized game development, and better hardware support took it to the next level. Sound, calculations, sprite and polygon rendering, player control, collision detection—these are just a few of the things that, just a few years ago, you could only do painfully, in assembly language that would run on only one processor. But Nintendo changed that.

GAME CONSOLES SHAPE THE FUTURE

Back in the 1970s, when Atari and the like debuted their game consoles, processors were expensive. So, consoles such as the 2600 and Intellivision had to rely on less processor power to do all the necessary tasks. In 1984, Nintendo was creating its new video game console, The Family Computer (or Famicom), which later became the Nintendo Entertainment System (NES) in the United States. By this time, chips were more affordable and easier to come by. So, when it created the Famicon, Nintendo gave it several processors, each with a specific task.

The breakdown went like this: The main CPU, the 6502, controlled the larger functions, such as math calculations, floating point instructions, and system management. Another chip controlled the creation and administration of graphics—how they appeared on the screen, and what sprites would do when they collided into one another. Yet another chip managed created, and played sounds. This whole system created a looser, more efficient structure, allowing programs to harness the power of each processor individually. The first Famicom games appeared in Japan in 1985, a year when Atari's 2600 was still king in America. But if you've ever seen a 2600 and Nintendo game side by side, you know that NES games blow 2600 games to smithereens.

A few computers of that day also used separate processors. The Commodore 64 had separate video, audio, and main processing chips. But Nintendo really showed the advantages of this type of system. The word was out: This was the way to better games. Commodore's Amiga series and Atari's ST series took the model to an extreme by including amazing graphics and audio processors, even while they had mediocre CPUs.

While game console makers flocked to multi-processor systems, PC manufacturers approached the idea with more caution. For a long time, IBM and the clone-makers thought their customers didn't want graphics. Computers used for businesses don't need high-powered graphics or polygons or full-on surround-sound stereo. What businesses needed was a "real" computer like a PC, right?

Some third-party manufacturers thought otherwise. Graphics card manufacturers, like Creative, created cards with better video processors, and that included their own RAM. The cards took on many time-intensive tasks, and the main CPU became free to do other things. CGA, the first PC graphics standard, turned to EGA, and then to VGA and SuperVGA. Soon, "Graphics Accelerator Cards" like the 3Dfx™ and ATI series appeared. These cards assisted the video card and gave enhanced performance to graphics-intensive applications (games!). They rendered polygons into the tens of thousands and applied textures for a "real-life" look.

The same push for improvement happened in the sound world, too, though the battle ended pretty early. Two cards, the Ad-Lib and the Sound Blaster®, appeared in the early 1990s. By the middle of the decade, the Sound Blaster was an unofficial standard. Today it comes in nearly every new PC and creates and plays sound unimagined a decade ago–full stereo music and effects, sounds that even rival real life. The screeches in Grand Theft Auto sound as if they're outside your door.

For game developers, cards made programming even easier. Each card came with drivers and libraries that could be inserted into new games. A new game could look and sound fantastic right out of the box, with no need to rewrite basic sound and graphics routines. Flat, 2D games with tinny sound gave way to fully rendered 3D worlds filled with music and sounds around every darkened corner. In Unreal, the growls fall from the platforms above. In Quake 3: Arena, you can actually hear the sound of someone getting fragged two rooms away. Quick! Run! Frag the fragger!

THE FUTURE OF GAME DEVELOPMENT

It may seem like we've come to the end of game development's road of progress. But this is by no means a dead end. There will always be room for advancement and improvement. Some developers believe easier programming and game development tools make for worse games. This is not true. Sure, there are a lot more games out there because they are so easy to crank out, and that ease of creation has caused some poorly done games. But better games are also appearing, because real artists can work on a game and create a great game, not a degraded version of it. Gamemakers can also focus more on the production values of the game, and not the technical details.

The typewriter didn't create bad writing, just more of it, both good and bad. In any artistic endeavor, it's the output that is to be judged, not the tools that made it.

Previously, it was necessary to learn the specific language of a processor before even trying to write a game for it. Now, with tools like TGF or The Pie GCS, gamemakers can create games in a matter of hours. Easier programming tools give professionals a broader range of talent to pull from. And it gives amateur developers stronger tools to hone their skills.

Games and game development are becoming more popular due to the increasing ease of entry into the game development field (you no longer have to be a programmer). There is a demand for artists, animators, and designers. As a result, there are larger and more diverse teams working on games.

GAME GENRES

To design and develop computer games, you'll find that, as in most professions, you will need a common vocabulary to communicate with all the people involved in the life of a game title. Among the most important terms is "genre." Genres in computer games, as in movies and books, help the designers form a unified vision, help businessmen sell the games, and help the audience know what they are getting.

 GameDictionary.com (www.gamedictionary.com) is an online resource you can visit to brush up on the terminology of the game development industry.

The concept of the genre in computer games starts simply, but it also gets rather complex. The field of game development has more forces and influences at work on its product in the computer field than in any other medium. In printed fiction, genres started simple, like the thriller, then branched off into subgenres, such as the "legal thriller" or "psychological thriller." Having subgenres branch off main genres is simple to understand for everyone involved, from the writer to the reader. But in computer games, many factors create many genre hybrids and combinations. Things are also moving so fast that there is barely time to develop a consensus on how genres should be divided and labeled.

In the following sections, we will look at the many genres, subgenres, and hybrids of computer games. You will need to know the genre of your game before you design it, but chances are, if you have an idea for a game, it already fits into one of the genres discussed below. Genre is important at this point, because it will help determine the amount of art, technology, time, and money you will need for your game. And if you plan on getting your game published, you will need to be able to quickly and clearly position your title in the publisher's mind by comparing it to other games, and discussing your game, in terms of its genre.

Maze Games

ON THE CD

Maze games have been around almost longer than any other genre. These are the very familiar games like Pac-Man and Ms. Pac-Man. Maze games are simply that—you run around a maze, usually eating or gathering something, while being chased by something. Maze games started in 2D with an overhead view of the maze. You can easily make maze games with The Game Factory.

Many people don't realize that from a design point of view, the modern high tech full-blown 3D games are simply a case of the player being brought into the maze. Players still chase, are chased, gather power, and die in a maze. An old example can be seen in Figure 4.7.

FIGURE 4.7   Crak Man was not well-received by any audience.

Board Games

When a traditional board game like Monopoly, Clue, or Sorry is recreated on the computer, it still keeps its original genre classification of "board game." The game usually looks much like the original game, with no innovation in game play, no original use of computer technology other than to make the game function as it does in real life, and usually no artistic improvements on the original game board and pieces. Initially, the challenge of programming enough artificial intelligence for the computer to play the game was enough to keep the developers busy, so new innovations in art and game play had to wait.

More recently, board games in the computer world have been moving away from straight copies of their 2D ancestors, to newer 3D versions. These newer games sport a 3D look, as the pieces move and have animated cut scenes at highlights or low points (victory and defeat points) of the game. Still, they are not usually innovative. They are simply more lavish productions. Some players and designers argue that this takes away from the game itself, as the animation and videos in many cases slow the game down.

Card Games

Computer card games like Solitaire, Poker, Hearts, and Strip Poker are a huge genre. And, like board games, these titles have so far seen little innovation in most ways. Hardwood Hearts by Silver Creek Entertainment is a well produced card game (see Figure 4.8) that is showing some really cool innovations, such as multiplayer modes and custom decks.

Battle Card Games

Battle card games came about with the Magic The Gathering craze, which spawned such card games as Spellfire, Legends of the Five Rings, and Pokémon. Battle card games play very much like traditional card games, only with pretty pictures and an emphasis on being collectible. Naturally, the decks are open-ended; if users buy more cards, they become more powerful. Their move to the computer has been much like traditional card games' move to the computer, with little real innovation.

Quiz Games

Quiz games are big, especially online, and TGF makes them easy to create. Games like You Don't Know Jack, Jeopardy, and Trivia Wars are some of the biggest in this genre. The logic behind these so-called "multiple-choice

FIGURE 4.8   A screen shot of the innovative *Hardwood Hearts*. A demo can be downloaded at www.silvercrk.com.

games" is rather easy. All the games have to do is display a question and three or four answers. The hard part is in the researching and organizing of all the content—the questions and answers. Figure 4.9 shows a typical quiz game interface.

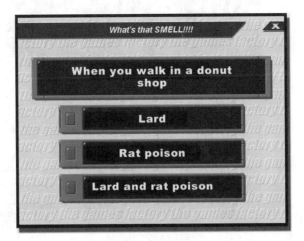

FIGURE 4.9   A typical quiz game interface.

Puzzle Games

Puzzle games include Tetris, Dr. Mario, and others. Usually, there are pieces falling from above, which players have to line up before they hit bottom. The player must fit them all together in the most efficient manner, to leave no open spaces between the pieces. The pieces become more complex and fall faster as the game progresses.

Shoot 'em Ups

Space Invaders, Asteroids, Sinistar, Space Battle, and the original Spacewar are examples of this genre. (In Part 2 of this book, we make a shoot 'em up game.) These are the 2D games where you are in a ship in space and you shoot things before they hit you—aliens, missiles, and such. Space Defiler is a typical shoot 'em up and can be seen in Figure 4.10.

Side Scrollers

Side scrollers are what made id big. Remember Commander Keen in the "Invasion of the Vorticons?" The original Duke Nukem, Prince of Persia 1,

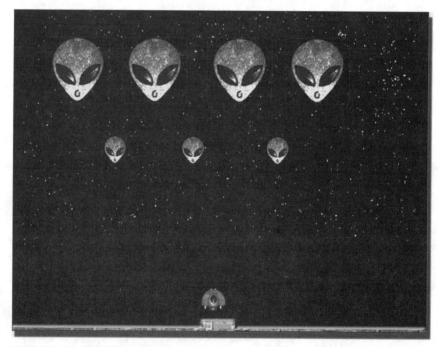

FIGURE 4.10 Space Defiler, a shoot 'em up you can make with The Games Factory.

FIGURE 4.11   Zeb is a side scroller made with The Games Factory.

and Zeb are also examples. Zeb was made with The Games Factory. Side scrollers usually have the hero running along platforms, jumping from one to the next, while trying not to fall into lava or get hit by projectiles. A typical side scroller interface is shown in Figure 4.11.

Fighting Games

There are many fighting games. Examples include Street Fighter 2, Samurai Showdown, Martial Champion, Virtua Fighter, Killer Instinct, Battle Arena Toshinden, Smash Brothers, and Kung Fu (see Figure 4.12). Fighting games started as flat 2D interfaces and now feature full 3D arenas and animated characters. The focus in a fighting game is the almost endless fighting moves and special moves that you can use against your opponent.

Racing Games

Racing games center around the concept of driving fast around different tracks. Wipeout, Destruction Derby, Mario Kart, and South Park Derby, to name a few, are all racing games. Some 2D racing games have a scrolling road and the sprite of the car moving over the surface. With the explosion of the color Game Boy on the scene, these games are making a comeback.

FIGURE 4.12 The Kung Fu game is a fighting game made with The Games Factory.

Flight Sims

A flight simulator (sim) attempts to simulate real flying conditions by giving you control over such things as fuel, wind speed, and other instruments, and control over the flaps and wings of your craft. A sim will respond with the same limits as a real plane, as opposed to a more simple flying game, where you can't control much. Wing Commander, X-Wing, and Microsoft Flight Simulator are all flight sims. A screen shot from a flight sim is shown in Figure 4.13.

Turn-Based Strategy Games

In games such as Breach, Paladin, Empire, Civilization, Stellar Conflict, and Master of Orion, players take turns making moves. These games require a lot of strategic thought and planning, much like chess.

Real-Time Strategy Games

Populous, Command and Conquer, Warcraft, and Syndicate are a few popular real-time strategy games. In these games, you don't have forever

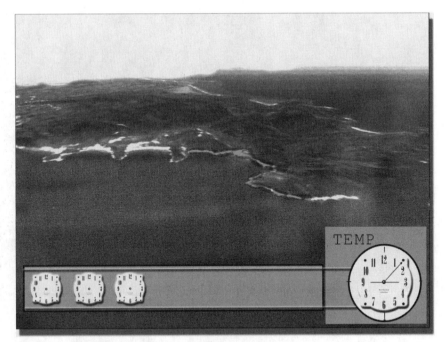

FIGURE 4.13   A flight sim mock-up for a game company.

to take your turn before the next person moves. Faster players can make many moves in a short period of time. These games are also a bit like sims, since you are usually overseeing a large battle or war, and the building of towns and outposts. Resource management is important—such as in Warcraft, where you have to determine the amount of gold you can get before you run out and can build no more.

Sims

Sim City, Sim Earth, Sim Ant—Sim Everything. In these games, you run a simulation of a town, world, or ant colony, making decisions and managing resources. These are often called "God Games," because you are playing the part of God in the game world.

 In the discussion that follows, the terms first person *and* third person *refer to the point of view of the player. Just as in literature you can write in first person ("I shot the rocket") or third person ("She shot the rocket"), there are points of view in gaming, as well.*

FIGURE 4.14   Screen shot from Sorcerer, a First-Person 3D game.

First-Person Shooter (FPS) 3D Games

These games include Castle Wolfenstein 3D, Doom, Duke Nukem, Quake, Dark Forces, and Sorcerer. The focus in these games is on technology and atmosphere. These games attempt to put you into the action, as you are literally looking out of the eyes of the character, seeing and hearing what they see or hear. As you can see in Figure 4.14, the point of view is from a person on the street.

First-Person 3D Vehicle-Based Games

These game are much like the first-person shooter games, except that they put you in a vehicle, such as a tank, ship, or giant robot. This genre is more similar to an FPS shooter game than a racing game, because you are not simply driving as fast as you can to cross a finish line. Your goals are more

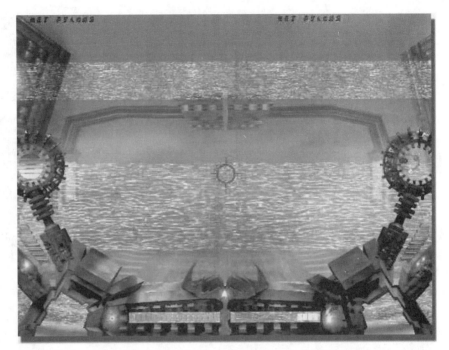

FIGURE 4.15   Screen shot from Dead Reckoning, a first-person 3D vehicle-based game.

similar to the ones in an FPS game—kill or be killed. Examples of vehicle-based shooters are Descent, Dead Reckoning, and Cylindrix. Figure 4.15 shows a screen shot of a vehicle-based shooter game.

Third-Person 3D Games

Tomb Raider, Dark Vengeance, Deathtrap Dungeon, and Fighting Force are all third-person games. Although there are games where you can switch from first- to third-person perspective, most games are designed primarily to be one or the other. Tomb Raider in first person is not as much fun, since it is designed around seeing Lara Croft jump, roll, and tumble. In first person, you would not see these acrobatics. In Figure 4.16, you can see a third-person game. Notice how you can see the spell effects that you cast (the protection circle) when in third-person mode. Likewise, when playing a first-person shooter, like Quake 3 Arena, you depend on speed and accuracy in battle to win—that is the point of the game. If you were able to play Quake 3 in third-person mode, you would die an awful lot since you would not be able to run, aim, shoot, and run some more as quickly.

FIGURE 4.16 Screen shot from Sorcerer in third-person mode.

RPGs (Role-Playing Games)

Wizardry, Ultima, NetHack, Dungeon Hack, Might and Magic, and Daggerfall are all RPGs. These games emulate the traditional pen-and-paper games where you play characters who have a lot of significant attributes, such as health, intelligence, strength, and areas of knowledge and skill. RPGs are like a simulation of an adventure.

Adventure Games

Zork, Hitchhiker's Guide to the Galaxy, and King's Quest are all adventure games. In an adventure game, you walk around and try to fulfill a quest or unravel a mystery. You typically collect information and items. Battle is light and not the focus of this game type.

Full Motion Video Games (FMVs)

FMV, or Full-Motion Video games include MYST, RIVEN, and . . . well, no other FMV game is worth mentioning. These games require a lot of art and animation or video production, and little of anything else. There is simply no room for effects, because FMV is a limiting genre at present. In an FMV, you mostly watch a movie and then select what portion of the movie to watch next, much like a computerized version of the "choose your own adventure" books.

Educational and Edutainment Games

Some games or interactive products fall under this genre. Whether a game fits into this genre depends mostly on its purpose, rather than on its content or use of technology. A first-person game would be an edutainment title if its intention were to educate and entertain, as would a quiz game. These genres are instructional and informative. The edutainment variety attempts to make learning fun, while the educational variety is straightforward learning.

Sports Games

Sports is a huge-selling genre all by itself, but also another genre label that doesn't completely convey the technology, game play, interface, or other aspects of the game. In fiction, a thriller that takes place at a football game may be called a "sports thriller." An inspirational nonfiction book with a sports theme may be called "self-help/sports." But in games, people often don't say "quiz game/sports" or "quiz game/football" or "third-person football simulation"—everything is lumped under "sports."

Screen Savers/Desktop Toys

While not games, and not even very interactive for that matter, these products are generally entertaining, so they are usually lumped in with games and interactive products. These are fairly lucrative products that you can make with The Games Factory, like the screen saver in Figure 4.17, which was made for a Web site.

Genre Madness

Even with all the genres listed above, there are lots of games that cross over and combine the genres. Generally, a good game in one genre will have elements of other genres, such as puzzle-solving in a 3D game. Breakouts into new genres often occur where technology permits. For example, many fighting games started out as side scrollers for the 2D platform and evolved into 3D shooters or 3D games. Duke Nukem is a good example. Duke's progress is shown in Figures 4.18, 4.19, and 4.20.

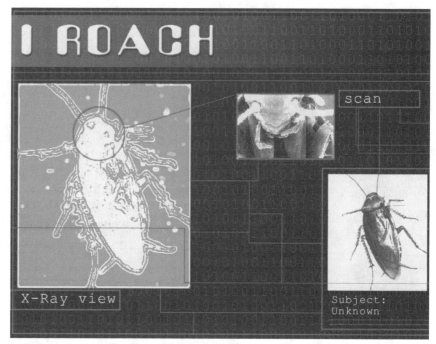

FIGURE 4.17 *Swarming Roaches* is a screen saver that Goldtree made as a novelty giveaway for a local Web site.

FIGURE 4.18 The original 2D side scroller Duke Nukem.

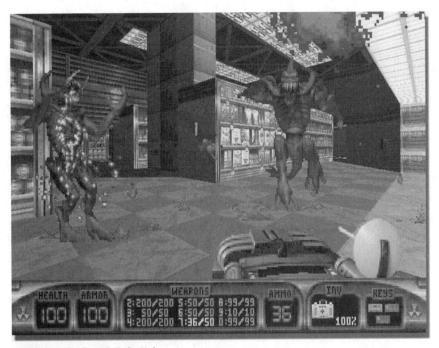

FIGURE 4.19   The first 3D Duke Nukem.

FIGURE 4.20   The latest Duke Nukem, using the Unreal Engine.

CHAPTER REVIEW

When designing your title, keep genre in mind. It is the first step in communicating your vision clearly to all involved. Once you have a clear idea of your game ("it's a first-person adventure game with shades of military simulation"), you can describe it in visual terms on paper, then break it down into the elements that will comprise the design document. In the next chapter, we'll look at the elements of design.

5

ELEMENTS OF DESIGNING A GAME

So far we have looked at the most fundamental parts of game design and development: your equipment, the building blocks of a game (sights and sounds), the truth about game design and development (facts and fallacies), and finally the genres, or classifications, of games. Now we are at last ready to look at the stage of game design where you actually start designing the game; where you start to marshal your resources, explore your limits, form your ideas, and put it all down on paper. This chapter will help you generate a design document in the early stages of developing your game. We'll also look at the game treatment and game proposal, which can be important parts of getting your game published.

All too often, people start generating their design documents and jumping right into development all at once. While recording your ideas and other information, and prototyping and testing as you go, can be invaluable, an unbridled jump into development can be a waste of time and will usually physically and mentally lock you into a tight spot. It is far harder to change the course of something that has momentum than to set it rolling on the right path to begin with.

This is not exclusively a beginner's mistake. Often, newbies to game development will do a better job at this phase, precisely because they are newbies and have to plan out everything they are going to do. Planning is important and can not be stressed enough.

Not planning can be disastrous if you are putting a lot of time, talent, and money on the line—dashed hopes can throw a small team or business asunder. Don't jump right into this stage of breaking out the specific elements of your game, or you will develop yourself into a corner. Building the proper groundwork is essential. Otherwise, you may design and develop a game which no one wants, which you can't legally use, or which represents wasted time and money.

The actual elements of a computer game are no secret. They are just mysterious to most people because they think of the design document as something that you just dash off. They think that having enough pages to impress any reader is sufficient. They have trouble filling these pages as they struggle through each item, trying to fill in the blanks. The truth is, it is only after you have decided upon your game idea, genre, and the overall feasibility of the game idea, that you will be ready to tackle this phase. The elements of your game should flow on paper, once you know what your game is.

 Design documents are not fill-in-the-blank forms. If you approach creating them this way, you will be frustrated, and your game will not be half as good as it could have been had it been planned up front. Design documents are the end result of your game idea. They are not game ideas waiting to happen; they are guidelines for the areas you should develop in your game. But as we'll see, they are not the end-all.

There are three phases of game design—predevelopment, development, and post-development. We are most concerned with predevelopment at this point. During predevelopment, you should be defining your limits and strengths, researching the feasibility of your game idea, and, of course, defining and refining it.

Before you develop a game, you must determine if your audience will like that game. As mentioned previously, you have to design for an audience, whether it is for one person or a million. And you have to know who these people are: which computer systems they like or dislike, and other factors that we'll explore below.

Along with what type of computer system you design for, your audience will determine how complex your game will be, how long it will take to play, and even its content. You should design with the best technology in mind; but obviously that's limited by the technology you are familiar with and have access to. We will look at this in the latter part of the book.

In designing a game, you should include *only what you need*. This is important to say, because many designers throw in all the elements they can think of, and in a predetermined order. What the *proper parts of a game are* is not at issue here; what will *make a game successful* is. Remember, any bold and conclusive statements that you've heard, stating what a game *has to be*, are wrong. The truth is, a game must be fun for the intended audience. What a game should be, or should contain, continues to evolve and is never set in stone.

GAME ELEMENTS

Now we are down to the elements of a game. We could just list them here, but where's the fun in that? Anyone can just list game elements and attempt to fill in the blanks, but it takes more than that to design a game worth developing. Important: anyone can make a game, but few can make a game worth playing.

Element One: Game Type

We looked at game genres previously in detail. Now is the time to fill in the blanks. Write down your game type from the following list. You need to at least know this tidbit of information.

1. Action—Lots of frantic button-pushing
2. Adventure—The story matters
3. Strategy—Nontrivial choices
4. Simulation—Optimization exercises

5. Puzzle—Hard analytical thinking
6. Toys—Software you just have fun with
7. Educational—Learning by doing

This is a good start for your design decisions and will greatly simplify the other decisions. The basic genre you develop will determine the focus on technology, art, content, and research. It will even determine the approximate size of your team, budget, and other resources.

As you decide about your game's main genre, you should also make notes about the other genres or game types that you hope to incorporate into it. Keep in mind that adding, or layering, genres, on your game increases everything—time, money, and resources needed, and the complexity of the project. After you have a good idea of the type of game you want to do—depending on your strengths and weaknesses—you are ready to move on to the next step.

Element Two: Game Idea and Game Treatment

You are now ready to write your game idea down, but not the treatment. The idea and the treatment are two very different things, and people often confuse the two.

Game Idea

A game idea is just that, an idea. You should write it first, to convey your game idea to others.

Game Treatment

A game treatment is written after substantial research, design, and even development has been done. It serves primarily as a selling document to pique the interest of publishers, investors, and department heads in larger companies. This is a concise document for an already well-formed game project. In other words, while the game idea represents the sum total of what you plan for the game, the game treatment is a distillation of a much larger body of work and only touches upon the highlights of the project.

Initially, you should write a rough draft of your game idea that presents as much information as possible about the game, as clearly and concisely as possible. It should spell out the general resources (time, talent, and cash flow) that the game will require, and why you think it is such a great idea. You can then use this document to discuss and research the feasibility of the game.

As the game project gears up, you'll need to line up resources and (possibly) team members, determine needs, develop budgets and schedules, and define the game to a great degree. The original idea will change, evolve, and grow more solid. This will generate a mountain of useful information.

At the end of this stage, you'll write the game treatment, which will explain the exciting game development effort you have underway.

Most of the advice floating around the Internet tells you to write the treatment first, before other documents. This is not the best advice. This comes from people looking at a game proposal and attempting to reverse engineer (an attempt by someone to determine this information after the game is completed) it.

The treatment *generally* contains the following items: the (proposed) title, the genre, the feel of the game play, the overall look of the game, features that you plan for the game, and any marketing information that will back up the feasibility of the title. Money, budgets, and dollar amounts should wait until after the publisher is interested in your game.

As a selling document, the treatment should open with the most marketable feature of you or your game development effort. If you are a top-selling developer, or if you developed a technological wonder or an artistic masterpiece, those facts should be presented first.

Be careful. This document is deceptive to many because of its brevity, but writing this short and concise document in an effective way requires a great deal of industry knowledge and writing skill. What you are attempting, in as few words as possible, is to get a publisher or investor to invest in your idea. This document is the equivalent of the query letters writers send out to get book and article publishing deals, and the cover letters that accompany business proposals. These are all selling documents and contain the same basic elements.

Even if you are making a game on a small scale, you should still get in the habit of writing down your ideas and documenting the development of your title. This will give you a focus that will benefit your title, and the practice will clarify your thoughts and clear the way for new thoughts to bubble up.

Element Three: Technology

This element consists of the game platform and the technology needed to play the game.

You should know what the system requirements are for your final game. Will it require a CD-ROM drive, a special video card or peripheral, a certain amount of RAM, or other special resources? What operating systems, drivers, or special software will the user need? These are all considerations the publisher will want to hear about.

Element Four: Audience

Several questions are important here.

- Who did you develop the game for, and why?
- Did you get audience input?
- What were their suggestions?

Keep in mind the previous sections of this book, dealing with game design and the audience.

Element Five: Team

You need a team, even if you are the only one working on your game. Here are some questions to ask.

- What team members will you need, and what jobs need to be done?
- Who are your team members, and where will you get them from?
- What are their strengths and weaknesses?
- How will you manage them; and do you have any experience managing people?

Element Six: The Design Document

So what should a design document contain? The design document comes from having a good game idea, along with the breakdown of the elements needed to develop that idea into a game. Publishers always want to see a design document, and with good reason, because it represents a complete game, along with the elements it takes to make a complete game. It is what the developer aspires to create.

Looking at an existing design document can be very useful as a guide. But remember that it is for someone else's title and most likely will not be a perfect fit for your game. Like the game treatment, a design document is a product of your game; it should come after you've fleshed the game out, not at the start. If you are doing a 3D shooter that is action-oriented, you may not have a need for a strong background story. In fact, that may be a detriment to the document from a development and selling point of view.

To illustrate the design document, Appendix A includes a sample design document. This is probably not the "fill-in-the-blank" form most of you were hoping to find. But reading and adapting it should serve as a guide for you in defining your game, rather than being a "fill-in-the-blank" exercise. Take note of the elements of this design document, but realize that your own game may have none, more, or all of the elements listed in that document.

Sample Design Document Outline

If you'd like to follow along with an actual design document, Appendix A contains the complete version of a design document for a 3D shooter. You can also use this as a basic template for creating your own design documents.

The CD-ROM included with the book also contains this design document / template, in Microsoft Word format.

ON THE CD

What Is a Design Document?

A design document is often overlooked in the rush and excitement of a game idea. After all, if you have a unique idea that could conceivably be a great game, why would you want to waste your time working on something that doesn't really get you any closer to the end product?

Many times, even relatively large development teams don't spend the time to create a fully functional design document. Most game developers will try to stay away from unnecessary work, but the long hours spent creating a thorough design document will actually save countless hours later down the development road. You might be lucky enough to create a very good quality game without a design document, but the key word in this is "lucky." Most often, a game that begins without a properly developed design document will be delayed for months or may not even be finished.

Creating a design document is similar to creating a movie script. In it, you will write details of an exact story (if you have one—for example, racing games would probably not have a story), an overview of the characters or opponents you are intending to create, detailed descriptions of every level, and so on.

If this is the first time you've ever considered creating a design document, there are a few things you should be aware of.

First, the design document is not chiseled in stone. It can and should evolve as the game does, but it shouldn't be drastically altered. The design document will serve as a sort of road map to how the project will develop and should be as complete as possible. That being said, you should change it when necessary, to include a new character or a change in the plot. Design documents are team oriented and therefore should include as many contributions as possible from the individuals who make up a team.

Sometimes, one person is the main author of a design document. If this is you, be careful not to be offended if someone suggests that you change something in the document. Input from others is important to the process, and it can give you invaluable information.

Appendix A should serve as a good guide to creating a design document. Feel free to change what you see there for any projects you are working on. Remember that creating a design document is an inexact science. Not all games are alike, nor are all design documents.

Also, proofread carefully! You would be surprised at the number of simple spelling errors that appear in most design documents. While everyone misses a word now and then, you should try your best to keep grammar and spelling mistakes to a minimum. This may not seem important to you, but again, you don't know who might end up reading your document.

Importance to Team Members

A design document is important to all team members, for a number of reasons. For a potential publisher, it details the game and provides a vision of what you are hoping to accomplish. For a development team, its purpose is rather simple; it sets out the responsibilities of everyone involved.

Depending on the team member, a design document will mean different things. Producers will use it to make their estimates, while programmers may look at it as series of instructions for carrying out their part of the project. Artists will use the design document to help them visualize the characters they need to create. Designers often use it to scope out important elements, such as the mood for a level. Audio personnel need to have a basis for developing sound effects and music. The design document may be the only place they can truly acquire the appropriate knowledge.

 While the design document is very important, it doesn't take the place of meetings among the members of the development team. Having team members share thoughts at regular intervals is very important. These meetings don't have to be formal. They can be in person or over some electronic medium, such as a discussion board. Like most things, it's not really important how they occur, just that they actually do.

Things to Include

Now that you have a basic understanding of design documents, let's look at the components or ideas that make them up. Many teams will include information such as legalities, target audience, and market analysis for a game in their design document. While this can work, it would make more sense to include those types of "business-related" materials in a game proposal to a publisher, something we'll look at in more detail later in this chapter. It's counterproductive to have team members scrolling through pages of information that they really don't need to review.

Game Overview (Storyline) This may be the most important piece of the entire design document. Without a solid story or game overview, the later steps will be much more difficult to create. Be very thorough with the game overview. If you leave something out, go back and fix it immediately. Sometimes the smallest details can make a big difference in a large project.

Because you don't know exactly who will read your design document, make sure to use as many details as possible, just as you would if you were creating a good storybook. Many teams place background information (information that tells how the situation shown in the game came about) in its own category, but because it relates to the story, you can put it in the game overview section. However, some genres, such as a sports simulation, wouldn't need a background section.

Levels The next item to address is the levels that make up a game. If you do a thorough job in the preceding step, this one is very easy. You compile a list of levels, in the order in which they will be encountered in your game, adding any details you feel are necessary. Some optional materials to include about the levels include ideas such as the layout, and a general description of the placement of enemies. Try to create a mood for a level at this time. If you do, a designer or artist can simply browse this information to get a feel for what needs to be created.

Creating a set of maps for the levels can be helpful to the members of the team, especially the programmers and level designers. These maps can be very detailed pictures, but they more likely will be a set of simple lines, circles and squares that form a rough layout of the levels. You can see an example of this in Figure 5.1.

Heroes and Enemies The next section of the design document deals with the characters in your game. Like the level section, the character section should almost fall into place if you've created a detailed game overview.

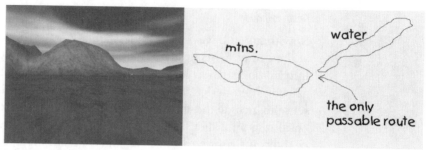

FIGURE 5.1 A level with a map.

There are two basic types of characters in most games: a hero, and enemies. You can include details of the hero, such as background information or rough sketches. These will help team members understand what they're trying to accomplish. For every hero, you should also include a list and description of animations that apply to that character. Depending on their role in the story, you can also include descriptive ideas of their intelligence level and strength, and basic information about how they react to the rest of the characters. Again, this information will be beneficial to the team when they are working on those characters.

After you finish with the heroes, create a section for enemies. This could include anything (human or not) that will attack a player. For instance, in an FPS, you might include a dinosaur; or in a space combat game, you could include an asteroid. Follow the same basic procedures that you did in fleshing out the heroes, making sure to include similar details and sketches where appropriate. For reference, Figures 5.2 through 5.4 contain sketches of the raptor that we will be using in our game project.

FIGURE 5.2 A rough sketch of a raptor.

FIGURE 5.3 The raptor with some color.

FIGURE 5.4   A 3D rendering of the raptor.

Finally, you need to include information about the types of weapons the characters will have access to. Include detailed descriptions of every weapon that can be accessed by either type of character. Sketches can be valuable for everyone on the team. Also, create a list that details the damage that each weapon will cause, along with the type and quantity of ammunition for each weapon (see Figure 5.5).

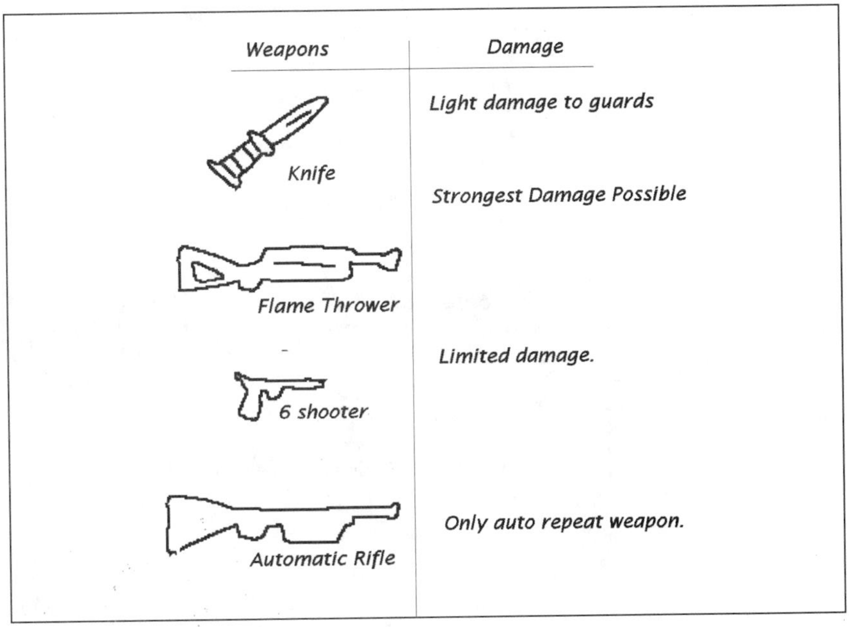

Weapons	Damage
Knife	Light damage to guards
Flame Thrower	Strongest Damage Possible
6 shooter	Limited damage.
Automatic Rifle	Only auto repeat weapon.

FIGURE 5.5   List of weapons and damages.

Notice that the sketches in Figure 5.5 are very simplistic. You can make the sketches as detailed or as simple as you wish. Often, it's more important to get them drawn than to worry about how great they look. You can always go back to them and clean them up later.

Menu Navigation   Another very important element is creating a list that details the game's menu navigation. It helps you keep track of how parts of the game are linked to other parts, and is particularly important to the programmers. You should create the main menu and a simple illustration of how the screens will be linked together. You don't need anything fancy, but all of the menus should be included. For example, you could use something like Figure 5.6 to display information about the opening screen of a racing game.

User Interface   The user interface goes hand in hand with the menu navigation system. For convenience, you could place them under the same category, because they deal with many of the same ideas. The information for this category can be text-based information about what you are planning to do, but ideally, some type of sketch works the best. Like most of the de-

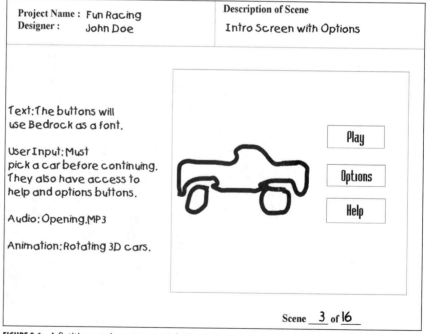

FIGURE 5.6   A fictitious racing game opening screen.

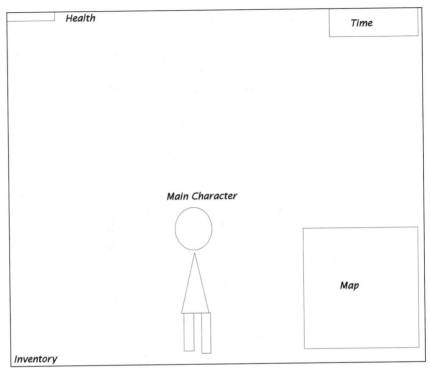

FIGURE 5.7   A user interface example.

sign document, this section doesn't have to be fancy. But details are important. (see Figure 5.7).

Music and Sound Effects   This section is important to the audio personnel on the team, and to the programmers who will use their sounds in the game. You can discuss the tools that you plan to employ, the types of sound effects you have in mind, and possibly detail the music you have in mind for the levels that you listed earlier in the process.

In the first draft of the design document, the most important details to include here are which audio formats and sound API (Application Programming Interface) you are planning to use, along with what types of music and sound effects you are planning. For instance, you should decide if you are going to use MIDI, WAV, or MP3 files for the music, and if you'll need things like explosions or footsteps for sound effects. You should also list the genres of music you're planning, such as rock or pop. This keeps the programmers and audio personnel informed, so that they are not surprised two months into the project.

Single or Multi-Player The next step focuses on the game play itself. If you worked hard on the game overview, you may have already covered this, and this section will be much easier. If not, start by determining if the game will be single player, multi-player, or both. For example, if you are planning an FPS clone like Quake, you might decide that it is single player only. If you are doing a sports game like basketball, you'll probably want to have multiple player support. Sometimes the information in this area of the document is discussed in other areas, but you shouldn't worry about duplication of ideas. This is especially true on a first draft, as you can always change the document later.

If you're designing a single player game, you can probably describe the game experience in a few sentences and perhaps break down some of its key elements. For example, if it's a Quake clone, you could begin by setting up the location of the game. Next, you could detail the types of enemies that players will face, and the route to complete the game, such as that players have to finish 10 levels before the game is over. You could also list how the game ends, and what happens if a player doesn't finish a given level on time. You might also include a projection of how long players will take to finish the game, and how a player wins the game.

Just as a multi-player game is harder to design than a single player game, it's harder to create the design document.

A multi-player game description starts the same way as a description of a single player game. Take a few sentences to describe the basics of the game play. The design document for the basketball game mentioned earlier could start by mentioning the type of game it is. For example, if it is a street ball game, a college game, or an NBA or international rules game. You might also decide what types of options the game will include, such as franchise mode for a professional game, or what types of parks you'll include for a street ball game.

Now is also a good time to decide how many players will be able to play simultaneously, and how you plan to implement the client-server or peer-to-peer system. For instance, do you plan to use something like DirectPlay® or another API, and how many players do you plan to allow to play against one another. In our basketball example, you need to decide how many people can play on a team. You don't need to have complete technical details, but at the least, you should discuss the client-server vs. peer-to-peer system issue. Optimally, in this section you will also discuss potential pitfalls that are common in multi-player games such as dealing with communication lag time.

Miscellaneous and Appendix The final area of the design document should discuss miscellaneous information that may be specific to a certain type of genre, or that doesn't fit neatly into another category. You can name this category anything that works well for you. For example, suppose you decided to do a basketball street game and you wanted to include information about the way the basketball players will dress, so that you can keep track of players from both teams. For example, you could have one team play in white shirts and another in red shirts. If you have comments to make about several different topics, split the discussion up, to keep everything easy to read and follow. The appendices are a good place to put items such as sketches or concept drawings. This way, you can refer the reader to an appendix instead of cluttering up your text.

Wrapping It Up   After the design document is finished and everyone on the team has had a chance to read it and suggest changes, you should print a copy for everyone. Keep the original in a safe place, where it will not be altered unless the necessary parties agree. For example, if you leave the document on a server where everyone can access it, team members may decide to alter it on their own, which would ultimately defeat the document's entire purpose.

Element Seven: The Game Proposal

The game proposal is a much more formal document than the design document. Its general purpose is to be used to approach a publisher for possible funding for your project. If you are planning to develop the project with your own money, a game proposal is probably unnecessary.

A game proposal takes the design document to a higher level and involves several issues that should not be included in a design document. For example, it should include information such as technical specifications, and marketing, financial, and legal issues. After the design document has been thoroughly digested by the lead programmers or the senior members of the team, it should be included with the game proposal. We won't break down a game proposal in great detail here. But for a quick overview, refer to Figure 5.8.

GAME MARKET

The game market is a good place to begin. You can determine a market simply by looking at titles that are similar to the one you are developing. By looking at sales figures, you can figure out how large a market a particular style or genre has, and your potential for sales. An excellent source of game market data is www.pcdata.com. You can search for information

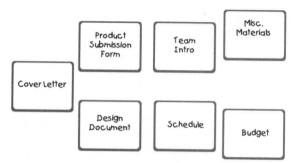

FIGURE 5.8 Basic parts of a game proposal.

such as PC sales, Macintosh Sales, and even home education sales. Figure 5.9 shows an example of the data available at PCData. If you are planning a game to run on multiple platforms, you should try to break this information down among them.

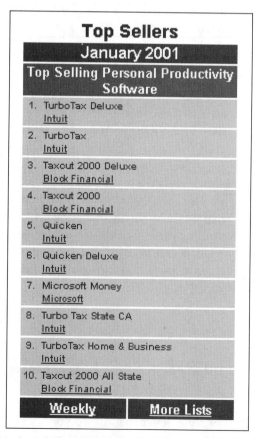

FIGURE 5.9 Example from PCData showing market sales for February 2001.

TECHNICAL INFORMATION AND ASSOCIATED RISKS

The most important things to list in this area include the teams members' development experiences in developing a game similar to the one you are working on. For instance, if the lead programmer has developed 3D engines in the past, mention this experience. On the other hand, if this is your team's first 3D engine, you should also convey this as well. If you are using third party software, such as a code library or sound effects, you should list them as well.

In any project there are technical risks. You should try to provide the possibility of a workaround if you encounter one. For example, you could purchase a 3D engine from company XYZ if the engine you are working on does not pan out.

REQUIRED RESOURCES AND SCHEDULING

The final area to include is the required resources and scheduling information. The schedule should include an estimate of the project's length, along with specific milestones that occur along the way, such as an alpha or beta product. The required resources should include all financial estimates, such as the cost of employees, hardware, and software.

CHAPTER REVIEW

In this chapter, we looked at the main parts of good game design, and at how to document that design. Nailing down your game type and the elements that go into creating your game is just the start. We then saw how to bring these decisions into your design document, and looked at the importance of the game treatment and game proposal.

There are no set rules for game design and development. Still, with the material from this chapter, you shouldn't have a problem creating a functional game treatment, design document, and game proposal for yourself or a team.

One of the greatest things about game development is that the genres are so flexible and the technology is so powerful. There are no barriers to entry. In fact, it is incredibly easy to get started in game development. It is all about knowing what tools and resources you have at your disposal and where you want to go with your ideas. In the next chapter, we'll use some of those ideas and finally begin to make a 2D game.

6

INTRODUCTION TO GAME MAKER

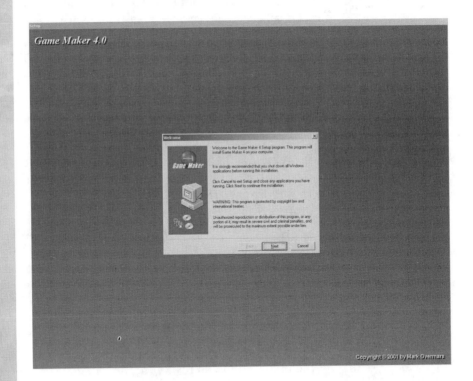

This chapter introduces you to Game Maker. The program's name is indicative of its ease of use; with the Game Maker you can make computer games without writing a single line of code. Using easy-to-learn drag-and-drop actions, you can quickly make professional look-ing 2D games. The games can include any number of elements, including backgrounds, animated graphics, and music and sound effects. After you have mastered the drag-and-drop actions, you can move on to the simple built-in programming language that lets you add advanced functionality to any game. To top it all off, Game Maker is free of charge and allows you to create standalone games that you can distribute freely.

ON THE CD

Game Maker 4.0 is on the CD-ROM that accompanies this book, in a folder called GameMaker. You can also get it from the Web site of its programmer, Mark Over-mar. To get the latest version, go to http://www.cs.uu.nl/~markov/gmaker/ index.html.

INSTALLATION

Game Maker is easy to install.

1. Put the CD-ROM included with the book in your CD-ROM drive.
2. In Windows Explorer or My Computer, open the folder called *GameMaker*.
3. In the *GameMaker* folder, run *gmaker.exe*. This starts the installation process. You'll see a screen similar to Figure 6.1.
4. Click the Next button to display the license agreement. Be sure to read the License Agreement before proceeding. Then, click the Next but-ton. This opens the Product Information materials.
5. Read the Product Information materials. When you're done, click the Next button to display the Installation Directory options (it should look like Figure 6.2).
6. Choose the directory where you want to install Game Maker, and click the Next button. You can navigate to a directory of your choice, but the preferred method is to use the default setting of *c:\Program Files\ Game_Maker4*.
7. Choose a name for the Program Group for Game Maker, and click the Next button. You can change to a different group, but the preferred method is to use the default setting shown. The installation program will start copying files to your installation drive and directory (see Figure 6.3).
8. When all files have been copied, the Finished Setup screen will appear. Click the Finish button to finish the installation and run Game Maker (see Figure 6.4).

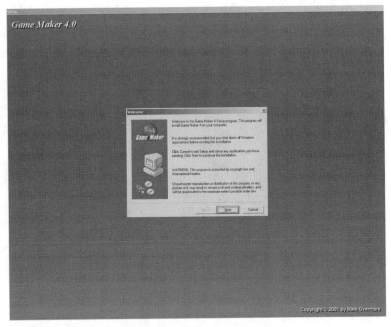

FIGURE 6.1   Beginning Game Maker installation.

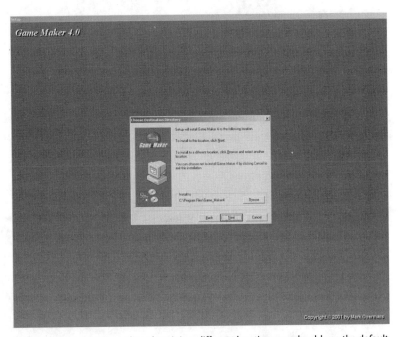

FIGURE 6.2   Unless you need to place it in a different location, you should use the default directory.

FIGURE 6.3 The files are being copied to the hard drive.

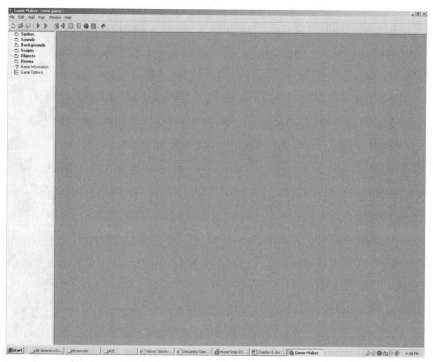

FIGURE 6.4 The interface of Game Maker.

GAME MAKER INTERFACE

Game Maker is so easy to work with because everything has been designed with simplicity in mind. In Figure 6.4, you can see the various elements that make up Game Maker Integrated Development Environment (IDE). These are discussed below.

Resource Explorer

At the upper left is the Resource Explorer. This displays the various resources that can make up a game project: Sprites, Sounds, Backgrounds, Scripts, Objects and Rooms. Along with the resources, you'll see Game Information and Game Options. You'll also see a standard type of menu and toolbar at the top of the screen.

The Resource Explorer gives a tree-like view of all the resources in your game. Here's how it works:

- To open a resource, right-click it.
- If a resource has a "+"next to it, you can click the "+" to expand the tree view and see the resources inside of it.
- If a resource has a "−" next to it, you can click the "−" to collapse the tree view and hide the resources inside of it.

Figure 6.5 shows resources with the "+" sign. You can click the "+" to expand the view of these resources. Figure 6.6 shows the Resource Explorer after the user clicked on the "+" signs for Sprites and pac-mans to open them up.

FIGURE 6.5   The unexpanded Resource Explorer.

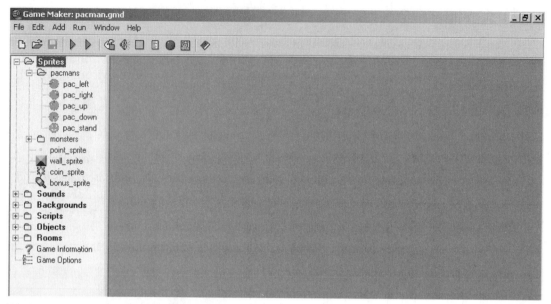

FIGURE 6.6 Resource Explorer with items expanded.

Menus and Toolbar

The menus and toolbar appear at the top of the IDE. The following sections explain what you'll find there.

File Menu

The File menu includes the usual options, as listed below.

- New: Creates a new game project.
- Open: Opens an existing game file.
- Save: Saves an existing project with its current name. The first time you save a project, it will prompt you for a name.
- Save As: Saves a project, but prompts you for a name first.
- Create stand-alone: Creates a standalone game that can be run like any standard Windows program.
- Import scripts: Imports scripts from an outside file. Scripts are small pieces of program code used for advanced features. They are not covered in this book.
- Export scripts: Saves a script.
- Preferences: Lets you set various preferences for Game Maker.
- Exit: Exits the program.

Edit menu

The Edit menu contains commands that affect a currently selected resource, such as a sprite, object or room. The commands that are available depend on the currently selected item.

- Insert resource: Lets you insert a copy of the selected resource before the currently selected item.
- Duplicate: Makes a copy of the current resource and adds it after the currently selected item.
- Add group: If resources are combined, they are called a group. Adds a group into the project.
- Delete: Deletes the current resource.
- Rename: Lets you rename the current resource.
- Properties: Lets you edit the properties of the current resource.

Add Menu

Lets you add new resources. You can add a new resource of any type from this menu.

Window Menu

Contains the usual commands to manage the different windows:

- Cascade: Displays all windows so that they are partially visible.
- Arrange Icons: Arranges all the windows when they are minimized as icons.
- Close All: Closes all open windows.

Help Menu

Lets you access the help information for Game Maker.

CHAPTER REVIEW

In this chapter, we walked through the installation of Game Maker and looked at some of the basics of the IDE. Although this is a good introduction, there is much more to learn about Game Maker. We'll look at Game Maker in more detail in the next chapter, when we create our first game.

YOUR FIRST GAME MAKER PROJECT

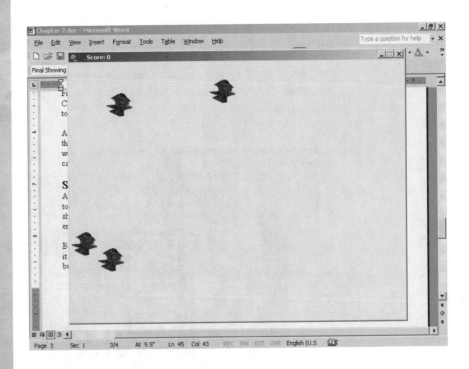

B efore we start using Game Maker, we need to learn about a few of the ideas behind the program. Understanding the various ideas and elements will help tremendously when we create a game.

GAME MAKER BASICS

Games created with Game Maker take place in one or more rooms. These correspond to the levels that you see in a game. For instance, a Pac-Man type of game would have a room with a maze, Pac-Man, and the Ghosts and Pellets (see Figure 7.1 for an example). Game Maker is only 2D, so the rooms are flat. However, you can give a 3D appearance to a room by designing the graphics appropriately.

Objects

All rooms contain objects. These include anything that is used in the room. For instance, the objects in a Pac-Man game would include items that play-

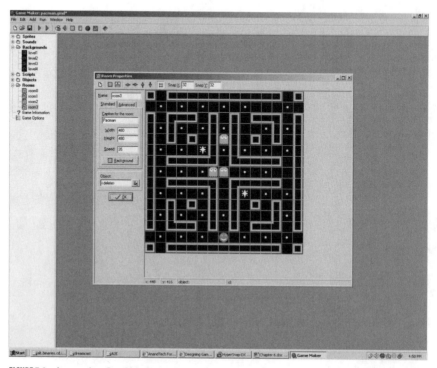

FIGURE 7.1 A room in a Pac-Man game.

ers control, such as Pac-Man; stationery objects, such as the maze; and computer-controlled objects, such as the Ghosts.

Sprites

For objects to appear on the screen, they must have an associated image. In Game Maker, sprites are used for this purpose. Sprites generally are composed of many separate images. You can see an example of a sprite made up of several sprites in Figure 7.2.

Events

As sprites move around the room, they have things happen to them. For example, they can collide with walls and other objects. These encounters are called *events*. Events also include user actions, such as when a player clicks on an object. It is these events that allow us to create games in Game Maker.

When an event occurs, you as the developer can establish what happens. For instance, if two objects collide, you can make them rebound. You

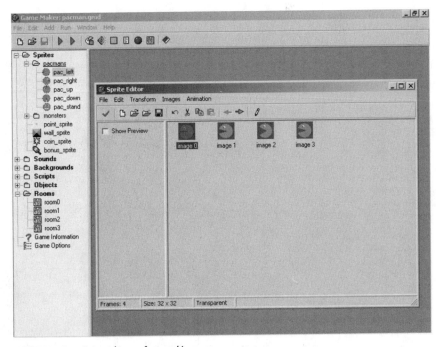

FIGURE 7.2   A sprite made up of several images.

can also create an object for which you can set its speed and direction, or even have it play music.

CREATING A GAME

It's time to get going. Let's create a game. Start up Game Maker. You'll see a screen like the one shown in Figure 7.3.

 The game that we'll create in this chapter is available on the CD-ROM that accompanies this book. Look for chapter 7.gmd in the Projects directory. You can open it and look through it, or follow along by creating the project yourself.

Next, we'll create the objects that will make up our project. Here's how:

1. Right-click on Sprites in the Resource Explorer. You'll see a menu like the one shown in Figure 7.4.
2. Select Add Sprite from the menu. You'll see the Sprite Properties window, which looks like Figure 7.5.

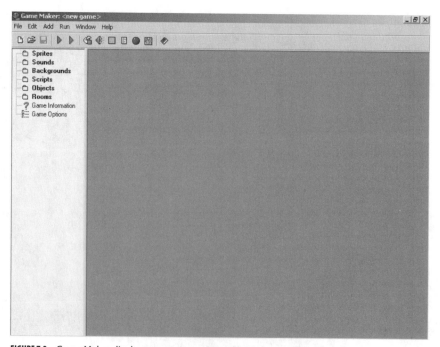

FIGURE 7.3 Game Maker displays an empty project when it first opens.

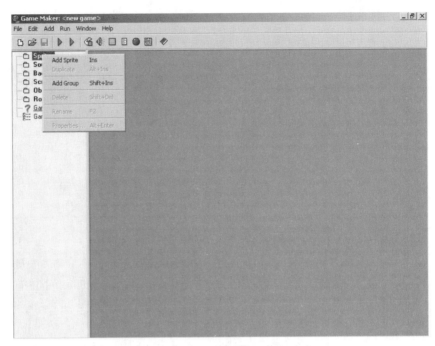

FIGURE 7.4   Right-clicking a resource allows you to add it to the project.

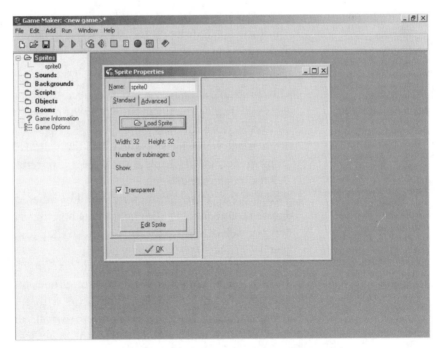

FIGURE 7.5   The Sprite Properties window allows you to create or alter a sprite.

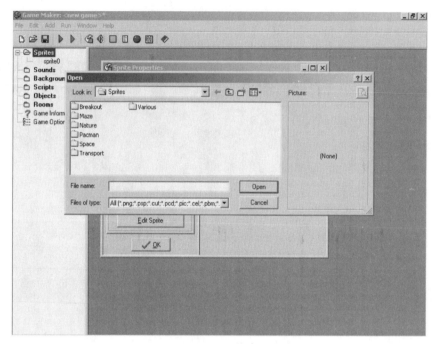

FIGURE 7.6   This allows you to select the sprite you need for your project.

3. Click the Load Sprite button. You'll see an Open dialog box, as shown in Figure 7.6.

1. From this window, choose the *Space* folder (you may have to choose the *Sprites* folder first, to get to it). Select *Asteroid.gif* from the list of files. This will display the file in the Sprite Properties window. Click the OK button to close the window.

2. Right-click the Objects resource and then choose Add Object from the pop-up menu. This displays the Object Properties window (see Figure 7.7 for an example).

3. Beneath the "Object Properties" window label, click the button that is located immediately to the right of the box that says "<no sprite>." This lets you select a sprite for the object, so that you can use it in the project.

4. Select <sprite0> in the pop-up menu that now displays.

5. In the Object Properties window, locate the toolbar at the far right. In the first row of the toolbar is an icon with red arrows pointing in every direction. Drag this icon onto the small window immediately to its left. When you let go of the button, you'll see a window like Figure 7.8.

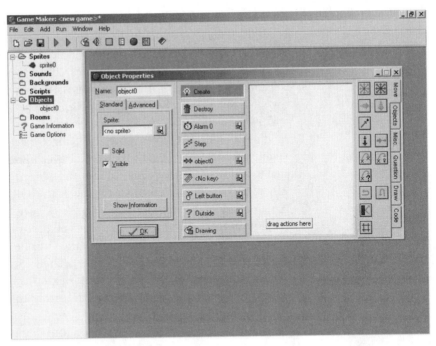

FIGURE 7.7   The properties for the object.

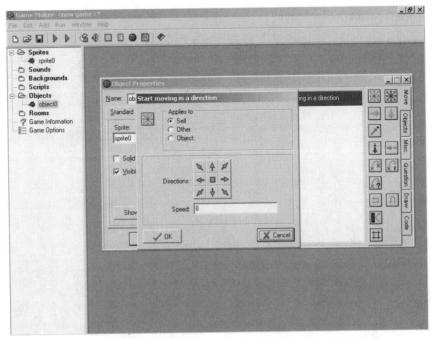

FIGURE 7.8   This window lets you give an object a direction when the game is first opened.

6. Click all eight direction arrows (this specifies that the object can move in all directions). Then set the speed to 3 and click the OK button. You'll be returned to the Object Properties window.

7. Click the button labeled "Left button" (third from the bottom in the column of buttons to the left of where you just dragged the eight arrows). This lets you create actions for the events that will occur when a player left-clicks the object.

8. At the far right of the window, click the Objects tab. When the tab opens, drag the icon that looks like a trash can onto the window to its left. Now, when a player left-clicks the object, it will be destroyed. When the next window displays, click the OK button. The Object Properties window should now look like Figure 7.9.

9. We'll now set the bounce action that will occur if the object attempts to move outside the game area. Click the Outside button (second from the bottom in the column of buttons). Then click the smaller button within it and choose Boundary from the pop-up menu.

10. Click the Move tab in the toolbar. This brings up choices for how the object will move.

11. Drag the "Bounce against objects" icon into the window that is located to its left (it's the second one from the bottom, with a red arrow

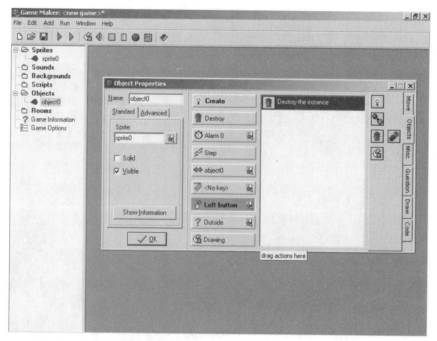

FIGURE 7.9 The properties for this object.

bouncing off a blue barrier). In the screen that appears, click the button to the right of the "against" field, and choose "All Objects." Then, click the OK button.

12. To save your changes to the object, click the OK button in the Object Properties window. The Object Properties window will close. You'll also need to click OK in the Sprite Properties Window if it is open.

Now that we've created an object and given it properties, we'll create a room and put some copies of the object in that room. Here's how:

1. From the Resource Explorer (remember, it's at the upper left), right-click on Rooms and then select Add Room from the pop-up menu. You'll see the Room Properties window, as in Figure 7.10.

2. Now, we'll set up the background for the room. Click the Background Button. In the new window, click the Background Color button and then choose a light blue color. Click the OK button to return to the previous window, and then click OK. You'll be returned to the Room Properties window.

3. At the bottom of the window, you'll see an object selection box. Click on the icon and choose Object0 from this list—it's the object we created earlier.

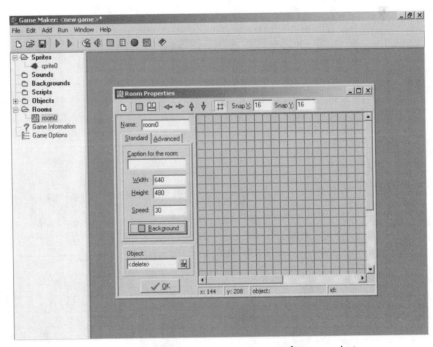

FIGURE 7.10   The Room Properties window lets you set up a room for your project.

4. Click several times within the blue background area. Each time you click, a new object of the same type is created in the room.

5. When you've created a few objects, click the OK button to close the window.

SAVE AND RUN

Congratulations! You've finished your first game! It's a very simple game that allows you to "shoot" asteroids from a simple screen. Any asteroid that isn't destroyed bounces around the screen. Although it's a simple one, creating this game has allowed us to learn a lot about Game Maker. This will make future game development much easier.

It's time to save and run the game. Here's how.

1. On the File menu, choose Save. Give the file a name, and click the Save button. Game Maker will automatically add the extension "gmd" to the name you choose.

2. On the toolbar, click the green triangle, below the Run menu item. Your game will start running. You'll see a screen like Figure 7.11.

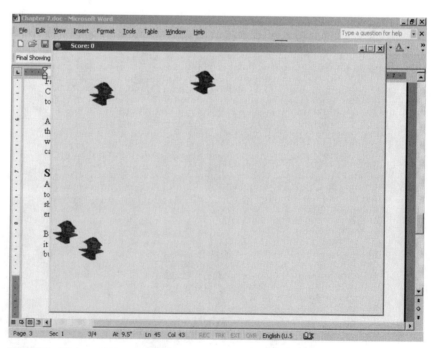

FIGURE 7.11 The game being executed.

Try out the game to see if you can zap the asteroids in the project. You can stop the game at any time by pressing the ESC key on your keyboard.

CHAPTER REVIEW

Now that we have successfully developed a simple game, we have a good basis for future work. In this chapter, we learned about a variety of very important items, such as the resources that make up a project (rooms and objects), and how to put together a basic project. In the next chapter, we'll create a space shooter using Game Maker.

2D SPACE SHOOTER

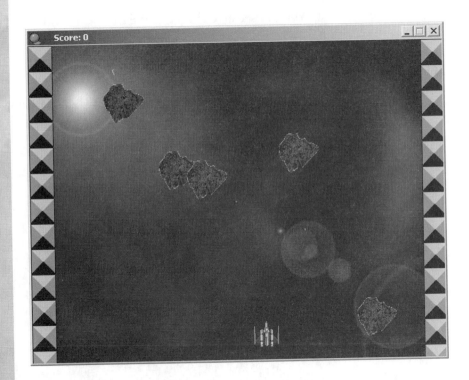

n this chapter, we'll expand on what we learned when we created the simple asteroids game in the previous chapter. We'll add the following things:

- A ship that is controlled by the left and right arrow keys
- A space backdrop
- The ability to shoot projectiles that destroy the asteroids
- The ability to handle collisions between the ship and asteroids, and between the asteroids and left/right borders
- A simple scoring system

You can see an example of the final game in Figure 8.1.

SETTING UP THE GAME

To begin, start up the Game Maker. This will create a new project automatically. It should look something like Figure 8.2.

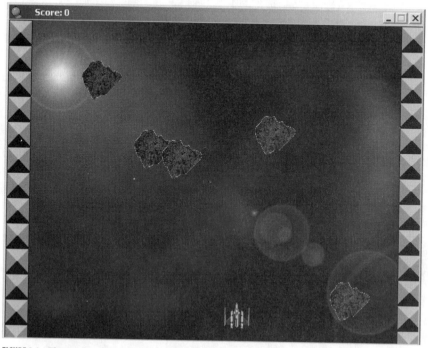

FIGURE 8.1 The game we'll create in this chapter.

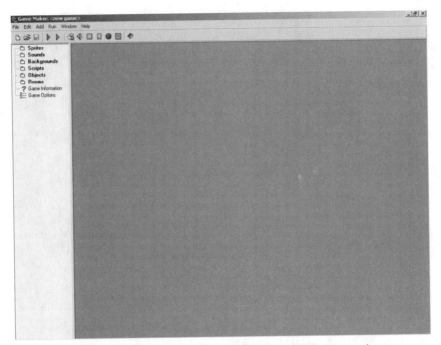

FIGURE 8.2   A new project is automatically created when the Game Maker is opened.

Sprites

We won't need to design any of the graphics used in this chapter. The Game Maker comes with graphics that we can use with very little alteration. Instead, we'll focus on these built-in graphic elements. We'll start with sprites, including an asteroid, a space ship, a projectile, and a border for the left and right sides of the screen.

Making the First Sprite

1. To add a sprite, click Add Sprite from the Add menu, as shown in Figure 8.3. This calls up the Sprite Properties menu, as shown in Figure 8.4.
2. Click the Load Sprite button. An Open dialog box will appear, as shown in Figure 8.5.

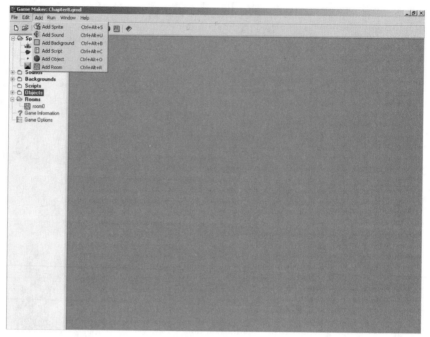

FIGURE 8.3   Adding a sprite.

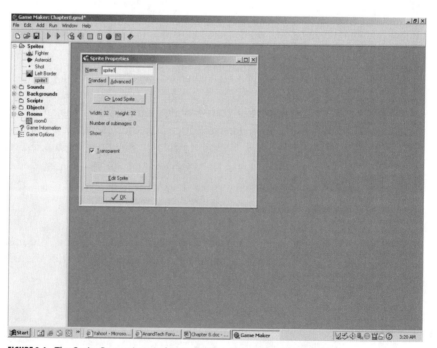

FIGURE 8.4   The Sprite Properties window is displayed when you click Add Sprite.

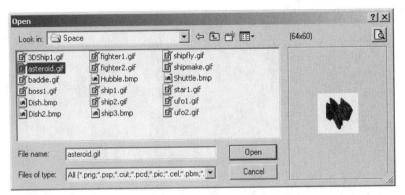

FIGURE 8.5 An Open file dialogue box allows you to add graphic images to your project.

3. Open the Game Maker default folder (usually *C:\Program Files\Game_ Maker4*). Then choose the *Space* folder, which will be inside of it.
4. Click the *asteriod.gif* file and then click the Open button. This will import the graphic image into the Game Maker. You'll see the asteroid image, as shown in Figure 8.6.
5. The *asteroid.gif* file contains several individual frames that make up an animation. We'll remove all of the frames except for the first one. To start the process, click the Edit Sprite button to open the Sprite Editor window, as shown in Figure 8.7.

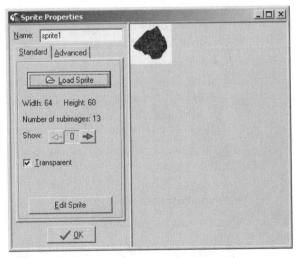

FIGURE 8.6 The image is imported into the Game Maker.

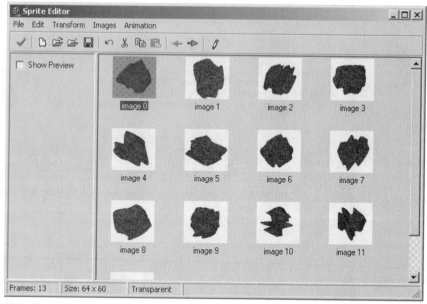

FIGURE 8.7 The Sprite Editor allows us to add and remove frames from an animation.

6. Click Image1 and then either press the Del key or choose Delete from the Edit menu. This removes Image1 and will remove the image from the animation.

7. Delete the other images, until only Image0 remains. The Sprite Editor should now look like Figure 8.8.

8. Click the close box (the "X" in the upper right hand corner). If Game Maker asks if you wish to save the changes, choose Yes. You'll be returned to the Sprite Properties window.

9. Click in the Name text box where it says Sprite1 (or Sprite0), and change the text to Asteroid. This gives the name Asteroid to the sprite. This isn't necessary in a simple game, but it can make a big difference in a project with a large number of sprites or other elements. The Sprite Properties window should now look like Figure 8.9.

10. Click OK. You've now finished making this sprite.

Making the Rest of the Sprites

It's time to add the other sprites to the game. The following list shows the sprite name, and the Game Maker 4 file, to use for each one. Figures 8.10,

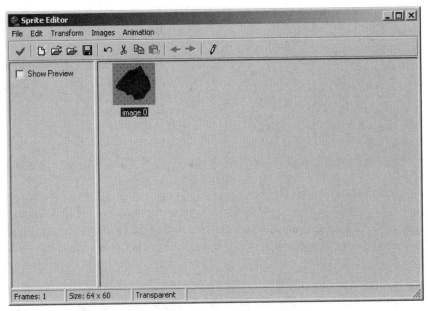

FIGURE 8.8   The Sprite Editor with only one frame remaining.

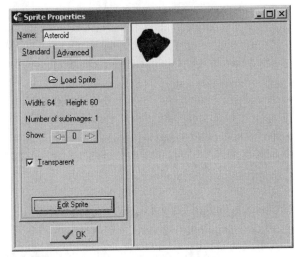

FIGURE 8.9   Sprite Properties are now finished for the Asteroid.

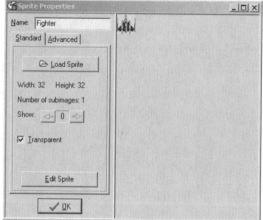

FIGURE 8.10 The Fighter properties.

FIGURE 8.11 Left Border properties.

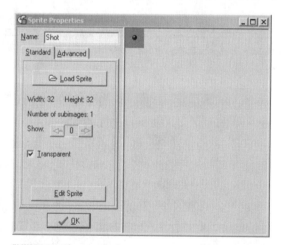

FIGURE 8.12 Shot properties.

8.11 and 8.12 show the Sprite Properties for each sprite, so that you can compare your work with them.

Sprite Name	Graphic File Name and Location
Fighter	...*Game_Maker4\Space\Fighter1.gif*
Left Border	...*Game_Maker4\Maze\Wall.gif*
Shot	...*Game_Maker4\Various\dot.ico*

We'll use the Left Border sprite for both the left border and right border objects, instead of importing a different file for each one.

To create the other sprites, use the table shown above. Follow the steps that you used earlier to create the Asteroid sprite, while making the changes shown below.

- Steps 1-3: Same as above for each sprite.
- Step 4: For each sprite, call up the image file listed in the Graphic File Name and Location column of the table.
- Steps 5-7: If the image contains more than one frame, delete the extra frames. If it doesn't, skip to step 8.
- Steps 8-10: Same as above, but in step 9, change "Asteroid" to the name in the Sprite Name column of the table shown above.

Sounds

It's time to create some sounds. This is the item below Sprites in the Resource Editor at upper left of the Game Maker's IDE. We're going to add a single sound that will play when a collision occurs between a shot and an asteroid.

1. Choose Add Sound from the Add menu (see Figure 8.13 for a view of this menu).

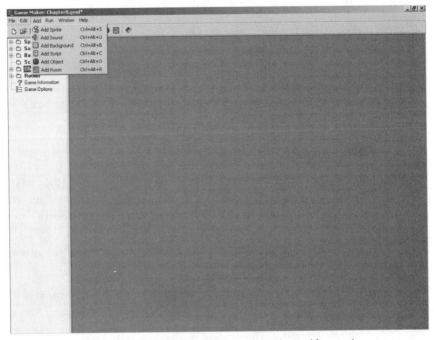

FIGURE 8.13 The Add menu, with the Add Sound menu option (second from top).

2. In the window that appears, click the Load Sound button. This displays an Open dialog box that lets you choose a sound file for the explosion.

3. In the Game Maker 4 installation directory (again, this defaults to *C:\Program Files\Game_Maker4*), open the *Sounds* directory.

4. Load *explosion.wav*.

5. Rename the Sound element to Explosion and click the OK button.

Background

Now, we'll add the background image, a space scene.

1. Choose Add Background from the Add menu.

2. In the window that appears, click the Load Background button. This displays an Open dialog box that lets you choose a background.

3. In the Game Maker 4 installation directory, open the Backgrounds directory.

4. Load *space1.jpg* and click the OK button.

 If you don't have space1.jpg in the directory, you can download the free sprite pack from the Game Maker Web site (http://www.cs.uu.nl/people/markov/gmaker/download.html).

Objects

Now that we have sprites and a background, let's turn the sprites into objects. We can then interact with them. Among many possibilities, we can test collisions between them and can use the keyboard to control them.

We'll begin by selecting the Fighter.

1. Choose Add Object from the Add menu. This brings up an Object Properties window that looks like Figure 8.14.

2. As shown by the "<no sprite>" entry in the first column of Figure 8-14, no sprite is currently selected. To start selecting a sprite, click the button to the right of the "<no sprite>" entry. A drop-down menu displays, as shown in Figure 8-15.

3. In the drop-down menu, select the Fighter sprite that we created earlier.

Now that we've selected it, we'll turn the Fighter into an interactive object. First, we'll create a basic movement for it.

As shown in Figure 8.14, the Object Properties window includes a set of buttons, with labels such as Create, Destroy, and Alarm. These buttons

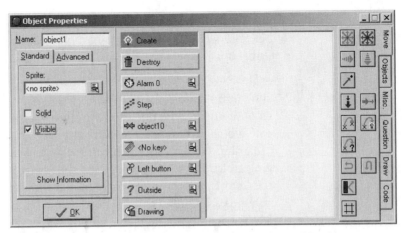

FIGURE 8.14   The Object Properties window controls many aspects of the object.

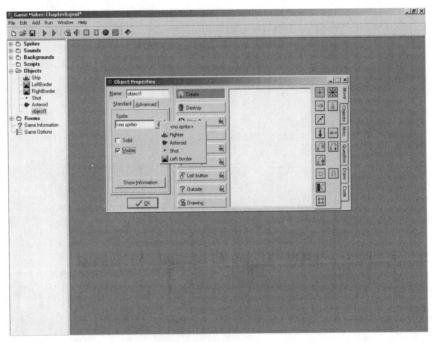

FIGURE 8.15   A drop-down menu is used to select the sprite.

let you specify interactions with the objects that you create. We want the Fighter to move left and right along the bottom of the screen. Here's how to set this up:

1. Right-click the button labeled "<No key>." You'll see a menu, as shown in Figure 8.16.
2. Choose <Left>. The title on the button changes to Left. This will indicate which button you are currently working with.

   Earlier, we saw how you can create actions for an object by dragging an icon from the toolbar (on the far right) into the blank area to the left of the toolbar. Each of the tabs at the far right of the toolbar contains a different set of actions. We'll be using the Move tab to select the action that happens when a player presses the left arrow key.
3. Place the mouse pointer over the button that has two "X" figures on it. Notice that the button's label appears: "Jump to a given position" (see Figure 8.17). Now, click and drag that button to the empty box located immediately to its left. You'll see a display like Figure 8.18.
4. Click the Relative option and then enter –10 (negative 10) for the X value. This means that the object will move 10 pixels to the left when the left arrow is pressed. Click OK to close the window.

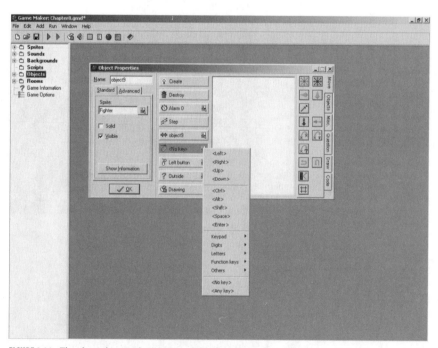

FIGURE 8.16 The drop-down selections available for movement.

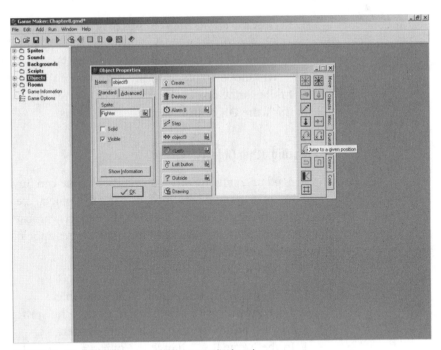

FIGURE 8.17   The information about a button is displayed.

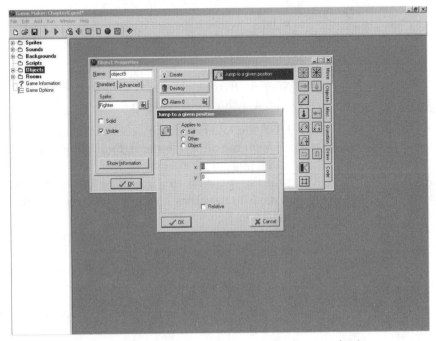

FIGURE 8.18   "Jump to a given position" is opened automatically when you select it.

5. Repeat the earlier steps in this procedure, with the following changes:
   - Choose the <Right> key instead of the <Left> key.
   - Enter 10 for the X value (not negative 10). This means the object will move 10 pixels to the right when the right arrow is pressed.
6. In the Name box at the upper left, change the object's name to Ship.
7. Click the OK button.

Creating Other Objects

We need to create the other objects before we can finish the ship. First, call up the sprite named Left Border. Using this object, create objects called Left Border and Right Border. Both of the objects can use the same sprite, because the sprite only dictates how the object appears. You don't need to set an action for either of these.

To create the Left Border Object:

1. From the Add menu item, click Add Object.
2. Click on the button to the right of the <no sprite> box.
3. In the pop-up menu, choose Left Border.
4. In the Name box, change the object's name to Left Border.
5. Click the OK button.

To create the Right Border Object:

1. Follow the steps you used above for the Left Border object, but type Right Border in the Name box, rather than Left Border.
2. Click the OK button

Now, we'll create an object called Shot, using the Shot sprite. We'll also set a single action for this object.

1. From the Add menu item, click Add Object.
2. Click on the button to the right of the <no sprite> box.
3. In the pop-up menu, choose Shot
4. Drag the "Start moving in a direction" button (the red one with 8 arrows) into the blank area to its left. You'll see a window like the one shown in Figure 8.19.
5. Click the arrow that points straight up (see Figure 8-20). Set the speed to 8, and click the OK button.
6. In the Name box, change the object's name to Shot.
7. Click the OK button.

This Shot object will automatically move straight up as soon as it appears in a room.

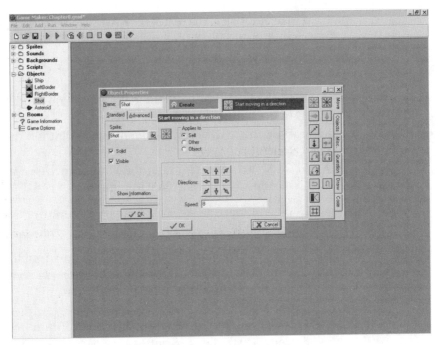

FIGURE 8.19   The "Move in a direction" options.

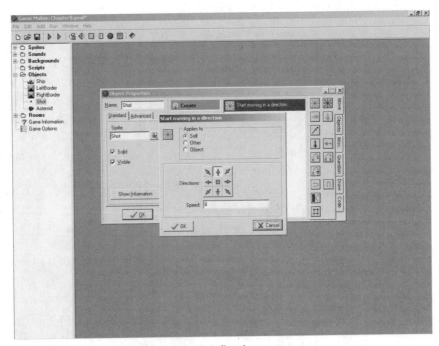

FIGURE 8.20   An option selected for moving in a direction.

The last object to create is the Asteroid object, for which we'll use the Asteroid sprite. We'll set it to move in any of three directions: down and left, straight down, or down and right.

1. From the Add menu item, click Add Object.
2. Click on the button to the right of the <no sprite> box.
3. In the pop-up menu, choose Asteroid.
4. Drag the "Start moving in a direction" button into the blank area to its left.
5. Click the three arrows in the bottom row (see Figure 8-21). Set the speed to 2, and click the OK button.

We also need to set what happens when the Asteroid hits the room borders, and make sure the object has the correct name. Here's how:

1. Click the Outside button (the second one from the bottom).
2. Drag the "Jump to start position" button (the one with an "X" and a light bulb) from the toolbar into the blank area, and click the OK button.
3. Drag the "Start moving in a direction" button from the toolbar to the blank area. Click the bottom row of arrows, and set the speed to 2. Then click the OK button.

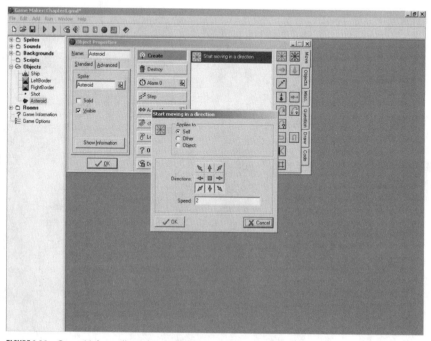

FIGURE 8.21 Game Maker will randomly choose one of the directions.

4. In the Name box, change the object's name to Asteroid.

5. Click the OK button.

Collisions

Now that we've created all the objects, we need to set how the Ship object will react when it collides with one of them.

1. In the Objects part of the Resource Explorer, double-click the Ship object. In the column of buttons, you'll see a button called "Ship" with two arrows on it. This specifies what happens when two Ships collide. Since we'll only have a single ship, we won't worry about this. Instead, we need to select one of the other objects.

2. We'll make the Ship move 20 pixels to the right if it collides with the Left Border. First, right-click the "Ship" button and select Left Border from the pop-up menu. Then, drag the "Jump to a given position" button (the one with two "X's") from the toolbar to the blank area. As shown in Figure 8-22, enter 20 for the X value. Then, click the OK button.

3. We'll make the Ship move 20 pixels to the left if it collides with the Right Border. First, right-click the Left Border button and select Right

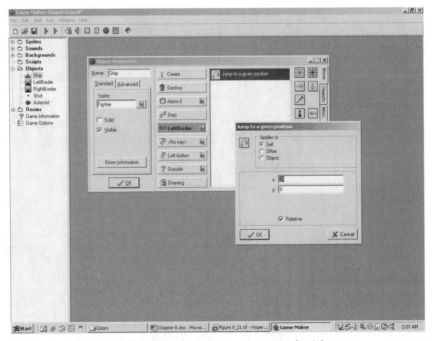

FIGURE 8.22   A collision with the Left Border requires us to move to the right.

Border from the pop-up menu. Then, drag the "Jump to a given position" icon from the toolbar to the blank area. As shown in Figure 8-23, enter –20 (negative 20) for the X value. Then, click the OK button.

The only other objects we need to check for collisions with the ship are the Asteroids. We can use the Destroy Instance and End Game actions for this. They are located in the Objects and Misc. tabs, respectively. You can close the object properties for the ship.

We also need to set up the actions that occur when an Asteroid collides with the Left Border and Right Border. Open the Asteroid object properties and select the Collision button. Use the drop-down list to set the collision for the Asteroid and Left Border and then drag the Bounce Action. Do the same for the Right Border. Next, choose the collision with the Shot object. If this occurs, we'll begin by destroying the Asteroid instance (Object Tab), playing a sound (in Misc. Tab), and we'll finish by setting the score. Figures 8.24, 8.25 and 8.26 display these actions.

Rooms

Now that we have the collisions all set, the next step is to create the environment in which the collisions will occur. The Game Maker uses rooms

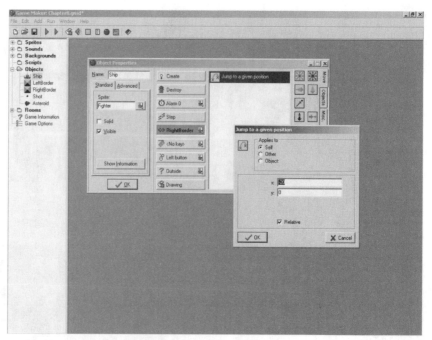

FIGURE 8.23 Right Border collisions require us to move to the left.

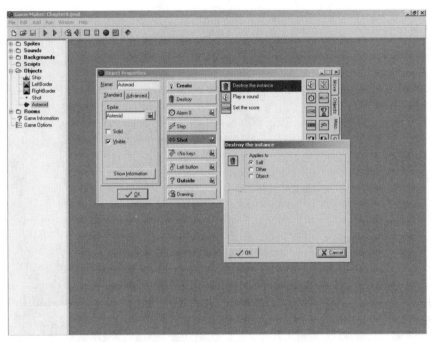

FIGURE 8.24   Destroy the asteroid if it collides with a shot.

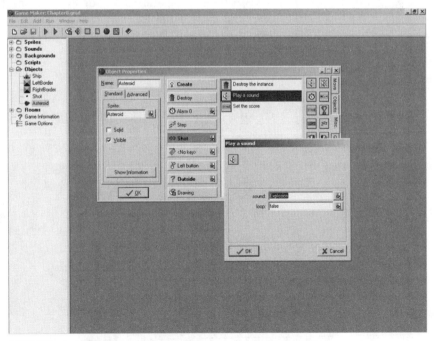

FIGURE 8.25   An explosion is played if a collision occurs with the shot object.

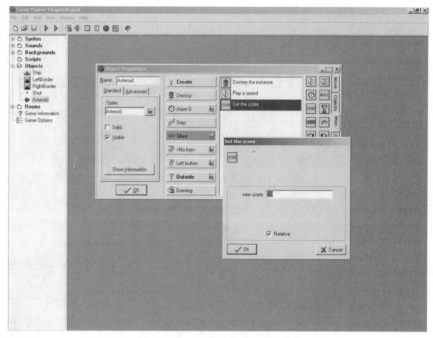

FIGURE 8.26 You should add a value to the score if a collision occurs.

for the screen areas in a game. Click Add Room from the Add menu to create a room and display it on the screen. You'll see a grid window that will eventually make up the play area of the game (see Figure 8.27).

The next step is to click the Background button. This will display a dialog box like Figure 8.28.

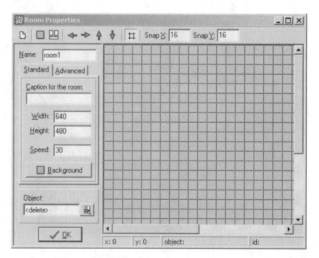

FIGURE 8.27 Room Properties for a newly created Room.

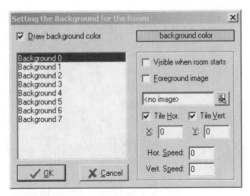

FIGURE 8.28   Setting up the background.

Choose Background from the drop-down box that initially contains <no image>. Choose the "Visible when room starts" button and then click the OK button. Change the width and height to 540 and 400 respectively (this is the same size as the background image).

To place the objects in the room, you need to select them from the Object drop-down list and then single click inside the grid to place each object. For example, select Ship and then place it near the bottom middle of the room (see Figure 8.29).

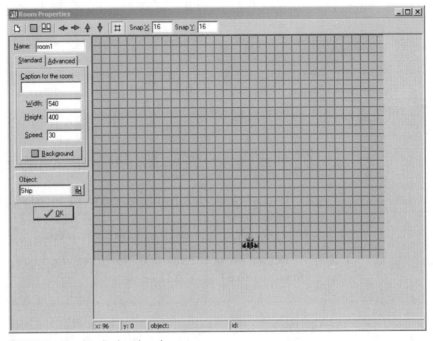

FIGURE 8.29   The ship displayed on the screen.

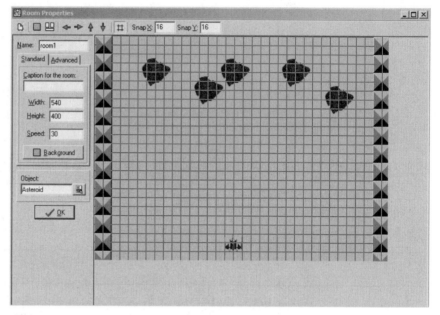

FIGURE 8.30 The final screen layout.

From here, arrange the objects as shown in Figure 8.30.
Click the OK button to save the layout and close the window.

Figures 8.29 and 8.30 are displayed without the background to make it easier for you to see their placement.

TESTING

The game is now finished, so the next step is to save it to a name and location that you will remember. Once you have saved it, you can run the game in any of these ways:

- Click the green arrow below the word "Add" on the menu
- Press the F5 key.
- Choose Run Normally from the Run menu

Regardless of the method, you'll see the final game. It should look something like Figure 8.31.

FIGURE 8.31   The shooter is finished.

CHAPTER REVIEW

In this chapter, we designed a complete space shooter game and learned about as much as we can about the Game Maker without getting into its scripting capabilities. In the next chapter, we'll take a look at a new development tool, The Games Factory.

9

INTRODUCTION TO THE GAMES FACTORY

I n the following chapters, we will actually make a game, step by step. It will be exciting to see your creations come to life on the screen as we work through the tutorials. Once you have made a 2D game, you have the basis you need to go further into game development. Much of what you learn here will apply to more complex applications and tools later on. You will find it easier to pick up new software and tools and learn them after having learned one application. We will be using The Games Factory (TGF), thanks to the wonderful people at Clickteam (See Figure 9.1).

Once you are comfortable with TGF, you will be able to use it to produce games and interactive applications with ease. TGF is a very powerful 2D game creation package. It contains state-of-the-art animation tools, sound tools, multimedia functions, and fabulous game structuring routines that make it very easy to produce your own games—with no programming.

You can also make slide shows, interactive tests, presentations, and screen savers with TGF.

We will start by installing TGIF and getting familiar with its major functions.

ON THE CD

On the CD-ROM in the back of the book, you will find both 32- and 16-bit versions of TGF. If you are running Windows 3.xx, you need the 16-bit version. If you have any other Windows operating system, use the 32-bit version.

STARTING THE INSTALLATION

If you have Windows 3.xx, you must install the 16-bit version of The Games Factory. All other Windows users should install the 32-bit version.

FIGURE 9.1 Clickteam makes The Games Factory, Install Maker, and other fine products. Please visit them at www.clickteam.com.

1. Put the CD-ROM containing The Games Factory in your CD-ROM drive.
2. In Windows Explorer or My Computer, open up the CD-ROM drive and find the folder that contains the 16 bit or 32 bit version you are installing. Double-click this file to start the installation.

Installation

The installation procedure is very similar for both the 16- and 32-bit versions. During the installation you will be given the choice to install the Unregistered, Home, or Pro version (see Figures 9.2 and 9.3). You should install the Unregistered version.

This is a normal Unregistered version of TGF, but as a special contribution to this book, Clickteam has removed the time limit. You can use TGF as long as you like, but you will see a startup screen each time you start it up. Also, you cannot save standalone games, screen savers, or Internet applications.

This Unregistered version allows you to save your creations as GAM files (*.gam* files). This means that anyone wishing to play your game needs to have TGF installed on their computer. As mentioned above, to save standalone games, screen savers, and Internet applications, you'll need to

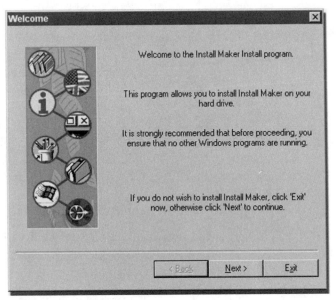

FIGURE 9.2   The welcome screen.

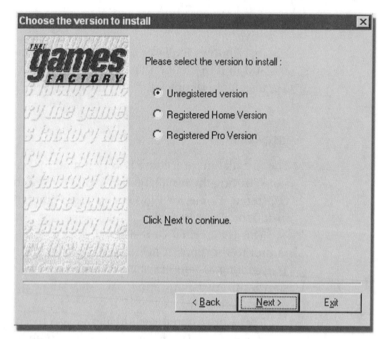

FIGURE 9.3 Unless you are a registered owner of TGF, you should select the Unregistered option.

go to www.clickteam.com and register TGF. You can buy a registration code that will allow you to run either the registered Home version or the registered Pro version. You don't need to download anything, because the necessary files are included on the CD-ROM. All you have to do is reinstall TGF, select the proper registered version from the menu during installation, and enter the registration code, as shown in Figure 9.4.

Both the registered Home and Pro versions of TGF can save standalone games, screen savers and Internet applications. However, games saved with the Home version have an end screen and cannot be sold for profit. The Pro version saves standalone games that have no end screen and that can be sold for profit. For purposes of this book, we'll assume that you have selected the Unregistered version from the CD-ROM at the back of this book.

Here's how to complete the installation.

1. TGF will now install itself and ask if you want to read the README file. It's a good idea to do so. Click Finish at the bottom of the screen when you are ready to move on.

2. The next screen asks if you want to install either Video for Windows® or a QuickTime™ video driver for showing AVI and QuickTime-com-

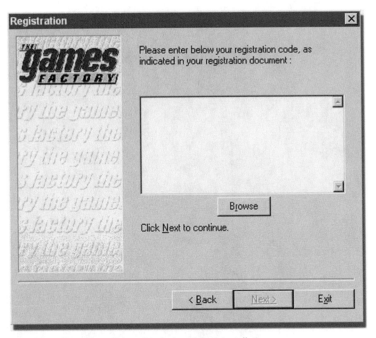

FIGURE 9.4   The registration code window during installation.

patible video clips. Unless you want to install one of the drivers, click Next. The next screen asks you to type in your full name. When you have done so, click Next.

3. On the next screen are two check boxes, one for the 16-bit version and one for the 32-bit version. If you are running Windows 3.xx, the 16-bit box will be checked. Otherwise, the 32-bit box will be checked. (See Figure 9.5.)

4. For 32-bit Windows users, there is a check box for DirectXDirectX®, which is Microsoft's graphics driver. Unless you specifically don't want to install DirectXDirectX, check the box. If you experience problems using DirectXDirectX, you should change the graphics driver. For 16-bit users, there is a check box for Win G, which is Microsoft's graphics driver. If you need it, install that driver.

5. At the bottom of this screen is the default directory that The Games Factory will use. Unless you specifically want to enter a different name, click the Next button.

6. If the directory doesn't exist, you will be asked if you want to create it. Click the OK button to proceed.

7. Now wait while The Games Factory installs. When installation is complete, click the Return to Windows button to return to Windows.

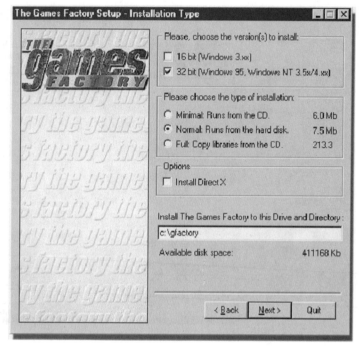

FIGURE 9.5 Installation Type screen.

Now you can double-click the icon for The Games Factory to run the program.

To follow along with the tutorials, copy the three tutorial files from the CD-ROM (in the samplegames\tgflibs *folder) into the TGF Library folder. (If you did a default installation, the folder will be called* C:\GFactory\Libs.*) DO NOT copy the folder itself—only the three files in the folder.*

A Quick Introduction to TGF

TGF is centered around three main editing screens that allow you to control the three main parts of your game:

- The **Storyboard Editor** lets you specify the order of the levels in the game.
- The **Level Editor** lets you specify which characters, backgrounds, and objects to put in your level, and how to animate them.

- The **Event Editor** lets you assign the actions and responses that will make your game come alive.

You can easily move from one editor screen to the next by clicking the Editor icons from the toolbar at the top of each editor screen. Some of the functions of the screens overlap, so it's a good idea to use the Handy Hints along the way. Don't worry if you don't remember what each one looks like. As you move the mouse pointer over the icons, a text balloon will appear, telling you what each one is.

The following sections describe the functions of each of the editor screens. For more information, see the sections of The Games Factory user manual that relate to them.

Storyboard Editor

Most games are composed of several different levels. This screen lets you add levels to your game, copy levels, and change the order of the levels. This is also where you decide on the size of your playing area, add and edit professional-looking fades to each level, and assign passwords to enter each level (See Figure 9.6)

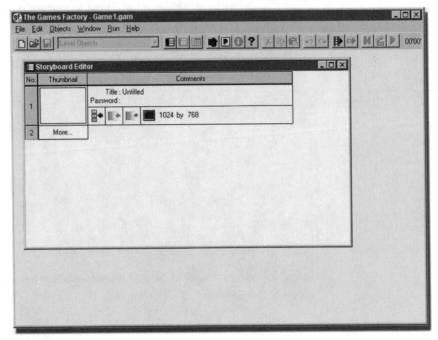

FIGURE 9.6 The Storyboard Editor.

Until you have created a level, the only way to move out of this screen is to right-click in the "Thumbnail" area and then and select the "Edit this level" option.

Level Editor

The Level Editor (see Figure 9.7) is the initial "blank page" for each of your levels. It displays the play area and is where you enter background objects and the main characters of your game. You generally access this screen from the Storyboard Editor screen.

This screen lets you access the libraries of all the different objects that you can use in your game. It also lets you create your own animated objects, text, and other object types. Basically, all the objects that you want to play with have to be placed on this screen first before you can start manipulating them. You can also change the animation and movement of objects here, and change the basic setup of all your objects. You will frequently find that before you can manipulate an object from the Event Editor, you must make sure that it is set up correctly in the Level Editor.

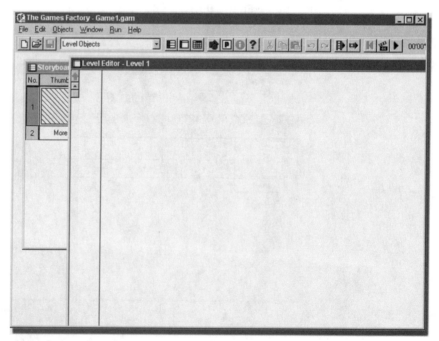

FIGURE 9.7 The Level Editor.

Event Editor

This is where your game will really come to life. You create interactivity here by assigning actions. When you are experienced with The Games Factory, you'll spend most of your time here. For example, you specify all of your game's events here.

As shown in Figure 9.8, the Event Editor is set up like a spreadsheet (you can only see the top "spreadsheet row" in the figure). By filling in the rows and columns, you can assign relationships to each object in your game. This setup makes game building easy, since you can visually see what happens in your game. Examples of the game play elements you can build here include aliens colliding with a spaceship; the main character collecting a power-up or getting hit by a missile; setting a time limit; and assigning a sound event. You can create an explosion, destroy an object, add to the score, subtract a life, or even specify complicated events, such as changing the direction of a character or a randomly moving object.

That was the quick tour of TGF. We saw that a game is built in TGF in three stages. First, you lay out the flow of your game in the Storyboard Editor. Then, you lay out each level and its objects in the Level Editor. Finally, you use the Event Editor to assign relationships and behaviors to your objects.

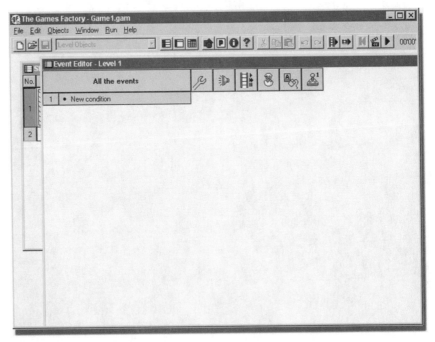

FIGURE 9.8 The Event Editor.

For the next chapter, you will need to have TGF installed and running, if possible, since we will be digging deeper into it. Be sure to first copy the sample folders from the CD-ROM to the proper folder for your installed copy. Otherwise, you will not be able to use the sample game tutorials with TGF software.

CHAPTER REVIEW

This chapter covered how to install The Games Factory and introduced you to the three editing screens in which you'll spend most of your time. In the next chapter, we'll get to work creating a game.

10 BEHIND THE SCENES OF THE GAMES FACTORY

Now we'll will take you through the step-by-step process used to construct a very basic shoot 'em-up game with The Games Factory. We'll call our retro-creation Space Defiler (See Figure 10.1), our own version of Space Invaders™. You will see that, with TGF, you can create a game that does a lot more than what the original Space Invaders could.

Retro gaming is still rather popular. People still love to play Pac Man, Asteroids™, Space Invaders, and other older games. Many can be found online in the form of Java applets that can play in your Web browser window. A great site for this is http://spaceinvaders.retrogames.com.

LOADING SPACE DEFILER

The CD-ROM for this book includes the finished Space Defiler game. Start up TGF and then select the Open option from the File menu. Navigate to the sample game folder on the CD-ROM. Open that folder, then open the *spacedel2.gam* file, as shown in Figure 10.2. As you're searching for that file, notice that TGF shows a thumbnail preview of the GAM file (see Figure 10.3).

FIGURE 10.1 Space Defiler, a retro-creation using TGF, inspired by Space Invaders.

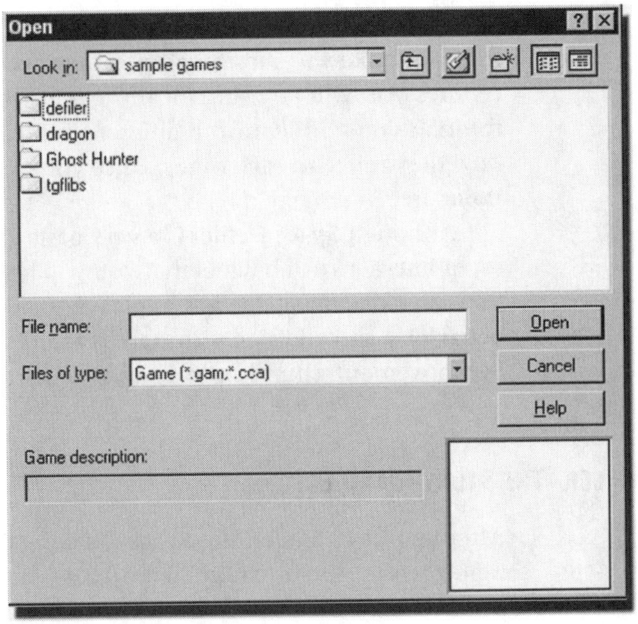

FIGURE 10.2 Opening the *spacedel2.gam* file.

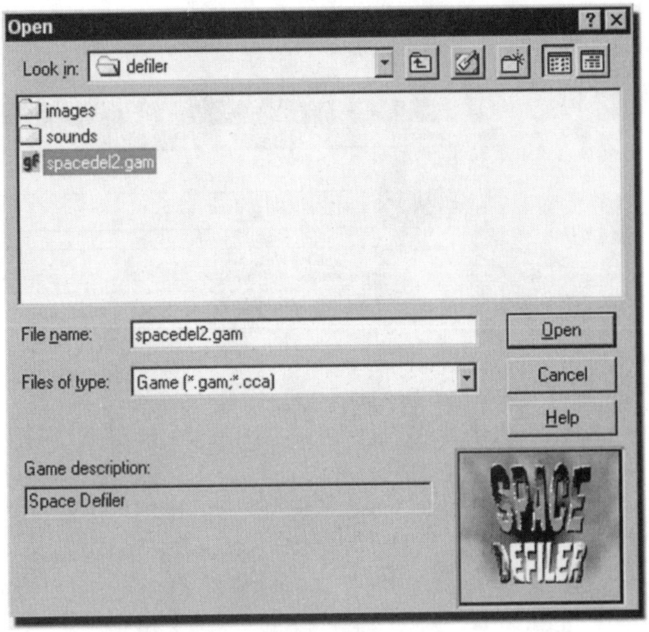

FIGURE 10.3 Opening the *spacedel2.gam* file. Notice the thumbnail of this game in the lower right-hand corner.

Space Defiler will show you the basics of creating games with TGF. But these will take you a long way in game development, since a lot of the procedures you will be using for this game are basic to all games. With this tutorial, you will learn the different functions of the Editor screens and how they relate to each other. Once you understand those basics, you are home free.

Although Space Defiler is a very basic game, it will introduce you to a set of interactive behaviors that you will be able to add to and expand on. You can make any game as complex as you like by adding levels, monsters, behaviors, and additional complexity, and by changing elements such as the movement, sounds, power-ups, and scoring.

SPACE DEFILER—THE STORYBOARD EDITOR

After you have loaded the Space Defiler game, you'll see the Storyboard Editor screen, as shown in Figure 10.4.

Starting from the top of the screen, let's look at the various features of the Storyboard Editor screen. Many of the features are the same for all of the Editor screens, but what they actually perform on each Editor screen can be quite different. So you may want to get used to looking at what screen you are in before clicking buttons.

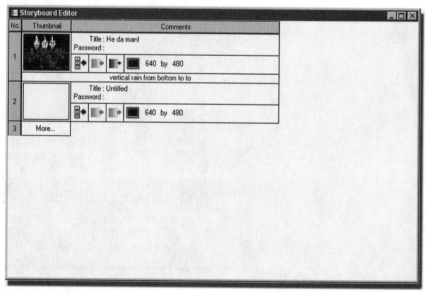

FIGURE 10.4 The Space Defiler Storyboard Editor.

At the top right of the main TGF window are the standard Windows manipulation icons: Minimize/Maximize (Maximize), Restore, and Exit. By clicking these you can control the window size or close the application. It's important to mention this because the different editors also have their own set of window manipulation icons below the Windows ones. If you click the wrong icon, you could accidentally close TGF, when all you really wanted to do was close a specific Editor screen.

At the top of your screen The Games Factory's header bar. This displays the current game name—in this case, *spacedel2.gam*. Next to this is the name of the current Editor screen, Storyboard Editor. Below this is the main menu bar. From here you can save your games, change the size of the screen, change preferences, access the Help pages, and customize your display.

Below the menu bar is The Games Factory toolbar. From here you can quickly and easily move around the Editor screens by clicking their icons, save games, cut and paste objects or events, and conduct test runs of your games (see Figure 10.5).

Each level is displayed as a thumbnail, or very small screen shot, in the main window area of the Storyboard Editor. By default, the thumbnail is displayed next to the number of the corresponding level, as shown in Figure 10.6.

FIGURE 10.5 Toolbar icons.

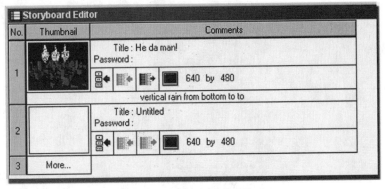

FIGURE 10.6 Closeup of the Storyboard Editor's level window.

Next to the thumbnail are the comments for that level, the title of the level, and the password. To change these, simply click the text that you want to change with the left mouse button. You can then edit or add a title or password.

Underneath the comments are several buttons, as shown in Figures 10.7–10.10. These buttons denote a multimedia level, which is what all your levels will be by default. If you were to make your level an animation frame, this icon would change.

You can add a fade-in transition to your level by using the icon in Figure 10.8. You can add a fade-out transition to your level using the icon in Figure 10.9. You can select the size of your play area by using the button in Figure 10.10. The play area can be much larger than the screen size, if you want. Then you can scroll around it, using one of the scroll functions.

By clicking the numbers in the play area sizing icon in Figure 10.10, you can enter your own screen sizes. You can type the size, or by clicking

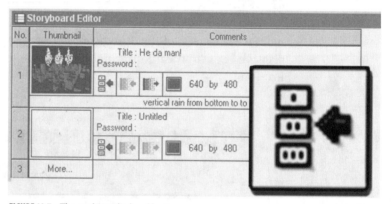

FIGURE 10.7 The multimedia level button.

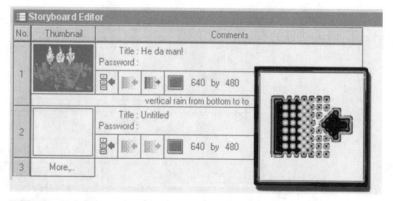

FIGURE 10.8 Fade-in transition button.

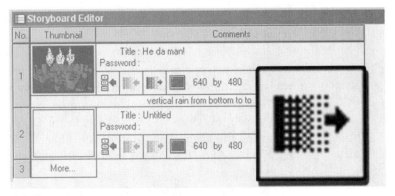

FIGURE 10.9   Fade-out transition button.

FIGURE 10.10   Play area size button.

the monitor icon, you can pick one of the standard monitor sizes. Space Defiler is set at 640 × 480, the lowest standard monitor size. This lets the game play faster than with a larger screen size.

Now that you've got a general idea of what all the different features are on the Storyboard Editor, let's look at how to use the Level Editor to put all the objects on the screen. We'll return to the Storyboard Editor in more detail soon.

SPACE DEFILER—THE LEVEL EDITOR

If you are just opening the Space Defiler file, right-click inside the thumbnail to get the pop-up menu. Select Edit the level/Level Editor. This will take you to the Level Editor.

If you open a new file at this point and then open the Level Editor, you'll see a white, empty screen.

When you open the *spacedel2.gam* file, you see the screen as it looks in the game, along with several items arranged in a vertical row on the left (see Figure 10.11). In the next chapter, we will look at getting those items into the editor. Once you have been in the Level Editor or the Event Editor using the thumbnail from the Storyboard Editor, all you have to do is click the icons on the toolbar to move through the different Editor screens in the future.

Now that you are in the Level Editor, notice that the toolbar at the top of the main window is the same as on the Storyboard Editor screen. However, now you can access the object libraries in the Level Objects drop-down menu in the toolbar, as shown in Figure 10.12. Notice also that on the left side of the screen is an Object window, in which you can see all of the objects that have been used to create Space Defiler.

When there are many objects in a level, not all will fit inside that window, so there is a scroll bar to look through them. Scroll the object libraries now. You will find many premade items that you can use. Click on a couple of libraries. Notice that when you select a library, it appears in the left-

FIGURE 10.11 The Space Defiler Level Editor, with objects and a background.

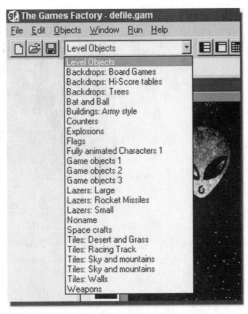

FIGURE 10.12   The Level Objects pull-down list.

hand vertical window of the Level Editor. When you change libraries, all the items go away, unless you have used one. If so, that item is retained.

You can also make the window a "moveable window," using the "Objects-Display objects in a movable window" option from the menu bar at the top of the screen.

If you move your mouse pointer over the objects in the Object window, a "Handy Hint" shows you the name of each object, as shown in Figure 10.13. You could now select one of the objects with the left mouse button and then place it anywhere on the screen.

Go ahead and try things out now. Just don't save the file!

If you had fun placing objects all over the level screen, select them with the left mouse button and use the Delete key to erase them. You must do this before you continue, or you will change the contents of the other Editor screens. If that happens, what you see will no longer correlate with the contents of this book.

Also, try moving the mouse pointer over the objects that have already been placed on the screen. You can click and drag with the left mouse button to move them around. Now, go to the scroll bars at the side of the screen, and try moving around the play area using them. You will notice that there is a gray area, which is the edge of the play area. Any objects placed here will not be shown on the screen when you play your game.

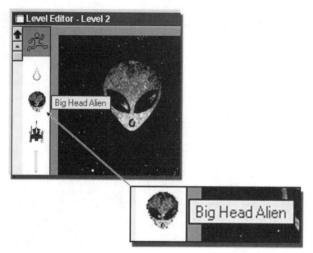

FIGURE 10.13 Handy Hint balloon over an object in the Level Editor.

But it can be a useful "holding area" for placing objects in a level, which you can move onto the play area later by using the Event Editor.

Now let's look at the menu options for each object. Different types of objects have different menus. Right-click on the backdrop object (the background). As shown in Figure 10.14, you'll see the options for that ob-

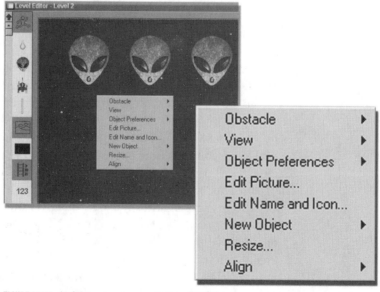

FIGURE 10.14 Right mouse menu over space backdrop.

ject (look, but don't change anything). Now, right-click other objects on the screen. We'll be using the various pop-up menus in a later tutorial.

Now that we've had a quick tour around The Games Factory's more basic features, let's look at how the game plays! To be sure that you haven't changed the game, simply reload it. To do this, click the File menu at the top of the screen, then select the Open option. Now open up Space Defiler, right-click in the thumbnail, and select and open the Level Editor.

Look at the top right of the toolbar. There are several control buttons there which control the testing of your game. For now, we are just going to use the Play/Pause button and the Restart button, as shown in Figure 10.15.

The controls for the game are Left/Right (cursor keys) and Fire (the Ctrl key). Now click the Play button. Move around and take some shots. To stop the action, click the Play button (which is now the Pause button) again. When you want to finish playing, click the Restart button to reset everything.

SPACE DEFILER—THE EVENT EDITOR

To get into the Event Editor, click the icon on the toolbar at the top of the screen. You'll see a screen that looks like Figure 10.16. The Event Editor is where you specify the action and strategy of your game. This is where you add sound and explosions, move onto the next level, and display Hi Score tables—the list of events is almost endless. We will look more closely at how to change and edit the events and actions in the Event Editor in the next chapter. Right now, we'll look at the logic of the Event Editor.

The first time you call it up, the Event Editor basically consists of one horizontal line. It's like the first line of a spreadsheet before you enter any information. In Figure 10.16, many events have already been entered. At the top of the Event Editor is a row of icons that represent possible actions.

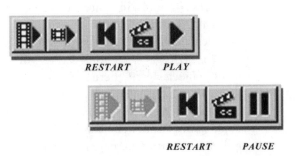

FIGURE 10.15   The Play/Pause buttons and the Restart Button.

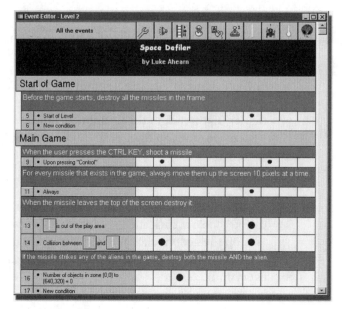

FIGURE 10.16 The Space Defiler Event Editor.

To the right of those icons are all the objects that were placed in the game from the Level Editor.

At the left of the screen is a vertical column of gray "event lines." Look below the heading "Start of Game." Notice that next to each gray event line, there is a grid of boxes. Each box lines up with an object icon at the top of the screen. Under the "Start of Game" label, you'll see the text comment "Before the game starts, destroy all the missiles in the frame." The dots in the "Start of Level" line (line 5) are what make that happen. We'll cover how to insert and edit events and actions in the next chapter.

The horizontal line at the top of the Event Grid in Figure 10.17 shows how this line looks in Space Defiler. "All the events" is the heading for the vertical column, which is where you insert all the events for the game. We'll cover this after discussing the icons in the horizontal bar at the top.

The icons at the right of the "All the events" heading refer to the level's objects. Here, there are icons for all of the objects (except the backdrop) that have been placed on the play area. You can see the enemy objects here, as well as the player's ship and the missile (see below for more detail about these). There will also be icons for any object that you use for bullets, or that you create from within the Event Editor, even if they are not already on the play area.

FIGURE 10.17   The Event Grid in Space Defiler.

NOTE   *How to shoot an object is described in the next chapter.*

The first six icons denote Game Objects, and are always on the event grid by default. The following list shows them in order, as shown in Figure 10.18.

- **Special Conditions**. Performs special functions when an event occurs.
- **Sound**. Plays or stops sound or music, including CD tracks.
- **Storyboard**. Allows you to start, stop, and change levels, as well as control the flow of the different levels of your game.
- **Create New Object**. Allows you to place or create a new object on the screen at certain times, or due to certain events.
- **Mouse and Keyboard**. Lets you control how the player interacts with the mouse and keyboard—interactivity!
- **Player One**. Allows you to change lives and scores.

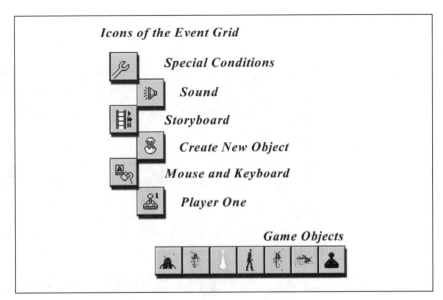

FIGURE 10.18   The six icons on the Event Grid.

Before we go any further, use the vertical scroll buttons on the right side of the screen to move down through the events until you see events 18 and 19 at the bottom. The screen should now look like Figure 10.19.

There are three event lines within the group "Missile Destroys Aliens." Going from left to right, in lines 18 and 19 are two events that involve the two alien head entities and the missile object.

The logic in lines 18 and 19 is spelled out by a combination of text and pictures: **Collision between missile and enemy**.

To see the rest of the logic in lines 18 and 19, move the mouse pointer over the dots in the grid to the right. As you move left to right, you'll see the Handy Hints listed below:

> **Play sound sample.**
> **Add 10 to the score.**
> **Destroy the ship object.**
> **Destroy the missile object.**

Notice how the pattern for these two events is identical, except that a different alien is destroyed in each of the two lines. Since the two events refer to two different ships when they are struck by a missile, logically each event destroys a different ship.

Look through the rest of the events. Move the mouse pointer over the various dots, so that you can see which actions are associated with which objects. As you see this relationship unfold, you will see the simplicity of game creation with TGF.

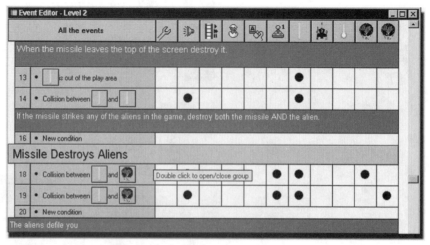

FIGURE 10.19 The Space Defiler Event Editor, events 18 and 19.

Creating Event Lines

Let's quickly create an event line and add some actions to it. This is very much like working with a standard spreadsheet and is very easy. You use menus to create all options, and all the information is entered for you.

1. To create a new event line, move the mouse pointer directly over the text "New condition" on an empty event line. *New condition* means that this line is completely empty. Notice that it has no grid next to it.
2. Right-click the text. You'll see a dialog box like the one in Figure 10.20. Notice that when you move the mouse pointer over an icon in the New Condition window, a Handy Hint shows you what that icon is.
3. Right-click the Storyboard controls icon. A pop-up menu will appear.
4. Click the Start of level option in this menu.

You will now be taken back to the Event Grid, and the new event will read *Start of level*. You've created your first event! All you need to do now is to add an action associated with that event. (Notice that there are no actions on the line.)

To add the actions:

1. Go across the empty check boxes on line number 10 until you get to the box underneath the missile icon.

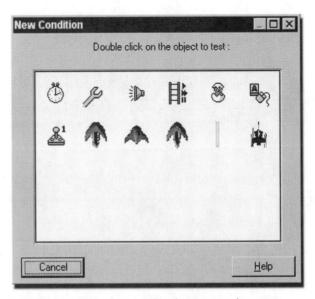

FIGURE 10.20   New Condition window that pops up when a new condition is added.

2. Right-click the empty box. You will see a menu of all the things you can do to the missile object, such as movement, animation, direction, position, and so forth. We will look at all these options in the next chapter.

3. Move down the pop-up menu. Click on the Destroy option. You will be taken back to the Event Grid. You'll see a new event line with the logic that states: **At the start of the level destroy the missile object.**

CHAPTER REVIEW

We've now seen the basics of using TGF. When you are comfortable with the concepts presented in this chapter, move on to the next chapter, where we'll create a game from the ground up.

11

MAKING A GAME YOURSELF WITH THE GAMES FACTORY

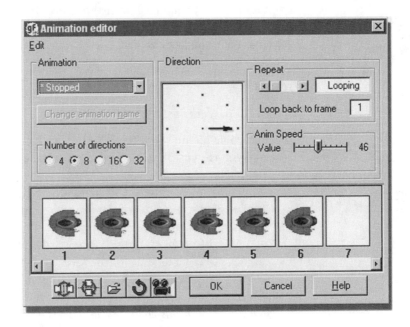

G et the caffeine pumping in your system and prepare your mind— you are ready for the serious stuff. In this chapter, we'll go deeper into TGF and really get our game tweaked out. We will attempt . . . drum roll, please . . . to make Space Defiler from the ground up. By the end of this chapter, you will be able to lay out multiple levels, or-chestrate game effects, play music off an audio CD from within your game, and more.

CREATING SPACE DEFILER YOURSELF

Now that you've had a guided tour around TGF, let's look at how Space Defiler was assembled. We'll will move faster when it comes to areas we covered in the last chapter. For instance, we'll cover how to create a new event line without telling you exactly how to do it each time, since that was covered in the last chapter.

Create a File

To create a new file in TGF:

1. On the File menu, select New. If Space Defiler is open, The Games Fac-tory will ask you if you want to save the changes you have made. Choose No.
2. You will be asked to select a playfield size. Choose 640 by 480, then click OK. This screen size will let the game run faster because it is small, but it is still big enough to be playable.
3. You will now be taken to the Storyboard Editor, with an empty level 1 display. To enter a name for the level, click the "Untitled" text within the level 1 display, enter the name you would like, then press Enter.

 Although the point of this chapter is to have you build Space Defiler from the ground up, you can go to the CD-ROM and open the file spacedel2.gam *to look around the finished version of Space Defiler.*

4. Right-click the empty Thumbnail.
5. From the pop-up menu, click the "Edit this level" option, then the Level Editor option. You will then be taken to an empty Level Editor screen, ready for you to place your objects.

To place new objects on the screen, go to the Level objects text box on the toolbar and click the pull-down button at the side of the text (See Fig-ure 11.1).

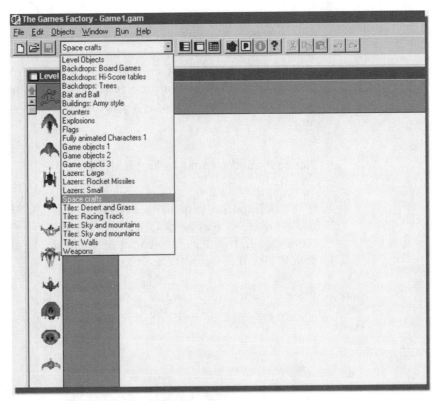

FIGURE 11.1 The pull-down Level Objects button.

Now look through all the different object libraries until you get to one called *(Tutorial) SPACE DEFILER.* Click this library.

You will now have all the objects from this library displayed in the Object window down the left-hand side of the screen. Notice that there are large icons in this window. These icons each stand for a different type of object, as shown in Figures 11.2, 11.3, and 11.4.

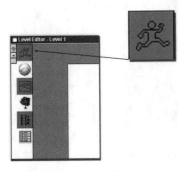

FIGURE 11.2 The Active Objects icon denotes active objects.

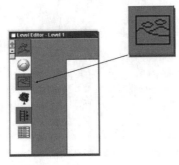

FIGURE 11.3 The Backdrop icon denotes backdrop objects.

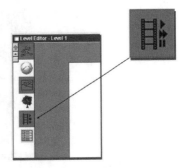

FIGURE 11.4 The Storyboard icon denotes storyboard objects.

Try moving your mouse pointer over the different objects in the window. A Handy Hint box will tell you what each one is called. It's useful to know what these are, because before we place the active objects of our game on the play area, we are going to put a backdrop into place, align it perfectly with the edges of the screen, then lock it into place so it cannot be selected or moved while we are putting all the other objects on the play area.

Placing the Backdrop and Locking It in Place

To place the backdrop on the screen, go to the Object window and click the Backdrop icon, called Space Defiler Backdrop. Now move the mouse pointer over the play area—anywhere will do—then press the left mouse button again. This places the backdrop object on the play area. Your screen should look like Figure 11.5.

When the backdrop object and the size of the play area are identical, The Games Factory will automatically align the backdrop object to fit.

FIGURE 11.5 The Space Defiler background on the playfield.

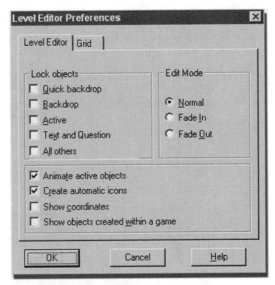

FIGURE 11.6   The Level Editor Preferences window.

We are now going to stop the backdrop object from being selected every time you click it with the mouse. This will make it far easier when you start putting other objects on the play area. Go to the toolbar and click the Preferences icon. You will see the Level Editor Preference window, as shown in Figure 11.6.

In the Lock objects heading, put a checkmark in the Backdrop option box by clicking in it. This means that you have locked the backdrop into place. Now click the OK button.

If you lock the background or any other object in place, don't forget that you did it! There is no indication that something is locked in place, other than the fact that you cannot move it—it simply doesn't respond to your cursor. This may be confusing if you forget you locked it.

Now try clicking the backdrop object. You cannot! As you saw from the different options in the Preferences dialog box, you can lock many different types of objects into place. To unlock the backdrop object, click the Preferences icon and then click the Backdrop object checkbox again.

Placing Objects on the Screen

Now that we have a nice backdrop for our game, we are going to place the active objects on the play area: the enemies, the missile, some obstacles,

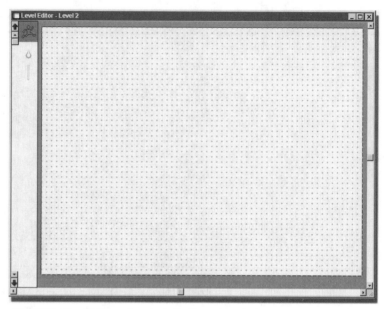

FIGURE 11.7 The grid is used to precisely align objects in the game.

and the player's spaceship. The trick to getting all the objects lined up so neatly on the screen is to use the grid tool. To do this:

1. In the toolbar, click the Preferences icon.
2. In the Preferences dialog box, select the second tab, called Grid. You'll see the Grid preferences in Figure 11.7.
3. On the Grid tab, you will see several options. Set them as follows:
   Origin. This sets where the grid starts. Leave it at zero.
   Square size. This sets how far apart the "line up points" of the grid are. The larger the number, the farther apart the points, and the less fine control you have over where an object is placed. Click the numbers in the Width and Height boxes and change them to 10.
   Snap-to. This option button is at the bottom of the dialog box. Click it. This means that any object you place on the screen will snap to the grid points.
   Show grid. Click this if you want to see the grid as you work. Some people prefer not to have the grid visible.
4. After you've made any changes, click the OK button to take you back to the Level Editor screen.

We're now ready to start placing the objects on the screen. Because the grid is enabled, you will see the objects jump a little when you drag objects across the background, because they snap to the grid. If you went back to the Preferences dialog box and made the grid squares larger, you would see the objects jumping more.

Let's put a single object on the screen.

1. Go to the Object window and click and object to select it.
2. Move the object to where you want it on the screen. When you're ready to set its position, *left-click* again. This places a single copy of the object. You can also place multiple copies by *right-clicking*. This keeps you from having to return to the Object window every time you want to place the same object. This is handy for placing an army of drones, or building a maze dungeon with many obstacles.

Now, let's use the right mouse button to lay out a wave of Space Defiling aliens!

1. In the Object window, click the big alien head.
2. Move move the mouse pointer over the play area. Go to the top left to start placing aliens. Select the place where you want to place the first alien, but don't click yet. Remember not to place it too close to the edge of the screen, or it will go off the screen when you play the game. We'll be placing the alien heads in a row in the center of the play area, as shown in Figure 11.8.

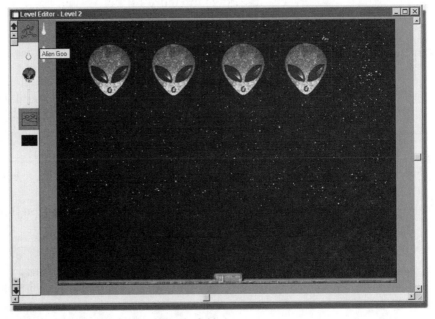

FIGURE 11.8   The big alien heads on the playfield.

You can still scroll around the display area using the scroll bars even when you are placing an object.

1. To place the alien heads, right-click to place *all but the last one,* as shown in Figure 11.8.
2. For the *last* alien, click the *left* mouse button instead. This gets you out of the mode where you're placing multiple objects and frees up the mouse pointer. You should now have a line of alien heads evenly spaced across the top of the screen, as shown in Figure 11.8.
3. Go to the Object window and click on the Player's Ship. Move to the bottom of the play area, slightly above the bottom of the screen. Then left-click, to place one copy of it.
4. Go to the Object window and click on a Space Defiler Obstacle. Place a row of about four of these immediately above the Player's Ship. Re-member to right-click for all but the last obstacle, then left-click for the last one. Try not to have them too close to the ship—give it some room.
5. Next, place the bullet, Missile, anywhere on the screen. When we use the Event Editor, we will remove any missiles from the display when the level starts. We're putting it on the screen now so that it will ap-pear in the Event Editor and we can assign behaviors to it.
6. Scroll through the Object window until you find the Score object. Place that on the bottom of the screen, out of the way of everything else, as shown in Figure 11.9.

Assigning Movements to Objects

The Level Editor makes it easy to assign movement and animation to ob-jects. Right-click an object in the layout area. You'll see the pop-up menu shown in Figure 11.10.

We'll look at two of these options now: Movement and Edit Anima-tion.

- **Movement** has an arrow indicating that more choices are available—Change or Edit, in this case.
- **Edit Animation** will open up the Animation Editor if selected.

It's important to understand the distinction between movement and animation in TGF. Animation refers to having an active object function like a short movie, by playing frames over and over. This can make the object appear to be walking or running in place, among other things. Movement refers to having the active ob-ject move around the screen, and to how the object is controlled.

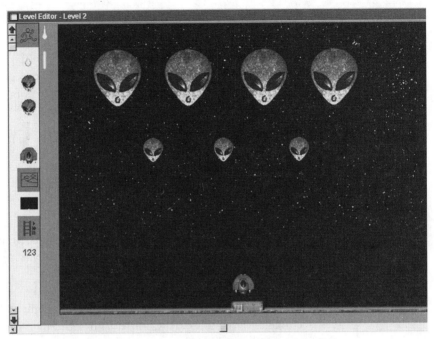

FIGURE 11.9   The objects all laid out in the Layout Editor for the Space Defiler game.

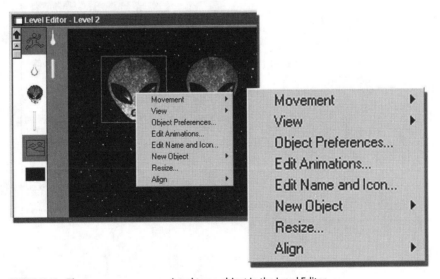

FIGURE 11.10   The pop-up menu associated to an object in the Level Editor.

An active object can have more than one animation assigned to it. We will look at that next.

Examples of Animation include:

- Walking. Legs moving back and forth, and arms swinging. Remember, this doesn't mean that the object is actually going anywhere.
- Running. Like walking, only faster.
- Dying. A body falling to the ground.

Examples of Movement include:

- An active object follows a path on its own.
- The player controls an active object to make it move.

Notice that Animation and Movement are often used together. When an active object uses Animation to make a walking motion, and it uses Movement to actually move along the screen, this creates the illusion of walking.

For a good illustration of these points, go to the Level Editor and right-click the big alien head. The same menu as in Figure 11.10 appears. Select Change Movement. The Choose a movement window will appear, as shown in Figure 11.11.

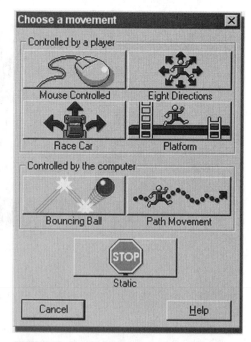

FIGURE 11.11 The Choose a movement window.

As you can see, you can make the object computer- or player-controlled. For our Space Invaders-type game, the alien heads are controlled by the computer.

Remember how the aliens in Space Invaders move back and forth? We'll use the Path option to control that. This option lets you select a track the object moves on, whether it loops or plays once, and the speed of movement. And, most importantly, it allows you to test the object's movement.

Play with the options for awhile. When you're done, click the Cancel button. Then, right-click the Spaceship, and select Edit Animation from the pop-up menu. This opens the Animation Editor, as shown in Figure 11.12.

In the Animation Editor, you will see three main areas: the Animation window (top left), the Direction window (top center), and the Animation Frames window (unlabeled, at the bottom). The Animation window has a pull-down text box that lists the animation tracks for many events for each active object. This is used later in the Event Editor, where you can make a character that uses the default walking animation switch over to the dying animation track when he gets hit.

To specify a different animation for an object, you can pull this list down and choose it. There will be an asterisk next to the selections that contain an animation. Pull down the list. As you'll see, in this case, there are two: **Stopped** and **Getting Hit**. The Stopped animation shows the Player Ship swaying, and the Getting Hit animation distorts and changes the ship's color.

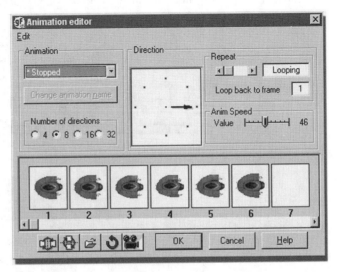

FIGURE 11.12   The Animation Editor.

When you add your own active objects, you will be brought to this window. Even if an object is not animated, you will still have to import the images here. To do this, click the Create New Object icon on the toolbar and select the active object. Double-click in the first frame, and then click the Open Folder icon in the Picture Editor.

Checking Your Work

To have a look at what you've done so far, click the Play button on the toolbar (see Figure 11.13). To pause the game, click that button again. You can also use the Rewind button to reset the game. You should have a field of alien heads moving around the screen and dropping big wads of alien goo down at you. Try pressing the left and right arrow keys. These should let you move the spaceship horizontally in both directions.

Now that we have the basic objects on the screen, we need to add some actions, sounds, and other elements. To do all this, we'll go to the Event Editor. But, before we do this, we need to save the work that we have done.

Saving a File in TGF

If you have created anything unique in the previous exercises and want to keep it, stop and save your work now! From the File menu, choose Save As. Select the drive and folder that you want to save to. Next, type the name you want to give the file. If you are using Windows 3.1, this can be up to eight letters long, and must always have *.gam* as the extension (for *.GAM* file). For any other version of Windows, you can enter up to 256 characters. Once you have safely saved your work, close your file.

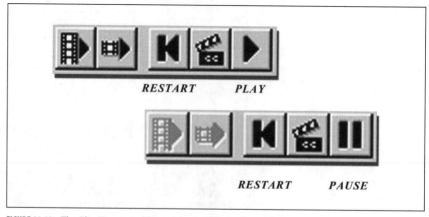

FIGURE 11.13 The Play/Pause and Restart buttons from the toolbar.

Making Space Defiler Events and Actions

In the previous section, you saw how easy it is to place objects on the screen. Now, we'll add the ability to fire missiles, destroy aliens, add sounds, and change the score. For this section, open the file *spacedel2.gam* and right-click the thumbnail of level 2 in the Storyboard Editor. Click the Event Editor option (see Figure 11.14). This opens the Event Editor, which is where your gaming really comes to life.

We'll now go step by step through creating a complete set of events that brings Space Defiler to life. A lot of what you will learn in this chapter is basic to all game creation using The Games Factory and other applications.

First, we'll see how to create comment lines. These are important because they provide you with notes to refer to in the Event Editor. Although Space Defiler is a very simple game, writing comments in the Event Editor is a very good habit to get into. When you start writing longer, more complicated games and applications, you will need to refer to these comments.

We'll also see how to define groups of events. This also makes your event editing much easier to follow and lets you simplify writing your game.

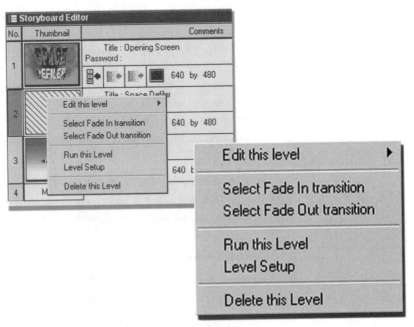

FIGURE 11.14   The pop-up menu to get to the Event Editor.

Creating a Group of Events

First, we'll create a group of events called "Start of Game Actions." To do this:

1. Right click the number 1 on the New condition line.
2. Select the Insert option from the menu, then the "A group of events" option from that menu. You'll see a dialog box asking you to enter the name of the group.
3. Type in the text "Start of Game Actions."
4. Make sure that the "Active when frame starts" option button is selected. It will be selected by default, but check to make sure, anyway.
5. When you have the name entered, either press Enter or click the OK button.

You should now have a group called Start of Game Actions. Event line number 2 will be indented slightly, showing that it's in that group.

Creating a Comment Line

Now, let's make line number 2 a comment. Right-click the number 2 in this line. Select the Insert option, then the A comment option. You'll see a dialog box where you can select the font, color, and background color of your text. We are going to use the standard font, but we'll write in white.

1. Click the "Set font color" option, then click the white square. Next, click the OK button.
2. Click the "Set back color" option, select dark green, then click the OK button.
3. Click in the top left of the empty text box. Now you can type in the words that you want in the comment. Enter the text "Before the game starts, destroy the missile in the frame to make sure only the missiles fired from the ship are used in the game."
4. lick OK.

You now have a comment with a green background and white letters. If you have made a mistake, you can edit your comment line by right-clicking the text of the comment, then selecting the Edit Comment option.

Creating an Event Line

It's time to get down to the nitty-gritty of creating your game! We are going to insert an actual event, Start of level, which means that all the actions associated with this event line will be performed when the level begins. This event will be in the Start of Game Actions group.

To create the Start of level event:

1. Right click on the text "New Condition" of event line number 3. You'll see a dialog box titled New Condition, with the subheading Double click the object to test.
2. Move your mouse pointer over the Storyboard controls icon (the Handy Hint text will tell you which one it is as you move your mouse pointer over the objects), and either double-click or right-click it. You'll see the window shown in Figure 11.15.
3. Click on the "Start of level" option. You will have an event line number 3 that reads "Start of level."

You can now insert an action. But if you are working on your own game from the ground up, before you go any farther, take the time to save your game.

Adding Actions to Event Lines

Next we are going to insert an action into event line number 3, to destroy the missile.

Destroying Objects

Right-click in the empty box below the missile icon, on line number 3. You'll see a large menu of all the possible actions that you could do to the

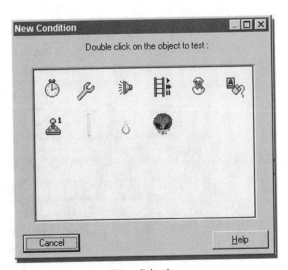

FIGURE 11.15   The New Condition dialog box.

missile. Click on the Destroy option. You will have a complete event line that will destroy the missiles at the very start of the level, within the group Start of Game Actions.

Now it's time to start adding the rest of the events. Create a Group called Main Game. Next insert a comment. The text of the comment line should be: "When the user presses the Ctrl key, shoot a missile."

Testing the Keyboard for a Specific Key

During the game, you will want certain keystrokes to do specific things; in this case, the Ctrl key will fire a missile—*Interactivity, baby!*

Here's how to set this up:

1. Right-click the "New Condition" text.
2. Use the right mouse button to select the Mouse pointer and Keyboard icon.
3. Select the Keyboard option from this menu, then select the "Upon Pressing a key" option.
4. You will now be asked to press the key that you want to associate your actions with. Press the Ctrl key, as shown in Figure 11.16. You will now be taken back to the Event Editor screen, with an event line that reads "Upon pressing 'Control.'" You are now half way there!

Shooting an Object

Now that you've made your event line to test what happens when the Ctrl key is pressed, you need to find something to shoot.

1. Go to the empty box directly underneath "Player's ship" on the same line as the event line we just created. Right-click the box and select the "Shoot an Object..." option from the pop-up menu (see Figure 11.17).

FIGURE 11.16   The Control, or Ctrl key.

FIGURE 11.17   The relationship between the event created and the object it affects.

2. You will see a dialogue box that shows all the active objects in the current level. We want to use the Missile object as our bullet, so select that, then click OK.

3. You will now be asked to select a speed and direction for the bullet. By default, the speed is 100, which is very fast. Use the mouse to move the pointer to 50.

4. Next, select the direction to fire in, which, in this case, should be up. To do this, click the "Shoot in selected directions" button.

5. Select the direction that you want to fire the bullet in from the "direction clock face." You can select/deselect directions by clicking the black buttons around the clock face, as shown in Figure 11.18. To *select all directions*, click the small icon at the bottom left. To *deselect all directions*, click the small icon at the bottom right. For now, make sure you have just one arrow, pointing straight up. If you select more than

FIGURE 11.18   The direction clock face.

one direction, The Games Factory will select directions at random as the game plays. We'll use this feature later, on the aliens.

6. Now click all the OK buttons to take you back to the Event Editor screen.

You should now have a complete event line, so that when you press the Ctrl key, a missile is fired up the screen.

Now, save your game before you go any farther!

The Aliens Shoot Back

What fun would it be if the aliens just sat there? They need to shoot back, and this is where the real *defiling* comes in. To make the aliens shoot back, go to the Level Editor and follow the same steps we used earlier to place a missile into the scene; only this time, choose the alien goo object. Place this under the missile object in the Level Editor, simply to keep things neat.

Back in the Event Editor, follow the same steps to tell The Games Factory to destroy the goo object at the start of the game. Also, have it destroy the goo if any goes off the screen, just like the missile.

Next, go to the Event Editor. This is where we'll make the aliens fight back.

1. In the Event Editor, create a new event by right-clicking the "New condition" line and then right-clicking the clock face.
2. Select the Every option from the pop-up menu.
3. In the window that pops up, set the time to 1 second. This means that the event will take place every one second.

 Warning! *The default time value here is minutes. If you fail to move over to the seconds (middle) window, and accidentally set the event at "every 1 minute" instead of "every 1 second," it will look like your event is not happening at all, because nothing will happen for a full minute.*

4. Now go to the empty box directly underneath the big alien head, on the same line as the event line we just created. Right-click it and select the "Shoot an Object ..." option from the pop-up menu. You will see a dialog box displaying all the active objects from the current level. We want to use the alien goo object as our bullet, so select that, then click OK.
5. Next, you will be asked to select a speed and direction for the bullet. You should make it a bit slower than we made the player's missile, both for game play reasons and for aesthetics. By default the speed is

100, which is very fast. Use the mouse to move the pointer to 50 or below.

6. Now, let's set how the aliens shoot. Click the "Shoot in selected directions" button and deselect the arrow that points up (by clicking the little black square it is pointing at). Now, they won't shoot up. To make them shoot down, click the down, or 6 o'clock, arrow. Then, click the squares immediately to the left and right of the 6 o'clock position. Remember that selecting more than one direction makes TGF select a direction at random. This can be annoying if you're shooting at something, doing this for the aliens gives a nice random feel that adds to the game.

7. Press all the OK buttons to take you back to the Event Editor screen.

8. Then, press the Play button to check your work.

Adding Sound Effects

You're probably anxious to add some sounds to your game. Try running the level with no sound event (or turn your speakers down), and then running the level with sound. You will see firsthand how important sound is in a game.

To add sounds, follow this procedure.

1. Right-click the empty box beneath the Sound icon on the active event line.

2. Select the "Play sample" option from the menu. You will then be taken to a file selector.

3. Choose the drive you want to use. You can click the button under the Drives heading to pull down a list of the available drives.

4. Look down the list of directories (use the scroll bars) until you find one called *samples*. Double-click this directory.

5. Look down this list until you find weapons. Double-click it. You will now have a list of all the noises in the *weapons* directory.

6. Scroll through the list of all the noises until you get to one called *phaser03.wav*. Click on it, and then click the Play button on the right side of the dialog box. You'll hear the sound. You can preview all the available sounds this way. Just select another sample and preview it using the Play button. You can also move to another sound directory. To do so, double-click the samples directory, then choose the directory you want.

7. When you are happy with the sound that you want to play every time a missile is fired, click the OK button.

Later in this chapter, we'll see how to add music to your level from a CD.

Moving an Object by Changing Its Coordinates

It's time to specify how objects move. Let's get started.

1. First, create a comment on the next line, containing the following text:"For every missile that exists in the game, always move them up 10 pixels at a time."
2. Create an Always event on the line after that. To do this, right-click the New Condition text, then right-click the special object. From the Always/Never option, select the Always option.
3. Now insert an action on the Always event line, beneath the missile icon. Right-click the empty box. In the pop-up menu, select the Position option (see Figure 11.19).

To specify how the missile moves:

1. From this menu, select the Set Y coordinate option.
2. Click the Edit button. This will take you to another Expression Editor.
3. Click the "Retrieve data from an object button."
4. Right-click the missile from the objects displayed.
5. When you select the missile, it will produce a menu. Select the Position option.
6. From the menu, select the Y coordinate option.
7. You will now have the text Y("MISSILE") in the text box of the Expression Editor. Without changing this text, add –10 to the end of the text, so that you have an expression that reads Y("MISSILE")—10. This means that every time The Games Factory cycles through the Event Editor, it will always subtract 10 from the Y coordinate of the missile.
8. Click the OK buttons to take you back to the Event Editor.

This method of movement is actually somewhat redundant in this game, since we are already firing the missile at the speed of 50. But this exercise does show you that you can move objects around quite easily by

9	• Upon pressing "Control"		•								•
For every missile that exists in the game, always move them up the screen 10 pixels at a time.											
11	• Always								•		

FIGURE 11.19 The relationship of the Always action to the missile object.

changing their coordinates. This will help you in the future with more complex games.

Testing the Position of an Object

Keeping track of objects in the game can be important for its efficiency. For now, we will start with a simple exercise in object tracking. Insert a new comment on the next event line that reads: "When the missile leaves the top of the screen, it is not needed any more, so destroy it."

Now, we'll insert an event on the line below it to test the position of the missile.

1. Right-click the New condition line and select the missile from the dialog box.
2. Select the "Position-Test position of the Missile" option.
3. In this dialog box, you can test the position of the missile in several different ways. Move the mouse pointer over the different buttons and look at all the options available.
4. Click the "Is the object outside?" button. Note that from here, you could select more than one button. You can deselect a button by clicking it again.
5. When only the "Is the object outside?" button is depressed, click the OK button to take you back to the Event Editor. You will now have an event line that reads (Missile) is out of the play area.
6. Insert an action to destroy the missile, on the same event line (see Figure 11.20).
7. Insert the following new comment: "If a missile strikes another missile, destroy it."
8. Insert the following Event: **Collision between (missile) and (missile).**
9. Right-click the New condition text, right-click the missile object, and select the "Collisions-Another object" option from the menu.

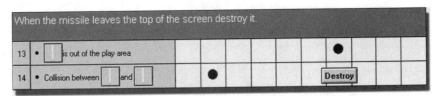

FIGURE 11.20   The relationship between the missile object and the action to destroy it if it goes outside of the play area.

10. In the dialog box, click the missile, then click OK. You will have an event line as described above.

11. We are doing this in case the player is very fast on the keyboard and fires too many missiles that end up running into each other. If they do, the missiles will destroy each other. This can also be useful if you apply the same action set to any other two objects in a game.

12. Next, insert another action in this group to destroy the missile.

 You can copy the action from one of the other event lines by clicking and holding on one of the Destroy tick-marks, then dragging it into the empty box beneath the Missile icon, on the **Collision between (Missile) and (Missile)** *event line.*

Before going on, save your game!

Destroying an Alien

For your missiles to have an effect when they hit an alien, we need to assign that behavior as well. We will create the necessary events for this next.

1. On the next line, insert the following comment: "If the missile strikes a big alien head, destroy the missile AND the alien."

2. Insert the following event: **Collision between (missile) and (big alien head).** To do this, right-click the New condition text, then right-click the Missile icon. Select the "Collisions-Another object" option. Now, select the big alien head object.

3. Insert the following event next: **Collision between (missile) and (alien head)**.

4. Insert the following event: **Collision between (missile) and (baby alien)**.

You should now have three event lines. On the first one, let's make a sound for when a missile hits an alien:

1. Insert a sound action on the first event line, **Collision between (missile) and (big alien head)**.

2. Pick something appropriate for an explosion. To do this, Right-click the empty box under the sound icon, select the "Play sample" option, and look in Samples-Impacts until you find the sound you want.

3. Copy the sound action into the lines for the alien head and baby alien. You will now have that sound being played every time a missile collides with any of the aliens.

Destroying the Missile Upon Impact

For realism, we want the missile to be destroyed when it hits an alien. Otherwise, it will just keep going!

To do this:

1. Insert another Destroy action in the empty box under the missile on each line. (Right-click the box and select the Destroy option.) To save a lot of time, drag the Destroy action, using the left mouse button, into all the empty boxes beneath the missile, for when the missile collides with an alien.
2. Now, check your logic. Make sure that it is the big alien head that is destroyed when a missile collides with a big alien head, and not one of the others! If you make a mistake, you can delete it by selecting a check mark and pressing the Delete key.
3. Do the same for the other alien entities. The events should now look like the screen shot in Figure 11.21.
4. Save your game!

Keeping Score

Now we want to add to the score each time a missile destroys an alien. We can do so while still working with the same three event lines from the previous section.

1. Right-click the empty box underneath the Player 1 object and select the Score option.
2. Select the "Add to score" option. You'll see the dialog box shown in Figure 11.22.
3. You can choose how much to add to the score when a big alien head is destroyed. Since the aliens are big and nasty, let's enter 100. Then click OK.
4. Do the same for the other alien entities.

FIGURE 11.21   The two alien collision events.

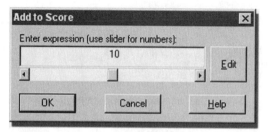

FIGURE 11.22 The Add to Score dialog box.

You can also make items deduct points when destroyed. To make an item worth negative points, type a minus sign before the number. This will create an item that the player does not want to hit. For example, to make levels harder later on, you can introduce friendly, or civilian, crafts you are not supposed to hit.

As you develop a game, you'll need to make decisions about how many points to award for hitting a target. Usually, the harder a target is to kill, the more points it will be worth. This type of decision in your game design is called game balance.

It Ain't Over Till It's Over

It's easy to forget that you need to tell the TGF when it is over—the game, that is. We'll have the computer look at the playing area. If all the aliens are dead and gone, the game is over. Insert a comment line, if you wish, that says the following:

"Check the area above the player's ship where the aliens are. If there are no more aliens, the game is complete."

Now we are going to insert an event to end the game when all the aliens have been destroyed. To do this, we'll test if there are any objects in a zone on the play area.

1. Right-click on the New condition text line.
2. Right-click the New Objects icon.
3. Select the "Compare to number of objects in a zone" option. You will be taken to a Zone setup screen. We'll tell TGF to check the entire 640 × 320 (pixels) playing area.
4. Click in the first box, Horizontal. Type a 0 in the box. Go to the next box on that line, click it, and type 640.

5. Next click the first box on the next line down, Vertical. Enter a 0 in the box.

6. Now enter 320 in the last box, to. You should have the four boxes filled as follows: 0 to 640, then underneath, 0 to 320. If you have done this successfully, click OK.

7. You'll see a dialog box where you can enter a number to compare to the number of objects in the zone that you just defined. In the top of the dialog box are several option buttons, which is where you decide how you are going to compare the number. By default, it is set at Equal. This is the comparison that we want to use, because when the number of objects is equal to zero, we want to end the game. Make sure the Equal option button is selected.

8. Now, enter the number you want to compare. In this case, it is 0, so make sure the text box at the bottom has a 0 in it. You can change it by using the slider, or by clicking the text box and entering the numbers directly.

9. When you have the comparison set to Equals 0, click the OK button.

Your event line will read: **Number of objects in zone (0,0) to (640,320) = 0**.

Finally, we'll insert an action to finish the game.

1. Go to the empty box below the Storyboard controls icon and right-click it.

2. From the menu, select the "End the game" option.

3. That's it! Space Defiler is ready to play! Oh yeah—SAVE YOUR GAME!

CHAPTER REVIEW

In this chapter, we expanded our knowledge of TGF and built Space Defiler. In the next chapter, we will take our development with TGF up a notch or two by introducing a new game type.

12

MAKING ANOTHER GAME WITH THE GAMES FACTORY

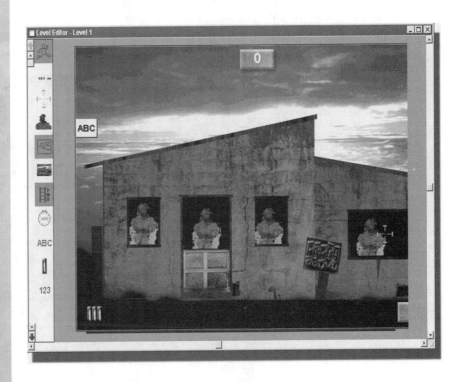

Okay, are you ready to make a game that will sell a million units and blow right off the sales charts? Well. hold on tight, because we are going to make Ghost Hunter (see Figure 12.1)—a surefire hit! Think about it—Deer Hunter, only with ghosts....

Well, the design needs work, but we will develop Ghost Hunter for fun. And behind all this fun, you will be learning the next step of working with TGF. We will be using several more features of TGF and doing a lot more actual development, as far as the tweaking of the assets and game flow. As you will see, Ghost Hunter offers a different viewpoint than Space Defiler. Instead of shooting up, we will be shooting at the targets. This will introduce a few new techniques to your growing TGF knowledge base.

In this chapter, we will not only learn new functions of TGF, but we will also learn a few new techniques to keep productions made with TGF organized and running smoothly.

Let's look at Ghost Hunter.

FIGURE 12.1 Ghost Hunter—a surefire hit.

LOADING GHOST HUNTER

To see the completed version of Ghost Hunter, choose Open from the File menu, go to the directory where you installed TGF, and then go to the *gametuts* directory. When you get there, load *ghosthunt*. When you have it open, we can begin.

GHOST HUNTER—THE STORYBOARD EDITOR

The first thing you will see is the Storyboard Editor. When you have loaded Ghost Hunter, you will have a Storyboard Editor screen that looks very similar to the one for Space Defiler, with all the same options are available (See Figure 12.2).

While we are here, let's look at a few more things you can do from the Storyboard Editor screen that we didn't look at in the last chapter. Click the Preferences icon and look at the dialog box, as shown in Figure 12.3.

In the box, you see one slider bar and two check boxes. The boxes allow you to remove the comments and the top bar, as shown in Figure 12.4.

The slider bar in Figure 12.3 lets you change the density of the display. This means that the thumbnail picture can be larger or smaller, as shown in Figure 12.4.

Setting the density lower can be useful as you get more proficient with TGF and don't need all the visual help. Making the thumbnails smaller

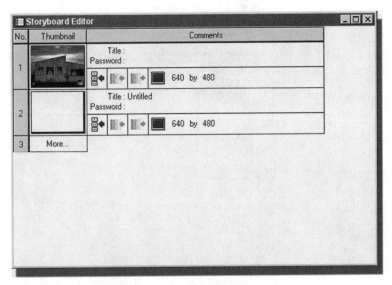

FIGURE 12.2 The Storyboard Editor, as used by Ghost Hunter.

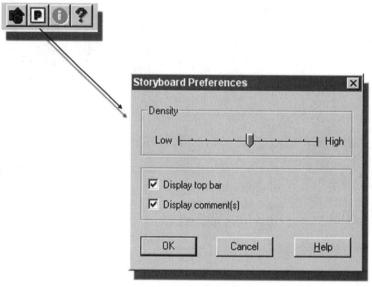

FIGURE 12.3 The Preferences icon and the Storyboard Preference dialogue box that pops up from the Storyboard Editor.

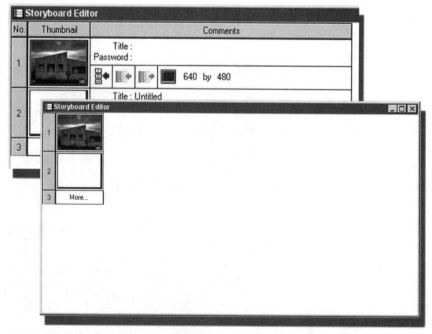

FIGURE 12.4 The Storyboard Editor with the comments and top bar deleted.

makes them harder to see, but if you have been working a lot on a game, you will be intimately familiar with the level names, layout, and general appearance. As your games become more complex and contain more levels, you'll find that you prefer the smaller thumbnails.

When you're done looking at or making changes in the Storyboard Preferences box, click OK to exit.

When you return to the Storyboard Editor, you'll see that for this game, the screen is set at a higher resolution, 800 × 600. Since almost all PCs today can display at least this resolution, we'll use it to make the game a bit bigger.

GHOST HUNTER—THE LEVEL EDITOR

Now, let's go to the Level Editor. Right-click the thumbnail of the level, bring up the "Edit this level" option, and select the Level Editor. Remember that you can look at all the objects in the editor by simply placing the moue pointer over them and reading the Handy Hint balloons. If you do this, you will see how Ghost Hunter was created and what objects are contained in the game (see Figure 12.5).

Notice that in the Level Editor, you can see all the ghosts, but later when you run the level, you will see that they drop down and hide (for

FIGURE 12.5   Ghost Hunter in the Level Editor.

good reason) soon after the game is started. When the game is running, all the ghosts will be hidden. Then, at random, they will emerge from hiding to scare you, and then hide again. You will only be able to shoot at them when they are out of hiding. As we'll see, you'll use the mouse to put the crosshair of your Ghost Vaporizer over them and then fire at them by pressing the left mouse button.

To make the ghosts look like they are actually hiding behind something and then emerging from behind it, we'll use a chopped-up copy of the backdrop. As we've seen before, active objects are placed on top of backdrop objects and display in front of them. To hide the ghosts, we'll make an active object out of part of the backdrop and use it as a Mask object in front of them.

This makes it look like the ghosts are hiding and popping up. As mentioned before, it also prevents them from being shot while they are hiding, thus increasing the challenge of the game. The mask that covers a ghost fits exactly over it, making the ghost invisible (that is, unless we do a sloppy job and place the ghost or the mask improperly).

GHOST HUNTER—THE EVENT EDITOR

To enter the Event Editor, click the Event Editor icon on the toolbar, or right-click the thumbnail if you have gone back to the Storyboard Editor. You will now be able to look through the events that make the game actions for Ghost Hunter, and read the comments. There are a lot more events than in the Space Defiler game. You'll also see a few new icons we will be working with. Figure 12.6 shows the Ghost Hunter Event Editor.

Notice also that groups are used to a much greater degree in this game. One reason is that the game is larger, and you will need to use groups more to help organize it. But groups are also used because you can deactivate and activate a group (and everything in it) during the game. This makes the game easier to control.

Scroll through the events and move the mouse pointer over the check marks in the boxes, to see the actions that are associated with the events. This will help you get a feel for the logic, or flow, of the game. Some of the first events you will see are the group deactivation events mentioned above. We will look at these more closely later. The deactivation events help speed up game play by preventing unneeded events from running. This will be useful in boosting performance when you start making larger and more complex games.

For example, you will notice a group of Level Won events, as shown in Figure 12.7. This group is inactive until it is needed, when the player wins the game. Then, it is activated and other groups are deactivated.

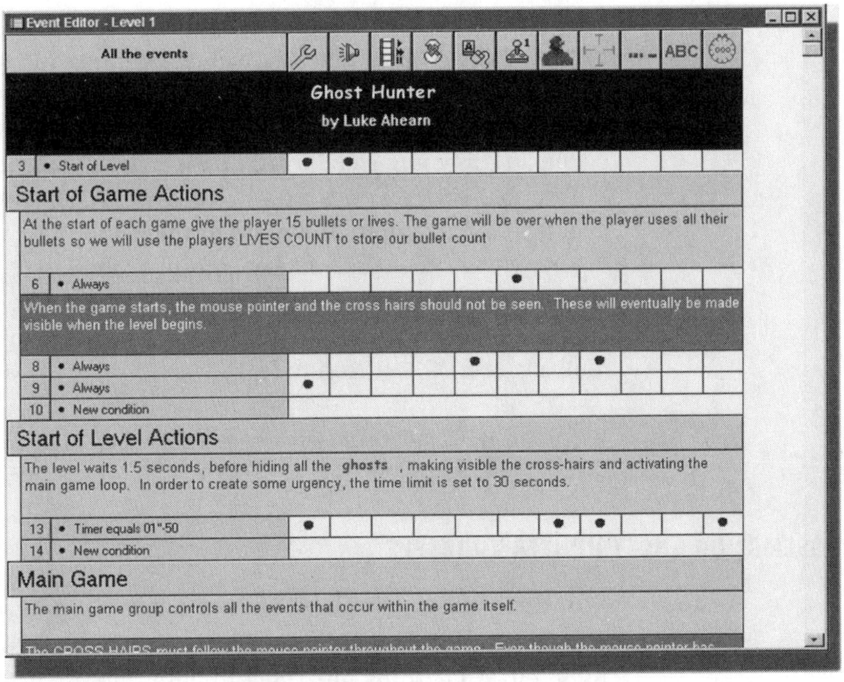

FIGURE 12.6   The Ghost Hunter Event Editor.

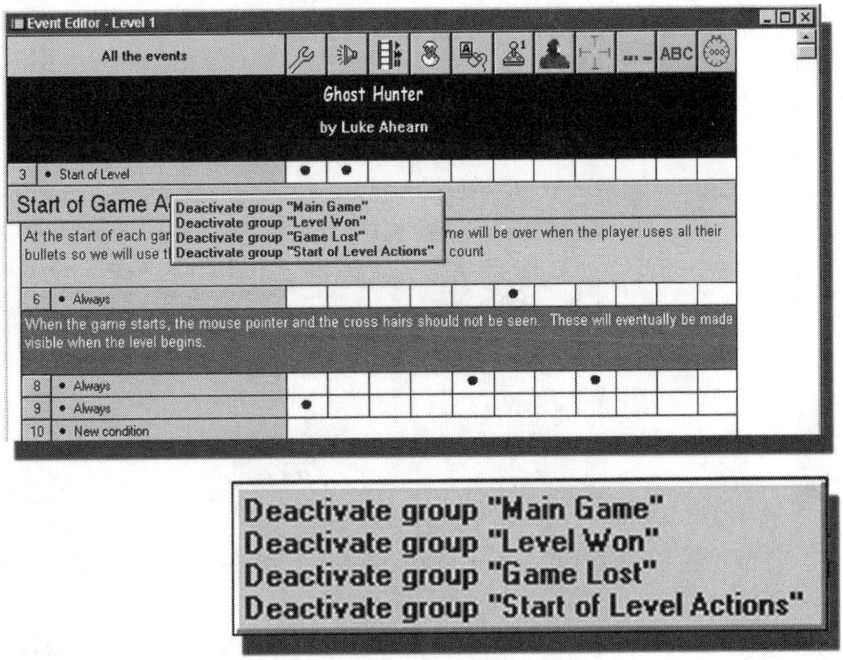

FIGURE 12.7   The events for activating and deactivating groups.

You can collapse a group of events by double-clicking its header. Do this to all the groups, and you will be see how this can make it far easier to move around the Event Grid. This will also make it easier for you to see the major steps of the game. Notice that there are five major groups of events in this game (see Figure 12.8).

Double-click on each group, to open it. When you'll do, you'll see the events that make up that portion of the game.

Now that we've had a look around in the Event Editor, let's play the game a little before we start to recreate it. This will give you a frame of reference for the events we are setting up. Use the Run Game button on the toolbar to run Ghost Hunter.

 When you're ready to exit the game, press Alt and F4 together.

ASSEMBLING GHOST HUNTER YOURSELF

Now that you've seen Ghost Hunter run, we'll go through the steps of assembling it. When you're done playing Ghost Hunter, load a new file. You should now be in the Storyboard Editor. Set the play area to 640 by 480 and then click OK.

The Ghost Hunter Level Editor

To get into the Level Editor from the Storyboard Editor, right-click the empty thumbnail and choose the "Edit this level" and Level Editor options.

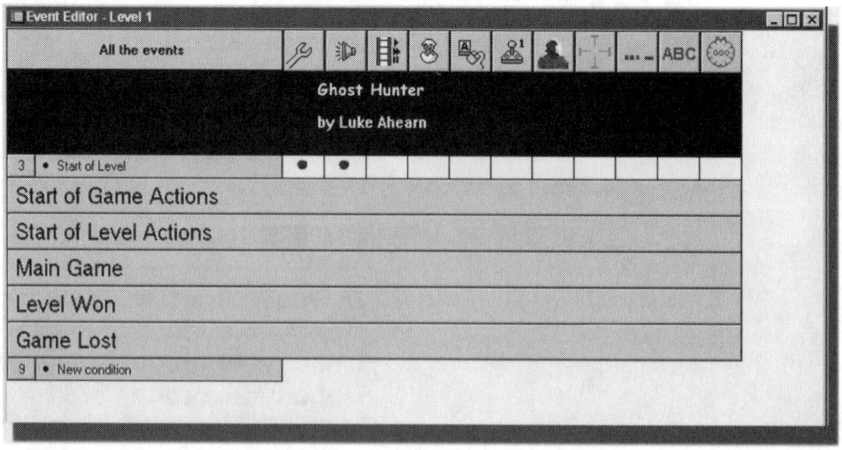

FIGURE 12.8 The Event Editor, with all events collapsed into group headings.

First, we need to get the assets and objects we will be using for this project. Go to the Level Objects pull-down menu on the toolbar. Click the button at the side of this menu to pull down a list of all the object libraries, and select the library called *(Tutorial) GHOST HUNTER*. You'll see the screen shown in Figure 12.9.

In this screen, you can see all the objects used to create Ghost Hunter, in the Object window on the left side.

Placing the Backdrop Object

The first thing to place is the backdrop object, called Background, onto the screen. Select it, then place it anywhere in the play area. As mentioned earlier, because it is exactly the same size as the play area, it will align itself automatically.

Placing the Ghosts

Next, click the active object for the ghost, named Ghost. Place three copies of it—in the window part of the house, on the door, and over the fence. Remember that it's a good idea to right-click to place all copies except the

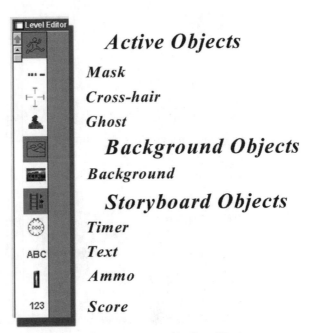

FIGURE 12.9   The library of items used in Ghost Hunter.

last one, for which you should left-click. When you've placed all the ghosts, line up the bottom of each one, so that it fits nicely into its area.

The Mask Object

Now, we'll place a mask object in front of the ghosts, so that we can make them invisible. Be careful to line it up with the backdrop perfectly. It should also cover up the bottom part of the ghosts a little. The mask will keep players being able to shoot the ghosts when they are hiding. Since they are behind an active object, the mask, they will be protected (see Figure 12.10).

 Notice that the mask is nothing more than the backdrop image copied, with the large areas being filled in with a color that is very different from the rest of the image. This "transparency color" will be invisible when it is placed on the play area.

 If you are creating your own mask object, be careful not to use anti-aliasing on it. A mask with anti-aliasing will have a colored line around it.

FIGURE 12.10 The mask (notice the blocks of color that will be used for transparency).

Placing the Crosshair Object

Now, let's place the object that we will use as the crosshair of our gun. Later, this crosshair will replace the mouse cursor in the game.

Go to the Object window and select the Crosshair object. Place it anywhere on the screen. It doesn't matter where you place it, since we are going to hide it at the very beginning of the level. We will deal with making it replace the mouse cursor later on, in the Event Editor.

Placing the Countdown Object

The countdown object keeps track of the time left in a level. Select it and put it on the play area in a place where you will be able to see it readily, but where it won't interfere with the ghosts, such as one of the corners.

Placing the Text Object

Now place the IT'S A SHAME! text object on the far left of the play area, at about the same height as the top of the ghosts.

Placing the Ammo Object

Place the ammo object on the bottom left of the play area. This is the display of the number of bullets that you have left.

Placing the Score Object

Place the score object on the play area near the countdown object. This displays the score during the game.

You should now have a screen that looks like Figure 12.11.

Changing the View Order of Objects

While we are in the Level Editor, let's look at a small but useful feature of TGF—changing the view order of objects. Let's say that you accidentally placed the mask object on the screen before the ghosts, then placed the ghosts over the top of the mask. You then noticed that the mask does not cover the ghosts, and the ghosts are on top of the mask object. If you had done this, you *could* fix things by deleting everything and starting over. But you don't *need* to take that drastic step. Instead, you could simply right-click the mask and change the order of the layers, just like you can in Photoshop, Paint Shop Pro, and other paint programs. What this means is

FIGURE 12.11 The Ghost Hunter Level Editor, with objects laid out.

simply that you can make the mask move forward and be on top of the ghosts.

To change the order of the layer of either the ghosts or the mask:

1. Right-click the mask object. You'll see a menu with several options, as shown in Figure 12.12.
2. Select the View option from this menu.
3. Now select the "To front" option. This will place the mask object "in front" of all the other objects on the screen.

This is a simple and very useful tool to be aware of. You may have noticed that your other options were to bring the currently selected object forward one or back one level. You can see how this will save you time if you have many items on the screen, or if you decide to add another active object and have to get it behind the mask. You can put it in and then change its order.

FIGURE 12.12   The pop-up menu from the mask object.

Changing the Game Setup

Before we go on, let's look at the Game setup menu. We are going to change the game setup because some of the objects we are using need to have their initial values changed. We also want to hide the mouse pointer, and the menu bar that is normally displayed when you do a full run of your game using the Run Game button (see Figure 12.13).

1. From the File menu, select the "Game setup" option. Be careful not to select the General setup by accident. You'll see the dialog box shown in Figure 12.14.
2. On the first "layer" of the dialog box, enter a name for your game in the Title text box.
3. Enter your name underneath in the Author text box.
4. Go to the Window layer by clicking its tab at the top of the dialog box, as shown in Figure 12.15.

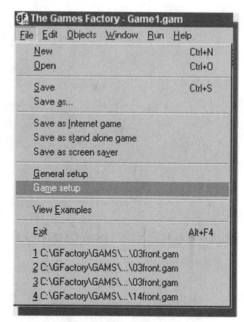

FIGURE 12.13 The Game Setup menu.

FIGURE 12.14 The About tab of the Game Setup dialog box.

5. Make sure that all of the check boxes are unselected. This will stop the menu bar and heading from being displayed when you run your game.

6. Select the Players tab. In the Lives box at the bottom right, change the Initial setting to 15. You can enter the numbers directly by clicking the text box, using the Delete key to clear the box, and then entering 15 (see Figure 12.16).

7. Change the Maximum value to 15 also.

8. Click the OK button.

 We didn't look at several options in the Game Setup dialog box, but we will get back to these later.

The Ghost Hunter Event Editor

After you have those changes made to the Game Setup dialog box, and you have all the game objects placed the way you want them on the play area in the Level Editor, go to the Event Editor. To do this, select its icon from the toolbar at the top of the screen (see Figure 12.17).

Now, we'll insert some events. We'll start with a Start of level event, then put in some actions.

1. Right-click the "New Condition" text of event line number 1.

FIGURE 12.15   The Window tab of the Game Setup dialog box.

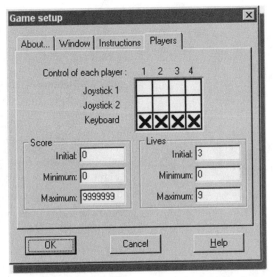

FIGURE 12.16   The Players tab of the Game Setup dialog box.

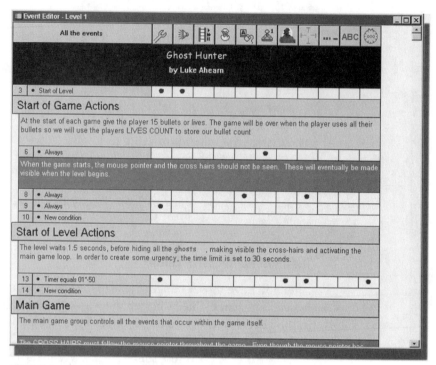

FIGURE 12.17 The Ghost Hunter Event Editor.

2. Right-click the Storyboard icon, then select the "Start of level" option from its menu.

Playing Music

We want to play some music at the start of this level, so we'll insert an action to do this on this event line. We'll also add add four actions to deactivate other groups of actions, as mentioned earlier. Since we have not yet created these groups, TGF will not let us deactivate them yet.

1. Right-click the empty box directly beneath the Sound icon.
2. Select the "Play and loop music" option.
3. Select a file. If you have done a normal installation of The Games Factory, the sound files will be on your hard drive in the default installation folder.
4. Navigate to the sound file directory, and under it, to the directory called *Midi*. Find the file named *Melanitr.mid*. Select this file, and click the OK button.

5. You will now be asked to enter the number of times you want the music to loop. Enter 99, and click the OK button.

Notice the check mark under the sound icon. Move the mouse pointer over it. The event will read **Play music Melanitr.mid 99 times** (see Figure 12.18).

Inserting The Start of Game Actions Group

Now we'll create a group called Start of Game Actions. Remember that having groups lets you deal with many objects at once.

1. Right-click event line number 2.
2. Select Insert from the pop-up menu, and then select A Group of events.
3. Type "Start of Game Actions" in the text box, then click OK.

Inserting a Comment

We can now place events in this group. Make sure that each event line on which you insert a new condition is indented slightly from the left. This specifies that this specific event line is in the group directly above it.

Insert a comment on line number 3 that reads: "At the start of each game, give the player 15 bullets, or lives. The game will be over when the

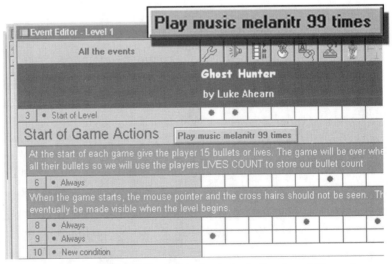

FIGURE 12.18   The pop-up Handy Hint balloon for the Start of Level event, Play music Melanitr.mid 99 times.

player uses all their bullets, so we will use the player's LIVES COUNT to store our bullet count." To do this, right-click the number of the event line. Select the Insert option, then select the "A Comment" option.

Of course, to make the comments stand out, you can change the text and background color. This also is useful for grouping the events visually. As your games get increasingly longer and more complex, color-coding the comments will help you keep track of your game.

Inserting an Always Event

In this section, we'll insert an Always event on line number 4. To do this:

1. Right-click the "New condition" text line.
2. Right-click the Special Object icon in the window.
3. From the Always/Never option that pops up, select the Always option.

Setting Lives

Now we will insert the Set number of lives to 15 action. To do this:

1. Right-click the box under the Player 1 object, on line 4.
2. Select the "Number of lives" option, then select the "Set number of lives" option.
3. Set the number to 15. You can enter the number in the text box, or use the slider.
4. Click OK.

Inserting a Comment

Insert the following comment on line 5:

"When the game starts, the mouse pointer and crosshair will not be seen, but the crosshair will be made visible when the game starts."

Inserting an Always Event

Insert an Always event on line 6, as you did on line 4. To do this:

1. Right-click the "New condition" text line.
2. Right-click the Special Object icon in the window.
3. From the Always/Never option that pops up, select the Always option.

Hiding the Mouse Pointer

Now, we'll use this Always event to hide the mouse pointer, so we can re-place it with the custom crosshair object. On the same line as the Always event, insert the Hide Windows mouse pointer action. To do this:

1. Right-click the empty box beneath the Mouse pointer and Keyboard icon.
2. Select the "Hide Windows mouse pointer" option.

Making the Crosshair Object Invisible

Insert another action on line 6 to make the crosshair invisible. To do this:

1. Right-click the box under the crosshair object.
2. Select the Visibility option.
3. Select the "Make object invisible" option.

We are hiding the crosshair at the start of the game to add to the game play. You may have noticed that when you run the game, the ghosts taunt you for a second before hiding—you can't shoot them at this time. This adds a bit of production value as a sort of introduction to the action of the game.

Inserting an Always Event

Insert an Always event on line 7. We'll activate and deactivate some of the groups here, but as explained earlier, you cannot do this until you have created those groups.

Save your game.

Inserting a Start of Level Actions Group of Events

Insert a group of events called Start of Level Actions on line 12. You must create this group on a line that is not indented, so it will function properly in the game.

When you have done this, line 8 should be empty, and should still be in the Start of Game Actions group, as shown in Figure 12.19.

Inserting a Comment

Insert the following comment on line 10:

Not Indented

Indented

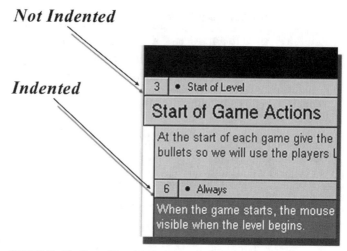

FIGURE 12.19 The Start of Level Actions group on line 9, not indented.

"The level waits 1.5 seconds before hiding all the ghosts, making the crosshair visible, and activating the main game loop."

To increase the game play, we'll create a sense of urgency and set the time limit to 30 seconds. Right-click the number in the border and select the "Insert-A comment" option. Enter the above comment line and click OK.

Setting the Timer

Now, insert an event on line 11: **Timer is greater than 50**. To do this:

1. Right-click the "New condition" text and right-click the timer object.
2. Select the Is the timer greater than a certain value?
3. Enter the time. By default, the value is 1 second, so you only need to change the 1/100 box. Click in it and enter the number 50, then click OK.

Changing an Animation Sequence

Insert a Change animation to hiding action under the Ghosts icon on line 11. To do this:

1. Right-click the box, select the Animation option, select the Change option, and then select the "Animation sequence" option.
2. In the dialog box, select the Hiding option.
3. Click OK.

Making the Crosshair Reappear

Now, we'll insert a reappear action on line 11, under the Crosshair icon. Right-click the box and, from the menu, select the Visibility option, then select the "Make object reappear" option.

Next, insert an action to set the counter to 30. Right-click the empty box under the countdown object on line 11, and then select the "Set counter" option. You will see a dialog box where you can either enter the numbers directly in the text box, or use the buttons on the slider to change the number. Make sure that the value entered is 30, then click OK.

Inserting the Main Game Group

Insert a group called Main Game, as outlined below.

You must do this on line 13, which is outside of the Start of Level Actions group. If you used line 12, which is indented, this would put a group within a group, which The Games Factory will not allow.

To insert a group, right-click the number of the line (13), select the "Insert-A group of events" option, type in the text, and click OK.

Inserting a Comment

Insert the following comment on line 14: "The Main Game group controls all the events that occur within the game itself."

Right-click the number, select the "Insert-A comment" option, type in the text, and then click OK.

Inserting Another Comment

Insert another comment, preferably in a different color: "The crosshair will follow the hidden mouse pointer throughout the game."

Even though the mouse pointer has been hidden, it is still there, moving about and functioning as though it were visible. If your game window is smaller than your screen size, the mouse pointer will reappear if you move it off the game and onto the Windows Desktop.

By taking the mouse pointer's X and Y coordinates, we can make the crosshair follow the movement of the mouse pointer.

Inserting an Always Event

Insert an always event on the next event line (line16).

Making the Crosshair Follow the Mouse Pointer

Now we will make the crosshair follow the invisible mouse pointer. Insert an action on line 16 to set the coordinates of the crosshair to be the same as the coordinates of the mouse.

1. Right-click the empty box under the crosshair object on line 16.
2. Select the Position option.
3. Select the "Set X coordinate ... " option.
4. Click the Edit button.
5. Click the "Retrieve data from an object" button.
6. Right-click the mouse pointer and keyboard object.
7. Select the "Current X position of the mouse" option.

You should have an action under the crosshair object that reads "Set position to X mouse." To set the Y coordinate to be the same as the mouse, do the following:

1. Right-click the filled box under the crosshair object on line 16.
2. Select the Position option.
3. Select the "Set Y coordinate ... " option.
4. Click the Edit button.
5. Click the "Retrieve data from an object" button.
6. Right-click the mouse pointer and keyboard object.
7. Select the "Current Y position of the mouse" option, then click OK.

This will set the crosshair object so that it always precisely follows the movement of the mouse pointer.

Save your game.

Inserting a Comment

Insert the following comment on line 17: "Every second, deduct 1 from the counter that holds the time limit."

Testing the Timer

Now insert an every 1"-00 event:

1. Right-click the "New condition" text of line number 18, then right-click the timer object.

2. Select the Every option.
3. Make sure the time entered is 1 second, then click the OK button.

Changing the Value of the Counter

1. Insert the subtract 1 from counter action.
2. Right-click the box under the countdown object.
3. Select the "Subtract from counter" option.
4. Enter the number 1 in the text box of the Expression Editor produced, then click OK.

Inserting a Comment

Insert the following comment on line 19: "Every 2 seconds, select one of the many ghost objects from the game, and if that ghost is currently hiding, run its appear from hiding animation." Right-click the number and select the "Insert-A comment" option.

Testing the Timer Every 2 seconds

Insert an event, every 2"-00:

1. Right-click the "New condition" text of line number 20.
2. Right-click the timer object, then select the Every option. Make sure the time entered is 2 seconds, then click the OK button.

Adding a Condition to a Timer Event

Now add a condition to the above event. To do this, right-click the text "Every 2"-00" and select the Insert option. Now right-click the Ghost object, select the "Pick or count" option, then select the "Pick 'ghost' at random" option.

Adding a Further Condition

Next, add a further condition to line number 20, "Ghost" animation Hiding is playing.
    To do this:

1. Right-click on any of the texts of line 20, and select the Insert option
2. Right-click the ghost, then select the Animation option.
3. Select the Which animation of "Ghost" is playing?

4. Select the hiding animation from the list in the dialog box.
5. Click OK.

You will have three conditions, all on one event line.

 You should move the every 2"-00 event to the top of this event line, so that The Games Factory will only go through the rest of the conditions once every 2 seconds. This will help to speed up your game play slightly, especially if you have many event lines like this. For example, if you placed the Pick one of "Ghost" condition at the top, The Games Factory would go through the actions of picking a ghost before looking at the other conditions.

Changing an Animation Sequence

Insert a Change animation sequence to Appear from Hiding action into line number 20. To do this:

Right click the box under the Ghost object on line 20.
1. Select the Animation option.
2. Select the Change option.
3. Select the "Animation sequence ... " option.
4. From the dialog box, select the Appear from hiding animation, then click OK.

Inserting a Comment

Insert the following comment on line 21: "Four times a second, select one of the ghost objects from the game, and if that ghost is currently hiding, run its appear from hiding animation."

Testing the Timer

Insert an every 00"-25 event on line 22. Right-click the "New condition" text, right-click the timer object, and select the Every option from its menu. Make sure that the time entered is 25 hundredths of a second, then click OK.

Picking a Ghost at Random

Insert a condition to line 22, Pick one of (Ghost). Right-click the text "Every 00"25" of line 22, and select the Insert option. Right-click the

Ghost object, select the "Pick or count" option from its menu, and then select the "Pick 'ghost' at random" option.

Testing Which Animation Is Playing

Now insert another condition to line 22, "ghost" animation Stopped is playing.

1. Right-click either of the condition texts on line 22.
2. Select the Insert option.
3. Right click the Ghost object from its menu, and select the Animation option.
4. Select the "Which animation of 'ghost' is playing?" option.
5. From the dialog box, select the Stopped animation.
6. Click OK.

Changing the Animation Sequence

Now, insert an action into line 22 to hide the "ghost" that has been picked. Right-click the empty box on line 22, underneath the "ghost" object. From its menu, select the Animation option, select the Change option, and then select the "Animation sequence" option. From the dialog box, select the hiding animation, then click OK.

Inserting a Comment

Insert the following comment on line 23: "If the player manages to click the mouse pointer (appearing as a crosshair) on a ghost, destroy the ghost and add 10 points to the score."

Testing the Mouse to See if It Has Clicked a Ghost

Insert a user clicks with left mouse button on "ghost" event on line 24:

1. Right-click the "New condition" text of line 24.
2. Right click the mouse pointer and keyboard object.
3. Select the "The mouse" option.
4. Select the "User clicks on an object" option. You will be taken to a dialog box.
5. Make sure that there are check marks in the "Left button" and "Single click" option buttons, then click OK.
6. Select the ghost object, then click OK.

Inserting Sound

Now we will insert two sound actions on line 24.

1. Right-click the empty box under the sound object, and select the "Play sample" option.
2. You will see a file selector. If you have done a normal installation, the sound files are in the default TGF directory. Look for the directory *samples*.
3. In the *samples* directory, look for the sub-directory *weapons*. It is from here that we are going to select the noise for the gun being fired.
4. Try the *gun3.wav* file. To preview the sound, click the Play button. Then click the Open button.
5. Insert a second noise, the yelp of the ghost, from the Ghost Hunter tutorial folder.

To insert a further Action in the same check-box, left-click in the box you want to add an action to.

Find a gunshot sound:

1. Click under the sound object again, then right-click the "New action" option.
2. Select the "Play sample" option.
3. Look again in the *samples* directory, but this time look in the Ghost Hunter sub-directory.
4. Look for the file *Ricchet2.wav*. Try playing it a few times.
5. If you are happy with your selection, click the OK boxes until you are returned to the Event Editor.

Changing the Score

We've set the sound that users will hear when a ghost is destroyed. Now, we'll tell TGF to change the score when that happens, as well.

1. Right-click the empty check box underneath the Player 1 object.
2. From the pop-up menu, select the Score option, then select the "Add to score" option.
3. You can enter the score by typing it, by clicking in the text box, or by clicking the slider. You can add any score you like, but let's add 10 here.
4. Click the OK button.

Destroying a Ghost

Now right-click in the empty check box underneath the Ghost object. From the pop-up menu, select the Destroy option.

Deducting a Life (Ammo)

Next, add an action to deduct a life from Player 1. In the context of this game, it means that Player 1 has used a bullet each time he fires the gun. When there are no more bullets, the game is over, since there is nothing else to do. This is an example of using set tools in a different way than they are labeled to make a better or more interesting game. Just because the word *life* is used, doesn't mean you have to literally make the action apply to a life.

1. Click the box underneath the Player 1 object, where you just inserted the action to add to the score.
2. Right-click the "New action" option.
3. Select the "Number of lives" option.
4. Select the "Subtract from Number of Lives" option.
5. Enter the number 1 into the text box, or use the slider bar to change the value.
6. Click OK until you are returned to the Event Editor.

Inserting a Comment

Insert the following Comment on line 25: "When the player presses the left button and misses, deduct 1 life and play the sample *gun04.wav*. The sound condition makes sure that these actions are not repeated very rapidly."

Testing the Mouse to See if the Left Button Has Been Clicked

Insert an event on line 26 to check whether the user has clicked the left mouse button. We are then going to add a condition to this, so the actions associated with this line will only take place if a sound is not playing—if the player has not hit a ghost.

1. Right-click the "New condition" text of line 26.
2. Select the mouse pointer and keyboard object.
3. Select the "The mouse" option.
4. Select the "User clicks" option. Make sure that the "Left" button and "Single click" option buttons are selected.
5. Click OK.

Testing to See if No Samples Are Already Being Played

Here, we'll make sure that the user has not already just killed a ghost. Insert a condition to line 26 to check that no samples are being played. Right-click the text of line 26 and select the Insert option. Then click the sound object. Choose the Samples option, then select the "Is a sample not playing?" option.

Playing a Sample and Deducting a Life

Now, insert actions into line 26 to play a sample and to deduct 1 from Player 1's lives (in other words, one bullet).

1. Right click the empty box under the sound object.
2. Select the "Play sample" option.
3. Look in the *samples* directory, then in the *weapons* sub-directory. From here, select the sample *gun04.wav*.
4. Right click the empty box under the Player 1 object.
5. Select the Lives option.
6. Select the "Subtract from number of lives" option.
7. Set the Expression Editor value to 1.
8. Click OK.

Inserting a Comment

Insert a Comment on line 27: "If all the ghosts in the game have been destroyed, the player has completed the level. Reveal the 'It's a shame!' message and activate the Level Won group."

Testing to See if All the Ghosts Have Been Shot

Insert the last "ghost" has been destroyed event on line 28. Right-click the "New condition" text, then right-click the Ghosts object. Select the "Pick or count" option, then select the "Have all 'ghosts' been destroyed?" option.

Playing Victory Music and Displaying Victory Text

As previously stated, we can't activate or deactivate a group until it has been created, so we will insert the action to activate the Level Won group after it has been created.

For now, you can insert several Actions on line 28.

First, insert an action to play some music. Right-click under the sound object, select the "Play music" option, then look in the *midi* directory and select the *soldier2.mid* file.

Now that we've chosen the music, insert an action to display the text "It's A Shame." We'll need to tell TGF where to display it. To do this, right click under the good shooting object, then select the "Display text … " option. You will now see a position selector. Enter 0 into the X coordinate box and 64 into the Y coordinate box, then click OK.

Inserting a Comment

Insert the following comment on line 29: "There are two ways in which the player can lose the game. The bullets can run out or the time limit can expire. In each case, the Game Lost group will be activated."

Inserting an Event

Insert an event on line 30. Right click the "New condition" text, select the Player 1 object, then select the "Compare to player's number of lives" option. Now make sure that the value is 0, and that the Equals option button is selected. Click the OK button.

Inserting Sound

Insert a sound action on line 31. Play a piece of music that you feel is appropriate to losing the game.

Comparing the Value of the Countdown Object to a Number

Insert an Event on line 31. Click the line's text, then select the countdown object. Next select the "Compare the counter to a value" option. Make sure the value it is being compared to is 0, then make sure that the Equals option button is selected.

Copying an Action

Click and drag the music action from line 30 down into line 31. This copies that sound action onto line 31.

Inserting a Group

On line 33, insert a Level Won group. Note that this must go on this line so that it falls outside of the Main Game group. If you were to place it on line 32, The Games Factory would be unable to run your game.

Inserting a Comment

On line 34, insert the following comment: "When the congratulations music has finished, restart the level, which keeps the score and allows the player to play again with all the ghosts back as they were at the start of the level."

Testing to See if No Music Is Playing

Insert an event on line 35. Right-click the line, select the sound object, select the Music option, then select the "Is music not playing?" option.

Restarting the Current Level

Insert an action on line 35. Right-click under the storyboard object, then select the "Restart the current level" option.

Inserting a Group

Now insert a Game Lost group on line 37.

Inserting a Comment

Insert the following comment on line 38: "When the game lost sound has ended, restart the game to clear the score and begin the entire game from the very start."

Copying an Event

Copy an event onto line 38. Click and hold on the "No sample is playing" text of line 35 and drag it into line 38. This will copy that event.

Restarting the Game

Insert an action on line 39 to restart the game. Right-click the box under the storyboard object, then select the "Restart game" option.

Inserting All Actions to Activate/Deactivate Groups

That's almost it. All we need to do now is go back and insert all the actions to activate and deactivate the groups at the appropriate time, now that we have created them. Go to line 1, right-click the box under the special ob-

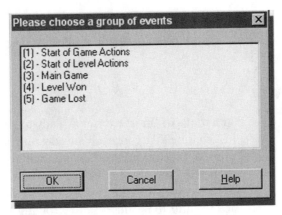

FIGURE 12.20   The dialog box where you activate and deactivate groups.

ject, select the "Group of events" option, then select the Deactivate option. You will see a dialog box where you can select the groups that you want to deactivate (see Figure 12.20). First of all, pick the Start of Level Actions group, then click OK.

Now, insert the rest of the actions into the same check mark. To do this:

1. Click the check mark. This will produce a dialog box which lists all the actions from within that check mark.
2. Right-click the "New action" option. You will see the same menu produced as when you first right-clicked under the special object.
3. Select the "Group of events" option.
4. Select the Deactivate option.
5. Select the Main Game group.
6. Now, deactivate the Level Won and Game Lost groups, using the method outlined above. Go to line 7 and insert the following actions: deactivate group—Start of game actions, and activate group—Start of level actions.
7. Right-click under the Special object, select Group of events, select Deactivate, Start of game actions, then click OK.
8. Click the check mark, right-click New actions, select Group of events, select Activate, select Start of level actions, then click OK.
9. Go to line 11 and insert the following actions: deactivate group—Start of level actions, and activate group—Main Game.
10. Go to line 28 and insert the following actions: deactivate group—Main Game, and activate group—Level Won.
11. Go to line 30 and insert the following actions: deactivate group—Main Game, and activate group—Game Lost.

12. Copy these actions into line 31 by clicking and holding on the check mark, then dragging it into line 31.

CHAPTER REVIEW

And that's it. Ghost Hunter is ready to take the market by storm. You have just completed a more advanced game in TGF. You've learned some functions and techniques to help you with organization while making a game with TGF, and also to help TGF run more efficiently.

Next we will take yet another big step in game development and create a game that adds to our growing bag of tools. Once again, we will change the perspective you have of the game world and attempt a different type of game to further explore the abilities of TGF.

CHAPTER

13

MAKING A MORE ADVANCED GAME WITH THE GAMES FACTORY

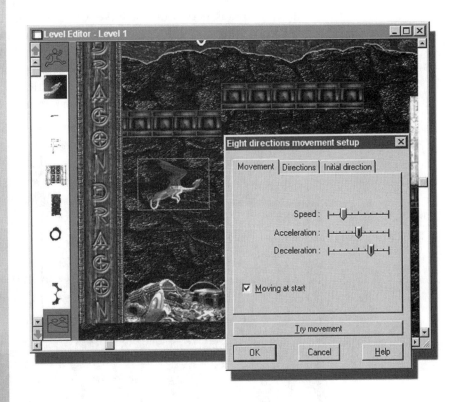

Okay. Ready to make another game? This time we will do a game that is a bit more advanced. We will explore a few more functions of The Game Factory. We will look at side scrolling on a screen larger than the play area. We'll also use groups to speed up game development and make the Event Editor easier to look at. We will be developing Dragon Flight (see Figure 13.1).

DRAGON FLIGHT

By now you should really have a good feel for the different Editor screens and their purposes. As you can already see, most of your game action is created in the Event Editor, and the levels themselves are assembled in the Level Editor. The Storyboard Editor allows you to control the flow of your game as a production—level order, transitions, and the progress of your game. Now we will look deeper into some fairly complex game-creation techniques, but don't be intimidated. We will go through these step by step.

Dragon Flight is a simple game where you are racing against the clock. The dragon is trying to take off out of its cave and has to dodge the walls and its own firetraps. Although simple in terms of game play, Dragon Flight uses some fairly advanced techniques to achieve the end result. Before we go any farther, let's load up the game and have a look around.

FIGURE 13.1 A screen shot of Dragon Flight.

Go to the File menu heading at the top of the screen, and select the Open option.

Now look for the directory *sample games,* and then look in the sub-directory *dragon* for the file *dragon.gam.*

Storyboard Editor—Dragon Flight Part 1

Let's have a look around the Dragon Flight Storyboard Editor and see the changes that have been made here, as well as looking into the various preferences that have been changed (See Figure 13.2).

First, go to the File menu in the toolbar and select the Game setup option. You can see on the first layer of this dialog box the author and title of the game. You can also see that the panic key has been enabled (See Figure 13.3).

The panic key is useful in case you panic during the game (like when your boss walks in when you are playing). If you press the key (F5), during the game The Games Factory will take you back to the Windows screen, leaving the game running in the background. The panic key turns off the sound and minimizes the display. When you click the button in the Windows taskbar to restore the game, the sound effects will work, but the looped music will not play again until the level is restarted.

Click the Window tab and look at the next layer. There are some significant changes here from the default settings. These have a dramatic effect on the final look of the game, and it is important to understand these changes (see Figure 13.4).

The first line is Maximized on boot up, which maximizes the window used to display the game when it is first loaded, not the game itself. Like

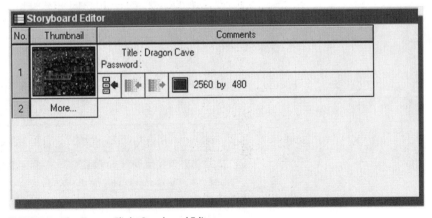

FIGURE 13.2   The Dragon Flight Storyboard Editor.

FIGURE 13.3   The Game Setup menu for Dragon Flight, with the panic key activated.

FIGURE 13.4   The changes made on the Window tab of the Game Setup menu.

FIGURE 13.5   The maximized game window (note that the game is not maximized).

any Windows application, The Games Factory uses a window to display your game. Having this option turned on will stretch the window out to fill the screen to the very edge (see Figure 13.5).

 Players will not be able to change the dimensions of the window using the mouse pointer when this option is enabled.

The Resize display to fill current window size option will fill whatever window size you are using with the game display.

 If you disable the Maximized on boot up option, you will be able to shrink or stretch the window used to display your game, using the mouse pointer to "grab" the edges of the window. Be careful, though. When the window is large, this option can dramatically slow down the game action due to the complicated nature of the calculations necessary to resize the display.

The Full screen at start option is for use on the 16-bit version only. It was designed specifically for use with the 320 by 200 graphics mode that is supported by the 16-bit version.

Changing this option will have no effect when used with any other window sizes, only on the 320 by 200. It allows very fast game play at a low resolution that still fills the screen. Notice at the top of this layer, the size of the window has been changed to 320 by 200, which means that only an area 320 by 200 will be shown. By enabling the Full screen at start option, you expand this small chunk of the play area to fill the screen.

Go back to the Storyboard Editor and look at the size of the play area. Notice that at 2560 × 480, it is much larger than the size of the screen (see Figure 13.6). The Window preference being set to 320 by 200 means that only a window 320 by 200 will be shown for this play area, and Full screen at start means this is expanded to fill the screen. This is a very important feature of The Games Factory. You can use it to change the way your games are displayed.

If you're running a 32-bit version of TGF (almost all of you will be), you can achieve the same effect that the Full screen at start option has on the 16-bit version. To do this, enable the Maximized on boot up and Resize display to fill current window size options. This will make the window being used to display the game fill the screen to the edge. Then the display is resized to fit this larger window.

 If you maximized the window without resizing the display, the screen will show a chunk of the 320 × 200 play area, surrounded by a huge black border.

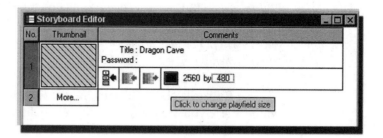

FIGURE 13.6 The playfield size is set larger than the screen size.

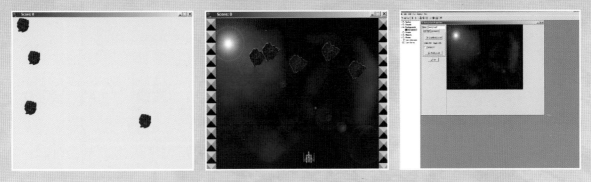

COLOR PLATES 1–3 Sample games created with GameMaker 4.0.

COLOR PLATES 4–6
2D games designed with The Games Factory.

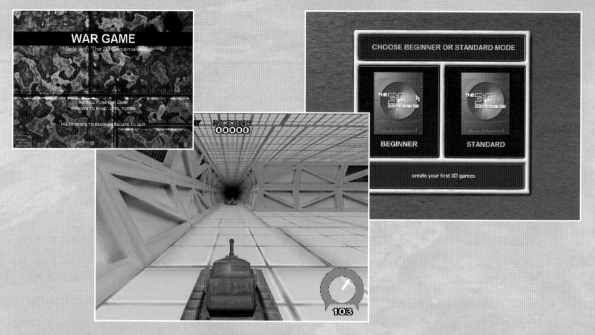

COLOR PLATES 7–9 The 3D GameMaker shooter.

COLOR PLATES 10–12 Discreet gmax allows us to create models for many applications.

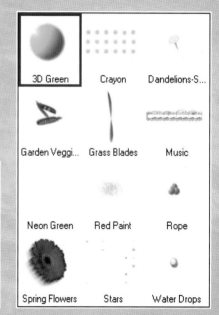

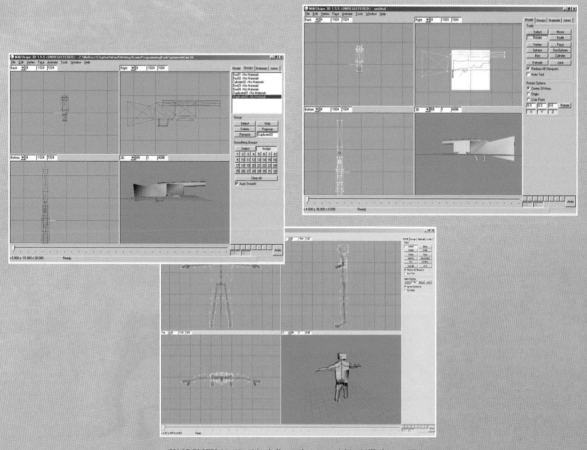

COLOR PLATES 13–14 Using Jasc Paint Shop Pro 7 to create a variety of 2D graphics.

COLOR PLATES 15–17 Modeling a humanoid in Milkshape 3D.

COLOR PLATES 18–20 Images from Max Resistance.

While having a look around the Window tab, notice that the Heading and Game to include menu bar options have been disabled. This means that when your game is run, there will be no menu at the top of the screen, and no heading telling what the game is (see Figure 13.7).

 Notice that only the actual play area window will be displayed. The only way to exit the game in this state is to use the Alt + F4 keys. The mouse pointer has been hidden in the Event Editor and is inaccessible. Even if it were there, there are no menus to click!

Since there are no other changes to look at here, click OK, or click Cancel if you might have made changes that you don't want to keep.

Now, let's look around the levels of Dragon Flight. First, notice that the play area size is 2560 by 480, a long horizontal strip.

The game world has been designed to be much longer (up and down) than it is wide (side to side) so that you can learn to use TGF to scroll the screen right and left. Having a long screen ensures that the whole level isn't visible all at once.

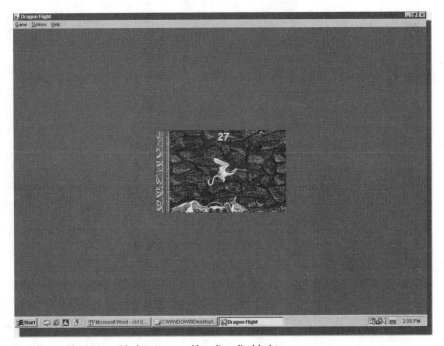

FIGURE 13.7   The game with the menu and heading disabled.

Level Editor—Dragon Flight, Part 1

Fire up the Level Editor. As you have done in previous tutorial games, run the mouse pointer over the different objects to see what they are and how they relate to each other. Not all of the objects that we are going to use are on this screen yet—they are being saved for later tutorials.

Move the mouse pointer over the Cave wall backdrop object and right-click it. Select the Obstacle menu option. Notice that the No option is selected. This means that active objects cannot collide with this object. This is the "wall" of the cave in the background. Our dragon is going to move through the cave with this wall in the background. See Figure 13.8 for the backdrop pop-up menu.

Look at the pop-up menus of the other objects. Notice that for them, the Obstacle menus all have the Yes option checked. This means that active objects can collide with them, as you'll see when you run the game. Be sure to Cancel out of the pop-up menus, so you can't accidentally change anything (or make a backup copy of the game first, if you want to experiment).

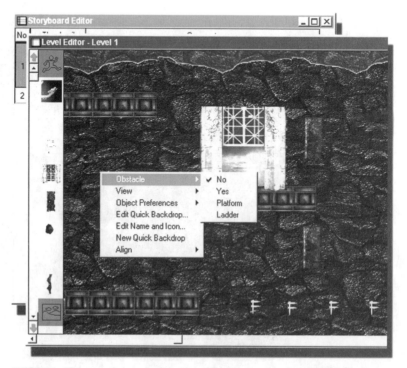

FIGURE 13.8 The pop-up menu for the cave wall, indicating that it is not an obstacle.

Now go and find the dragon object. It is on the far left of the play area, which is where the game starts.

Right-click the dragon object to show the menu options. Look at the Movement option and the Edit movement option. Notice that the Eight direction movement is being used. The maximum speed is set quite low, making the object slow, and the deceleration is set quite high, making the object slow down quickly. To make the dragon reasonably responsive, the acceleration is set quite high (see Figure 13.9).

While you are here, look around at the other objects. If you look at all the menu options for all of the different objects on this screen, you will recognize many functions from the previous chapters. Now, look at all the objects in the Object window. There are many different active objects in this game level, such as the cave walls.

 There are two different cave walls, which look exactly the same. But there's a difference! One will be indestructible, while you'll be able to shoot the other one out of the way during the game.

FIGURE 13.9 The Movement options for the dragon.

Before the difference in destructibility was created, the walls were identical. To make two different objects be exactly the same, put the first object on the play area. Right-click it. From the pop-up menu, select the New object option (see Figure 13.10). Make the second object an active object, then select the Edit name and icon option to change its name. Except for the names, the objects will be identical. You can then use the Event Editor to make them different from each other.

Scroll through all the other objects in the Object window. You'll see that the background has been made out of many different objects, placed individually on the screen. Using The Games Factory's many different libraries, you will be able to do the same thing to create similar backgrounds or platforms.

At the very bottom of the object library is the Counter object, which is used to display the time left, and a Lives object, which in this case, is used to keep count of the number of fireballs the player (dragon) has left.

When you are finished looking around the Level Editor, move onto the Event Editor by clicking its icon from the toolbar.

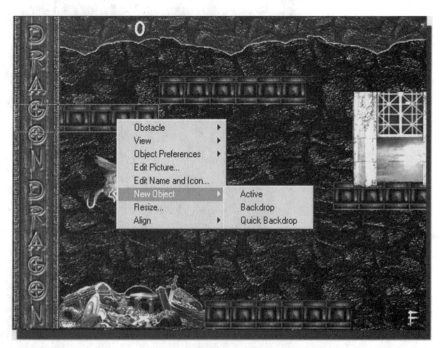

FIGURE 13.10   The pop-up menu in the Level Editor to make a new object from an existing one.

Event Editor—Dragon Flight, Part 1

One of the first things that you will notice in the Event Editor is that there are lots of objects displayed across the top of the event grid. In fact, there are so many that you may have to scroll through them using the scroll bar at the bottom. You will also notice two funny face icons—Group.Bad and Group.Neutral. Ignore these for now. We will discuss them at the end of the chapter.

 If you have a small monitor or are displaying at a low resolution, you can make all the events fit onto the screen. To do this, click the Preferences icon on the toolbar, select the display layer of the dialog box, then move the number of events on the screen slider to High. Experiment with this slider until you are happy with the result. This is similar to the Storyboard Display properties that we looked at earlier.

Read through all the comments in the Event Grid. These will clearly explain what has been done at each stage of the game. Remember that you can collapse groups, sort events, and manipulate the display for your convenience to see all the events.

An interesting side note: As mentioned at the beginning of this book, the drag-and-drop tools available to us now, like TGF, have made our lives as game developers a lot easier. So much so that we may take things like this first actual event line for granted. To tell TGF to allow the screen to scroll in this event, we only have to click one button and make a few menu selections. This used to take hours of extensive programming, but it takes just one line with TGF, as we'll see below. This event line makes the rest of the screen scroll about, using the dragon object as the center when it is moved. The dragon will always be in the center of the screen, while the play area moves around it.

Keeping the Dragon in the Center

To make the event to keep the dragon in the center, create an Always event. Then:

1. Right-click the square under the Storyboard Actions icon.
2. Click the "Center horizontal position in the playfield" button.
3. Click the "Center vertical position in the playfield" button.
4. Click the "Retrieve data from an object" button from these menus.
5. Select the dragon object to use its X and Y coordinates for the scrolling actions.

See Figure 13.11 for the menu progression of this function.

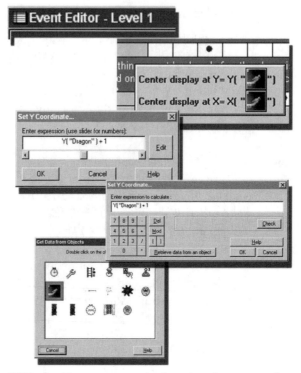

FIGURE 13.11 The menu progression for making the screen scroll with the dragon object.

Decreasing the Counter

In the game, the counter will decrease in value by 1 for every second that passes. This is the clock you are racing against. This event was created by adding the event line Every 1″00, then selecting the Subtract from Counter option, and setting the value to 1.

Moving Firetraps

To move the firetrap objects, start by making their Y values the same as the Y value of the dragon. This means that the firetraps are always "in the way" or in the same location as the dragon going up and down, but not side to side. The player has to shoot the firetraps to get past them.

You do this in a way much like setting the scrolling function above. Right-click the square below the firetrap, and then select the Position option from the pop-up menu. Select the Set Y coordinate option. Then all you have to do is click the "Retrieve data from an object" button and select the dragon object from the pop-up window.

During the game, the firetrap objects will get, or *retrieve*, their Y coordinate values from the position of the Dragon.

Use the Play button on the top right of the toolbar to see how all of these events and actions fit together. Then, save your game file if you are creating it from the ground up.

Level Editor—Dragon Flight, Part 2

Let's look at another significant feature of Dragon Flight—an easy one to pull off, but a very useful one. Look in the Object window for an object called the Real Collider. This is the object that is actually going to be tested for collisions instead of the dragon object. The reason is that the dragon object is fairly big—or the square image it is contained in is—but the body of the dragon is actually rather slender.

Because the flapping wings and flames make the dragon so big, players will never get through the cave if the entire dragon image is tested for collisions. So, we'll make things a bit more fair for them by testing another object.

By default, TGF detects collisions using each image's entire borders. Thus, a collision would be detected if any part of the dragon collided with anything else, including the flames and wings. Since we want the dragon's main body to be what causes a collision, we will use an active object created for this purpose, which has an outline shape that matches the dragon object. This also lets us have an impressive object that shoots lightening bolts off in every direction for effect, but that also has a small body for passing through the caves or tunnels of our game. Think of the problems if even the tips of a lightening bolt with supposedly no mass would cause a collision. See Figure 13.12 for a visual representation of these concepts.

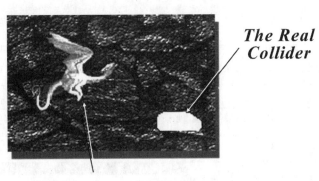

The Real Collider

The Dragon Object

FIGURE 13.12   The large dragon bitmap and the Real Collider objects, and how they function in the game.

Later, we'll use the Event Editor to make the Real Collider object invisible, and to give it the same X and Y coordinates as the dragon.

Event Editor—Dragon Flight, Part 2

Let's look at the groups, Lost Race and Won Race (see Figure 13.13). These groups perform groups of actions when the race is either won or lost. They are deactivated here to stop their actions from being performed during the game. When the game is won or lost, one of the two groups is activated, and the Main Game group is deactivated.

You can see that this very much simplifies your game creation.

Rather than having a condition on all the lines for the Lost Race group that tests to see if the game has been lost, the group is simply deactivated, then activated when needed. Also on this line is the action to make the Real Collider object invisible. The next significant new line is line 23. This is where the Real Collider object is given exactly the same position as the dragon.

To give the Real Collider object the same position as the dragon object, do the following:

1. Set up an Always event,
2. Right click the square under the special object, and select the Position option from the pop-up menu.
3. Select the Real Collider object.
4. Select the Select position option.
5. Set the position to 0,0, relative to the dragon object.

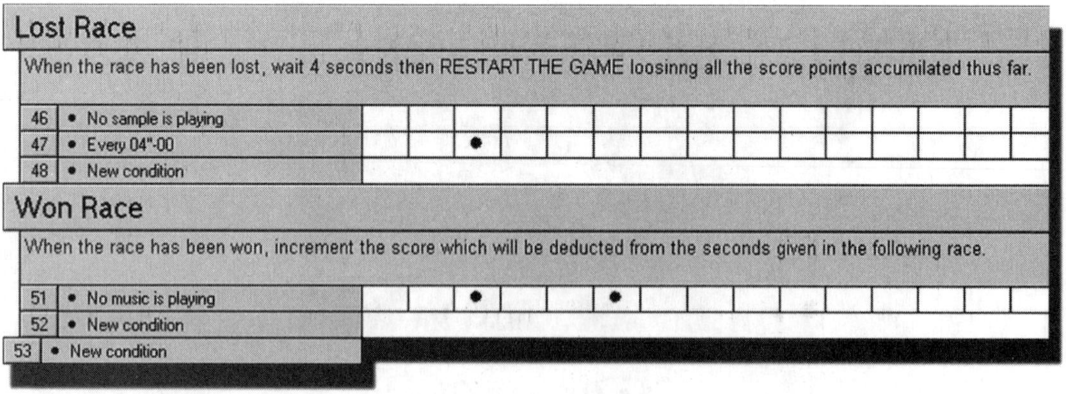

Lost Race

When the race has been lost, wait 4 seconds then RESTART THE GAME loosinng all the score points accumilated thus far.

46	• No sample is playing																			
47	• Every 04"-00		•																	
48	• New condition																			

Won Race

When the race has been won, increment the score which will be deducted from the seconds given in the following race.

51	• No music is playing		•		•															
52	• New condition																			
53	• New condition																			

FIGURE 13.13 The Lost Race and Won Race groups of events in the Event Editor.

Losing the Game by Collision

A user loses the game if the dragon hits the walls of the cave. We'll make this happen in line 25. We'll start by inserting an event that detects if a collision has occurred between the Real Collider object and the background. Remember, don't use the dragon object for this collision test. Here's what to do.

To set this line up correctly:

1. Select the New condition text.
2. Right-click the Real Collider object.
3. From the pop-up menu, select the Collisions menu option.
4. Select the Backdrop option.

As you can see, the Main Game group is now deactivated, to stop the game from continuing to run, and the Lost Race group is activated.

An explosion sample is also played on this line. The player's control is taken away here, and the dragon object is destroyed.

Because the Main Game group is deactivated here, all the lines that follow will be ignored when the game is lost. Only the lines in the Lost Race group will be active.

The Racing Flavor

The next line is the one that controls when the game is won. To give the game a true racing flavor, only the X coordinate of the finishing portal object has to be passed in order to win, making it a true "finish line."

To create the finish line, we'll do the following:

1. Select the Position option of the dragon object.
2. Select the **Compare X position to a value** option.

Here, the X position of the finishing portal is retrieved via the "Retrieve data from an object" button. The test then uses the **Greater than** comparison.

Notice that on this line, the Main Game group is deactivated and the Game Won group is activated. Also, notice that to stop the player from moving any farther, the player's control is ignored.

The Lost Race group, at this stage, waits four seconds and then restarts the game, which resets the score.

The Game Won group waits 1 second. Then, it restarts the level, which does not reset the score. It also adds 2 to the value of the score. We won't be displaying the score. It's used, instead, to subtract from the available time at the beginning of the game. Each time you win, you have less and less time to reach the end.

O.K. Let's see how it works. Run this version of Dragon Flight and see how the dragon collides with obstacles and how the won/lost game sections work.

In the rest of this chapter, you'll see how to get a finished, running race game!

Level Editor—Dragon Flight, Part 3

Now, let's add another important function. Look in the Object window and on the play area, and you'll see the fireball object. We'll use this to replenish your stock of Fire Breath, without which you would be unable to get past the various traps and obstacles.

You may have noticed the groups Group.Bad and Group.Neutral. These consist of bad objects and neutral objects, respectively. To find out which objects belong to which groups, right-click the objects on the play area, then select their Object preferences menus. This will show you which groups they belong to.

Event Editor—Dragon Flight, Part 3

Now, let's look at the event that will destroy all the fireball objects that might be left on the play area before the game begins. Also, we'll add a neat little start to the game, for effect. While the music is being played, the dragon will move down and along a path, as if it has just launched off of its perch and is ready to fly out of the cave.

As soon as the music that was played from line 11 has finished, this line plays another sound sample. It then deactivates the Start of Race Actions group, which stops the dragon from being moved any farther. It also launches you into the main game by activating the Main Game group.

Launching a Fireball

The next major event is blasting something with a fireball. First, we must check that we have some fireballs. To do that, we'll check to see if the number of lives (fireballs) is greater than 0. If it is, when the key is pressed, all the actions on this line will be performed.

To create this line:

1. Create the Upon pressing the key event.
2. Insert the Number of lives >0 condition.

3. Right-click the Upon pressing the key text.
4. Select the Insert option. The player 1 object is tested by selecting its Compare to the player's number of lives option.

Now associate the following action to this event line, using the Event Editor as a guide (see Figure 13.14):

1. Play a sample.
2. Create a fireball just in front of the dragon. Notice that the fireball is not fired out, and is in fact stationary when it is first created. It needs an event line elsewhere in the Main Game group to accelerate it. We'll control the fireball's movement in this way, to create a realistic effect of the fireball slowly accelerating.
3. Subtract one fireball (life), since one was just fired.

Accelerating a Fireball

Farther down is where the fireballs are accelerated, up to a maximum speed of 50. To do this, do the following steps, using Figure 13.15 as a guide:

1. Select the fireball object's Movement menu.
2. Select its Compare speed of "fireball" to a value option.
3. Using the Less than comparison, compare this with the value 50.
4. Place the action to set its direction in the check box first.
5. Insert the action to increase its speed afterwards, by left-clicking the box, right-clicking the "New action" text, selecting the Movement option, and then selecting the Set speed option.
6. Set the fireball to retrieve its own speed by using the "Retrieve data from an object" button, then adding +5 onto the end of the expression.

Taken together, these steps set the fireball's speed to its current value, plus 5.

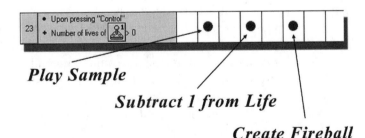

FIGURE 13.14   The events associated with the dragon's breathing a fireball.

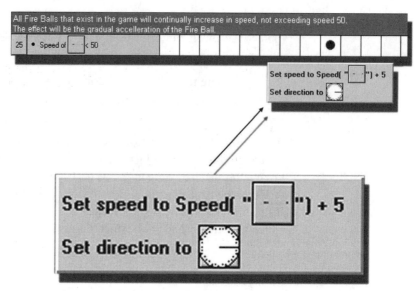

All Fire Balls that exist in the game will continually increase in speed, not exceeding speed 50. The effect will be the gradual accelleration of the Fire Ball.

25 • Speed of · · < 50

Set speed to Speed(" · · ") + 5

Set direction to

FIGURE 13.15 The steps for accelerating a fireball from a dead stop to 50, but no faster.

You can then set an action to destroy the fireballs if they collide with the background, and associate a sound sample with this action.

One last thing about the fireballs. To speed up and simplify game development, you can use the Bad and Neutral groups. For example, you can set an event to say, "Anything belonging to the Group.Neutral is destroyed when hit by the fireball." That way, you don't have to go through the motions for every object that you want destroyed when it is hit by a fireball.

Game Balance and Indestructible Walls

In this game, we have also placed some walls that react when hit with a fireball, but which are in fact indestructible. While the steps to do this are easy (we will look at them next), it's a good idea here to discuss this easy action's impact on the game.

It may seem cruel to have these walls, because players will no doubt waste precious time and fireballs trying to get through them. They will probably lose the game the first few times. But these initial defeats make the player want to play the game again and again, since they know what to do differently the next time around to win—or they think they do, until they hit your next trick.

Think of this as a gift to the players, since they will have a more enjoyable experience in the long run. They will gain a feeling of accomplishment after playing your game a few times and eventually winning. This illustrates the idea of game balance. As you can see, even a simple aspect of a rather simple game can enormously increase players' enjoyment. With game balance you literally are balancing the game play—too hard, and you lose the player to frustration; too easy, and players are done in a flash and become bored with the game's simplicity.

The walls also add a great deal to the game's atmosphere. Remember from our discussions on game design that interactivity is a very important aspect of game development. Game worlds that feel flat and dead reduce the playability of the game. Adding little things like this make a big difference in the quality of your game. This is called production values, professional polish, or tweaking. As some developers say, "God is in the details." Walls and objects that can be poked or prodded and tested for a result make the players feel that they are exploring a real world, and not just driving through tunnels.

Back to the Game Steps and Destructible Walls

Now we will also create weaker walls, that are destructible. These are actually animated active objects that allow a hole to be blasted through them. The walls won't be completely destroyed. The animation will be changed to create a hole, the fireball will be destroyed, and a sound will be played. And the dragon will be able to pass through the newly made hole.

Collecting Fireball Energy

During game play, the player can gather fireballs by having the dragon touch the fireball power rune object (the Ammo object). When this happens, we'll just add two to the number of lives and destroy the fireball power rune object. Remember that we're using the Real Collider object to keep track of where the dragon is and what it touches, not the dragon object itself.

Countdown

The countdown object keeps track of how much time is left in the game. If the value of this counter is zero, the player has lost. When this happens, the associated actions deactivate the Main Game group and the player's controls, as well as playing an appropriate sound sample and activating the Lost Race group.

Real Collider Hits Backdrop

The player loses the game if the Real Collider object (which tracks the dragon) hits any of the backdrop objects. The same actions are performed as above, with the addition of destroying the dragon object.

Real Collider and the Group.Neutral

This tests to see if the Real Collider object hits any of the other active objects that belong to the Group.Neutral. These include the walls (both weak and indestructible) and any of the firetrap objects or boulder objects.

That's it! You've just made another game with TGF. By now you should understand how this game was constructed, as well as why it was constructed in this way, using groups.

If there are any events you are finding hard to understand, try to recreate an event line on a spare "New condition" line. You can always delete it afterwards. Also, check out various actions and events by right-clicking them and selecting the Edit option. Notice that you cannot edit some of the very simple actions, such as Destroy.

CHAPTER REVIEW

In this chapter, we went step by step through the creation of a game in TGF. Now that you may be itching to get on with game developments of your own and to move on in TGF, the next few chapters will look in depth at some of the most commonly used tools in game development with TGF.

14 ADVANCED CONTROL OF ACTIVE OBJECTS

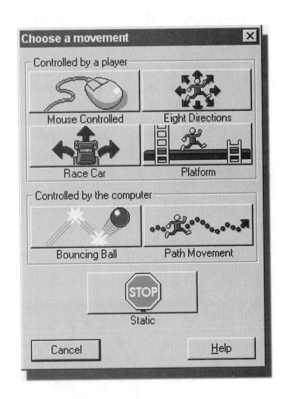

Now that you have a firm background in TGF, you will want to experiment on your own more. For example, start digging deeper into the menus. This chapter covers some of the most important things you will do with active objects in TGF.

You may have noticed that in the previous chapters, you were never called upon to create assets or animate objects. Over the next few chapters, we will look at ways to create and manage assets. We will start by looking at all the active objects and their movement menus, the text objects, and the backdrop objects—the mainstays of TGF games.

ACTIVE OBJECTS

Active objects are mostly used as the main characters of your games. These are the characters and objects we have been using to assign behavior and controls to. We did this by either allowing the player to use the mouse or keyboard, or we had the computer control the objects for us. You can also make your active objects animated, making them run, jump, or do whatever you decide.

Active objects are denoted by their icon on the object shelf on the Level Editor screen (see Figure 14.1). Open dragon.gam, the Dragon Flight file, from the last chapter. Grab the dragon active object and drag it onto the screen of the Level Editor.

You can also create your own active object by clicking the New Object icon in the toolbar of the Level Editor screen, as shown in Figure 14.2. You can then change the options by right clicking the object and choosing new characteristics. Don't worry about the images and object animation just yet. We'll cover those in the next chapter.

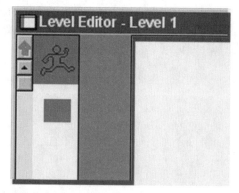

FIGURE 14.1 The Active Object icon in the Level Editor screen.

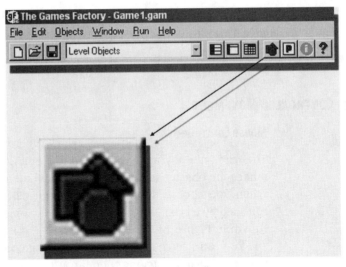

FIGURE 14.2   The New Object icon from the toolbar.

MOVEMENT

To change an object's movement from the Level Editor, right click the object, select the Movement option from its pull-down menu, and then select the Select Movement option. The menu in Figure 14.3 will pop up.

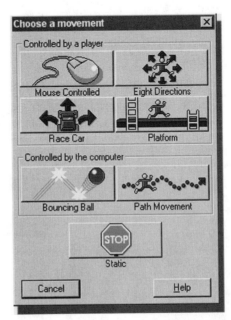

FIGURE 14.3   The Choose a movement pop-up menu.

The first area on this menu is the Player-Controlled Movement area. This allows the player to control the object in several ways, as discussed below.

PLAYER-CONTROLLED MOVEMENT

Mouse Controlled

The first type of player-controlled movement is Mouse Controlled. This makes the object exactly follow the movement of the mouse. Notice that when you choose this option (see Figure 14.4), the object will be surrounded by a box. This box represents the object's limits of movement, as shown in Figure 14.5.

You can stretch or shrink the area by grabbing the sizing handles with your mouse and dragging them around. Note that this box takes its position from the object, not from the screen. This means that if you move the object to a new position on the Level Editor screen, you may need to edit this box again.

The following movement parameters are used for several of the movements, so it's useful to get to know them.

Speed

Speed sets the maximum speed at which your object can move.

Acceleration

Acceleration sets the rate at which your object will reach its maximum speed. If your object is a car, for example, you may want the acceleration quite high. If it is a "heavier" object, like an elephant, you would want it set quite low.

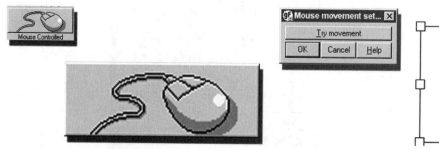

FIGURE 14.4   The Mouse Controlled icon.

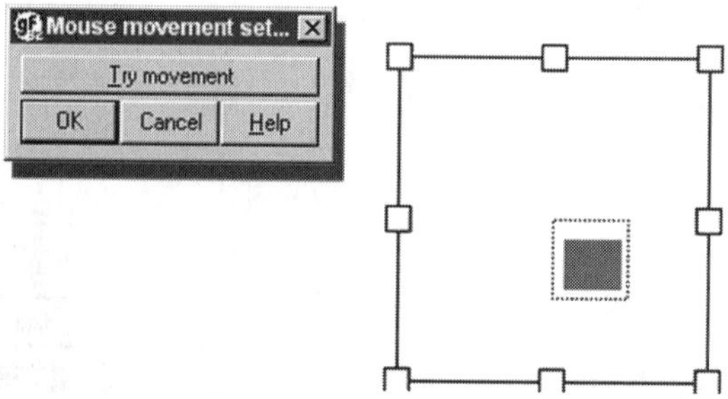

FIGURE 14.5   The mouse movement area control box.

Deceleration

Deceleration affects the rate at which your object slows down. A high value stops the object quickly when you release the key that moves it. A low value produces a very gradual slowing down, as though the object were really heavy, like an oil tanker.

Initial Direction

Initial Direction allows you to decide what the first direction of the object will be. If you select more than one direction, the computer will select a direction at random.

Moving at Start

Moving at Start toggles whether or not your object will be moving at the start of a game.

Try Movement

Try Movement tests your object's movement on the screen. To stop the object and return to the Direction Editor, press the Esc key, or click the Stop icon.

Eight Direction Movements

This movement control (shown in Figure 14.6) provides you with the classic eight directions that are used by a joystick. You can also use the cursor keys to control movement. There are several basic controls. Speed, acceleration, and deceleration have been described above. The Possible directions

FIGURE 14.6   The Eight Directions icon.

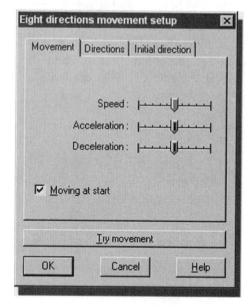

FIGURE 14.7 The Movement Direction dialog box.

option allows you to select or de-select the number of directions your object can move in. See Figure 14.7 for the Movement Direction dialog box.

To select or de-select a direction, click the relevant box. Possible directions are shown by having an arrow pointing to that box. In Figure 14.7, the only direction that the object could move is to the right.

Race Car

Figure 14.8 includes arrows that simulate a birds-eye view of a car's movement. As shown below, there are controls for steering, braking, and accelerating, which users can activate by pressing a key or using a joystick.

Action	Keyboard	Joystick
Accelerator	Up Arrow	Joystick Up
Brake	Down Arrow	Joystick Down
Turn Left	Left Arrow	Joystick Left
Turn Right	Right Arrow	Joystick Right

In addition to the speed, acceleration, and deceleration settings, there are three more options, as discussed below.

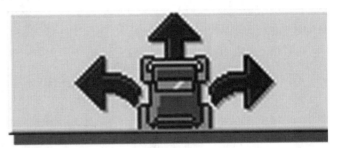

FIGURE 14.8   The Race Car icon.

Enable Reverse Movement

This option gives your object the ability to go backwards. With it turned off, the object can only move forward.

Directions

Directions lets you decide how many different directions the object can move. Selecting 4 will only give you left, right, up, and down; Selecting 32 will give you the smoothest possible direction changes.

You can easily create all the different animation tracks needed for each direction by using the Animation Editor. We'll discuss this later.

Rotating Speed

Rotating Speed sets the rate at which the object turns. A high value will allow tight corners to be turned, while low value reduces the cornering ability.

Platform Movement

This movement (see Figure 14.9) is used mainly to define platform game-type movement. This means characters who walk along a platform, viewed from the side, as in Commander Keen or Zeb. They are controlled by the cursor keys or the joystick. In addition to the usual acceleration, deceleration, and speed controls, there are a large number of controls particular to platform movement. You can make platforms and ladders that are obstacles out of backdrop objects.

 You must still test for a collision with a backdrop platform object; otherwise, your active object will fall through the platform as if it weren't there.

Gravity

As the name suggests, this option selects the effect of gravity. A high setting will make your object fall rapidly, allowing only short jumps.

Jump Strength

Jump Strength selects the jumping power of your character. Changing the gravity will also affect this parameter.

Jump Controls

Jump Controls are used to change the control system for jumps, as follows.

No Jump

This option turns jumping off for an object.

Up Left/Right Arrow

This option makes the object jump when the up arrow key is pressed at the same time as either the left arrow or right arrow key.

FIGURE 14.9 The Platform Movement icon.

Button 1

Button 1 uses fire button one, or the Shift key, to control the jump.

Button 2

Button 2 uses the second fire button, or the Control key, to activate a jump.

COMPUTER-CONTROLLED MOVEMENTS

There are two computer-controlled options: Bouncing Ball and Path Movement.

The first option is Bouncing Ball. As the name indicates, this option is used to let the computer move or control objects in your games—from a simple bouncing ball to an attack wave of aliens. It can even control objects that move on a preset path, such as a guard on patrol.

Bouncing Ball

This movement option (shown in Figure 14.10) is normally used to produce an object that bounces around the screen, like a ball. However, by changing several parameters and using the Event Editor, you can use this movement to control the movement of a host of aliens, or other enemies that will chase the player around.

Speed

Speed controls the speed of all the other types of movement.

FIGURE 14.10   The Bouncing Ball icon.

Ball Deceleration

When this option is set to zero, a ball will keep bouncing forever. Increasing this value gradually slows your object down until it grinds to a halt.

Bounce Randomizer

As the name suggests, this option makes objects bounce in a more random direction. As this number increases, so does the randomness.

Bounce Security

This option jiggles objects to keep them from getting stuck in corners. But as a result, the rebound effects are made slightly more random.

We will look at Bouncing Ball in a little more detail later.

Path Movement

The Path Movement option (shown in Figure 14.11) sets your object moving on a predetermined path, which you define. For example, you can create a patrolling guard who walks a set distance and then turns around, or who walks in a preset path around a corridor. This lets you control many parameters, and script some neat effects, such as the looping and speed that an object will move with on different sections of its path.

Path Editor

As shown in Figure 14.12, there are six different buttons that let you define the movement of an object, plus the speed bar, which changes the

FIGURE 14.11 The Path Movement icon.

FIGURE 14.12   The Path Editor Menu Window.

speed at which the object moves along its path. A path-type movement is entered using your mouse to define the path (see Figure 14.13).

New Line

This function will add a single line to the object's movement.

 If you already have a movement defined, New Line will be added at the end of it by default, unless you insert it somewhere else by choosing the insertion point with the mouse.

 New Line

 Tape Mouse

 Pause

 Loop Movement

 Reverse at End

 Reposition Object at End

FIGURE 14.13   The individual Path Editor option buttons.

Tape Mouse

This function allows you to set a very complex path movement. By holding down the left mouse button and dragging the mouse pointer around the screen, you set the movement you want.

 This function will change the speed of the object, depending on how fast you move the mouse around.

Pause

This function stops your object at its current position for a length of time that you define in seconds.

Loop the Movement

This function repeats a movement that you specify, over and over.

 Each time the loop repeats, this function repositions the object to its original starting position. So make sure that the path finishes at the object's starting point, or the object will jump around the screen.

Reverse at End

This function reverses an object's movement and sends it backwards along the original path. This function is good for a guard patrolling the grounds.

Reposition Object at End

This function puts your object back at its original starting position when it has completed the movement.

Try Movement

This function lets you try the movement before finally deciding upon it.

EDITING A PATH

Once you have added a movement to your object, you can edit it very easily in the Level Editor. To do this, select the object, then choose the Edit Movement option. This will open the Path Editor again. You can select individual points of the movement, or entire sections, by dragging a box around them. You can then manipulate these selected pieces by either deleting them, or using the Cut, Copy, and Paste options from the Edit menu (the drop-down menu at the top of the screen). You can simply drag one of the selected areas, using the left mouse button.

Inserting a Condition

After you've selected a point or area, you can add a condition to it by right clicking it. This lets you insert a previously defined condition at that spot, such as Set a Pause, Tape Mouse, and New Line.

BOUNCING BALL MOVEMENT

The Bouncing Ball movement is normally used to make an object bounce off obstacles on the screen. However, by setting all the parameters to zero, you will have a movement "blank page," which you can then manipulate entirely from the Event Editor. This is useful for enemy movements.

When you first select the Ball Movement Setup option, you will see a dialog box with three tabs (see Figure 14.14). As discussed below, each of these tabs controls different aspects of the Ball Movement.

Movement Tab

Speed

This option sets the maximum speed at which your object can move.

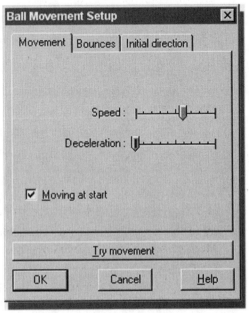

FIGURE 14.14   The Ball Movement Setup dialogue box—Movement tab.

Deceleration

Deceleration sets the rate at which your bouncing object will slow down. Having this option set to zero will bounce your object around endlessly.

Moving at Start

When checkmarked, the Moving at Start option causes the object to move in one of the directions you have chosen when the game starts. When this option is unchecked, the object will remain stationary until another object collides with it.

Bounces Tab

Number of Angles

This option (see Figure 14.15) sets the number of angles that it is possible for your object to bounce in. Setting it to 32 will result in the smoothest, most realistic effect. Setting it to 8 will result in an object that can only move left, right, up, down, and diagonally in between. This obviously would not be suitable for an object that is supposed to bounce like a ball does.

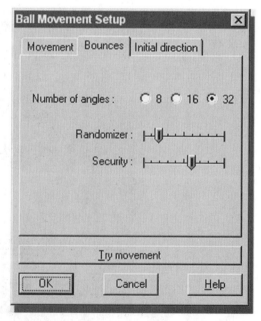

FIGURE 14.15 Ball Movement Setup dialogue box—Bounces tab.

Randomizer

This option gives your object a chance of bouncing off in a different direction from what you would normally expect. The higher the setting, the more unpredictable your bounces will be.

Security

This option jiggles your object around to keep it from getting stuck in corners. As a result, the rebound effects become slightly more random.

Initial Direction

This option allows you to choose one or more directions for your object to move when the game begins. If you choose more than one direction, TGF will choose one of the specified directions at random.

You can select and deselect the directions individually by clicking the box at the end of each direction arrow. A selected direction will have an arrow in that box; deselecting a direction will remove the arrow. You can select all possible directions by clicking the icon at the bottom left, or deselect all directions by clicking the icon at the bottom right (see Figure 14.16).

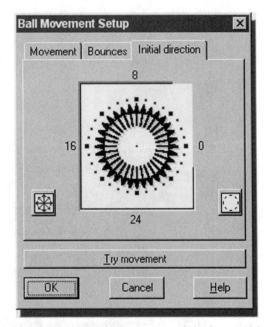

FIGURE 14.16 The Ball Movement Setup dialog box—Initial Direction tab.

BACKDROP OBJECTS AND QUICK BACKDROP OBJECTS

The following parameters all apply to both backdrop and quick backdrop objects, except that quick backdrop objects can be constructed without using the Picture Editor, if their appearance is relatively simple. This option is discussed in the next chapter.

Backdrop objects are normally used to "set the scene" in games. They provide backdrops for your players to move over, or to interact with. You cannot move backdrop objects or change their appearance when the game is playing, as you can with active objects. But you can change their position on the screen, as well as their size, shape, and color, from the Level Editor.

To make a backdrop object, you can select one of the many in TGF's object library. You can also create your own backdrop and quick backdrop objects, using the icon from the toolbar at the top of the Level Editor screen.

The usual way to change the appearance of a backdrop object is to use the Picture Editor (see the next chapter). As we'll see, when you change a quick backdrop object, you only use the Picture Editor when you have selected the Mosaic option.

All other changes to backdrop objects are made from the menu that you pull down when you right click the actual backdrop object in the Level Editor screen. The pop-up menu for the backdrop object is shown in Figure 14.17.

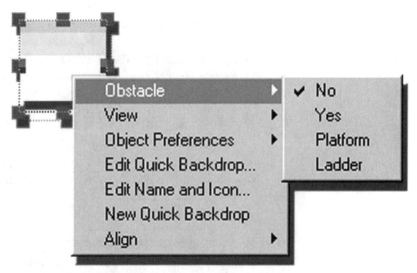

FIGURE 14.17 The Backdrop Object pop-up menu in the Level Editor.

Obstacle

You can change how other objects interact with a backdrop object by turning on or off the menu options here. There are four options:

No

This option means that the backdrop object will not be an obstacle to active objects. You will not be able to detect a collision between the backdrop object and an active object when this option is turned on.

Yes

This option means it will be possible to detect a collision with an active object. You must test for a collision with a backdrop object in the Event Editor and insert a stop action.

Platform

This option means that the backdrop object will act as a platform for active objects controlled by platform-type movement. This is not the same as the Obstacle option. You will not be able to detect a collision between a backdrop object and an active object that has been assigned a platform-type movement.

Ladder

This option will treat the backdrop object as a ladder when an active object using a platform-type movement. If the active object has an animation sequence, the animation will automatically be changed when the object climbs a ladder. If not, you could change ythe animation via the Event Editor. We will discuss Active-Actions-Animation later.

Edit Picture

The Edit Picture option allows you to change the appearance of the backdrop object using the Picture Editor. We will look at this in the next chapter.

New Object

The New Object option is available both for backdrop objects and for active objects. It lets you produce another object that looks exactly the same as the original object, except that the new object can be either a backdrop, a quick backdrop, or an active object. You can place this object on the Level Editor screen. Although the new object looks exactly like the original object, it takes on the qualities of whichever object type you selected. We used this in the last chapter, if you will remember, to create the indestructible and destructible walls.

New Quick Backdrop Object

This is only available from the menu of a quick backdrop object. It produces a clone of the original, but with a different name, one up in numerical order. For example, the first time you create a quick backdrop object in a game, it will be called Quick Backdrop 1. If you cloned that object using this method, the new object would have the same qualities as the original one, and would be called Quick Backdrop 2.

 This differs from using the right mouse button to lay down multiple copies of the same object. Using that method produces exact clones, with the same name. If you made a change to one, that change would occur to all of them.

Resize

This lets you resize your object by selecting the object and then dragging one of the sizing handles that appear around the object.

Align

This option lets you align a backdrop object. You can push it up against the left-hand or right-hand edge of the playfield, or center it horizontally using the Horizontally option. You can also align it against the top or bottom, or center it vertically using the Vertically option.

Special Options for Quick Backdrop Objects

The reason that there are two different types of backdrop objects is that for many purposes, it is only necessary to produce a block of color, or a gradient of color, rather than a fully rendered drawing.

For example, to produce a plain black backdrop, it is very easy to simply select a block color for a quick backdrop and then stretch it to fit the screen, rather than going into the Picture Editor and filling a picture. This makes simple structures, like platforms and ladders, very quick to produce.

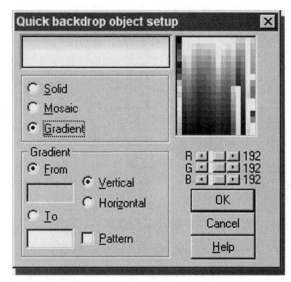

FIGURE 14.18   The Quick Backdrop Editor.

You have several options within the Quick Backdrop Editor, as shown in Figure 14.18.

Solid

The Solid option fills your object with a solid color, which you select from the palette.

Mosaic

The Mosaic option takes you to the Picture Editor. We will discuss this more in the next chapter.

Gradient

The Gradient option produces a smooth gradient from one color to another. To use this function, click the Gradient button, then click the From button. Now choose your first color from the palette. Then click the To button, and select the second color from the palette. You will see a smooth gradation of color, from the first color you selected to the second. You can change the orientation of the gradation using the Vertical and Horizontal buttons.

Pattern

The Pattern option uses a crosshatch to grade the colors from one to another, rather than smoothly fading the color.

Text Objects

Text objects are used to put text on the screen. You can use them for instructions, comments, end of game displays, or just about anything that requires text. There are some texts already in the object libraries, but you will no doubt want to make your own.

Only the options related specifically to text objects are described in this section. All the other options available have already been described for the majority of the other active objects. You can see the options for text in the pop-up menu in Figure 14.19.

To make your own text objects, select the Create New Object icon from the toolbar at the top of the Level Editor screen, then click the Text icon. The mouse pointer will be replaced with a cursor. Place the cursor at the point where you want the text to start.

You will also have a dialog box in which you can select fonts, styles, text sizes, and text color, as well as the justification style you want to use (see Figure 14.20).

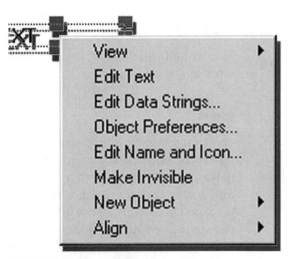

FIGURE 14.19 The Text pop-up menu.

FIGURE 14.20   The Text Options dialog box.

Selecting a Font, Style, Size, and Color

To choose a font, style size, and color for the text, click the Font icon (the one with "ABC" on it). This will take you to the dialog box shown in Figure 14.21.

The controls in this dialog box work the same as in most word processing programs. To make a choice in a box, scroll the box and then click on the choice you want. The Sample box gives you a preview of the style you have chosen.

The Text options dialog box has eight buttons, as shown in Figure 4.20. You can make changes to text by clicking any of the first six buttons. The

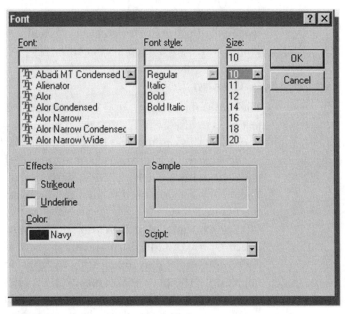

FIGURE 14.21   The Text Formatting dialog box.

OK button saves your changes and exits from the dialog box, while the Cancel button cancels any changes.

We've discussed the Font button above. The other buttons are described below, starting with the second button, and going from left to right.

The Color Selector

This is actually a shortcut to changing the text color of the text through the Font Editor. It brings up a palette from which to choose the text color.

Left Alignment

When you have more than one line of text, this option will align it all so that each line starts evenly from the left-most margin.

Center Align

This option will center all the text, as in a word processing program.

Right Align

This option aligns all the text against the right margin.

Import

This option lets you load text from existing .TXT files and place it into your text object. That way, you don't have to type the text in TGF. This lets you use a word processor to create text, while taking advantage of that program's tools, such as spell checking.

Edit Data Strings...

The Edit Data Strings... option (see Figure 14.19) lets you use one text object used to display different text at different times during the game. When you select this option, you'll see a dialog box like the one in Figure 14.22.

In Figure 14.22, three separate paragraphs of text have been entered, with the names shown. TGF assigns the numbers shown in the figure. These numbers are used to identify the paragraph when you display it in the Event Editor.

For example, an action you could insert under the text object on the Event Grid would be Display Para 1. This would display the text in that paragraph on the play area during a game. Once you have placed your text object onto the play area, you can right click it to produce its menu and edit it, as you can do with other active objects.

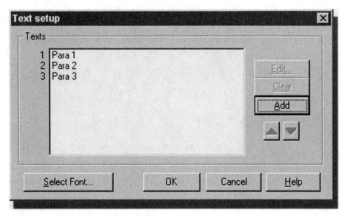

FIGURE 14.22   The Edit Data Strings… dialog box.

To edit or clear one of the numbered paragraphs, select the paragraph, and then click Edit or Clear. To change the order of the paragraphs, use the up- and down-pointing triangles at the right of the dialog box. To add a new paragraph, click the Add button. This takes you to a text box where you can enter the text for your new paragraph.

CHAPTER REVIEW

In this chapter, we looked at the basis for all TGF games—the active objects and their movement menus, the text objects, and the backdrop objects. These are the most common active objects in TGF, and the ones you will be working with the most. In the next chapter, we will look at asset creation using the Picture Editor and Animation Editor. These tools will round out your ability to make your own games and productions with TGF.

WORKING WITH PICTURES AND ANIMATION IN TGF

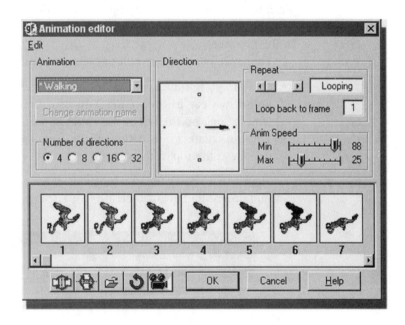

n our final dealings with TGF, we will look at how to create and manipulate assets for your games. Some of the most useful tools for the game developer that come with TGF are in the Animation and Picture Editors. These tools make it easy to import and deal with your assets in the game. They include animation functions that previously required you to work manually in another application like Photoshop, such as copying, rotating, and other tedious operations. First, we will look at the Animation Editor.

THE TGF ANIMATION EDITOR

Animation is a word that still strikes fear in the hearts of many who want to develop games, but TGF makes animation a lot easier with this tool. For example, if you have an animation of a creature facing one direction and want to make it walk in the opposite direction, you can do so by clicking just one button in the Animation Editor. We will look at that function later in this chapter.

There are two ways to edit or create an animated object using TGF:

- You can go to the Level Editor and open a library of objects from the pull-down bar in the menu. You can then pick an object from the Object Shelf on the left of the Level Editor.
- You can create a new active object using the New Object icon on the toolbar at the top of the screen.

Figure 15.1 shows the two methods of accessing an active object. You can pull down the Level Object lists, or click the New Object icon.

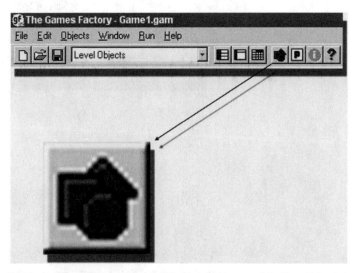

FIGURE 15.1 The pull-down menu for libraries of objects and the New Object icon.

Only active objects can be animated from the Animation Editor.

For this exercise, we will open an active object that already exists and analyze how the tools have been used to animate it. As we do this, you will see the steps required to create your own animated object. As we'll see, an animation can be made using either one image, or a few versions of an image.

1. Open a new blank game.
2. Start up the Level Editor, and open the Dragon Flight game library.
3. In the Object window, select the dragon object and place it in the middle of the play area of the Level Editor screen.
4. Right-click dragon object. In the pop-up menu, choose Edit animation. You should now have a screen similar to Figure 15.2.

Some of the things you can do with the Animation Editor are: change the name of your animation; run a preview of what it looks like when all the images are run together; create a different animation, depending on the direction your character is moving in; or create a different animation for any situation your character may get into (such as climbing and running).

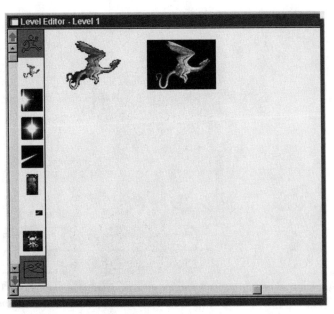

FIGURE 15.2   The Level Editor with the dragon object.

To select all the frames of an animation, use the Alt+A keyboard shortcut. This lets you move or delete a whole sequence of animation at one time. You can select multiple frames by holding down the the Ctrl key while you click on frames, or hold down the Shift key to select all frames between two selected frames.

Let's explore this screen a bit more (See Figure 15.3).

Animation Speed

As shown in Figure 15.4, at the top right of the window are the controls for the speed of the animation (the Min and Max sliders), as well as the number of times it will repeat itself before it stops (the Repeat box). You can select Looping by moving the Repeat slider below 1 with the arrow pointer. This will make the animation sequence repeat over and over.

You can also change which frame number the animation loops back to, in the Loops Back to Frame box. This is useful in a long animation if you only want to repeat certain parts. Say you are working with an animation of a man getting up from a crouched position and then running away. You may only want to play the first couple of frames of him being crouched down, then loop the animation back only to the running sequence as the man continues running.

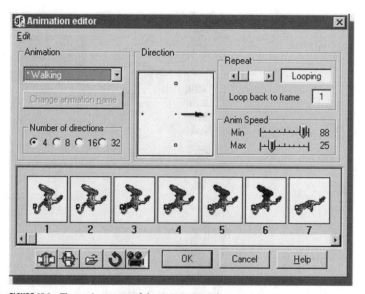

FIGURE 15.3 The main screen of the Animation Editor.

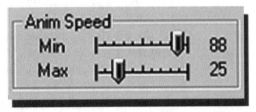

FIGURE 15.4   The animation speed control on the main screen of the Animation Editor.

An animation can have either one or two speed controls. An object that moves in place has a control only for its animation speed. Objects that move around the screen as their animation plays have an additional control, for speed of movement.

Minimum Speed

The *Min slider* in the Anim Speed box controls the speed when the character is *not moving around the screen*. Setting this to zero will halt the animation. Setting it higher will have the animation running all of the time. Of course, it may look unrealistic if your character is running frantically without moving!

Maximum Speed

The *Max slider* in the Anim Speed box controls the maximum rate of the animation *when the character is moving around the screen*. Note that the rate of animation will be proportional to the speed of the character, in between the Minimum and Maximum settings. To create a realistic running action, you may need to change the Maximum setting to a value that matches the character's speed across the screen.

For example, if you were to set a character's movement speed high and the animation speed low, it would appear as though the character was being dragged across the screen. If you had the animation speed high and the movement speed low, it would look as though the character were trying to run fast on an icy floor.

Animation Direction

This is a very useful feature that can seem hidden at first. Take a look at the Direction box, as shown in Figure 15.5. By clicking on the different direction squares in the Direction box, you can create a different animation for each direction that the character can move.

For example, look at the dragon animation for Dragon Flight and select the walking animation from the scroll list. You'll see that on the clock face, the 3 o'clock position (forward motion) and the 9 o'clock position (backward motion) have small solid black x's. These indicate that an animation is assigned to those positions. So the dragon has a different animation for forward and backward motion. For example, to add realism, you could have the dragon go slower and fly differently as it goes backward.

Counting all possible directions, you can have up to 32 different animated sequences for the walk direction of a character. This can help things look smooth. However, it will also be a real resource hog on your machine and is overkill for most purposes. A standard platform game has only four animations for walking.

FIGURE 15.5 The Animation Direction Clock Face.

An easy way to create several different directions from one animation is to click the "Create other directions by rotating this one" button. This will copy and rotate the current animation. It will also probably turn your objects upside down for some of the directions. But you can correct this using the controls that we discuss next.

Number of Directions Option Buttons

You can select the total number of different movement directions for an animation by clicking one of the buttons shown in Figure 15.6. Obviously, the higher the number of directions, the smoother will be the turning effect. This is particularly useful for race car movement. However, four directions is fine for a platform character.

As you set the motions for the various directions, you'll need to fill in many frames in the Animation Editor. You can save time by copying animations from one frame to another. To do this, use the Copy and Paste functions from the Edit pull-down menu.

Manipulation Icons

At the lower left of the Animation Editor screen are five icons that let you manipulate the frames of the animation being displayed (see Figure 15.7). Be careful when you use them, because it's easy to mess up your animation. The View Animation icon (the last one on the right) is safe, since it

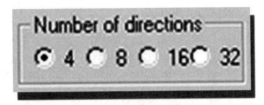

FIGURE 15.6   The "Number of directions" option buttons on the Animation Editor window.

FIGURE 15.7   The Manipulation icons in the Animation Editor window.

merely previews the whole sequence of images and shows what your animation looks like when it runs.

We'll cover the first three icons: Horizontal Flip, Vertical Flip, and Import.

Horizontal Flip

The Horizontal Flip function (first icon on the left) reverses all the images from left to right. This is useful when you have a character going one way and you want to turn all the frames to face the other way. An example of this is shown in Figure 15.8.

 Both the Action Point and Hot Spot will also be moved when you use this function.

Vertical Flip

This function (the second icon) turns all the images upside down. This is useful when you have created several new directions from your original animation, and some of the sequences are the wrong way up. You can even use this to make a character walk on the ceiling. This moves the Action Point and Hot Spot, as well.

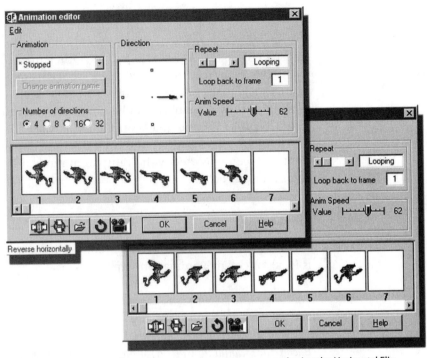

FIGURE 15.8   An example of an animated sequence being reversed using the Horizontal Flip function.

Import

This very useful function (the third icon) lets you grab one or more images from the disk and loads them into the Animation Editor. You can then manipulate or process them in the Animation Editor. As with most file loading operations, you can navigate to the drive and folder of your choice.

 You can load images stored as PCX, LBM, GIF, TIF, or BMP formats. You can even load FLC and FLI files, but beware: These files are normally very large, since they contain many separate images—usually more than 50. They will therefore use up large amounts of memory and storage space.

Capture Style

When you use the Import function, you will be asked to select a Capture style. This specifies the method by which you grab one or more images from the file you are loading.

Transparent Mode

Transparent mode makes the background color of the images that you pick transparent in the Animation Editor, rather than displaying the actual color. This keeps the background color from covering up other things that you may add to the image. If Transparent mode is off, the background color for the frames you grabbed will be transferred as well.

In Figure 15.9, the image on the left has been imported with Transparent mode set; its background color does not display. The image on the right has been imported with Transparent mode disabled; its background color is displayed.

Box Image Mode

Box Image mode imports a series of images using a single operation. This is ideal for creating animation sequences.

 The format and layout of an image file are important in the capture procedure. The first point in your picture should be set to the color used by your background (usually zero or transparent). The second should hold the color of your box (usually 1). Each image should now be surrounded by a one-point thick box.

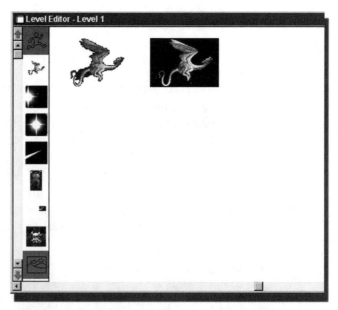

FIGURE 15.9 The images in the Animation Editor with transparent and non-transparent backgrounds.

In Box Image mode, you can select multiple images with the mouse by drawing a box around them. You can then import them all at once. In the Animation Editor, each image is pasted into its own animation frame, going from top left to bottom right. Make sure that the box completely encloses all the images you want to import. If there are ten boxed images on the screen, and you drag a selection area that completely encloses nine of them, but only half crosses the tenth, only nine of the images will be taken. Make sure Box Image mode is on if you select multiple images. If you draw a box around multiple images when Box Image mode is off, one image comprising the entire contents of the selection area will be taken and pasted into only one animation frame.

Full Window Mode

Full Window mode lets you grab the whole area inside the Capture window (not just inside your selection area) and paste that into your animation frame. This only produces one frame of animation, comprising the entire contents of the window.

If you have Box Image mode on at the same time you try to use Full Window mode, all the boxed images in the window will be grabbed and treated as separate frames of animation.

Creating Different Directions

As mentioned above, the Animation Editor allows you to quickly and easily create many different directions from one animation direction. Be aware, though, if you have several animation frames and 32 different directions, this will use a lot of memory. Also, remember that your object gets turned around in different directions. If you start with an object that faces to the right, when it is rotated to the left, it will be backward.

Creating and Editing a Single Frame of Animation

In this section, we'll look at an animation frame and then copy it to fill several frames, creating a new animation. To do this:

1. Create a new game file.
2. In the Level Editor, make sure you have only the dragon object on the playfield.
3. Right-click the dragon object to bring up the pop-up menu, then select the Edit Animation option to enter the Animation Editor.

4. In the Animation Editor, right-click the middle of the first frame.

5. In the pop-up menu, select the Edit Frame option. (You can also double-click the frame to automatically pop up the Picture Editor.)

When you are in the drawing screen, or Picture Editor, for the animation, you can decide the color, size, and shape of your animation frame. We will talk more about the Picture Editor later in this chapter.

In the Picture Editor, you can modify each frame individually to suit your own requirements. To save you from having to laboriously copy each frame, go to the Animation Editor. To modify a frame, right-click in that frame, and apply the following commands from the pop-up menu that displays.

Adding Animation Frames

You can create most animations easily by creating several frames that are slightly different from one another, based on one original image. When they are run quickly together, they will give the impression of fluid movement. Whether you are starting from scratch, or using one initial frame, it is far easier to copy each frame and then modify it as you go along than it is to draw each image for each frame, or modify each image by hand in a paint program.

You can add frames in two ways.

- Using the right mouse button. Right-click the first frame of your animation with your right mouse button, and then select the Insert option. This will insert a copy of your first frame into frame number two.
- Using the left mouse button. Left-click the image that you want to copy. Then hold down the left mouse button and drag the image to the frame you that you want to copy it to (in this case, frame number two). Let go of the button.

You can now open up the Picture Editor for that frame and modify it slightly. When you are ready, insert a copy of that frame into frame number three, which you can then modify further. By continuing this process, you can make a finished animation. You can check on your progress at any time by using the View Animation icon.

Resize Animation

The Resize Animation option allows you to automatically create several frames of animation that will gradually shrink or grow in relation to the frame you start off with. When you select the Resize Animation option, you will see a dialog box that looks like Figure 15.10.

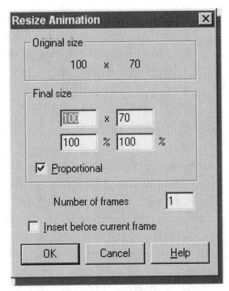

FIGURE 15.10   The Resize Animation dialog box.

This option was used to create the fireball powerups for the Dragon Flight game. We will recreate the fireball animation here.

1. Open a new, blank game file.
2. Go to the Level Editor, click the New Object icon in the toolbar, and then select the New Active Object option. You will now see the Create New Active Object Editor.
3. Double-click the first blank frame.
4. In the Dragon Flight directory, select the *fireq.bmp* image file. Capture that file and click OK.
5. Place a copy of the fireball on the play area. Notice that the copy of the fireball does not move.

You may want to create a quick backdrop object, make it solid, and choose the color black. This will show off your animation to better effect.

6. After you have the fireball on a black field, right-click to open the Animation Editor.
7. Right-click the first frame and select the Resize Animation option. Now you will be in the Resize Animation window, as shown in Figure 15.10 above.

8. Under the Final Size heading, select the size of the frame that you want to end up with. (Notice that under the Original Size heading of the window, the size of the frame that you are zooming from is displayed, in pixels.) You can either enter the actual size of the X and Y dimensions of the final frame (the number of pixels wide and high that the final frame will be) or you can enter a percentage ratio. For example, 50% would shrink that particular dimension by half.

If the Proportional option button is selected and you resize one dimension, the other dimension will be changed proportionally. For example, if you changed the width to 50%, the height would also be changed by 50%. With the Proportional option button deselected, you can change the dimensions independently. (But be aware that this distorts the image.)

The "Number of frames" option allows you to select how many frames will be placed between the original image and the grown or shrunken final image. The higher the number, the smoother the effect will be.

The "Insert before current frame" option will grow/shrink the object before the current frame. For example, if you select the first frame of an animation to shrink by half, and you insert ten frames between the current frame and the final image, the last frame will be the smallest. Looking backward from it, each of the next ten frames will be gradually bigger until you arrive back at the original frame.

By alternately increasing and decreasing an image's size, you can make an object appear to shrink and grow. This can sometimes be a useful effect.

Rotate

The Rotate option can be used to insert several frames of animation that gradually rotate clockwise or counterclockwise from the initial frame. You can choose the number of frames used to perform the rotation, from 4 to 32. The higher the number of frames, the smoother the rotation effect will be. The rotation frames will be inserted after the initial frame.

Morphing

The Morphing function allows you to change one frame into another, making for stunning transformations. You can use this function to make a human face morph into a monster or a spaceship smoothly change into another spaceship, rather than simply having the images snap from one to the next. You may have seen advanced versions of this technique in Hollywood movies. Now you can do it on your PC!

To morph an object, set up the Animation Editor with the first image in frame one and the "morph to" image in frame two. Right-click the first image, and you will be taken to the Morph Editor, as shown in Figure 15.11.

The easiest way to do this is to select your second (destination) object first, enter the Animation Editor, select the frame you want, copy it using the Edit function from the Animation Editor (top left), then exit the Animation Editor. Now select the first (start) object, enter the Animation Editor for that object, and paste the finishing frame after the frame you want first. You may have to enter the Edit mode and deselect the "Remove all" option, which will remove all previous animation frames if you try to paste a new frame into that animation sequence.

This function works best when there is only one frame for the original object. If there is more than one frame, delete the redundant frames so that you are only left with the start frame and the finish frame. You can leave part of the original animation if you want, but bear in mind that the morphing part of the animation will not start until the original animation has run. This can also use a lot of memory.

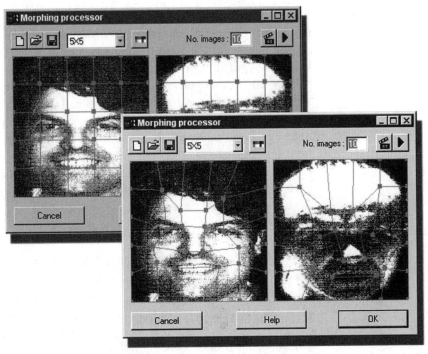

FIGURE 15.11   The Morph Editor before and after adjusting the morph points.

Using the Morph Editor screen, you can select the number of frames used to morph from the original frame to the final one. To do this, click the No. Images box. The more frames that you have, the smoother and more realistic the end result will be. However, this is also time consuming and uses a lot of memory. By default, The Games Factory uses ten frames for a morph, which is a compromise between smoothness of effect and speed of execution. You can also choose the definition of the change in the grid box at the top of the Morph Editor (by default, set to 5 X 5). Having a higher number here will raise the number of fine changes that are made in between each frame. Again, be aware that a very high definition combined with a large object will take a long time to do, and may use up lots of memory.

The icon actually starts the whole process off. When the Morph process has finished, you will be presented with a whole new animation strip, morphing smoothly from the first image to the last. In Dragon Flight, this function was used to give the dragon wings a nice blur effect as they moved. Two images of the dragon (one with wings up, and one with wings down) were morphed to create the effect.

Use of the Morph Grid

You can change the color of the Morph Grid using the icon. You may find this to be very useful, depending on the color of the images that you are morphing. The grid is used to define common points between the images that you want to morph between. The grid is composed of a number of "elastic bands" that you can stretch to fit various strategic points on the objects that you are morphing. For example, if you were to morph from one face to another, you would stretch the grid so that each point corresponds to an eye, nose, edge of mouth, and so forth. Make sure that each grid point on the second object is corresponds to the same point on the first one. For example, if the point one from the left and one from the top is placed on the eyebrow on the first object, the same grid points (one from the left, one from the top) must be used on the eyebrow of the second object, even if it means stretching a point across the image window.

 Make sure that you do not get grid points "crossing over" each other, since this will spoil the effect.

Setting the Hot Spot of an Object

The Hot Spot is an invisible handle, or anchor, that you can use to drag images around on the screen. It is also used as a reference for the X, Y co-

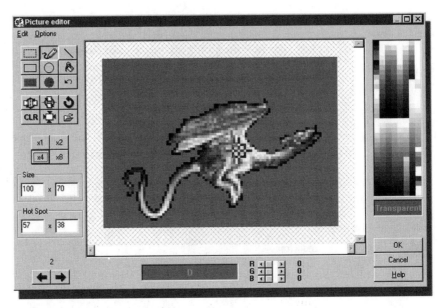

FIGURE 15.12   The Hot Spot on an object.

ordinates of objects. Each image can have its own separate Hot Spot. As a default, when you create a new active object, the Hot Spot is automatically positioned at the top left corner of each image (see Figure 15.12). You can, however, move it anywhere you like.

You can view the Hot Spot by going to the Options heading and selecting the Show-Hot Spot option. Try to position it centrally if your object is going to have several different directions; otherwise, it will "jump" when you change direction.

Setting the Action Point of an Object

The Action Point is the point where things like bullets are fired from objects. For example, if you had a large spaceship with a gun mounted, you would set the Action Point to the end of the gun barrel, where the bullet would first appear. You can show the Action Point by going to the Options heading and selecting the Show-Action Point option.

 The Hot Spot and Action Point can look the same, so double-check the menu to be sure the right option is selected.

The Picture Editor

The Picture Editor lets you create your own animation, background objects, icons, and quick backdrop objects. Because many of the features are identical for all these types of objects, they are summarized in this chapter.

We have already visited the Picture Editor, but Figure 15.13 shows the Picture Editor window for your reference as we go through the specific functions. In the center of the screen is the drawing area, where you will be working. If the area is too large to fit in this screen, you can either scroll around in it, zoom in or out using the zoom control buttons, or maximize the window, using the window manipulation icons at the top right of the window.

Zoom Icons

On the left of the screen are four buttons: x1, x2, x4, and x8. These let view the image at 1, 2, 4, or 8 times its normal size. This function does not actually change the size of the image, only how you see it.

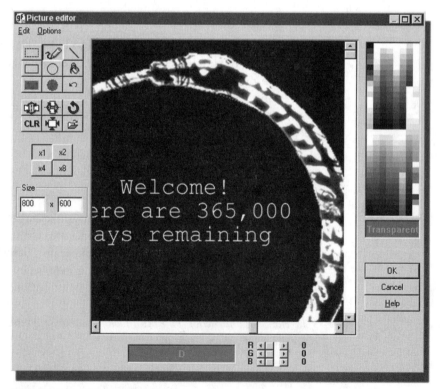

FIGURE 15.13 The Picture Editor window.

16 INTRODUCTION TO GCS

Film Strip

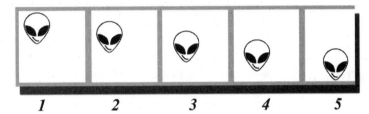

1   2   3   4   5

Game Frames

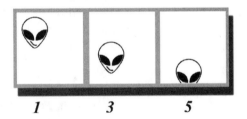

1   3   5

n this part of *Awesome Game Creation*, we will make a 3D game using The Pie 3D Game Creation System. We will refer to it as GCS from here on out. Special thanks go to Pie in the Sky Software (see Figure 16.1) for releasing the GCS free to the readers of this book. Please visit their Web site (www.pieskysoft.com) for information on the full version of GCS. The best thing about GCS is that it allows you to create an entire game without doing any programming.

You will see how much you can do with GCS using your own imagination to create 3D games that are comparable to Doom. Although you will not be doing any programming, things will get a bit more complex as we start to look into the third dimension. We will learn a new set of tools and techniques. But the basis you have from the first two parts of the book will serve you well, since you will still be using the vocabulary and processes you have already learned.

INSTALLING GCS

To install this version of the Pie 3D Game Creation System:

1. Put the CD-ROM from the back of this book into the drive, find the GCS folder, and click the Setup icon. The installation procedure will install everything you need and will also include an Uninstall option.
2. Agree to the terms of using the software, as shown in Figure 16.2.

FIGURE 16.1 The Pie in the Sky logo.

FIGURE 16.2 You must agree to the terms in order to install GCS.

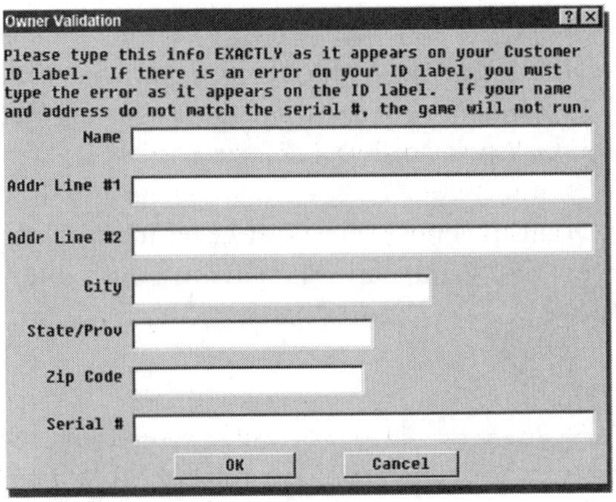

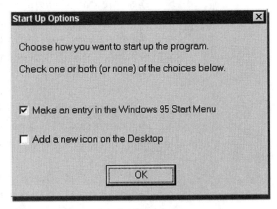

FIGURE 16.3   The installation directory screen.

FIGURE 16.4   This option chooses the program group.

3. Select the location where you want the software installed. It's usually a good idea to use the default directory, since many of the examples and instructions given later in this part assume a normal installation.
4. Next, we need to choose the installation directory as shown in Figure 16.3.
5. Now, choose the program group for the installation.

THE MAIN PARTS OF GCS

The Pie 3D Game Creation System consists of the following three main areas:

- Layout Editor
- Paint program
- Smooth-scrolling 3D game engine

The Layout Editor

In the Layout Editor (commonly called the Map Editor or Mapping Utility), you will handle almost all aspects of creating your games. You will work on one game level at a time, from a top view, using the toolbar icons to do the most common functions, such as copying, rotating, and placing walls. In addition, there are standard pull-down menus across the top of the screen.

There are some similarities to TGF in the terms and terminology we will be using, but in GCS, you are laying out a 3D world in two dimensions and can't see one entire dimension. You will have to mentally visualize what you are laying out, whereas with TGF, you could see exactly what was going into your game.

From the Layout Editor, you can choose File | Test Level to drop into the 3D world to test your layout and game play. The Layout Editor interface can be seen in Figure 16.5.

GCS Paint

The second part of GCS is the Paint tool for creating or retouching images. The GCS Paint tool has a set of features which allow the important control of image resolutions, contrast, etc. If you have trouble with these concepts, go back to Chapter 2. The GCS Paint interface can be seen in Figure 16.6.

The Game Engine

Ironically, you can't see the most important part of GCS—the game engine. And that is what we want in a book that has "no programming required" on the cover. The term *game engine* is a rather generic term that is used to describe the core application that runs a game. This engine is the software that runs when the user is playing the 3D game—you never actually touch

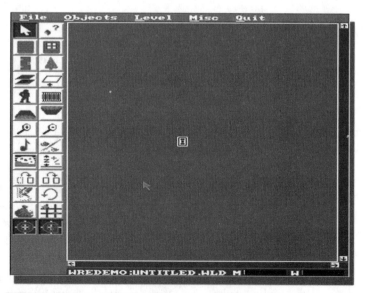

FIGURE 16.5 The Layout Editor interface.

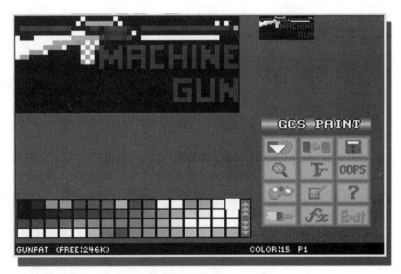

FIGURE 16.6   The GCS Paint program interface.

it in GCS. You simply build the levels and create the game on one end, and then the engine runs it on the other.

Following are some of the things the engine does:

Visibility Testing

The engine must decide which parts of the world are visible and which are hidden behind other walls or objects and should not be displayed on the screen. Visibility testing is not only important for how well the game looks, but also for how well it operates.

If this testing were not done, you would see errors such as objects showing through walls. Undoubtedly, you have played a game where you have seen this kind of error. If the testing were not done even for objects that you don't see, it would affect the speed and performance of the game. As you work with GCS, you will begin to get a feel for how you have to balance the amount of art you use, and you will become more sensitive to the way the engine will handle your world when it runs it.

Sounds

The engine must also play sounds and control the volume and the way the sounds are played back. As mentioned previously, sound is very important. It can make or break the "spell" of your game, or how immersed the player is in the game experience. A game engine typically will mix sound for depth and direction, on cue. It will juggle the number of sounds, prioritizing the order in which they are played, and canceling them, if necessary.

Collision Detection

The engine must also make sure that the player and enemies can't walk through the walls. It must detect collisions and dictate the behavior of the objects that have collided.

Artificial Intelligence and Behavior

The engine has the complex task of controlling all the moving objects in the game, from burning torches to sliding doors. For characters with complex behaviors, such as enemies, it uses Artificial Intelligence (AI) to control those behaviors.

All of the above—and a lot more—must be done in "real time," or as you are playing the game. These are just a few of the things a game engine must do and still keep up a decent frame rate.

 You will often hear the term frame rate, *referring to games—especially 3D games. Frame rate is the rate at which frames are created and displayed on the computer screen—just like the frames of a movie. One critical difference, however, is that when a movie's frame rate suddenly drops to half speed, the film itself is playing half speed. In a game, when the frame rate drops, the world is still moving at the same speed— you are just seeing half as many frames. So the movie you are watching is still running at the same speed, but it looks choppy.*

Figure 16.7 shows traditional film frames and the frames of a computer game—if they could somehow be put on film. Keep in mind that while film is static (it doesn't change), a game's frames can potentially be different each time. As Figure 16.7 shows, dropping frames in a game is a serious matter.

Running GCS

To run GCS:

1. Use the shortcut you established when you installed the program. Normally, this is one of the following:
   - Click the Start button and choose Programs. Then select the GCSWE group. From that group, choose GCSWE to start up GCS.

Film Strip

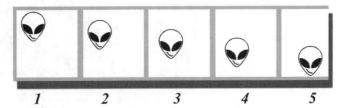

1   2   3   4   5

Game Frames

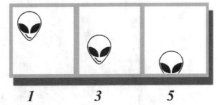

1   3   5

FIGURE 16.7   Film frames and computer game frames during rate drop.

- If you put a GCS shortcut on the Windows desktop, double-click that shortcut.
2. A window will open that looks like Figure 16.8. Wait for the time to countdown and then click the OK button.

Press a key to start DOS editor.

FIGURE 16.8   The window that opens when you start GCS.

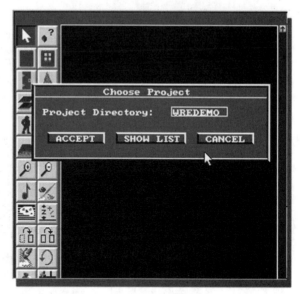

FIGURE 16.9 The Select a Project window.

To select a project file, as shown in Figure 16.9, you need to select Open an Existing Game Level from the File Menu. Remember that a Project folder is where all the level files are stored.

3. Click GDEMO.

4. Click the ACCEPT button to open the project.

 A red box will pop up, warning you that the colors are going to change on your screen. This is normal and is only GCS adjusting itself to use the same colors that the WREDEMO game will use.

GCS Main Screen

Now you should be looking at the GCS main screen (see Figure 16.10). There are pull-down menus across the top of the screen, icon buttons on the left side of the screen, and the viewport window in the middle. There is one white layered square in the center of the screen. You are looking at an empty level named UNTITLED.

Just as a word processor usually opens a document called *untitled* when you start it up, GCS starts with an untitled level as well. To load the demo that we will look at:

1. Choose File | Open Level on the main menu.

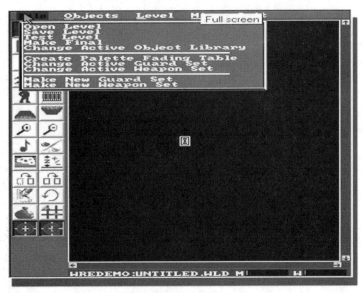

FIGURE 16.10   The main screen of GCS.

2. In the Choose Project box, you'll see the word WREDEMO. Click the ACCEPT button.
3. When you open an existing project, you'll also be asked to select a level from a scrolling list. Click Level #0 then click the OK button (See Figure 16.11).

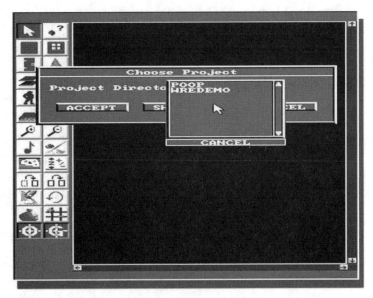

FIGURE 16.11   Opening a level that is stored in a project folder.

When the level opens, you will see in the viewport a top-down view of the level, like the plans of a house. The yellow lines are walls, and the blue squares are inventory items. The little yellow squares are enemy guards.

View Mode

If you want to see what each wall actually looks like, choose Object Properties from the View Menu (see Figure 16.12). Then move the mouse pointer around on the level and click various times. This is one way around the fact that you are looking down on your level and can't actually be in it to see the third dimension.

Test the Level

Before you modify the level, it would be fun to jump into the 3D world to actually see this level in 3D. To do this, choose File | Test Level (Enter 3D World).

Since the game engine will use Microsoft's Direct X/Direct 3D, the program must select which Direct X drivers and which video mode to use. The first time you start up the game engine, the program will try to choose the drivers and best mode automatically. Sometimes it cannot, and you will be prompted to make selections. Once those are answered, you should

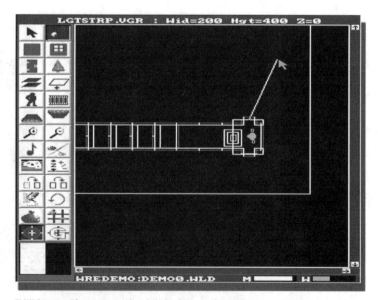

FIGURE 16.12   The View mode while looking at the walls in your level.

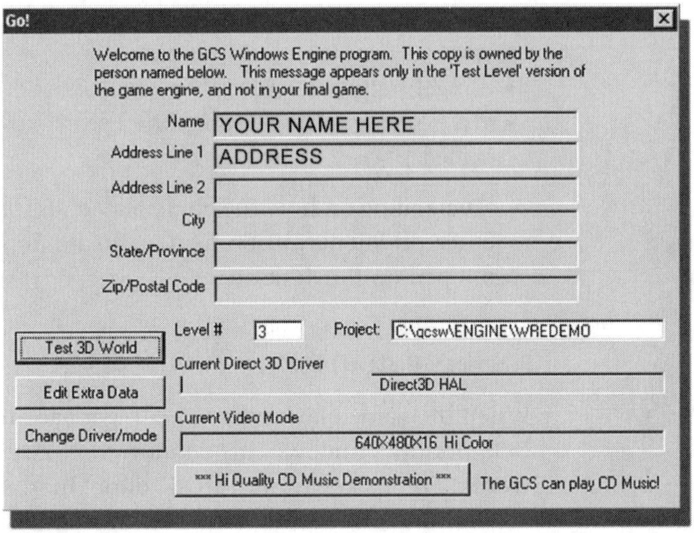

FIGURE 16.13   The Options screen that you see the first time you run the 3D engine.

have a dialog box on your screen with your name and address on it, as in
Figure 16.13.

*In the next chapter, we will talk in greater detail about choosing drivers and screen
resolutions for optimal performance.*

In addition, there will be three buttons available. Right now, let's click
the Test 3D World button. The 3D game engine will then start, and you
will be in the 3D world. If you get an error message, or something else goes
wrong, the problem is probably quite easy to fix.

Entering the 3D World

*When you first run GCS, it will choose a screen resolution for you that will most
likely work, but that may not be the best your video card can do. If the 3D world
screen appears to be low resolution, don't worry. Later we will look at how to run
and fine-tune your setup.*

Once you are in the 3D world, here are some ways you can explore:

- To move around, use the arrow keys or the keypad arrow keys. You
  can also move with the mouse. Move it up to go forward, down to go
  backward, and left or right to turn.
- To move faster, press the right mouse button.

- To fire your weapon, press the space bar, or press the left mouse button.
- To get help, press F1.
- To exit the 3D world, press the Escape key. (You'll also exit if you get killed!)

Depending on how the game play ends, the game engine may exit altogether, or you may just return to the desktop, with the game engine program open on the desktop.

Returning to the Level Editor

When the game play ends, you can get back to the world editor from the DOS prompt window. This window will either be blank or will have the words "Press a key to start DOS editor" in it.

If the title bar at the top of the window is gray, click it to make it the top window again. Then, press the space bar to go back into the Level Editor.

 Whenever you come back to the game engine after testing a level, the Level Editor will always be waiting in a DOS prompt box. It is very important that you restart the Level Editor, rather than starting up GCS again using the Start menu (or desktop icon). If you start GCS up again, you will have two copies of the GCS Level Editor running. This will lead to a crash, and possibly the loss of your level. If you are not sure if the Level Editor is already running, look on the taskbar at the bottom of the Windows desktop. A GCSWE button with the MSDOS logo on the left means that the Level Editor is already running. Click it to bring it up so you can press the space bar and return to the Level Editor.

CHAPTER REVIEW

Now that you have poked around GCS a little bit and you have it installed on your system, let's look at getting it to run as effectively as possible on your system. In the next chapter, we will look at and learn more about the technology behind the GCS 3D game engine and your computer.

17

RUNNING THE GCS
GAME ENGINE

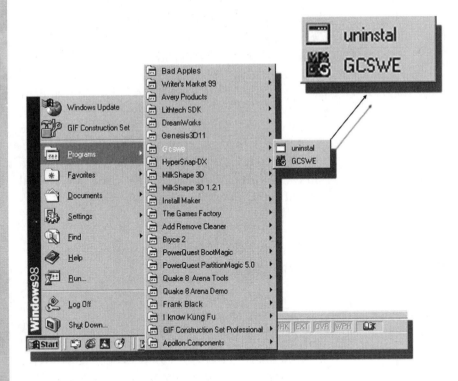

Now we will spend an entire chapter looking at all the options there are for setting up and running the GCS 3D game engine on your system. Simply setting up the engine to run at its best on your system can get complicated, with all the options presented and all the different technologies referred to. So, we will look at those options and technologies in great detail here. Don't let this chapter overwhelm you. Maybe the best way to use this chapter is if you really need (or want) to use it to speed things up. If you are happy with the default settings of GCS and it runs well on your system, then skim this chapter and come back to it later.

 The most important thing for you to learn from this chapter is the details of working and moving between the Windows and DOS environments.

As mentioned earlier, GCS is a Windows program; however, much of GCS is based in DOS. When we switch from the DOS Editor to the Windows 3D Engine, we are switching operating systems—literally making a big move in terms of how we should work on our computer. In The Games Factory, we were always in Windows. No matter how complex things were, we could always do a consistent operation to return to the main screen, or to exit the application. But in GCS, we have to always be mindful of the fact that we are jumping between DOS and Windows. You will always have to start the Level Editor from the DOS box or window, and you will return to it this same way. If you ever close the DOS window instead of going into the Level Editor to save your work, you will lose your work.

STARTING UP THE GCS WINDOWS ENGINE

To start, run GCS as we reviewed in the last chapter (we can make the instructions a bit shorter this time):

1. Click Start | Programs | GCSWE | GCSWE (see Figure 17.1), or double-click the GCS shortcut on the Windows desktop (if you have one).
2. Use the Level Editor commands to open the *GDEMO* project, and then open the *Level #0* level.
3. Choose File | Test Level. At this point, the GCS Windows Engine will start up.

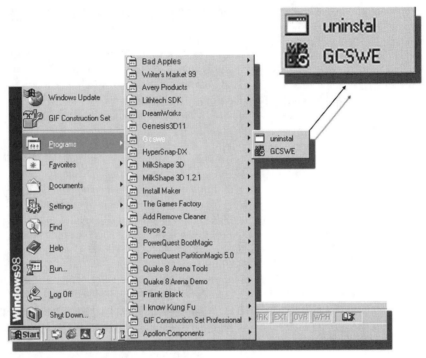

FIGURE 17.1   Shows the Windows Start menu and the GCSWE group.

Finding the Best Setup for the 3D Engine

As we saw in the last chapter, when you run GCS for the first time, you will see a dialog box like the one in Figure 17.2. Avoid the temptation to change any settings quite yet; let GCS select what it thinks is best and run the world.

When you enter the 3D game world, you will notice a yellow number on the upper part of the screen. This will appear only when you are testing levels, and not in the final game. This is the fps number, or frames per second display. Anything over 10 fps is pretty good, and the game will play pretty well. If the fps number dips below 5, it may start to get a little difficult to control your motion. You want to get this number as high as possible.

We will look at all the options available to you to make the GCS game engine run at maximum efficiency on your system. You should try a variety of video modes and 3D Direct (D3D) Devices to find the combination that works the best for you.

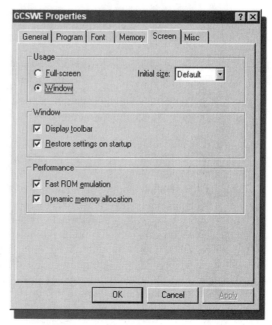

FIGURE 17.2 The dialog box that comes up the first time you run the GCS 3D game engine.

A good portion of game design and development—level editing, specifically—is spent balancing factors such as the available technology, the base machines most of your users will have, and the amount and size of your game's art and world geometry, all to make the best game possible. Some games call for huge worlds with little geometry, while others may call for small rooms with highly detailed art and models.

The Setup Options

The Pie 3D Game Creation System relies heavily on Microsoft's Direct3D® (sometimes called D3D). This is a set of pre-written code libraries that perform certain functions that are repeatedly used by games—such as drawing geometry, and handling the textures and art. When GCS needs any of these tasks carried out, it calls on D3D to do them. Since GCS relies on D3D, we will be looking at the several different modes of operation, the full screen modes, and the best setup for all these options. When a game is run for the first time, the GCS Windows Engine tries to make these selections for you, based on what is most likely to work. However, in some cases, the program cannot decide which is the best, or perhaps you may want to select a DirectDraw (DD) device yourself as you experiment to get the best performance.

Selecting a DirectDraw Device

To select a DirectDraw Device:

1. Start up GCS as before, by using the Test Level command on the Intro level.
2. In the game engine dialog box with the three buttons, choose Change Driver/Mode. This button just makes the dialog box go away so you can have access to the program's pull-down menu. You'll see the DirectDraw Device Select box (see Figure 17.3).
3. Make any changes you desire in the DirectDraw Device Select box, and click OK.
4. In the File menu of the game engine, choose Select DD Device. What to do here varies.

   - On most computers, there is only one choice, so it should be rather simple. But the selection box does let you see some of the features of your video card, such as whether or not it has hardware acceleration, and how much video RAM DirectX thinks the card has.
   - On computers which have a Piggyback-type hardware accelerator, there will be two choices. Some 3D accelerator cards, such as the Diamond Monster and Monster II, connect to your old video card without replacing it. If you have such a device, you will see more than one listing in the Select DD Device box. One will be your old

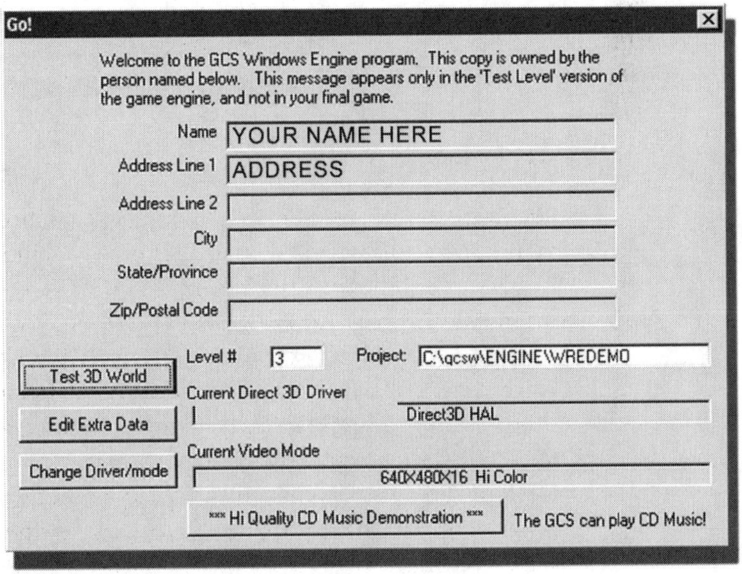

FIGURE 17.3   The DirectDraw Device Select box.

un-accelerated card, usually called Display. The other will be the accelerated device, called 3DFX or something else.

Choosing the accelerated device is usually the way to go. The only time you might want to try the Display device is if you are having trouble with the accelerated device and you want to try slower software emulation to isolate a problem. (You can also use this option when testing your game to see how it will run on a slower system without 3D hardware.)

 When you make a change to your DD Device, your options for the other choices will probably change as well. Therefore, after you change your DD Device, you must also change the D3D Device and the video mode.

Choosing a Direct3D Device

Microsoft's Direct3D Device dialog box allows you to select from a list of 3D drivers. Even though the game engine tries to make the best decision for you automatically, you may want to change it. To do this:

1. On the File menu, choose Select D3D Device. The number of options you get here depends on your computer and your video card (see Figure 17.4).

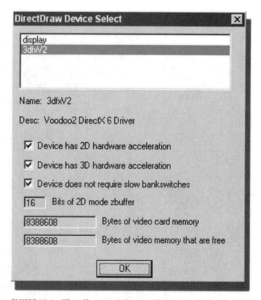

FIGURE 17.4 The Choose A Direct3D Device dialog box.

2. Choose a device. When you've finished choosing, click OK. The following are the most common choices:

- **Direct3D HAL.** This device represents your 3D acceleration hardware. This will usually (but not always!) be the driver which will give you the best performance. However, it is also the most likely to suffer from incompatibilities. If something seems wrong with the graphics, give the Ramp driver (below) a try. Also, some 3D accelerators (like the S3 Virge) will actually run slower than the software drivers. If the software drivers mentioned below work fine, but the HAL driver fails, send an e-mail to Pie in the Sky Software, with your exact video card, and they will try to resolve the incompatibility.

- **Ramp Emulation.** If you choose this device, all the 3D graphic computations will be done in software, and your hardware acceleration will not be used. Microsoft seems to be phasing out the Ramp driver, and if you have DirectX 6.0 or higher installed on your machine, it might be better to try the MMX™ or RGB software drivers if your HAL driver will not run correctly.

- **MMX Emulation.** This device uses multimedia extensions built into your CPU to accelerate the 3D graphics. If you have no HAL driver, try both this driver and the Ramp driver to see which one works better for you. If you have DirectX version 6.0 installed, the MMX driver may also use the 3D acceleration.

- **RGB Emulation.** This device is a software 3D graphics device like Ramp and MMX. Try this one out and compare it to Ramp and MMX on your system.

The full screen video modes that are possible change when you change the D3D Device. Therefore, you will automatically go into the Video Mode selection box if you change your D3D Device.

Choosing Screen Size

Your video hardware can change the resolution of your screen. If you remember, the more dots, the sharper the image. Also, the more dots, the larger the image, which takes more resources to display images, and more RAM and computer time to draw the 3D graphics. While high-resolution screens are great looking, they may cause your computer to fail if it runs out of video memory or if it becomes bogged down because there is too much information for the computer to handle. Images that have low resolution are blocky, but they require less work from the computer. See Figure 17.5 for the Choose a Screen Mode window.

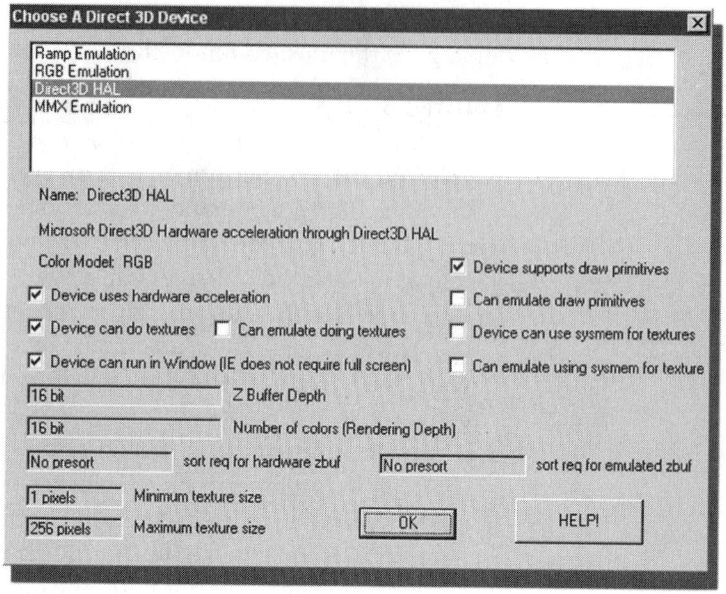

FIGURE 17.5 The Choose a Screen Mode window.

Remember that screen resolution is measured in width and height. A screen with a resolution of 640 × 480 has 640 dots from left to right, and 480 dots up and down, the total number of pixels being (640 * 480 = 307,200).

We are also concerned with color depth here. The lowest number of colors which GCS can work with is 256. This is called either 256-color mode or 8-bit color mode. GCS can work with 8-bit color, but in some cases, the colors won't look exactly right. The best choice is probably 16-bit color. It gives you 65,535 colors, which is plenty for excellent graphics, and it only uses twice as much video RAM as 8-bit color.

The most common mode to use GCS in is 640 × 480 × 16, which means a 640 × 480 resolution screen with 16-bit color. Keep in mind the difference between the art and images for the game, and the display mode. We are talking about display mode here.

There are also 32-bit color modes, which offer 16 million colors, but in practice they won't look any different than the 16-bit color modes, and they will use twice as much video RAM. If you have a video card with lots of RAM (12 MB or more), this shouldn't be a problem, however.

It is actually a bit of a mystery which video modes DirectX will make available. With some video cards, there are more than 50 modes to choose from, while on others there will be only three. Try to stick with the most common ones at first. The most likely to work are the following:

$640 \times 480 \times 16$
$320 \times 200 \times 16$

You can experiment with the other modes if you are inclined to, but working with the above common modes should cover your bases well.

Although GCS will run in 8-bit color modes (256 colors), you may have trouble with certain colors being drawn incorrectly. The 16-bit color modes are better if you can use them. The 8-bit color modes have the advantage that they use much less video memory.

The top selection of the video mode list is the Windowed option. If this is selected, GCS will run in a window on the Windows desktop. In this case, you cannot adjust the color depth from within GCS. If your Windows screen is set to 256 colors, then GCS will have to run in 256-color mode.

If you really want to run GCS in a window on the desktop, you can change the resolution and color depth as follows:

1. Exit from GCS and the Level Editor.
2. Right-click the desktop and choose Properties from the menu.
3. Click the Settings tab. You'll see the display in Figure 17.6.

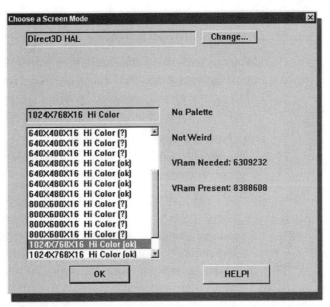

FIGURE 17.6 The Display Properties dialog box with the Settings tab showing.

4. Change the settings in the Color box (color depth) and Screen area box (screen resolution).
5. Click OK.

Using the windowed screen mode with 256 colors is not recommended. Direct3D does not appear to do such a great job with the palette management, and most of your colors will be inaccurate. This appears to be a DirectX weakness, because Microsoft's own demos exhibit this behavior when running windowed in 256 colors.

If Performance Is Terrible in All Modes...

Pie in the Sky Software has made sure that the frame rate is decent even on an old 120Mhz Pentium with no hardware acceleration. If the system is a better one than this and it still runs poorly, you may have a problem, or you may have over-designed your game. If this happens, consider getting a new computer or a 3D hardware card. The best bet is probably a new 3D card. If you are running an older Pentium-class computer without a 3D card, you'll be surprised when you see how much it improves your performance. Of course, more RAM will help as well, as we discussed earlier in the book.

For a list of video cards that work well with GCS, see www.pieskysoft.com.

Windows Engine Game Options

When you test your level and the Windows Engine starts, you have access to an Options menu that lets you make changes which affect the control of the game and the graphics quality.

To use these options during 3D game play:

1. Press and release the Alt key.
2. Click the option you want, or use the arrow keys to highlight that option and press the Enter key.

See Figure 17.7 for the pull-down menu of options.

Some menu options, including changing screen size or driver, will not operate unless you pause the 3D game first by selecting Reset from the File menu. To resume your game, select Go from the File menu after you are finished using the menu.

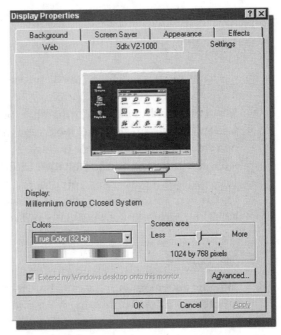

FIGURE 17.7 The Pull-down menu of options for the Windows Engine.

Horizon Bitmap

The game engine can display a horizon bitmap or a sky bitmap in the distance when you start using the Extra Features Editor. This option can enable or disable the horizon you have set. Turning it off can increase performance.

Wall Bumping (Collision Detection)

Ordinarily, walls are treated as solid by the game engine—you can't go through them. But with this option, you can do so. Even though in the game you will probably want most walls solid, it's convenient to turn off wall bumping as you test your level, so you can go directly through walls to get from place to place quickly.

Frames Per Second (FPS) Display

This option turns the frames per second display on and off (the yellow number in the upper left of your screen). Some people find the number very distracting when trying to see how the game will really look to the end user.

Correct Orientation

Leave this option off! This option was for the DOS game engine.

Bilinear Filtering

This option will do a smoothing operation on the pixels in your screen's image. This can make a level look much nicer, but on some video cards this can cost you significant performance; on many others it will have no measurable effect. Also, on some video cards this will tend to make dark outlines around the enemies and other shaped objects. So you will have to experiment to see what works on your card the best.

This option can be turned on and off before or during 3D game play.

Dithering Enable

Like the above option, this can change the quality of your graphics, but at a potential price. Try turning it on and off, to see which way you like it better.

Object Presort

Some video cards (only some hardware accelerated ones) will draw black rectangles around enemies, objects, door frames, and other objects that use transparency. Turning on Object Presort should eliminate the problem, if it arises.

Brightness

If your monitor is too dark to see walls and textures very well, you can use this option as a last resort. It only works when you change the setting before you start up the 3D world. Many video cards today come with their own utilities for boosting brightness that work very well, so only use the GCS option as a last resort. It will increase the brightness, but at a price, since your colors will become washed-out.

Joystick

This option lets you select or enable a joystick device. To calibrate your joystick, use the Windows control panel, and adjust the properties.

Mouse

This option lets you select or enable mouse control. In the unlikely event there are two or more mice on your system, you can choose the one you want to use with the Select option. You can also change the sensitivity in the x and y directions. You can hold down the right mouse button for forward motion, which is more convenient than walking forward by pushing the mouse forward.

Starting Up the 3D World

After you have selected your devices, video mode, and the options that work best for you, start up the 3D world by going to the File menu and selecting Go. In the process of making all these choices, you will do this a thousand times.

Returning to the Level Editor

When you want to return to the Level Editor from the game engine, press the Escape key. If you are using a nonstandard video mode (not 320 × 200 or 640 × 480), you may be asked if the video mode worked OK or not. This is so GCS can keep track of which modes don't work well on your system and can remind you if you try to use a nonstandard mode again.

When you exit the game engine, Windows will return you to a DOS prompt box, with a message that reads "Press any key to start the DOS Editor." Press any key (the space bar is convenient).

If you exit from the Windows Engine, and you aren't returned to the Level Editor as you would expect, look for the Level Editor window on the Desktop. If you don't find it there, check the taskbar at the bottom of your screen. Each program that runs in Windows has a rectangular icon on the taskbar, as shown in Figure 17.8.

One of those blocks should be the Level Editor (it says "GCSWE" and has an MS-DOS icon). Even if it doesn't look like it, the program is still running. To call it up again, click the icon for the Level Editor.

 If the window with the message "Press a key to start DOS editor" is on the screen, but it ignores your key presses, then probably that window is not the active window. Click the title of the window once with the mouse to make sure the window title is blue, not gray. Then try pressing the space bar again.

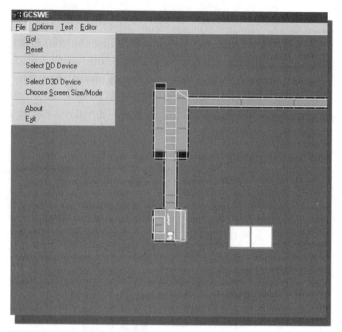

FIGURE 17.8 The Windows taskbar and the running applications.

Warning! Whatever you do—don't go to the Start menu to start up GCS again, if you still have a copy of the Level Editor running! This will crash your computer, and you may lose your level design! Make sure you don't already have the level Editor running, by looking at your taskbar on the bottom of the screen, before you try to start up a new one from the Start menu!

Tips for Using GCS

Accessing the Menu When There Is No Mouse Pointer

If you are running the game engine in full screen mode, there is no mouse pointer. To access the menu, press and release the Alt key. The game play will halt and a menu will appear. After you make your selection, the menu will disappear, and the 3D game play will continue.

Some menu commands require that the 3D game be paused first with Reset on the File menu.

Getting Back to the Desktop Temporarily

If you are in full screen mode, you can temporarily halt GCS and go back to the desktop by pressing and releasing the Alt key, and then selecting Reset from the File menu. To return to game play, select Go from the File menu. Sometimes this will fail, because DirectX cannot get control of the keyboard back.

Changing Screen Mode During Game Play

It is possible to change the screen mode during game play.

1. Press the Alt key and release it to bring up the menu.
2. Select Reset from the File menu. This will stop GCS.
3. Select Choose Screen Size/Mode from the File Menu.
4. Select a new video mode, then click the OK button.
5. Select Go from the File menu to restart the 3D world where you left it.

CHAPTER REVIEW

Well, that was the whirlwind tour of probably the most tedious part of GCS. Now we can focus more on making the game world. While these aspects are a bit tedious, they are very important to the overall quality of your game—how well it looks and runs. The effort spent here will ensure that you can make a game that pushes the limits in terms of quality and performance. Further, knowing all the terms and technology described in this chapter will be very useful if you plan to move up to a more complex development environment in the future. In the next chapter, we will look closer at the 3D Game World Editor.

18

LOOKING DEEPER INTO THE 3D EDITOR

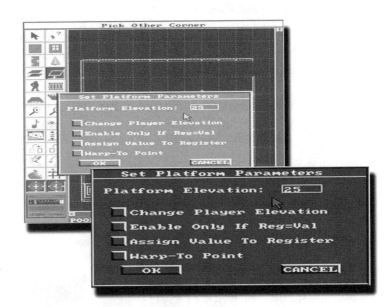

n this chapter, we will take a closer look at the various options of the Level Editor. The figures will show you a lot. However, you may want to start playing with the icons and changing a level around. This is often the best way to learn. If you do this, make sure to make a copy of the level first, by using the File | Save As command. Instead of just accepting the name of the level, give it another name. Then feel free to modify it without the worry of losing the original level.

In general, the right-click should get you out of most active functions.

LEVEL EDITOR

Select and View Icons

The Select option is available by default (see Figure 18.1). When you use this, you are ready to select objects from the viewport to move, copy, elevate, rotate, and so forth.

The View icon is the one with the question mark. When you click this icon, you go into View mode. Then, as you move around the viewport, you can see what the walls look like by watching the upper left corner of the screen (see Figure 18.2).

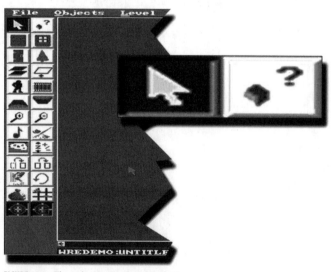

FIGURE 18.1 The selection in the viewport.

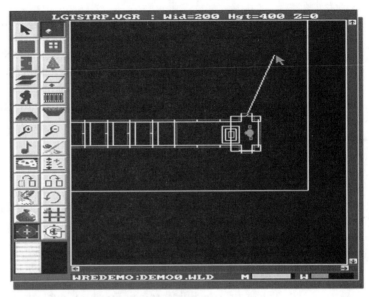

FIGURE 18.2   The View mode of the Level Editor.

Object Placing Icons

The Object Placing options can be seen in Figure 18.3. You click these icons when you want to add a new object to your 3D level.

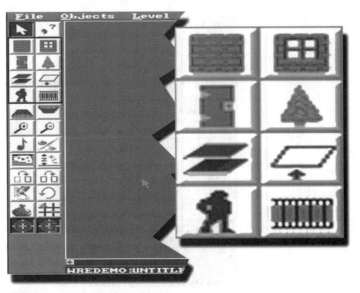

FIGURE 18.3   The Object Placing icons.

The **Wall** option adds walls to your levels.

The **Shaped Wall** option is for walls that have black pixels. The black will be treated as clear, or invisible, in the 3D world (color masking). If you make a wall with a black rectangle in the middle, the wall will have a window cut out that the player can see through.

We will go into much greater detail about the rest of these options in a later chapter.

Magnify

To zoom in and out (see Figure 18.4) you use the + and – keys on your keyboard. The + magnifying glass zooms in. The – magnifying glass zooms out.. Each press zooms you in (or out) again.

Fog

To set up the ability to see Fog in a level, you need to choose Light System2 Settings form the Project menu (see Figure 18.5)

Editing Icons

There are several options available when you have an item selected, such as the rotate object selection seen in Figure 18.6.

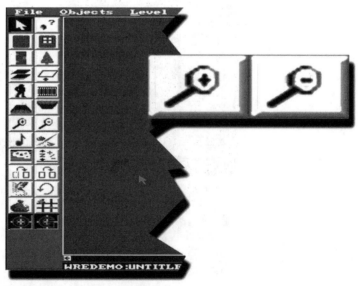

FIGURE 18.4 The screen is magnified.

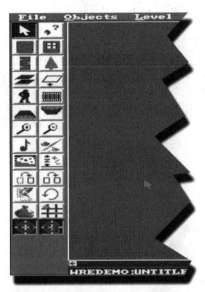

FIGURE 18.5 Setting up Fog.

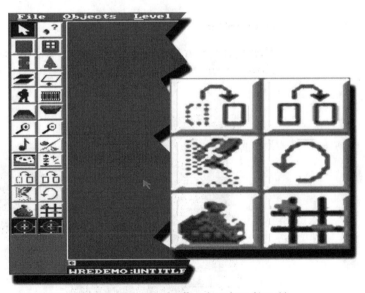

FIGURE 18.6 The Editing options only affect the selected item(s).

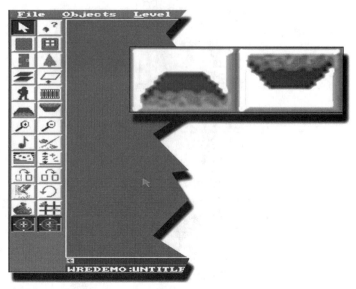

FIGURE 18.7 Exploring objects in the editor.

Object Explorer

If you select Explore Objects from the Edit menu, you will have the ability to quickly browse your level (see Figure 18.7).

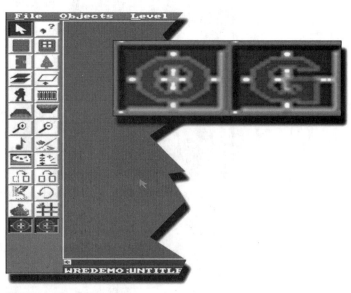

FIGURE 18.8 The Grid option.

Grid Option

To turn the grid on or off, select Show Grid from the Options menu.

Music Icon

You can add music to your level by choosing Midi Music Box from the Level menu (see Figure 18.9). You can specify a suitable MIDI file that exists in a directory, or you can play MIDI music from a CD.

Now that you have been introduced to GCS and have looked around a little (you even entered a 3D game world and then came back to the Level Editor), we can move on to the next step, creating game project files. This is important to understand so you will not be confused as to where certain files may be, and how things work in GCS. You will prevent many problems from happening if you set up your game files correctly.

CREATING GAME PROJECT FILES

GCS creates a separate project directory for each game that you create. When you start a new game, GCS asks you to name the project for that game. Each project is an entire game and can have multiple levels. For example, you might have a project or game that features a haunted house and call it HAUNTED, and then have many levels, like cemetery, floor-1, dungeon, and attic.

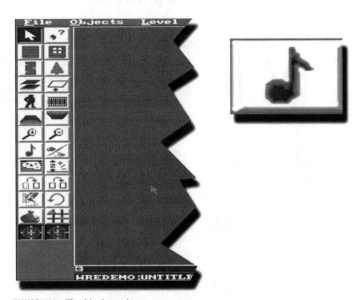

FIGURE 18.9   The Music options.

To start a new project in GCS:

1. Start GCS.
2. The first dialog box that comes up asks you to select a project. To make a new one, click the name box, and enter a name for your new project that is eight or fewer characters (don't include an extension. GCS will add it for you). Then either press the Enter key, or click the OK button.

When you click the Accept button, GCS creates a directory with files that the 3D game engine needs for the 3D world you are about to detail. This directory will have the same name as your project. So if you made a project called *myproj*, GCS will create a new directory with that name. Assuming you installed GCS in the directory *c:\p3dgcs*, the full name of the project directory would be *c:\p3dgcs\myproj*.

The Project Directory

GCS places many files in the project directory. These include the picture files for your game's background, the damage indicator artwork, and so on. At the beginning, these files are stock, or default, entities. After you have created your directory, you can edit these files to customize the game. We will look at how to do this in a later chapter.

Putting Walls and Objects in a Level

All the trees, enemies, and wall pieces that make up the 3D world are called objects. Rooms and hallways must be made from fixed-length sections of textured wall. It's easy to predefine the sizes of textured walls or other objects, but we'll cover that later. The point is that doing your 3D layout is simply a matter of selecting the objects you want to place, and then placing them.

 You must have at least one solid wall in your level, or you will get an error message when you test the level. Be sure to place at least one wall section before attempting to run the game engine.

Putting Walls into Your Layout

Now we are ready to start laying out a test room. To get started:

1. Choose Edit, Place New Object in Level, Solid Wall and Open Image Select Box.
2. Select a wall texture from the scrolling list (see Figure 18.10).

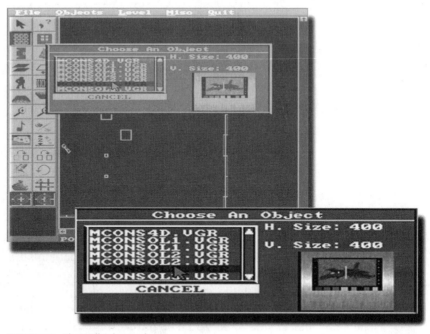

FIGURE 18.10   The Wall Selection box.

When you click the name, you will be in Place mode. As you move your mouse around on the viewport and click, you will be placing your wall around.

Below, you'll be dragging the wall. Unlike in most other programs, you do not hold the mouse button down to drag things. As you drag the wall around, it will always hang in an east-facing orientation.

To place the wall, move it to where you want it to go. When you're there, click to fasten the lower end of the wall to the grid. You'll see another wall section, which follows the mouse and is attached to the first wall you put down.

After placing a wall, you have the following three options:

- Get out of wall-placing mode with two right-clicks. This leaves your first wall but cancels that second, unplaced wall.
- Detach the new wall section with one right-click. You can now drag the new wall and place it.
- Choose a direction for the new wall, and click to make it permanent. After doing this, you will have placed two walls that are attached.

When you are starting a new layout, you will want to make big rooms and hallways with all the same wall type. So it's best to choose option three above. You can always go back later, delete a wall here and there, and re-place selected walls with another type, for variation and customization.

Using Magnify Mode

As we saw earlier, Magnify mode lets you magnify your view of the current level. Just to review, to change the magnification, first press one of the Magnify buttons (+ or −).

Putting Up Trees and Other Stand-Up Items

The symmetrical objects option lets you draw stand-up objects like trees or floor lamps. These are shaped objects that look the same from every direction. When you click the icon, you'll see a list of object names, as shown in Figure 18.11. Move the mouse pointer across the list to see the various images in the lower left-hand corner of the screen. Then click the object you want. You'll be put back into Place mode.

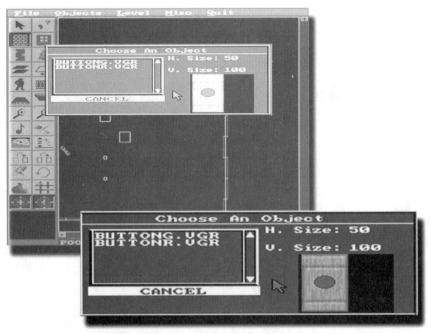

FIGURE 18.11 The Symmetrical Objects Selection box.

This Place mode is a little different, though. The direction doesn't matter for stand-up items, since they always rotate to face you. You don't need to anchor one end first, and then swing it to the proper direction. These are called anchored sprites.

To place a stand-up object, drag the square to the place you want, and click to place it. The square shows a rough representation of the horizontal width of the object. This is so you can judge its distance from walls. When you click to place the stand-up object, another potential stand-up square appears, attached to the mouse pointer. You can drag and place this one, or you can right-click to get out of Place mode.

You usually should turn off the grid before you click the Tree icon. When you're placing things like floor lamps and wastebaskets, the grid is usually more of a hindrance than a help. Click the Grid icon to toggle the snap-to-grid feature on and off.

Platforms

Platforms are rectangular areas in the 3D world that sense the presence of the player. One of the most common uses of a platform is to raise the player when he steps on one. Another function is to use the platform as a trigger for a teleport device to another level. In fact, this is how most level-switches are implemented with GCS.

Rectangular platforms are, by default, not drawn; they are completely invisible.

Usually, rectangular platforms are placed right in front of tunnels or staircases. When the player walks up to the staircase, the game switches levels, as if the player had traversed the staircase.

As mentioned above, one common use is to raise the player. Let's say you create a box out of wall panels, and you want the player to be able to jump up on the box and stand there. Without a platform, the player would sink down into the box, instead of standing on top of it. The box needs to have a platform over it so that when the player is within the platform's boundary, the player's feet are lifted to the height of the platform's z value.

Creating a Platform

To create and place a platform object, choose Platform from the Edit menu (see Figure 18.12).

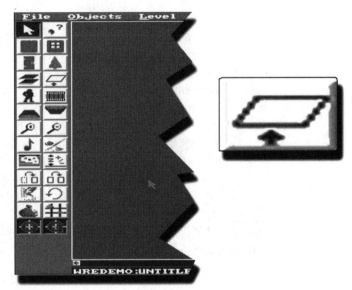

FIGURE 18.12 The Platform selection.

A dialog box comes up with some options. You can set the platform to be visible. This actually just makes a floor polygon in the same place as the platform. If you choose to do this, you will be asked to pick a color. In addition, you will have to choose the function of the platform. Warping to a different level is a common one.

If you select warping, you will have to know the entry point number of the destination level. Don't worry if you don't know what an entry point is at this point. We will discuss this later, as well (see Figure 18.13).

Putting the Bad Guys In

Placing enemy characters is as easy as placing stand-up objects. You get a dialog box of options for each enemy. When you are finished making choices, click the OK button. You'll be put into Place mode. You are then asked to choose a direction for the enemy to face (north is toward the top of the screen). After you decide on the facing direction, click where you want your enemy to be in this level.

You will usually want to turn the grid off before placing enemies. Otherwise, the Layout Editor may place your enemies in the middle of walls when attempting to align your enemy with the grid.

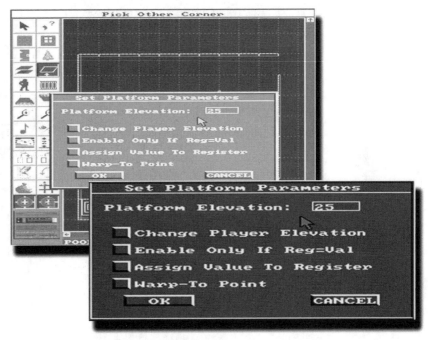

FIGURE 18.13   The Set Platform Parameters dialog box.

After you place them, the enemies can be copied, moved, and rotated like any other object, using the normal Copy, Move, and Rotate icons. However, there is a maximum number of 32 enemies on any one level. As you learn more about the characters in GCS, you will be able to set parameters to control how the enemies patrol (randomly or centered in one spot) and to control other behaviors. Enemies will also notice players and start shooting and chasing them and other neat behaviors. You can also change their appearance by editing their artwork files. We will look at all these options later.

CHAPTER REVIEW

If you have not done so already, you may want to run a test on a level. Go through this chapter. Drag out a few walls, select one wall, and click the Door icon to assign the door properties to it. Go with all the default settings, and then run your world. If you are unable to get your test level running, you may need to go back and try the options in Chapter 17 on running the 3D game engine. It may not be set up properly on your system. Once you are comfortable with that, turn to the next chapter, where we will start laying out a game level.

19 MAKING A 3D LEVEL

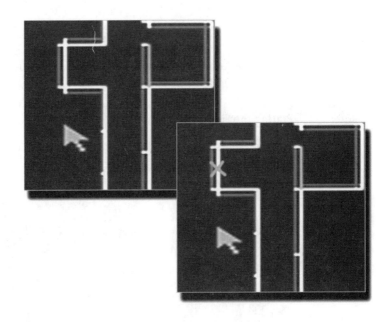

L aying out good game levels is really easy with GCS. In fact, you can lay them out in minutes. This chapter will take you through your first basic game level.

For this chapter, we will lay out the most basic of game levels. We will start by placing the player's starting point, then we will set up the walls that make up the hallways and chambers of our level, and then we will add a door or two. Finally, we see how to populate the level with the enemies. After you have gone through this basic process, you will see that you will be able to make game levels that are almost endless, since you can attach them to each other for a large and complex game.

DESIGNING THE LEVEL

We will do a basic level where you enter through the front door (which will be sealed behind you).

Placing the First Wall

To start, select Solid Wall from the edit menu. This will bring up the dialog box where we choose the art that goes on the wall we are about to place, as shown in Figure 19.1.

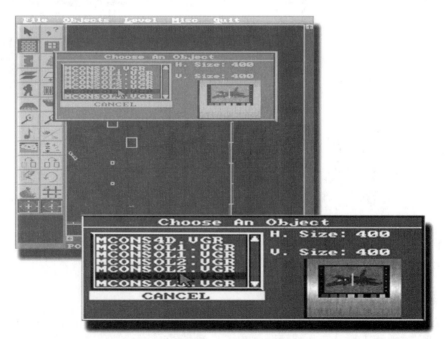

FIGURE 19.1 The dialog box for choosing the art that goes on the wall you are about to place in the game level.

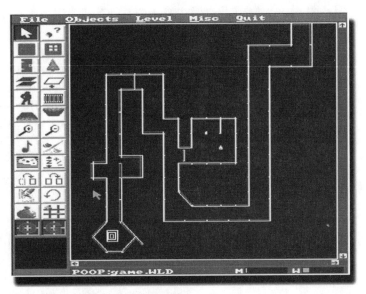

FIGURE 19.2   The floor plan of our test level.

We will use just a simple wall that looks like a rock texture—you can start filling in the floor plan by laying out walls when you are comfortable with doing so (see Figure 19.2).

Using the snap to grid features, we will be able to make our level very quickly. All the walls will line up beautifully.

Each level can contain a maximum number of 700 total objects.

Editing Your 3D Levels

After you have started laying out the walls of your level, you will undoubtedly want to start manipulating and editing the level to a greater degree. The following tools and functions will take you farther than before, where we discussed the basics of the Level Editor. You have already read how to place walls and other objects; now we'll look at how to edit your layouts.

Grid Snap

In making a room, it is very important to get your wall panels to fit perfectly against each other. Gaps even 1 cm wide can result in unsightly bright lines between walls. This is the reason for grid snap. When using grid snap, your walls will naturally line up along the grid. You don't have to worry about misalignment.

The only problem with grid snap is that it makes it difficult to put a wall in a position that is halfway between the grid lines. You can enable or disable snap to grid in the Options menu. This is very useful when you are working with walls of different sizes. However, sometimes it is better to turn the grid off and use object snap, as described below.

When using very fine grids like 50 units or smaller, you will have to turn off object snap, or the two effects will interfere with each other.

Object Snap

Object snap is very similar to grid snap. The difference is that this feature snaps new objects to existing walls, rather than to a fixed grid. This is very handy when you need to join walls that are not aligned along a grid snap line. This may seem to make grid snap extraneous, but in reality, grid snap is better because you can always close your rooms and hallways with grid snap. If you mix different-sized wall sections, you can still connect the walls with no gaps by using object snap instead of grid snap. However, you may have a problem when it comes time to close a room. When you mix wall sizes, you may find there is no wall section that will fit nicely in the left-over gap. If you use walls of 400 cm width and 400 cm grid spacing, you will never have this problem.

Warning! *Avoid the temptation to turn both grid snap and object snap off and place your walls free-form. If you zoom to a high enough magnification, you can actually get quite close this way. However, you will find that if you try to make rooms and hallways this way, errors will pile up as you place long strings of walls. Eventually, you will be faced with so many nasty gaps between your walls that it will be next to impossible to repair.*

Selecting Objects

It is very common to put down walls that you decide to remove later. This process of trying to make something better than what you first created is called tweaking; all the pros do it. There are several things you can do to walls that have already been placed. These include moving, deleting, copying, rotating, and raising and lowering. As with many Windows programs you may have used, these functions are implemented in a two-step process. First, you select which objects you want to operate on, and then you press the tool icon to make the action happen.

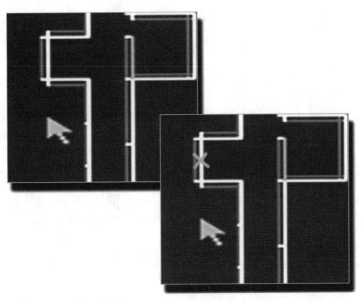

FIGURE 19.3   A selected object.

When you click existing walls or objects while you are in Selection mode, selection rectangles appear on those items. To select several objects at once, click the center of each object, and "x" them one by one. Or, you can click where there is no object, and draw a rectangle around a whole region. Figure 19.3 shows a screen with one selected object.

 To make a rectangle to select multiple objects, you left-click and drag the mouse (while holding the button down).

Most of the editing tools leave items selected. Sometimes, when you've finished all your editing, you may want to deselect all the items you have selected. To do this, right-click in an empty spot. The tools that are most commonly used are the Move, Copy, Delete, and Rotate icons.

Moving Walls or Whole Rooms

To move a wall (or another object) from one spot to another, first select the ones you want to move. Then click and drag it around the screen. It's as simple as that.

For example, let's say that your layout has an office cubicle. You want to move the cubicle down a wall. Here's what you would do:

1. Use the selection tool to make a rectangle around everything in the cubicle (such as a desk, plant, partition, and wastebasket).
2. Click and drag the selection box.

GCS will move all the objects down and put them in the right spot, relative to where the partition meets the wall.

One problem you may encounter as you move objects is that the grid doesn't let you move them exactly where you want. One way to solve this is to make the grid spacing finer with grid snap. You can also turn grid snap off, but that might be undesirable when trying to match up walls. Of course, if you are just moving symmetrical objects, you don't really need the grid. If the grid is really preventing you from putting a wall just where you want it, the object snap feature should let you join walls perfectly, even with grid snap turned off.

Copying Groups of Objects

The Copy function is identical to the Move function, except that the original objects stay in their original positions. A copy is placed at the new position.

Erasing Groups of Objects

The Delete function does just what you'd expect. Select the objects you want to discard. Hit the Del button. All the objects that are selected are now gone forever.

Rotating Groups of Objects About a Point

The Rotate function is really fun to use. Select your objects and click Edit | Rotate. You can then choose from the various options.

Adjusting Altitude

The elevation adjustment tool also operates on selected objects. You can raise a whole cluster of objects by a specified amount, or you can move them all to a specified height. Although these two functions may sound the same, they aren't, as you'll see below.

Raising Objects by a Specified Amount

Let's say you want to raise a cluster of many objects up by 50. To do this:

1. Select all the objects and then click the View | Object Properties.
2. Enter 50 in the Z text box, and click the OK button.

This function moves each selected object 50 up from its initial height. Look at the upper right set of objects in Figure 19.4. As shown there, this function preserves differences in elevation among the objects that you raised.

To move the objects back down, you would perform the same steps, but you would enter an elevation of –50 cm. The negative number would move them back down.

Raising Objects to a Specified Height

This time, let's say you want to move a cluster of many objects *so that they end up at the same height,* no matter how they started out. To do this:

1. Click the Absolute button. This specifies that all objects will move to the height that you enter, no matter where they started.
2. Follow steps 1 and 2 from above.

This function moves each selected object to the *absolute height that you entered,* no matter what its original elevation was. Look at the lower right set of objects in Figure 19.4. As shown there, the objects are now at the same height, even though they didn't start out that way.

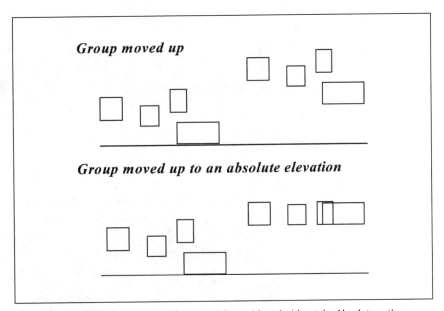

FIGURE 19.4   The difference between Elevation Adjust with and without the Absolute option checked.

Please note that the figure is not from GCS, but is only an illustration of the concept.

Changing a Wall Into a Door

To turn a wall into door, select the wall, and then choose the Object Properties dialog box. Next, select the Is a Door checkbox. You can actually make multiple doors at once by selecting several walls. Usually, though, you will want your doors to open in different directions, and to have different keys. We'll go into more detail on making doors later.

Editing Object Attributes

Each wall in your level has various attributes. These attributes control how the wall is drawn by the 3D game engine, and how the wall interacts with both the player and with enemies. To see a wall's attribute, select that wall. Then select Edit | Object Properties from the pull-down menu. You will see a list of settings for the wall (see Figure 19.5). These settings are discussed below. The default is for all these settings to be turned off.

 Warning! *It is not advisable to set the attributes for entire groups of selected objects. This practice leads to serious errors. Always select objects and set their attributes one at a time, and test your level frequently. While this makes level-building slower and more tedious, you will save yourself a lot of frustration and time in the long run.*

FIGURE 19.5 The Wall Settings dialog box.

Don't Draw Backsides

Each wall has a front and a back side. This is great when you are making a room within a room, where you want to see both sides of the wall. This makes level design easier, as discussed below.

However, having the 3D game engine do calculations to draw both sides of a wall can be a waste if the player would never see the back of the wall (the outer wall of a dungeon level, for instance). For walls where one side is never visible, the Don't Draw Backsides option speeds up the frame rate, since the 3D game engine doesn't have to draw the unseen side.

Pay attention to your walls, and to which side is their front and back. Since both sides are drawn by default, the walls will appear normal when you test your level. However, when you turn on the Don't Draw Backsides attribute for a particular wall, that wall will appear invisible when seen from the back, even though it's still there!

If you have set a wall to Don't Draw Backsides and it seems invisible, select that wall and use the Invert command (Ctrl+I) to flip it. Now the (visible) front of the wall will be facing you, so you can see it.

Warning! *Only use the Don't Draw Backsides attribute with walls! You will run into serious and critical errors if you use this feature with any other object.*

Don't Fade With Distance (Full Bright)

This attribute is used with lights, torches, glowing keys, and other objects that seem to have their own light sources. This attribute turns off fading and shading for the particular object that you selected. When you select this option, the object will always be bright.

Don't Draw if Far Away

You can speed up the frame rate of your level by setting this attribute for small objects. Why slow down your computer by having it do the calculations necessary to draw objects that are too far away for you to see anyway? This also applies to objects inside buildings or rooms that are way on the other side of your layout. Use this feature to tweak your finished level to make it run at the optimal frame rate by not drawing objects you can't see.

Can't Bump Into Object (Collision Detection Off)

By setting this attribute, you allow the player to pass through the object as if it were a ghost or hologram. This is great for making curtains, for example. This is a feature that you will need to use when making door frames; otherwise, players won't be able to get through your doorways. You might also want to use this feature to cut down the frustration level of players who get stuck in dense areas of foliage or in crowded rooms.

Set Wall Lighting by Angle

You can enhance the 3D look of your level with this feature. Walls with a north/south orientation are shaded differently than walls with an east/west orientation. You'll see that corners look especially good when you select this attribute.

Object Won't Show Up on Radar

The name for this attribute is a holdover from a previous attribute. Originally, GCS had a radar device, and this data was also used for wall-bumping and for detecting guards. The radar was not very popular, so it was removed when the Windows version came out. But the name lingers on. Now, this attribute simply controls whether enemies can walk through the specified wall or not. You have to use this feature when you make door frames that you want enemy characters to walk and shoot through.

Set FTC (Floor-To-Ceiling) on Solid Walls

This attribute tells the 3D game engine not to draw any object that would normally appear behind the selected wall. Use this for walls that extend from the floor to the ceiling and cannot be seen through. By preventing unneeded calculations, this function maximizes the frame rate.

For best performance, make sure you set this attribute on every *solid* (not windowed) wall that goes from floor to ceiling. However, be careful when using this feature. To prevent errors, use it only at the end, when you're done developing your level.

 Warning! Never use the Set FTC attribute with a windowed wall, fence, or any other wall panel that the player can see through, since everything behind the wall would then be invisible.

Adding Doors to Your Game

Knock and the door shall be open . . . actually you need the green key card.

Doors add so much to a game—interactivity, the feeling of suspense, the opportunity for exploration. For designers, doors are a great tool to work with. Think of the possibilities! *The player will need the green key card to get through this door, but the green key card is beyond a room full of sleeping guards, suspended over a pit of lava, and behind an electrical force field (hehehe-hehehehe, evil designer laugh).* Also, locked doors force players to search through your beautiful level and to make sure that they look carefully at every texture you created for keys.

Doors are extremely easy to make. In short, the whole process consists of selecting a normal wall section, clicking the Object Properties menu option in the Edit menu, and then setting a few parameters.

Look at your layout and decide where you might want to place a door. Select the existing piece of wall and then choose Edit | Object Properties. It doesn't have to look like a door. You are free to make "secret" doors out of any solid wall. You can make a secret door part of a continuous stone wall or a bookcase.

 You cannot make doors out of symmetrical objects like trees—only walls.

To make a door:

1. Place the object in which you want to have a door into your level.
2. Choose Selection mode by right-clicking the object, or by clicking the Selection tool icon.
3. Click once on the center of the door-to-be.
4. Choose Object Properties from the Edit menu.. A dialog box will display, with some text boxes and buttons (see Figure 19.6).Fill in the numbers as explained below, or use the defaults.
5. Use the buttons to set parameters, as explained below.
6. Click OK.

Your door should now be functional.

Door Parameters

Resistance to Forced Entry

This number determines how hard it is to open or break the door.

- **0:** Merely bumping the door breaks it, and it then stays open forever.
- **1:** The door can be opened by shooting or kicking. Increasing this number increases the difficulty of breaking the door.

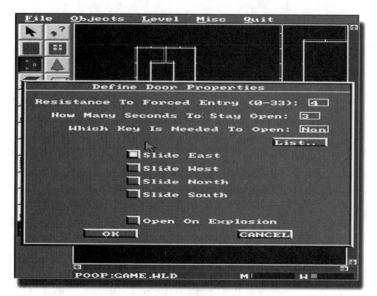

FIGURE 19.6 The Door Properties dialog box.

- **2–8:** If the player bumps the door while shooting his weapon, the door will be weakened. Repeated attacks will further weaken it.
- **9–31:** If the door is set to resistance 31, the door can only be damaged by jump-kicking it. This takes some practice by the player, but it is a fun action to master. Please note that on levels where you have a texture-mapped ceiling, the player cannot jump, for technical reasons. Therefore, it is best to leave doors like that for outside areas or for those indoor areas with high ceilings.
- **Higher than 31:** The door may as well be a wall. Doors with resistance set higher than 31 will not be affected by the player at all.

How Many Seconds to Stay Open

When the door is opened by enemies, or by the player, it stays open for a while before automatically closing. Doors will not close on the player. They will stay open until the player gets about 800 cm away. Set this number to determine how long the door stays open for enemies.

Which Key Is Needed to Open

This number selects which key will be needed to unlock the door. The player must have this key in his inventory to get through. If the player does not have the right key, an icon of the needed key will show up in an inventory window on the game play screen. The keys are coded by color.

Warning! If you have changed the default inventory item pictures, these colors might not be accurate. If you modify the picture images for the keys, it is up to you to keep track of what color keys you have modified.

Open on Explosion

Checkmark this box to make the door open if an explosion from a hand grenade, or another source, occurs close to it.

Tips for Placing Doors

Door Frames

You need to set certain object attributes to make your door frames operate properly. To do this:

1. Select the wall your door frame is on.
2. Select the Edit | Object Properties .
3. Click the Can't Bump into Object button. This allows the player to pass through the wall the door frame is on.
4. Click the Object Won't Show up on Radar button. This allows enemy characters to pass through the doors. It also allows enemy characters to shoot through the doorways.
5. Select the Don't Draw Backsides option. This will help with 3D game engine performance. But remember that if you ever reverse the wall object that contains this door, you will need to go back to the Level Editor and flip the wall so the door frame is visible.

How to Avoid Graphical Problems with Doors

The normal door movement is to slide sideways, into the wall on either side of it. However, this can cause problems if you aren't careful. When the door and the artwork slide to the left or right, the wall section that is moving does not stop at the door frame. It remains the same size and will pass through space and walls without discretion. In other words, the wall/door panel comes out through the side of a wall when it opens. You, as game designer, are responsible for making sure that the door panel is hidden when it slides sideways.

The easiest way to deal with doors is to put them in hallways. Make sure that the hallway has some inaccessible space on the side the door panel slides into (see Figure 19.7). Otherwise, the player may be in a room at a time when an enemy opens the door, and the door panel will slide through the supposedly solid wall of the room and ruin the atmosphere of the game.

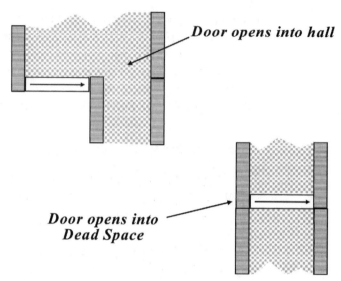

FIGURE 19.7   The proper and improper placement of a sliding door.

Another problem that can frequently occur is that the door slides out along another wall panel lengthwise and can be partially seen through the wall it is in. Here, the door and the wall panel are exactly overlaid in the 3D world and are fighting to be displayed, since they are both in the same location. The graphics then break down, and you will see a shimmering mess of vertical strips.

To avoid this, recess your door into a door frame a little bit. By *door frame*, we mean that you build a square of dead space on either side of the door. Then, place your door at the entranceway. However, if you set the object to be a door, and leave it here, you will run into the same effect described above. Offset the door 200 cm, so it will not be aligned with any other walls when the panel opens.

Please note that the snap-to-grid feature will make this offsetting impossible if the grid is set to the standard 400 cm. To solve this problem, lower the resolution of the grid or turn the snap-to-grid feature off:

1. Click the Grid tool and change the grid setting to 200 cm.
2. Select the door with the Selection tool, and click the Move icon.
3. Move the door one 200 cm grid line back, so that the door is now centered in the frame.

Now when the door opens, the panel will slide safely into the dead space. Of course, you can set your grid spacing to as little as 50 cm to inset the door just enough to keep the "scalloping" from occurring. It's best to be zoomed in before setting your grid to such a fine spacing.

If you make a door, but you can't go through it when you test your level, read the previous section on door frames. Likewise, if enemies won't walk through or shoot through your door, the section on door frames will explain the attributes that must be set to make the door function properly.

Putting Enemy Characters in Your Game

No 3D action game is complete without enemies. You can place up to 32 enemies in a level. Placing them is as easy as placing trees, but with more options.

To place an enemy:

1. Click Default Enemy Set in the Level menu. Pick one of the available options.
2. Next, Choose the settings that you want for the guard by choosing Enemy Orders/Params in the Edit menu. It displays a box shown in Figure 19.8. These settings are discussed below.
3. Click OK.

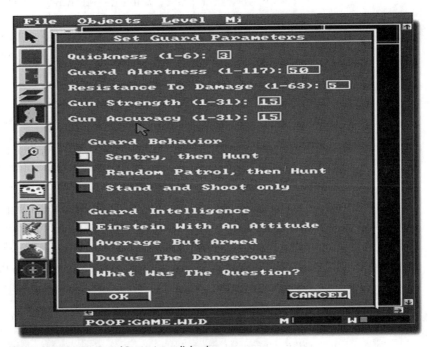

FIGURE 19.8 The Set Guard Parameters dialog box.

First, you must determine the properties of the enemy units. The following parameters adjust their strength and behavior:

- **Quickness**. This property determines the quickness of the enemy's movements.
- **Step Size**. This property determines how fast the enemy moves, by adjusting the distance traveled in each walking step.
- **Resistance to Damage**. This property sets how much damage the enemy can sustain before succumbing.
- **Gun Strength**. This property controls how much damage is inflicted on the player when the enemy strikes or fires upon the player.
- **Gun Accuracy**. This property controls how often the enemy will hit the player with his weapon.
- **Range**. This property sets how close an enemy must be before his attacks harm the player.

Guard Behavior

- Sentry, then Hunt: The enemy stands still until he sees the player, then chases after the player in attack mode.
- Random Patrol, then Hunt: The enemy walks about at random and then chases the player when he sees him.
- Stand and Shoot only: The enemy stands still. If he sees the player, he will remain in current position, but he will shoot.

Guard Intelligence

- Einstein With An Attitude: The enemy is highly alert.
- Average But Armed: The enemy is somewhat alert.
- Dufus The Dangerous: The enemy is not very alert.
- What Was The Question?: The enemy is so oblivious that he will almost never attack a non-shooting player.

The basic behavior of the enemies is always the same. They ignore the player until alarmed, and then they hunt the player down relentlessly. What causes them to become alarmed is a complex calculation.

What Alerts an Enemy?

Initially, all enemies are in a casual state. The only event which can cause enemies to become alarmed is seeing the player. However, not all enemies will become alarmed right away upon seeing the player. Whether or not they recognize the player as hostile depends on the intelligence setting, the viewing angle, and what the player is doing.

The most intelligent enemy units will recognize the player on sight from any angle and become alarmed. The least intelligent will not become alarmed even if the player is standing in front of him, blasting away. All enemy units will become alarmed if they take a hit from the player, however.

The view angle is very important in determining if an enemy will become alarmed. If the player is directly behind an enemy, the chance of alarm is much less. Also, for the most part, the enemies can't see through walls. If an enemy comes near a slain fellow enemy, it may become alerted.

The player's chance of being detected also depends on the player's actions. If the player is running around shooting weapons, he is much more likely to be spotted than if he is standing still.

All information about the player's running, jumping, or shooting is boiled down into one number, called the profile. The bigger the profile, the easier the player is to spot. Running or moving quickly will raise the profile. Shooting a weapon raises the profile drastically. Being wounded will also raise the profile.

How Enemies Behave

Enemies shoot when they are alarmed. If the player is out of range, enemies will not continue shooting, but they will snake toward the player. At the halfway point, enemies will stop and take at least one shot. If the player is within range, enemies will shoot repeatedly before venturing closer.

These steps will be repeated until the enemies are so close that there is no point in coming any closer. Then they will just stand and attack continuously.

If an enemy gets hit by the player's weapon, the enemy's shooting is interrupted for a moment. How much damage is done to the enemy depends on many factors. The range and accuracy of the player's weapon are very important. You can adjust these parameters by editing the text file *weapons.txt* in the game engine directory.

In addition, the resistance to damage setting determines how much damage an enemy unit absorbs when hit by the player's weapons. If the enemy is damaged enough, he will attempt a retreat. If he runs into a wall as he flees, he will turn and fight to the death.

If an enemy gets very far away from the player as it retreats, he may return to the non-alarmed mode, but this is very infrequent.

Once you have laid out the basics of a level and have run a test, you should be able to play in your own 3D first-person shooter. But it is not yet your own, really. That will come later, as we'll see.

CHAPTER REVIEW

In this chapter, we looked at many of the basics included with GGS. In the next chapter, we will look our look at GCS by concentrating on the paint program that comes with GCS (GCSPAINT). We will start learning how to use the tool that lets you customize and change the objects to make the game your own.

20 USING GCSPAINT AND ARTWORK IN YOUR GAME

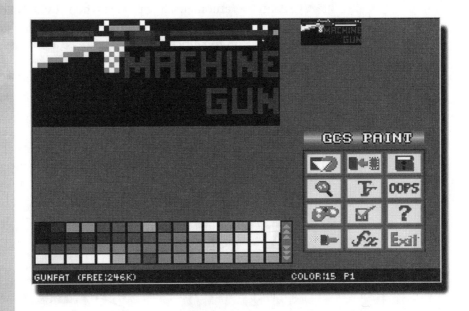

Wｅ will now depart the Level Editor for a while to look at the paint program that comes with GCS, and at some technical facts you will need to know about dealing with images. The paint program is called GCSPaint. With GCSPaint, you can import and edit images for use in the Level Editor and your game. We will look at GCSPaint in greater detail toward the end of this chapter.

 This chapter covers the use of GCSPaint, which is included with the GCS package. You should probably use a more advanced tool such as Paint Shop Pro if you find yourself needing more features. Additionally, much of the GCSPaint refers to the older versions of GCS that were DOS-based. This information has been left in the chapter but can be ignored if necessary.

GCSPaint was automatically installed when you installed GCS. You can access it from the Level Editor, as shown in Figure 20.1, or you can run it by finding the icon to launch it from Windows, as discussed below.

 There are two different color depths we will be discussing in GCS. One is the color depth of the original artwork. In GCS, all the artwork for your game must be in 256-color VGA files (we discuss making the VGA file later).

You can also run the game engine with the color depth of your system set to 16-bit or 24-bit color. Although all the artwork on the walls and floors is 256-color, the fading to black with distance requires thousands of

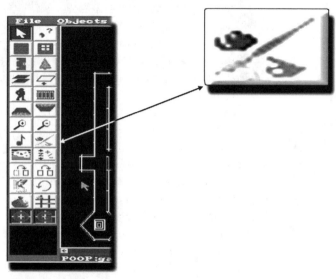

FIGURE 20.1 The icon in the Level Editor to launch GCSPaint.

colors to represent the continuous fade to black. Thus, there is a graphical advantage to using a 16-bit or 24-bit color video mode, even though all the original artwork is 256-color. This is because the game engine takes every color—pure red, for example—and then creates hundreds of colors from it to fade to black. So to fade red (RGB 255,0,0) to black (RGB 0,0,0), the game engine must display colors such as the following:

RGB 255,0,0

RGB 254,0,0

RGB 253,0,0

RGB 252,0,0

Notice that the amount of red decreases as the color approaches black.

MEMORY AND IMAGE RESOLUTION CONCERNS

We will look at GCSPaint in greater detail toward the end of this chapter. Right now, we will look at some of the technical aspects.

Earlier, we mentioned that each pixel of a 256-color piece of artwork takes up one pixel's worth of RAM. Each pixel can take 1, 2, or 4 bytes of texture RAM, depending on the video mode that a user has chosen.

- 256-color mode requires 1 byte per pixel of storage.
- 16-bit color requires 2 bytes per pixel of storage.
- 24- or 32-bit color requires 4 bytes per pixel of storage.

Therefore, a 64 × 64 picture for a wall section would take 4,096 (4K) pixels. In 16-color mode, this would take up 8,192 bytes of texture RAM. This means that if you wanted to make a game with no weapons, inventory items, or enemies, you could probably have 290 different wall images in your levels. This is because 290 8K wall panels will use up approximately 2.3 megabytes.

In your real game, you will, of course, want inventory items, enemy characters, trees, and weapons. This all takes up space. In a given GCS game level, you will most likely have at least 20 or 30 unique wall sections. You can see that managing your resources is important.

Let's say you wanted high-resolution artwork for your wall panels. The engine can't take any image that has a dimension bigger than 256. The largest image that could work is 256 × 256. This image contains 65,536 pixels, or 16 times more than our 64 × 64 image. This means 16 times fewer unique art elements for the wall panels in your levels.

In practice, you should never go higher than 128 × 128 for most games, but with the speed of computers today, you may want to push the limit. Just be aware of how the game engine works, and what the limit is, so you don't waste time creating a game that no one can play.

GETTING IMAGE FILES INTO THE 3D WORLD

As we've seen, in GCS, levels are made out of objects: trees, enemies, ammo, and walls are all objects. We've seen that walls are built panel by panel, just like modular construction. Erecting another wall is nearly the same as placing a tree or a health-pack. These objects are the 3D portion of the 3D world. Objects are geometry.

Almost every kind of object has an image file associated with it. These images are the artwork, called textures or texture maps, that is placed on the surfaces of the objects.

In GCS, all images must be VGR files. If you want to use *GIF*, *PCX*, or *BMP* images, load them into GCSPaint one by one, and save them in the VGR format.

 You don't need to know this, but for those of you who are curious, the VGA *file format is the format of MVPPAINT, which was written by David Johndrow years ago, and is the format GCS uses. A* VGR *file, which the engine uses, is simply a rotated* VGA *file. This is because of programming issues that cause images to draw faster in different situations, depending on how they are oriented.*

Images and Objects Together in a 3D World

The 3D world is empty at first. Other than the need for at least one wall, you can literally test an empty level and wander around in oblivion. As we've seen, in the Level Editor, you fill this void with walls and objects.

Each object has an image stretched over it by the 3D game engine. This stretching of the artwork or images you assign to the objects to fit the geometry is often called *texture-mapping a polygon*, or *adding art to your geometry*.

When you are using the 3D game editor, it is as if you are building a world constructed entirely of white wall panels. Each time you select a blank wall, you assign the image that will be stretched over it. Usually, the wall object is larger than the image, so to get the image to fit the wall, the game engine must stretch it out. As the image increases in size, you will start to see individual pixels. Because of this, the resulting image may or may not be acceptable.

You have to be aware that the game engine will stretch and compress images to fit the objects they are on. If you assign a square image of say, a person, to a very tall, thin wall, you will have a sideways-compressed image of a person on that wall. It would look like a fun-house mirror reflection.

So you can't just tell the game engine to put an image into the game. You must tell the game engine how big to stretch the image. For a brick wall section, this is fairly straightforward. Most typical walls are 400 × 400 units in size.

Bitmap Image Resolution vs. 3D World Size

Inside the virtual 3D game world, distances are measured in centimeters, but the unit of measure really doesn't have any impact on world design. The thing to remember is that in the 3D world, a square wall panel that is 400 units long, looks as if it were about 12 feet long. But the length of the wall has nothing to do with the resolution (or size) of the picture that the game engine paints on this 12 × 12 wall panel. We could stretch a 32 × 32 pixel image there (it would appear blocky, though), or we could put a 64 × 64 pixel image, or even a 104 × 64 image (see Figure 20.2).

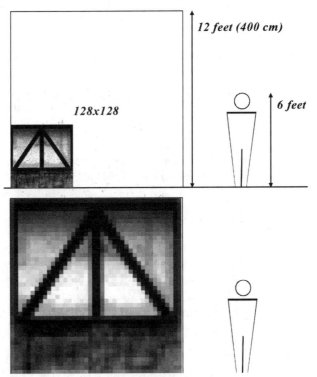

FIGURE 20.2   At the top, the average game wall is 400 cm long (about 12 feet); at the bottom, the typical 128 × 128 image stretched across it.

In the 3D world, the typical wall is 400 × 400 centimeters, and the art on it is usually 128 × 128 pixel size or smaller. The 128 × 128 pixel limit is for the image artwork only.

***Warning!** You can make the game engine stretch a tiny image, such as an 8 × 8 pixel image, across a huge 800 × 800 cm wall panel. However, it will look terrible (see the "Pixel Rip" section in Part 1). You may also cause a numerical overflow in the 3D calculations if you try to do a stretch or compression that is this extreme.*

Typical Dimensions

The typical wall panel is about 400 × 400 cm in size and has an image on it that is 64 × 64. In general, stick to the following dimensions:

- Images should have horizontal and vertical dimensions of about 32-104 pixels
- Wall dimensions should be between 50 and 600 units wide

You should not encounter critical errors or overflows with these safe dimensions. However, you might experience trouble when making very short, wide walls, say 800 × 50. So be careful when making steps or guardrails.

Although it doesn't affect the speed or smoothness of an image, having random wall dimensions like 477 × 613 cm makes it hard for you to match up the walls of adjacent rooms when laying out a level. On the other hand, it should be noted that there is no reason to keep all image sizes nice and neat, because images are stretched to the wall size and do not affect the layout of the level.

***Warning!** The above note does not apply to floor and ceiling panel artwork, which must be either 64 × 64, 128 × 128, or 256 × 256 pixels in size.*

Walls with Shapes and Holes—Windowed Walls

Walls are not limited to rectangular shapes. They can even have large cutouts. Examples are walls with windows, doors with rounded tops, a prison cell wall made of bars, or fences with gaps you can see through. All these are as easy to do as solid walls.

The trick is to make the cutouts "invisible." For example, if you want a brick wall with a big round hole in it, here's what to do:

1. Load the brick wall image into GCSPaint.
2. Set the painting color to black. This *must* be the first color in the palette, with the color number *0*. You can read the color numbers on

the bottom of the screen in GCSPaint. Choose your black from the upper left corner of the palette grid.

3. Use the Circle tool to paint a big solid black circle on the image of the wall.

When the game engine draws this kind of wall object, it stretches the image exactly like a solid textured wall. The only difference is that it never paints the color 0 (black). So whatever was behind the wall shows through (color transparency again).

So, Why Bother Having Two Types of Walls?

There are two reasons.

- You will want to be able to use black as a color on many occasions in your game, without it always being treated as clear.
- Windowed walls take more time to draw, because there are more computations involved. It is much more efficient to have two types of walls.

 You can use a lot of windowed walls in your levels. There is no real limit. In fact, you can define all your walls as windowed walls, but you might find that it will hurt the performance because the frames per second will drop off and the game will not appear as smooth.

Symmetrical Objects

Symmetrical objects are things like trees, floor lamps, and chairs. Unlike walls, which are stationary and can be looked at from various angles, symmetrical objects always look the same. The viewing direction does not matter, because they always rotate to face you. These stand-up objects are also called *anchored sprites* and will always turn to face the player (see Figure 20.3).

So to make a tree, you just need to draw a tree on a black background. The game engine draws the tree facing the player. It doesn't draw any of the black background between the leaves or around the outside edge of the image.

The important thing to remember about symmetrical objects is that they are stretched out over a rectangle, just like the images on the walls. The panels that these images are stretched onto have horizontal and vertical size in centimeters, just as walls do.

Just as with walls, be careful about holes in symmetrical objects. If you want to make your own shrub, don't try to have see-through areas be-

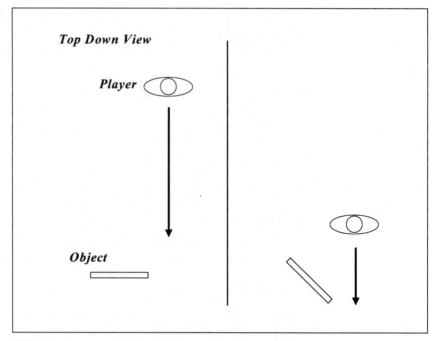

FIGURE 20.3 A symmetrical object will always rotate to face a player.

tween each leaf, or you may use too much of the program's resources. Keep the transparent (black) areas limited, and not very complex. With most reasonable trees, chairs, and other objects, you won't bump up against the program's limits.

Ceiling and Floor Images

Typically, you make floors from repeating tile patterns, which repeat in both the north-south and east-west directions.

Because your image will be repeated on the floor, the patterns you put on your image will be discontinuous as you go from one panel to the next. Sometimes you want this effect, such as when you are making floor tiles that look like square tiles. However, when you make a dirt floor, you don't want users to be able to see the tile boundaries. You'll need to blend the color on the top of the image with the pixels on the bottom, and blend the left with the right side. GCSPaint can handle this for you in the f/x submenu. You can smooth the edges of your image to improve their appearance in your 3D world.

VGA vs. VGR Image Files

As mentioned before, the 3D game engine can read two types of image files: *VGA* files and *VGR* files. Typically, all your walls and other objects are *VGR* files, and all the big things, like the backdrop, are *VGA* files.

The file types are so close in format that they are interchangeable for the most part, without a problem. For example, if you copied a 64 × 64 pixel file called *WALL.VGR* to *WALL.VGA*, you could still read it as a *VGA* with GCSPaint. However, you would notice that the image was rotated 90 degrees on your screen.

This explains what a *VGR* file is. It is just a rotated *VGA* image. The 3D game engine can read artwork more efficiently if the images are rotated 90 degrees. So the *VGR* file format has the pixel data rotated 90 degrees internally. You never know this when you bring up your images with GCSPaint, because GCSPaint puts them up on the screen right side up, although the image is on its side in the *VGR* file.

The only files that need to be rotated by the game engine are those that are in the 3D game play world. Pictures of the hit point guys (*HTPT0VGA*), the game play screen (*BACKDROPVGA*), and the weapons identification fat files (*GUNNONEVGA*) all are put on the screen as regular flat pictures, not in the 3D viewport. That is why they are *VGA* files.

The wall panel artwork, however, needs to be rotated 90 degrees. Although there's no need to do so, you *could* do this by saving your artwork as a *VGA* file. But if you do, make sure that you rotate the picture 90 degrees before you save it. Then rename the *VGA* file as a *VGR* file, so that GCS will let you import it.

There is really no reason to do this, except to illustrate the difference between *VGR* and *VGA* files. Just be aware of which type of file you need to load or save for which type of objects.

 An idiosyncrasy of GCSPaint is that it never asks you whether you want to save as VGR *or* VGA. *If you call GCSPaint from the icon in the GCS program, you will always be saving as* VGR, *although you can read both* VGR *and* VGA *files. On the other hand, if you quit GCS and run GCSPaint from the DOS command line, all images you save are written to* VGA *files. This is good, because some bigger files that you might like to edit, like* BACKDROP.VGA *or* BACKG40.VGA, *are too wide to be saved as* VGR *files. So to edit these large* VGA *image files, you need to exit GCS and run GCSPaint from the DOS command line.*

USING GCSPAINT

With GCSPaint, you don't need to hire an artist to create and edit graphics for your 3D project. GCSPaint is an image workshop that contains all the tools and special effects you'll need to create original artwork or to manipulate existing images. At the beginning of this chapter, we looked at how to start GCSPaint. If you are in the Level Editor, click the GCSPaint icon. The Level Editor will suspend operation and the GCSPaint screen will pop up.

The main menu for GCSPaint is located at the lower right side of the screen. The current palette of 256 colors is located at the lower left of the screen, as shown in Figure 20.4.

GCSPaint Help

Click the **?** icon for an introduction to GCS Paint's many features. The Help screens explain how to use each tool and special effect as you click the various buttons on the main menu.

The rest of this chapter discusses many of the features of GCSPaint. However, there isn't room to give as much detail as we'd like. For information not given below, use the Help feature, as outlined above.

Disk Commands

To access these commands, click the disk icon in the main menu. You will see the following options: Create New Image, Load Image, Save Image, Merge Image, and View as Tile. We will look at all these below.

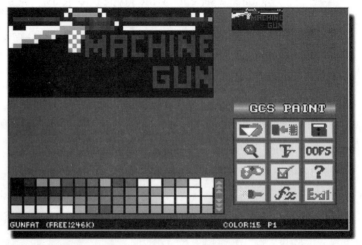

FIGURE 20.4 The GCSPaint main screen.

Create New Image

When you create a new image, a screen with a size box will appear. Drag the size box to the desired dimensions for your image. Please note the maximum image size in GCSPaint is 192 × 150. If you want to work on larger images, exit GCS and run GCSPaint from the DOS command line. Now you can work on full-screen 320 × 200 images.

Save Image

This function (obviously) lets you save images. GCSPaint saves images in the *VGR* format. Limit your file names to eight characters, because of the DOS naming convention. If you need to save your image in the *VGA* format, you will have to run GCSPaint from the DOS prompt (in a standard installation, this is *c:\gcsw\GCSPaint.exe*).

Loading GCSPaint from the DOS prompt lets you save large images like title screens and background images. However, always conserve memory by keeping your images small. Typical walls should be 64 × 64, and typical characters should be about 60 pixels tall. You can scale down large images with the Resize command. Try to maintain a reasonable balance between appearance and size when saving your images.

You should also avoid leaving a lot of unused black background in your images. Use the Move command to put your images in the upper left corner of the screen. Then use the Resize command to crop the excess black background.

 Warning! *Always test images that will later become shaped and symmetrical objects, to make sure that they don't have too many holes. Remember that black (color 0) is not drawn by the 3D game engine, making black areas transparent. Having too many see-through holes can sometimes cause critical errors when you test your levels.*

An easy way of testing for this pitfall is to use the color replacement feature to change areas drawn with color 0 to a bright color. Then you can clearly see how many invisible holes are in your image. Use color replacement again to refill those unintentional holes with a color other than color 0.

Merge Image

This command lets you merge (combine) two separate images. However, a problem arises when you try to merge your current image with an image that is larger. A warning will flash momentarily at the bottom of the screen, and the operation will fail. To merge the current image with a larger image, first use the Resize command, without scaling, to make your current image big enough to accommodate the image you are merging it with.

View as Tile

You will undoubtedly be working on wall, fence, or foliage artwork for your project. As mentioned earlier, this is usually done by repeating (tiling) a smaller image to fill a larger space. A common problem with using this kind of repeated or stacked artwork in your 3D world is that distracting patterns appear. Edges look harsh and ill-fitting. This command gives you a preview of what your image will look like when multiple copies of it are placed side by side or stacked one on top of each other in your 3D world.

Hidden Main Menu

Large images sometimes cover up the main menu so you can't see it. To view the hidden main menu, move your mouse pointer to where the main menu normally appears and press the space bar. After you select a command, the main menu disappears again and your image fills the whole screen.

Palette

As mentioned earlier, GCS works with one palette of 256 colors. All the images that you use in your game must use this palette. Each color has a number from 0 to 255.

The palette box displays 64 of the 256 colors on the lower portion of the screen. To see the other 192 colors, click the arrows on the right side of the palette box.

Select a Color

To select a color to work with, click that color in the palette box. You can also pick up a color from your image. To do this, move the mouse pointer to a pixel that has the color you want, and right-click.

Hidden Palette Box

Large images sometimes cover up the palette box so you can't see it. To view the hidden palette box, move your mouse pointer to where the palette box normally appears and press the space bar. When you select a color, the palette disappears again and your image fills the whole screen.

Load a Palette

Images do not always come with their own palettes. An image without a palette appears in wild colors when you load it, because it is drawn using a default palette. Remember that GCS uses only one palette of 256 colors at a time, so make sure that you are loading the same palette that will be used throughout your game.

Modify Palette

You can customize your own palette. You can change each individual color by adjusting its red, green, and blue components. You can also work on several colors at once with the trend option.

Match Palettes

GCSPaint gives you the option of matching the palettes of imported images to the palette currently in use. This is particularly helpful when you are using scanned images for your game. This feature enables you to make all kinds of artwork compatible with the palette that you are using for your game.

Save Palette

You should always save the palettes of images before you try to match them to the master palette of your game. If the palette-matching operation doesn't turn out well, you will want to reload the image with its original palette and try again.

 Warning! *If you don't first save the original palette, the original image may be ruined forever, and you won't have a second chance.*

Draw Tools

GCSPaint equips you with many powerful drawing tools: lines, rectangles, circles, ellipses, and polygons.

Interpolation

This command creates a morphing effect between two polygons. You can specify the number of intermediary shapes in the morph. You can also set the number of colors involved in the morph.

 Warning! Be aware that the operation will fail if original polygons have too many sides.

Settings

You can set preferences for GCSPaint. Choose this command to specify the brush size. You can even design brush patterns. In addition, you can set prompt delays to suit your needs. Memory settings are also adjustable.

Text

Two CHR files come with GCSPaint, although you can put public domain BGI files in the same directory as well. Select the size and style of the text you want to put in your image. If your text operation fails, it's probably because the text was too big for your image. Try again with smaller letters, a more compact font, or a larger image.

Color Tools

GCSPaint also comes with the following color manipulation tools:

Fill. You can fill areas of color with either solid colors or patterns.

Color Replacement. This tool lets you switch colors in your image. This is a big time-saver, since you don't have to add the new color to your image pixel by pixel.

Random Replacement. This handy tool lets you replace a percentage of a color in your image with a new color. This is especially useful when doing artwork that requires a haphazard pattern, such as dirt floors or carpeting.

Color Phase. This tool fills an area with a gradient. Pick a color and start the phase on that color.

Color Sunburst. This is similar to the Color Phase tool, except that it makes gradient fills in rounded areas. Pick a color, then start the sunburst on that color.

Special Effects

Outline

Trying to draw borders around areas by hand can be tedious at best. Select this tool, and your border is done in a flash! Your outline can be done with or without filled-in corners. Pick the color that you want to outline, then start the outline on that color.

Anti-Aliasing

This tool helps prevent the optical illusion that often occurs when two highly contrasting colors are placed directly next to each other. This tool also helps eliminate the sawtooth appearance of diagonal lines in low-resolution graphics.

Merge/Blend

This tool allows you to superimpose another image over your current image. You can control the transparency of the image that you are importing. Be sure that the image you are importing is smaller than your current image. If you try to import an image that is too big, the operation will fail.

Brighten/Darken

You can use this tool to brighten or darken lines or rectangles in your image.

 Warning! *Be sure to say* ***NO*** *to the prompt that asks you if you want the operation to affect the whole image and its palette. You never want to change the palette, since this would make the image incompatible with all the other images in your game.*

Smooth Image

This is one of the coolest special effects that GCSPaint has to offer. You can smooth all the pixels in your image, or you can apply the tool to the edges of your image. You can control the intensity of the operation: light, medium, heavy, and extremely blurred. Other stunning effects include negative image, grainy glass, and double image. The pixel wrap-around feature is especially useful when working on wall panels.

Contrast

There are times when you want to adjust the contrast of your image. This tool is just about as easy as fine-tuning the contrast button on your TV!

Rectangle Tools

These tools include Copy, Move, Overlay, and Erase. In addition, you can flip, rotate, and resize your image.

Zoom

There are times when you need to move in close to work on the details of your image. Zoom makes this possible. The best thing about this tool is that most of GCSPaint's features can be applied while in Zoom mode. It is also possible to save the zoomed in part of your image as a separate file.

Warning! *A prompt warns you not to save the zoomed section under the same file name as your original image, so you don't overwrite it.*

Oops

You can cancel just about any operation in GCSPaint by selecting the Oops icon on the main menu. Usually, prompts warn you that certain operations can't be undone. Another way to cancel an operation is to click your right mouse button.

CHAPTER REVIEW

Now that you understand the graphic formats, how they fit into the game, and how to use GCSPaint, we are ready to move on to the Advanced Features Editor, which is an extension of the DOS Level Editor in many ways. You will learn some of the additional effects and features of the Windows Engine to further tweak your game level.

21 THE EXTRA FEATURES EDITOR

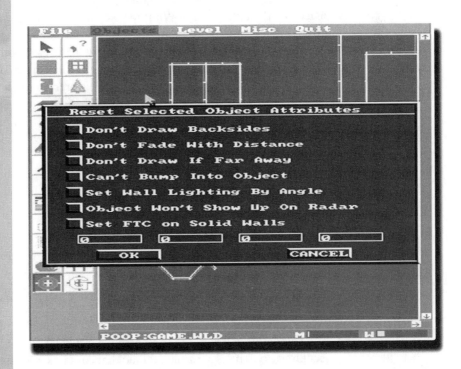

Why are we forced to do all this jumping around from DOS to Windows and now into the Extra Features Editor? First be aware that the game engine that runs the game, the game editor, and the paint program are all separate programs. To develop even one of these applications is quite a bit of work. So when the game engine was rewritten and upgraded, several concessions were made so that the original DOS editor would not have to be totally rewritten.

This chapter deals with the older versions of GCS that were not Windows based. Therefore, if you are using version 3 or above (the demo included is a Windows version 3), you can skip over this chapter.

The original GCS game engine was a DOS-based engine and was replaced by the aptly named Windows Replacement Engine. This new Windows engine was a great improvement over the original DOS-based engine, but to take advantage of the many features that have been added to extend the capabilities of the game engine, an intermediary editor had to be written. This was called the Extras Features Editor, since it edited the extra features of the new game engine. These features are obviously not available in the DOS editor, so we have to deal with them while we are out of the DOS editor and not yet into the Windows engine. This section shows you how to access these features.

THE GCS EXTRA FEATURES EDITOR

In addition to the improvements in graphics technology, there have also been some new features added to the game engine. These dramatically increase the visual impact of your game levels and also increase the flexibility you have in controlling the appearance of your games. You can use these new features by using a part of the Windows engine called the Extra Features Editor.

This editor will make changes to a file called *EXTRA??.TXT* in your project directory. This is a simple text file that contains information about floor and ceiling tiles, as well as lighting effects and other things.

EXTRA??.TXT is a file name where the question marks are replaced with a level number. In the real game, the file would probably be named something like *EXTRA001.TXT*.

Starting the Extra Features Editor

You will remember that when we test a level, the first thing we get is the dialog box in Windows with your name on it and the following three buttons at the bottom left: Test 3D World, Edit Extra Data, and Change Driver/mode (See Figure 21.1).

We already looked at two of the buttons in great detail. Here, we will look at the Edit Extra Data button that takes us to the EFE (Extra Features Editor).

To get started, click the Edit Extra Data button. The client area will now show a top view of your game level, similar to that of the DOS Level Editor. However, you will not be able to move or place walls or objects with this editor. They are on the screen just for reference. When the editor is running, you will be able to place floor and ceiling panels down and change various settings.

You can zoom in and out using the + and – keys on the keypad, and you can use the scroll bars to move around on the image. If the + and – keys do not appear to work, click the title of the main window. The title bar for that window should turn blue (or the active color), and the little dialog box's title bar should turn gray. Then, the + and – keys will function.

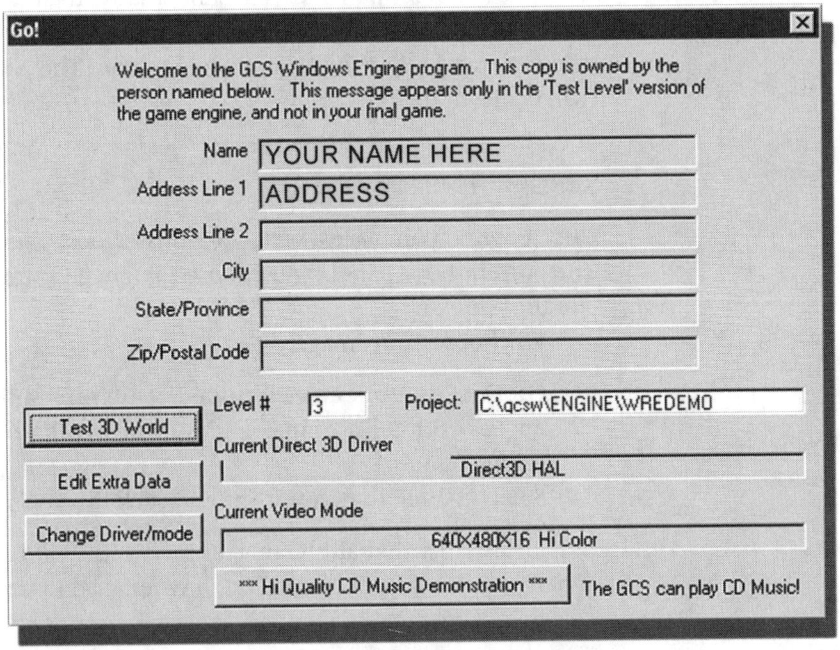

FIGURE 21.1   The dialog box in Windows with the Edit Extra Data button.

Placing Floor Panels

The floor and ceiling panels in the GCS are based on a 400 × 400 grid of squares. You can control the size of the panels you put down, but the size must be an even multiple of 400 units. The bitmap artwork that covers the panel will repeat over and over again to fill in panels that are larger than 400 units. It is more efficient to use large panels to fill in space, rather than many smaller panels.

To make a floor panel, click once on your level. A small 400 × 400 floor panel will be created in your level at the default height of 0. To make larger panels, click and hold down the mouse button, and then drag the mouse. The panel will grow or shrink to its maximum dimension as you move the mouse. When you let go, the panel will be created. When you enter the 3D world next time, your floor panel will be there.

 Warning! You must exit the Windows Engine and start it again in order for your changes to appear in the 3D world. If you go directly from the Extra Features Editor to the 3D world by using the Go menu item, your most recent changes will not appear in the 3D world even though you have saved your changes.

Deleting Floor Panels

To remove a floor panel, click a panel that you already placed. An "X" will appear in the middle of the panel. It is now selected. Then go to the Editor menu and select the Delete Panel option. The panel will disappear and will be deleted.

Choosing the Floor Image File

Just as when you place a wall, you must choose the artwork file to use for the current floor panel. You choose the image from a list before you create the panel.

To choose your image:

1. On the Editor menu, select the Set Texture option. A dialog box will appear with a list of image files from which you can choose floor or ceiling panels.
2. Select the file that you want and click the OK button.

Please note that all the images in this list will be loaded into memory when your level loads, regardless of whether they are actually used or not.

Adding to the List of Available Floor/Ceiling Textures

You can add images to the list of available textures. To do this:

1. Click the "Add more textures to list" button that is located below the list of available textures in the Set Texture dialog box. This will bring up another dialog box with two lists of image files. The list on the left side is a list of *VGA* files in the *FLCL_LIB* (Floor Ceiling Library) object library directory.
2. To look at the available files without selecting them, click on each file that you want to see. As you do, the preview window in the center of the dialog box shows you what the artwork looks like.
3. When you find a piece of artwork that you would like to add to the level's floor or ceilings, click the arrow underneath the preview picture. This will add the image to the level.

You can add more images if you like. You can also remove images from the right-hand list with the button below the list (see Figure 21.2).

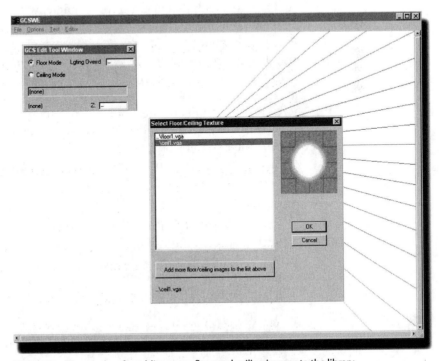

FIGURE 21.2   The window for adding more floor and ceiling images to the library.

There is a quirk of the EFE that requires you to save your changes and exit GCSWE after making changes to this list. When you return to the EFE again, the list will be updated with your changes.

Making Ceiling Panels

Making ceiling panels is the same process as making floor panels. It is just a matter of switching from Floor Mode to Ceiling Mode. The Editor menu has two items labeled Floor Mode and Ceiling Mode. To place ceiling panels, click Ceiling Mode. When that is done, the level will be redrawn without the floor panels, and you will be ready to place ceiling tiles. When you make them, they will be created at a default height of 400 units above 0.

Floor panels will not be drawn on the screen at all when you are in Ceiling Mode.

Gray and White Panels

You will notice that some panels in the drawing are white and some are gray. The panels that are the same texture as the current drawing texture are white. The panels that have a different texture than the currently selected texture are drawn in gray. For example, when you use the Set Texture menu item to set the current texture to *Floor1.vga*, all the panels that are already in your level that are *Floor1.vga* panels will turn white, and all those that are from another file will turn gray (see Figure 21.3).

Another way to change the Floor/Ceiling Mode is to use the modeless dialog box that is constantly on the screen when you are using the EFE. There are two option buttons, called Floor Mode and Ceiling Mode. Click these buttons to switch between Floor and Ceiling Modes. See Figure 21.4 for the modeless dialog box.

This dialog box is useful in other ways, also. You can use it to get information about a floor panel:

1. Click a floor panel to select it. An "X" will appear on the panel. Notice that the name of the image file is now in the dialog box, and the height appears in the Z box.
2. To select multiple panels, click several floor panels, one at a time. If all the panels you select have the same height, the Z box will contain the height. Otherwise, it will indicate "Various."

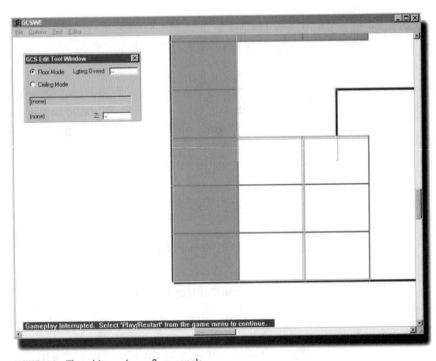

FIGURE 21.3   The white and gray floor panels.

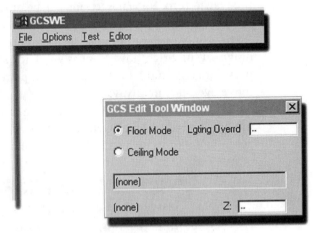

FIGURE 21.4   The modeless dialog box for switching between Floor and Ceiling modes.

Adjusting the Height of Floor or Ceiling Panels

You can adjust the height of a floor or ceiling panel. To do so:

1. Select the panel (or panels).
2. In the Z box of the GCS Edit Tool window, type in a new height. All the panels you have selected will move to the specified height.
3. To deselect the panels after you change the height, right-click anywhere on the layout. All the selected panels will be de-selected.

Level Settings

Each game level can have its own settings. You can make changes in the dialog box shown in Figure 21.5. Then, select Save Extra from the Editor menu. Your settings will stay set.

Fade Start Distance and Total Darkness Distance

If you wish, you can have the walls and floors fade to black as they recede from the viewport. The walls will be shown at maximum brightness until they are at a distance from the observer equal to the Fade Start Distance. This is in regular GCS units, where one typical wall section is 400 units. Total Darkness Distance is the distance where the brightness has faded all the way to zero. No wall sections will be drawn that are entirely darkened.

For example, say the Fade Start Distance is set to 1,000 units. Now say there is only one wall in your level. If you are close to the wall, it will be drawn at full brightness. Now as you back away, it will stay at full brightness until it is 1,000 units away; at that point it, will start to darken as you move even farther away.

Now assume the Fade End Distance is set to 3,000 units. If you keep moving away from that wall section, it will continue to darken until you get to 3,000 units away and it is faded all the way to black.

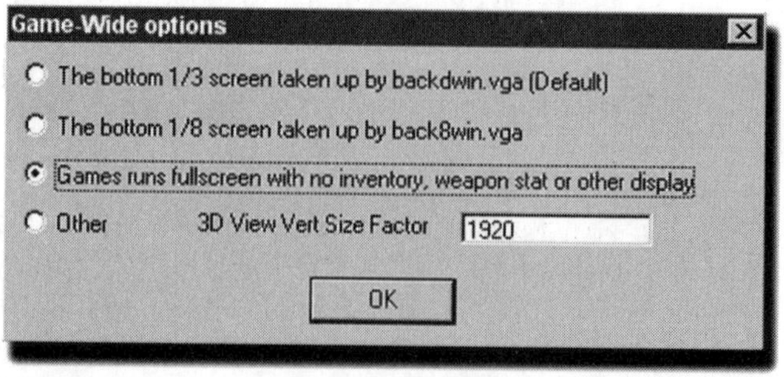

FIGURE 21.5 The Level Options & Stats dialog box.

Sometimes you want to set the Fade Start Distance to a negative value. This will cause a wall to be somewhat faded, even when you are right up against it. This is desirable when using special lighting effects, because otherwise, the lighting effects wash out when you get close.

For the fading with distance to work, the check box called "Fade to blk with distance" must be checked. However, even if it is NOT checked, the Fade Start Distance and Total Darkness Distance options do still set the Zero Point darkness. If you want all the walls to be at maximum brightness, make sure you make the Fade Start Distance a positive value.

Wall Fade Code 0 Point

The Wall Fade Code 0 point option sets the zero point for walls that have lighting overrides. The EFE will set lighting overrides according to the section on lighting effects. You can change the bias on lighting effects globally with this value.

Other Level Options

Fade Lights with Distance

The Fade Lights with Distance option lets you choose whether or not to have lighting effects diminish with distance. Sometimes this would be desirable when you don't want faraway lights to "show through" when surrounding walls are not drawn because they have faded to pure blackness. If this is not an issue, leave this option off for better realism.

Use Zbuffer on Floors

If you plan on having floors and ceiling panels at varying heights, you must turn this option on, even though it will hurt animation speed performance. If all your floor and ceiling panels are the same height, you can get a performance boost by turning this option off for the current level.

Background Options

Red, Green, and Blue

The boxes in the Background section of Figure 21.5 set the color of the background of the 3D viewport. This is the color that shows through between the gaps of the walls and floor panels. You can set this color using the RGB numerical mixtures we talked about previously.

Most of the time, you will want the background of the 3D world to be black, which would be the following settings:

Black = R0, G0, B0

White = R255, G255, B255

Dark Blue = R0, G0, B64

Horizon Texture

You have the option of using a horizon texture bitmap. This could be a wide mountain scene that moves as you turn in the 3D world. It is drawn behind all walls and objects and looks like it is far away because of its movement. This movement is called *parallax movement.*

The image must be a 256-Color *VGA* file. It is usually a very large one, maybe 1,024 pixels wide or larger.

The XSCL and YSCL boxes let you stretch the horizon texture horizontally and vertically. The left/right speed lets you fine-tune how much it moves when you turn in the 3D world. You'll need to experiment by by trial and error to get the speed right, so that the horizon does not appear to spin faster than the walls in your 3D world.

The same goes for the up/down speed, which is for when the user uses the A or Z keys to look up or down.

Setting Game-Wide Options

The dialog box shown in Figure 21.6 lets you change settings that affect the whole game, not just one level. At present, there is only one option, as shown in Figure 21.6.

3D View Verti Size Factor

Originally, a full third of the screen was covered in the DOS GCS game engine. Here you can choose the amount of the screen, as n/1920ths. This means that if you wanted the 3D view to use up half the vertical size of the screen, you would put the number 960, because 1920/2 = 960. If you want the whole screen to be used for the 3D view, put 1920 in here.

The VGA file called *backgwin.vga* is stretched into the remaining portion of the screen. You may change the size of *backgwin.vga* as desired. It is not fixed.

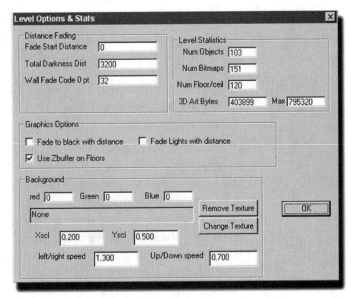

FIGURE 21.6   The Game-Wide Options dialog box.

Special Effects with the DOS Level Editor

Adding Light Sources

By adding light sources to your levels, you can make stunning visual effects. A light source is an invisible object in the 3D world that emits light in all directions. In GCS, you can make rectangular light sources of any size and put them anywhere in the 3D world. This is accomplished in the DOS GCS editor, as described below.

 A light source is really just a new kind of platform object. These are created using the Platform icon in the GCS Level Editor.

Light sources are flat rectangles, as viewed from the top view. The area within the rectangle is illuminated at maximum intensity. As you move away from the edges, the light will fall off linearly with distance when it gets outside the rectangle.

You will probably want to turn grid snap off when you make a light source. Usually, you do not want the edge of a light source to be on the edge of a wall; rather, you want your wall corners to be either decisively in the light rectangle, or in the fall-off area.

Adding lights to the 3D world is relatively easy using the DOS GCS editor. To add a light source:

1. Make a platform object.
2. Specify that it is *not* visible.
3. Select the Assign Value To Register option. Click OK.
4. A new dialog box will open. In the top box, it will ask you for the univ register and the value you want to assign. Enter a number between 192 and 223. For a light source of maximum brightness, enter 223.
5. You must also specify how far away from the platform's edges the light travels before fading out. After you decide on a fadeout distance, divide the desired range by 10, and put that number in the bottom box.

For example, if you want a light source to reach 1,100 units enter 110. The maximum range is either 1,280 units or 2,550 units, depending on if the DOS GCS editor can accept byte values greater than 127 or not.

You can also add negative light sources that suck light away. Any value less than 208 in the top box will suck light instead of adding it.

Warning! *The lighting effects are only calculated at the wall and floor panel corners. This means that to get smooth lighting effects, the range has to cover all four corners of a wall panel. Small lights that only include one corner of a wall panel will not give a very nice effect. Make your light sources large, unless you have small wall panels. There can be up to 32 light sources on a game level. More than 32 light sources will cause some of them to be nonfunctional.*

Lighting Effects

You can also modify the lighting on a wall panel. This can make a wall panel darker or lighter, or make it pulse or flash. To do this:

1. Place the wall in your level with the DOS Level Editor.
2. Use the Object menu to select Edit Attributes. This will bring up a dialog box with several buttons for selecting options for that wall object (seeFigure 21.7).
3. If you only have one wall section selected, there will be four red boxes along the bottom of the dialog box. To make this wall object have spe-

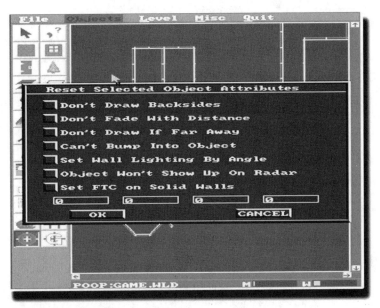

FIGURE 21.7   The Wall Options dialog box.

cial lighting effects, put a number between 1 and 63 in the *third* red box. A value of 1 means you want to darken the wall by the maximum amount. A value of 63 means you want to brighten it by the maximum amount.

As shown in Figure 21.5, the number that represents the zero point of illumination can be set in the Level Options & Stats dialog box. This is called the Wall Fade Code 0 Point setting. All lighting effect values greater than this number will lighten the wall section; all values below this number will darken the wall section.

For example, if the Wall Fade Code 0 Point is set to 48, any value greater than 48 that is placed in the third red box in Figure 21.7 will brighten the wall section. Values less than 48 will darken the wall section.

In addition, you can make a wall pulsate or flash intermittently. To do this, calculate a number based on a command code and an intensity value. Here's how:

1. Choose one of the following commands:
   - Command 2 Pulsate Phase 1
   - Command 3 Pulsate Phase 2
   - Command 4 Pulsate Phase 3
   - Command 5 Flash Intermittently

2. Multiply that command number by 32. Then add an intensity value from 1 to 31. Most of the time you would leave the intensity value at 31 for the maximum effect, but you can use lower numbers for milder effects.

Following are some examples of numbers to put in the third red box of a wall section:

- 63 for constant brightness added to a wall section's illumination
- 95 for pulsate effect using phase 1
- 127 for pulsate effect using phase 2
- 159 for pulsate effect using phase 3
- 191 for intermittent effect

Using Special Lighting Effects in Light Sources

You can also apply these pulsating and intermittent effects to lighting sources. Here's how:

1. First, make your light source, according to the instructions given above.
2. Select the platform object with the DOS Level Editor.
3. Open the Edit Attributes dialog box. Put a value in the fourth little red box. The value you enter should be calculated according to the previous section on wall section lighting.

 When applying these effects to a light source (platform object), make sure you put your number in the fourth (last) little red box, and not in the third, as you would for a wall section. If you put it in the wrong box, the lighting source will not work at all.

Using Cheat Keys in Your Game

GCS has five cheat functions you can invoke during a game, using the following codes:

- Kill all: Kills all enemies on a level
- Invincible: Turns on God mode
- Magic heal: Brings the player to 100% health
- Open doors: Opens all doors on the level for a few seconds
- Teleport n: Teleports the user to entry point #n

To use a cheat code:

1. Hold down the left Shift key.
2. Press the **c** key.
3. You will then be prompted to enter the cheat code.
4. After entering the cheat code, press Enter.

CHAPTER REVIEW

Now that you can take advantage of the special features in the Extra Features Editor, we are finally ready to make your game final. In the coming chapter, we will complete our 3D game.

CHAPTER

22

ASSEMBLING THE GCS GAME

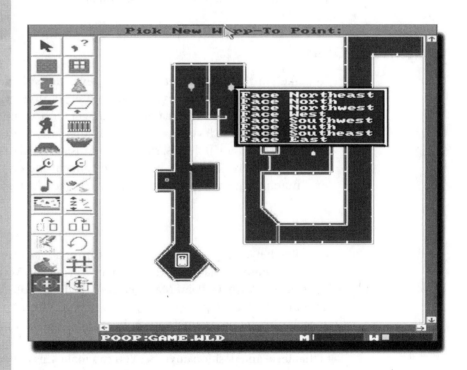

By now, you've learned how to lay out a 3D level, operate the paint program, and even enhance your level with the Extra Features Editor. Now you are ready to turn all those 3D levels into a game. The final step for all those levels in your project is to hook them all together with stairwells, transporters, or other devices. Then, you'll click Make Final to create the game.

Warning! It is very important to read this chapter carefully. If you don't do these steps just right, your final game will not function properly.

This chapter details creating levels with the DOS level editor. You can easily follow along even with the Windows editor (which is included on the CD-ROM) if you refer to the details in the chapters related to the editor.

CONNECTING THE LEVELS

To make your final game, each of your levels must have a unique level number. In general, it makes sense to set the starting level as level 0, the one next level 1, and so on. Later, you can get more complicated and have level 0 connected to levels 3, 5, and 10. In this case, there really isn't a sequential progression of levels, since the user is going all over the place. But for your first few games, it's best just to concentrate on having a unique level number for each level, and having a linear progression of levels.

Warp-To Points

Traveling between game levels is done through warp-to points. A warp-to point is merely a place where the player will appear. You set these points by using the Warp-To Point Manager from the Level pull-down menu. You can put as many warp-to points in a level as you like. You assign a name to each warp-to point after you set it. (see Figures 22.1 and 22.2.)

After you've defined a warp-to point, you can make the player travel to that level and position anytime. You can make this happen by using platforms, or by having an animated object execute the warp-to point command. Normally, the passageways between levels are done with a simple invisible platform placed around a stairwell wall piece. When the player walks inside the invisible boundary of the platform object, he is whisked to a different level and position.

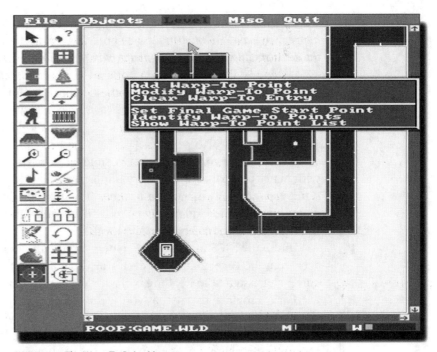

FIGURE 22.1 The Warp-To Point Manager.

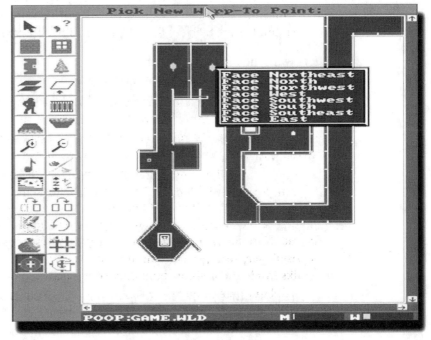

FIGURE 22.2 The Pick New Warp-To Point and direction selector.

The warp-to point is only a destination. It is the platform that makes the level switch happen. To make a connection between two levels, you must set a warp-to point in the destination level, AND also a platform in the original level.

Warning! *Warp-to points DO NOT work in test mode. All warp-to platforms or animated object commands will be ignored in test mode. They will work only in your final compiled game that you start with the GO.BAT batch file.*

As you make connections between levels, always keep track of them with pencil and paper. This is very important. Do not try to keep the level numbers and the warp-to point names in your head. Make a list of each of your level names and numbers.You will use the names and numbers to to assign connections between the levels.

Internally, GCS makes a table when you use the Warp-To Point Manager from the Level menu. For each warp-to point, GCS keeps track of the name you assigned to it, along with the level number and position.

For example, let's say that you want the user to start in level 0, walk up to a staircase, and then do a level switch to level 7. Assuming that you have already assigned a level number to each of your levels, you can go about setting that warp-to point. Here's how:

1. Open level 7 of your game (the level *to which* the player will go).
2. Click the Warp-to Point Manager menu choice in the Level menu.
3. Click Add, then click the spot where you want the player to appear.
4. Choose which direction the player should end up facing (north is toward the top of the screen).
5. Enter a reference name for this warp, and press the Enter key. Choose a descriptive name like "Back into the lobby from stairs," so you will know which warp-to point is what.

You will see a red dot in your level. This is the warp-to point. It is not an object in your 3D world. It is only a marker to show you that there is a warp-to point. If you zoom in, you will see that the dot has a spike sticking out, to show which direction you would be facing.

Because the warp-to point is not really a 3D object, the Box and Question Mark icon will not identify it. To see which warp-to point it is, bring up the Warp-To Point Manager and click Identify Warp-To.

Let's say that you've set the warp-to point at a lobby in level 7. That's where the player will appear when the warp occurs.

So now, you have set one warp-to point. To a functional passageway between levels, you have to specify where the player will warp *from*. In this case, we'll make a platform object in level 0 and place it in front of a staircase wall. Here's what to do:

1. Go to level 0.
2. Make the platform object, and make sure that the platform sticks out at least 150 cm from the wall.
3. When you make the platform, click the Warp-To box.
4. Click OK.
5. You will be given a list of warp-to points from which to choose. Select the one you just made.

You have now formed the connection between level 0 and level 7 of your game.

Warning! *Platforms can only do one function at a time, so only click the Warp-To button, and not any of the others. If you click more than one function for your platform, the platform might not work.*

You can make connections work both ways. This means that you can make the connection between level 0 and 7 be a two-way connection, so the user can come back through it. To do this, you do somewhat the reverse of what you did before. Just to review, will cover the process again in detail below.

First, make the warp-to point in level 0:

1. Open level 0
2. Click again on the Warp-To Point Manager from the Level menu.
3. Click Add, then click the spot where you want the player to appear.
4. Choose which direction the player should face.
5. Enter a reference name for this warp, and press Enter.

Now, make the platform in level 7:

1. Go to level 7.
2. Make the platform object, making sure it sticks out at least 150 cm. from any wall.
3. Click the Warp-to box.
4. Click OK.
5. In the list of warp-to points, choose the one you just made.

Warning! *A design challenge here is to make sure that you don't put the platform in level 7 that would make the user land in the exact same spot as where he is teleported in from level 0. This mistake causes an endless loop. The perplexed user bounces back and forth between the two levels indefinitely.*

Important Considerations

No Level Switches in Test Mode

The only way to test your inter-level connections is to click Make Final (which we will discuss in detail below). Then, exit GCS and run the game from the target directory. Level switch platforms and animated objects that give the level switch command will be ignored if you try out your levels in test mode.

Make Final Will NOT Work Unless You Have Specified a Game Start Position. To do this:

1. Bring up the Warp-To Point Manager.
2. Click the command to set the final Game Start Position. Don't confuse this with the Set Player Position command on the Level menu. That command is just for testing the 3D world.

After you specify and name the final Game Start Position, it will show up as a yellow dot with a spike. You can only have one Game Start Position. This initial starting point can be on any of your levels. The player does not have to start on level 0.

Using the Set Player Position Command

The Set Player Position command in the Level menu is only for using with the test command. This command does NOT set where the player starts in the final game—the position you set here is ignored in the final game. To set the starting position for the player in the final game, you MUST use the Set Final Game Start Point command from the Warp-To Point Manager Menu. This will set the location of the player when he starts up the final game using the GO.BAT batch file.

Make Final Will NOT Work Unless You Have Tested All Your Levels

Always use the Test Level command to test *all* you levels before you use the Make Final command. When you click Test Level, several files are created in your project directory. The Make Final feature uses these files to compile all your. *VGR* files and other files into compressed binary files. The upshot is that unless you have clicked Test Level for each level, the Make Final command will fail.

Any time that you make changes to any level in your project, you must test the level in the 3D world. Otherwise, when you click Make Final, your changes will not be reflected in the final product.

If you change the level number of a level using the Set Current Level Number command, you must click Test Level, enter the 3D world, and come back. Otherwise, that level will not be stored correctly. If you make a mistake and give two of your levels the same number, it will get confusing. Only one of the two levels will make it to the final game. The level that you tested last is included. Its twin is bypassed. Then in your final product, any warp-to points that were meant for the missing level would take the player to inappropriate spots, since the warp-to points weren't meant for that level.

When you click Make Final, only levels that have warp-to points assigned to them will be included in the final product. This makes sense, because if there is no way for the player to get to a level, there is no reason to include that level in the final product.

The Correct Sequence of Preparing for Make Final

To make sure you're ready to compile your game, follow these steps.

1. First go through all your levels and figure out where you want players to enter them.
2. Set the warp-to points, and write them down!
3. Then go through all the levels and put in the level-switching platforms.

Use your list to get the correct warp-to point names.

 Warning! *If you set a platform to a nonexistent warp-to point, you will get a critical error when you go over that platform in the final game.*

Don't forget to click Test Level after setting each warp-to point. Remember! If you don't test each level in the 3D world after changing it in any way, the changes don't get put into your final product!

Don't forget to set the final game starting point from the Warp-To Point Manager. If you forget, GCS will refuse to "Make Final."

When you're ready to compile your game, use the Make Final command. Here's how:

1. Open any of your game levels, and select Make Final from the File menu. The GCS game engine will start up, but instead of the normal dialog box, you'll see a list of all your levels.
2. In the list of all your levels, select the first one, so that it is highlighted in blue.
3. Click the Compile this Level button (see Figure 22.3).

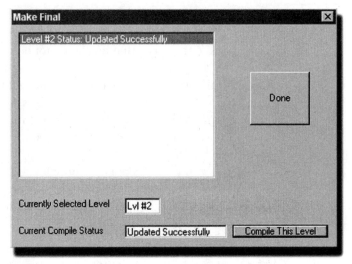

FIGURE 22.3 The Levels dialog box during the Make Final operation.

4. After the level is compiled, exit the game engine and go back to the Level Editor. Then repeat this process for your other levels.

When all your game levels have been "made final," your final game is ready for testing.

Trying Out Your Final Game

To try out your final product, exit GCS. Then change to the target game directory. In a normal installation, the target directory should be in the root of your hard drive and have the same name as your project. For example, if your project is named Blaster, and your GCS is installed on Drive C:, your final game target directory is named *C:\Blaster*.

To run your game, open a DOS Prompt box, change to your final game directory, and run the *GO.BAT* batch file.

You can run *GO.BAT* with or without command line options, as shown below:

GO.BAT Command Line Options

go	(for no sound)
go s1	(for sound; letter "s" and number 1, NOT letter "s" and letter "l")
go s1 j	(for sound and joystick control)

go sl m   (for sound and mouse control)

go sl m g   (for sound, mouse control, and God mode)

For these command line options, don't use slashes or dashes, as you may have done for other DOS applications.

You will notice that the game loads much faster from *GO.BAT* than from Test Level.

What to Do if There Are Problems

If *GO.BAT* doesn't run correctly, first make sure that you typed "sl," not "s" and the letter "l" (sl). This mistake is very common. As mentioned above, DON'T put slashes or dashes in front of the command line options, as you may have done for other DOS applications.

If the level-to-level connections aren't working, you can always redo them. Use the Box and Question Mark icon to tell you what each platform is set to do, and examine your warp-to points. You can overwrite their current values by erasing and replacing platforms, and using the Warp-To Point Manager to reset your warp-to points.

If you feel that your warp-to points are messed up beyond repair, or you are simply confused and want to start with a clean slate (because maybe you didn't write them down), exit GCS and delete the files WARP_TO.DAT *and* GAMESTRT.DAT. *Then, start putting your warp-to points in again from scratch.*

Warning! *If you remove a warp-to point, you must also remove any platforms that direct the player to the now-absent warp-to point. Warping to a deleted warp-to point can cause unexpected results, or a critical error.*

Common Problems in the Final Game

You might find it helpful to print the file *THEATERS.TXT* from your target *data* subdirectory. The first column is the warp-to point number. The third column is the level number. The next three numbers are the x, y, and z coordinates in the 3D world where the player should go to.

If weird things are going on such as that levels are missing in your final game, or you are appearing in totally unexpected places, you may have given two levels the same level number. GCS will not complain about this, but the final game will never work correctly if you do this. This will not normally generate critical errors, but it can make level switches go to unpredictable places.

Making an Installation Program for Your Final Game

ON THE CD

After you get the final game running the way you want on your system, you'll want to distribute the final product for others to try. To do this, we suggest you use Install Maker by Clickteam. It is on the CD-ROM in the back of the book. You should install it and follow the Wizard that will take you through the process of building a professional installation routine. Install Maker allows you to have custom bitmaps and README files, and to create install directories. Best of all, it allows you to create an uninstall routine.

Troubleshooting

What to Do if the Game Engine Won't Go Into the 3D World

First of all, to isolate your problem, always try the original and unchanged WREDEMO level (remember, we suggested you make a copy if you altered it). If that fails, then you know the problem isn't with the level itself; it must be with the driver or mode selection. If the DEMO levels work fine, but your level won't work, then the problem must be with your new level.

If the WREDEMO level will not run, how do they fail? Normally, what happens when you click the Enter 3D World button is that text messages will be flashing in the lower left-hand part of the screen as the game engine loads the various components of your game level. When all the data is complete, the video should go blank for a split second while it changes to the new full screen mode. Then the game engine should start.

If a level fails before the screen goes blank, the problem is probably with the installation or something that is preventing the level data from loading correctly. If there is a critical error or a set error, write the numbers down and contact Pie in the Sky at their Web site for assistance. Also, look in the ENGINE *directory for a file called* error.txt, *which is created when an error occurs, and send that along.*

If the error or crash occurs directly after the screen goes blank, it could be a DirectX graphics type of error. If this is the case, switching the DirectDraw Device, the D3D Device, or the video mode might solve the problem. The absolute most reliable settings would be using a DD Device of Display, a D3D Device of RAMP, and a video mode of 320 × 200 × 16. To change to these settings, start the game engine, but click the Change Device/Mode button instead of the Enter 3D World button. Then use the items on the File menu to change your settings to the following:

DD Device: Display	Use Select DD Device from File menu to set this.
D3D Device: RAMP	Use Select D3D Device from File menu to set this.
Display Mode: 320 × 200 × 16 Hi Color	Use Choose Screen Size/Mode from File menu to set this.

If this still fails, contact the Pie in the Sky Web site (www.pieskysoft) for assistance. Perhaps your problem is one experienced by others, and there is already a solution on the site.

If these settings DO work, you'll have to do some experimentation to find out whether the problem was the video mode you had chosen, or the HAL driver, or which setting was causing the problem. Make sure you do your testing on the unmodified WREDEMO level, since that is known to be a functioning game level.

Debugging Your Game Level

If the WREDEMO levels work fine in the 3D world, but a level does not, first find out if all your levels fail, or just one in particular. If you only have one level so far in your project, try adding a new level with just a few walls in it which are close to the start position. Try setting the *objdef* library to *Basiclib*, the active guard to *def_enem*, and the level number to 30 (or something you aren't using in any other level). If the WREDEMO levels test fine, but even this very simple level will not run in the GCS Windows Engine, there must be something wrong with the whole project. Write down any error numbers and print out the *error.txt* file which is created in the *ENGINE* directory when the game gets an unrecoverable error. Contact Pie in the Sky at their Web site for assistance, or check at www.pieskysoft.com to see if others have experienced your problem. There may be a solution there for you.

Troubleshooting Questions and Answers

1. I put platforms down in my level, and warp-to points, but it never works. I go there and stand right in the middle of the platform, but nothing happens.

Level-switching cannot occur when you are testing an individual level. You need to "make final," and then run the final game.

Also, make sure that you use the Test Level command after setting any platform. If you forget to test your level after making changes, the platform will not actually be in your final game. Use the **?** icon to check that your platforms are in the right place and are set correctly. If in doubt, delete your platform and replace it with a new one, but don't forget to click Test Level before making final again!

2. How do I put more than one kind of enemy on a level?

The Level Editor assumes you will have just one type of enemy on your game level. However, you may have several different types of enemies on your level. To add more types of enemies, you will need to use the Extra Features Editor and not the DOS editor.

3. When I save my files in GCSPaint, they don't get saved, or they are saved as the wrong file type.

There are a few different things that could be happening. First, if you want to save your images as *VGR* files, you must start GCSPaint from the icon that is on the GCS Layout Editor screen.

If you start the paint program by typing "GCSPaint," your files will be saved as *VGA* files.

If you save your *VGR* file in the proper directory, it may not show up in your Import list in the Library Manager dialog box. Be advised that although things that you add to the list usually appear at the end, this is not always so. This is dependent upon DOS file order on the hard drives, which is unpredictable. Look through the list carefully, and you can probably find your image.

4. How do I change the damage indicator guy for my game?

Exit GCS and bring up GCSPaint from the command line. You need to load the *VGA* file called *htpt.vga* from your project directory. You will see that this image file is a tiled repeat of the damage indicator, with varying degrees of damage in each picture. Feel free to change your damage images.

 Warning! *Do not try to change the dimensions of the little damage boxes, or the size of the whole* htpt.vga *image. If you do, the game engine may crash.*

5. Why does my sound not work in my final game? Why doesn't my joystick work?

The joystick cannot be used when you are testing levels. You need to add "s1" to the go command line ("go s1"). Make sure you use the number "1" and not the letter "l" in your "s1" option!

You must also add a "j" if you want joystick support. When you actually finish your game, you will probably want to use GCSMENU to create a way for your customers to choose sound on/off, joystick on/off, etc.

6. When I try to define written text for memos and animated objects to use, it never works.

You need to edit the file *pstr.txt* in your project directory, and then you must run the program *pstr.exe* on it to actually make your new text messages available for your game. The Help file on Text Messages explains how to do this. Be very careful not to ignore the two periods and the backslash when you type PSTR! Also, make sure you understand how to give each message in your *pstr.txt* file a different number when you are editing the file.

7. When I try to load my *.GIF*, *.PCX*, or *.BMP* file into GCSPaint, the screen flashes, and it refuses to load my picture.

The most common cause of this is that you are trying to import a picture that has too many pixels in it. The largest image that GCSPaint can handle is 200 × 200 pixels in size. If an image is more than 200 pixels high OR 200 pixels wide, the image will refuse to load. Please note that 200 × 200 is too large for a practical object in the GCS game.

If you are absolutely sure that your image is small enough in number of pixels, but the image is still being rejected, then perhaps your *.PCX* or *.BMP* file is not the right type. Since the GCS artwork must be 256-color, all *.PCX* or *.BMP* files that you import must be 256-color also. This means that 16-color files are not accepted, and neither are 16-million-color versions of these files.

8 Why is the computer beeping at me whenever I do anything with my level?

If you have added too much artwork to your level, memory may be full. See the explanation of the M and W meters in the previous chapters. And finally . . .

A Legal Notice of What You May Distribute

When you use the Make Final command, GCS makes a directory with the same name as your project. You may distribute all the files in this directory and the *data* subdirectory. These files comprise your game. The *.EXE* files in that directory are copyrighted by Pie in the Sky Software, but you have implicit permission to distribute them in unmodified form. The same goes for all the other files that the unmodified GCS puts in that directory when you "make final."

When the user installs the game files, make sure that the directory structure is preserved. This means that the *Data* subdirectory and its contents must be contained within the main game directory when the user types the GO.BAT command line to start the game.

CHAPTER REVIEW

In this chapter, we put together a final GCS game and learned how to run it. Now that we have worked through a complete game in the GCS, we'll turn our attention to a new development tool. In the next chapter, we'll go through the installation of the 3D Gamemaker and then learn to use it in the chapter after that.

23 INTRODUCTION TO THE 3D GAMEMAKER

O f all of tools we have looked at, perhaps none is quite as easy to use as the 3D Gamemaker. In this chapter we'll take a quick look at the installation of the software. In the next chapter, we'll use the 3D Gamemaker to build a complete game in a matter of minutes.

INSTALLATION

To install 3D Gamemaker:

1. Put the CD-ROM that accompanies the book into your CD-ROM drive.
2. Double-click My Computer and then the letter of your CD-ROM drive.
3. Double-click the *Applications* directory, then the *3DGamemaker* directory. Then double-click on the installation program called setup.exe. You'll see the screen shown in Figure 23.1.

FIGURE 23.1 The opening screen for installation.

FIGURE 23.2 The install area is highlighted.

FIGURE 23.3   The install wizard walks you through the steps.

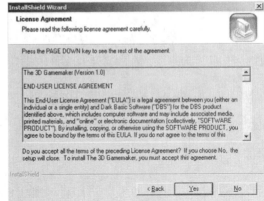

FIGURE 23.4   3D Gamemaker's License Agreement.

4. From the opening screen, put your mouse over the "Install the 3D Gamemaker" area. It will light up similarly to Figure 23.2.

5. When the area is highlighted, click the left mouse button to begin installing the 3D Gamemaker. This will display another window (see Figure 23.3).

6. Click the Next button to display the License Agreement, a portion of which can be seen in Figure 23.4.

7. Read through the License Agreement and then click Yes to continue the installation. Then choose Typical Installation from the window that is displayed next (see Figure 23.5).

8. The next screen, seen in Figure 23.6, asks you to choose the installation directory. Unless you have a reason to choose another, leave the default setting unchanged. Click Next to go to the next screen.

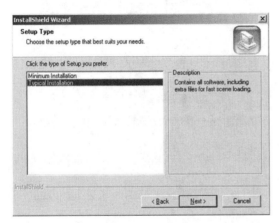

FIGURE 23.5   Choose the Typical Installation.

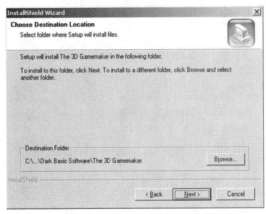

FIGURE 23.6   Choose an installation directory.

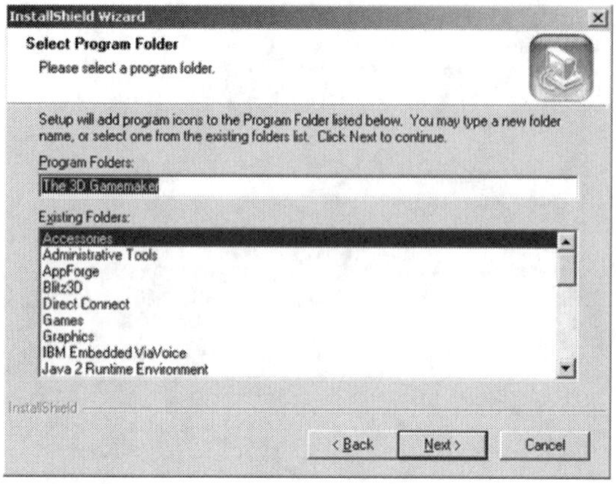

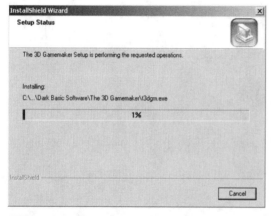

FIGURE 23.7 Choose a Program Group.

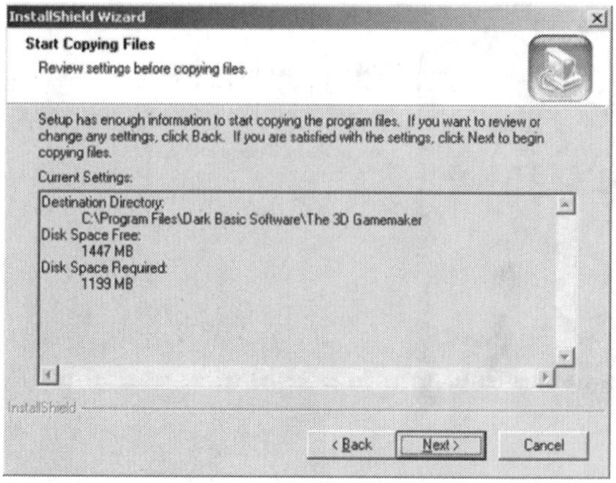

FIGURE 23.8 Review your settings and then click Next.

9. You'll see a a window that resembles Figure 23.7. Unless you have a reason to choose another program folder, leave the default setting unchanged. Click Next to go to the next screen.

10. The install wizard will display all the settings you have picked. You should review these settings (the defaults can be seen in Figure 23.8). If everything is OK, click Next. If not, you can go back and make the changes.

    The files will begin copying. You will see a window like Figure 23.9 that displays the progress of the installation.

11. After the files have finished copying, you are given an option of creating an icon on your desktop (see Figure 23.10). If you create an icon, you will have easy access to the 3D Gamemaker. Otherwise, you can

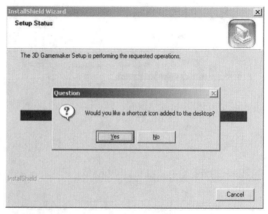

FIGURE 23.9 The files are copied to your computer.

FIGURE 23.10 You can add a shortcut to Gamemaker on your desktop.

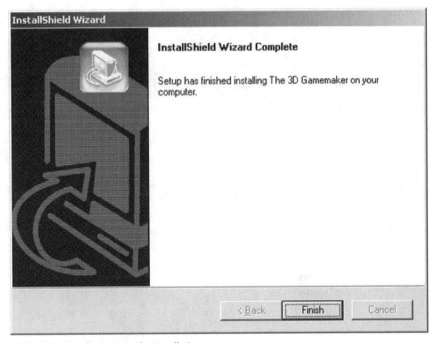

FIGURE 23.11   The final step in the installation.

run the program by choosing it from your Start menu. Click Yes if you want to place an icon on your desktop.

12. The final install screen is displayed. Click the Finish button (see Figure 23.11).

CHAPTER REVIEW

In this chapter we walked through the simple installation of the 3D Gamemaker. In the next chapter, we'll look at the simplistic IDE that was designed to work in a series of steps. By completing these steps, you can quickly build one of the many styles of built-in Gamemaker games.

CREATING A GAME WITH THE 3D GAMEMAKER

n the previous chapter, we walked through the steps required to install the 3D Gamemaker. Now that it's installed, we'll use it to develop a 3D shooter. The software comes with a variety of pre-built environments and 3D models that can be used in your creations. We'll use tanks as the combatants and a space environment for the scenery.

GETTING STARTED

In this section, we'll develop a simple game with 3D Gamemaker.

1. When you open the 3D Gamemaker, a screen like Figure 24.1 is displayed. This screen allows you to choose between Standard and Beginner modes of operation. For the example in this chapter, choose Standard.
2. After you select the mode, a second window will appear (see Figure 24.2). From this window, choose Make Game, the top selection on the list.
3. The next window that is displayed is the Standard IDE for the 3D Gamemaker. You'll see a series of icons across the top of the screen. Each of these icons represents a step in the creation of a game. Click the first icon. You'll see a screen like Figure 24.3.

FIGURE 24.1 3D Gamemaker allows you to choose Standard or Beginner operations.

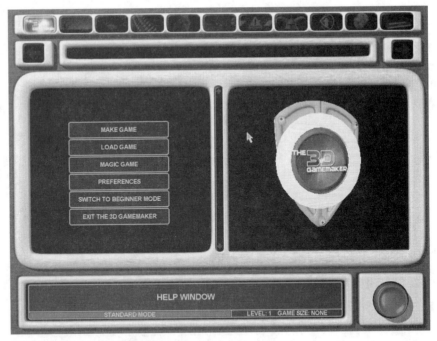

FIGURE 24.2   Choose Make Game from the menu.

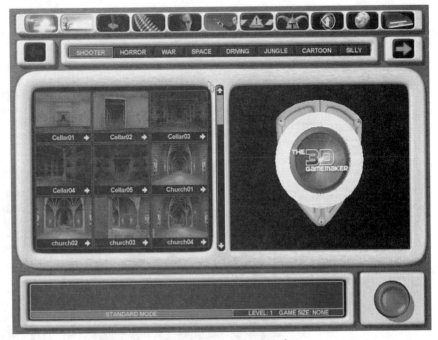

FIGURE 24.3   3D Gamemaker comes with several default types of games.

4. From the list of displayed genres, choose War. This will display a new screen like Figure 24.4, with available environments. Choose Corridors2 or something similar.

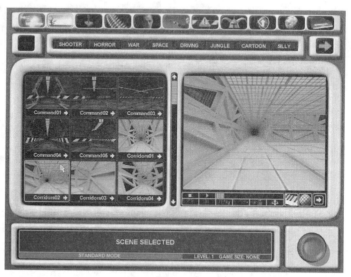

FIGURE 24.4 You can select from any of the pre-built environments.

5. Click the third icon in the list—the one that looks like a joystick. This icon lets you choose characters and objects to control in the game. Click on the Tank, as shown in Figure 24.5.

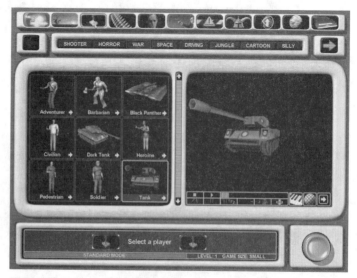

FIGURE 24.5 We'll control a Tank in the game.

6. As before, continue by clicking on the next icon to the right. Here, it's the ammo belt. This icon lets you select the bullets that you character will fire. Choose the Frag Bomb, as shown in Figure 24.6.

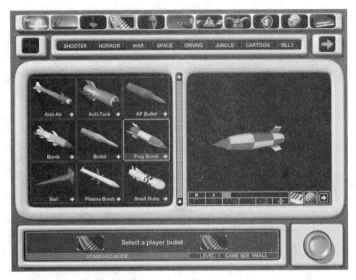

FIGURE 24.6   The Frag Bomb being selected.

7. Click on the next icon, a person. This icon lets you pick your enemies in the level. You'll see a list like the one in Figure 24.7. Choose Green Cobre.

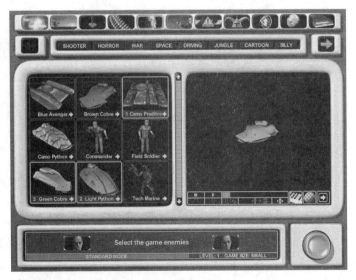

FIGURE 24.7   The available enemies.

8. Select the next icon, a man shooting a gun. This icon lets you choose your ammunition. You'll see a list like the one in Figure 24.8. Choose Gray Shell.

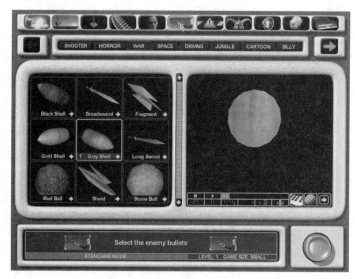

FIGURE 24.8 Available bullets in the 3D Gamemaker.

9. Select the next icon, with the triangular sign. This icon lets you select the obstacles that will be placed throughout the level. As shown in Figure 24.9, choose Debris.

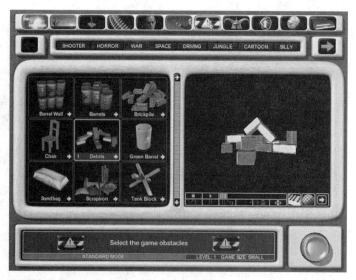

FIGURE 24.9 The Debris for the level.

10. Select the next icon, the horned helmet. This icon lets you choose the end of level boss. As shown in Figure 24.10, choose Dark Tank.

FIGURE 24.10   Dark Tank is the end of level boss.

11. Select the next icon, the arrow. This icon lets you choose game items. As shown in Figure 24.11, choose the Energy box with crosses on it.

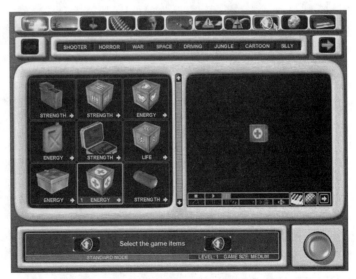

FIGURE 24.11   You can add Energy pick-ups to the game.

GAME SETTINGS

Now that we've established the basic elements of the game, it's time to establish the basic game settings.

1. Select the next item, the globe. This icon lets you set various settings for the game. Figure 24.12 shows the options.
2. Choose Set Objectives. This displays a screen like Figure 24.13. You can decide how you complete the game—in our example we'll use the default setting. When you have finished, click the arrow in the upper left of the screen.

FIGURE 24.12　The various game settings.

FIGURE 24.13　The game objectives.

3. In the menu that now displays, choose Game Difficulty from the list. This will display an options screen like Figure 24.14. This time through, leave the settings at their defaults. Later, after you try the level, if you decide it is too easy or hard, you can come back to these options.

4. Click the arrow in the upper left. In the menu that displays, choose Set 1 / 2 Player Mode. From the next menu, (see Figure 24.15) select Turn Based Play. Then, click the green arrow in the upper left.

FIGURE 24.14   The difficulty settings for the game.

FIGURE 24.15   The options for 1 / 2 player mode.

5. Now you are back in the main menu. Choose Game Volumes from the list. As shown in Figure 24.16, you can change the volume levels of in-game music and title score.

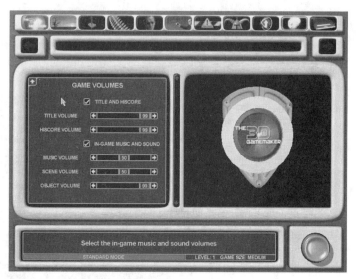

FIGURE 24.16 The Game Volumes can be changed.

6. In the screen shown in Figure 24.17, choose the fonts for the project. You can leave the default settings, or change to one of the available fonts shown there.

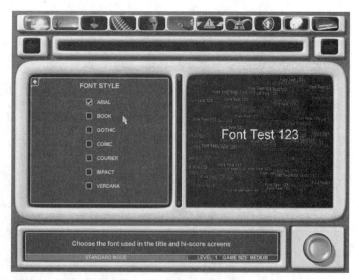

FIGURE 24.17 The various fonts that can be used by the 3D Gamemaker.

7. Figures 24.18 through 24.20 show the options for Game Appearance, the Opening Screen and the HiScore screen. Make your choices in each of these screens.

FIGURE 24.18   The Game Appearance options.

FIGURE 24.19   An Opening Screen can be changed.

FIGURE 24.20 The HiScore screen can be set up in many ways.

SAVING THE GAME

After making all of the selections, it's time to save the game. Click the icon in the upper right of the screen that looks like a disc (see Figure 24.21). Choose Save Game from the menu that is displayed.

FIGURE 24.21 Choose Save Game from the menu.

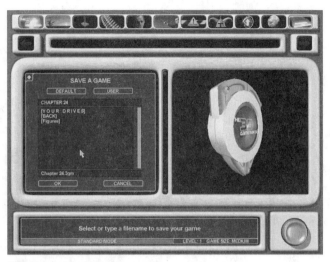

FIGURE 24.22   The Save Game menu.

The Save a Game menu is displayed. You can name your game anything you'd like. In the example seen in Figure 24.22, it is called *Chapter 24.3gm* (3D Gamemaker adds the *3gm* extension).

PLAYING THE GAME

After you save the game, the original menu will again be presented (see Figure 24.23). To play your game, click Play Game.

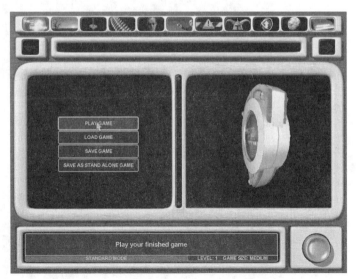

FIGURE 24.23   Click Play Game to start the game.

FIGURE 24.24 The opening screen of our game.

FIGURE 24.25 The game is being loaded.

When you execute the game, you will see the opening screen. This screen, seen in Figure 24.24, is the screen we could have edited, but didn't, earlier.

Press the Space Bar to begin the game. The game will start to load, as shown in Figure 24.25. When it is done loading, you'll see the game level, as shown in Figure 24.26.

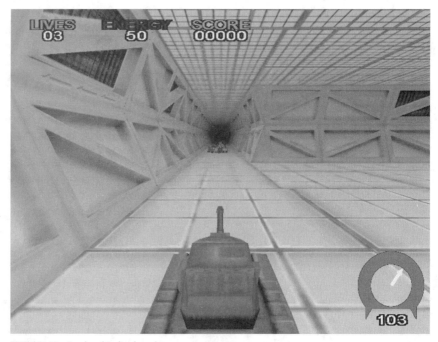

FIGURE 24.26 Our level is displayed.

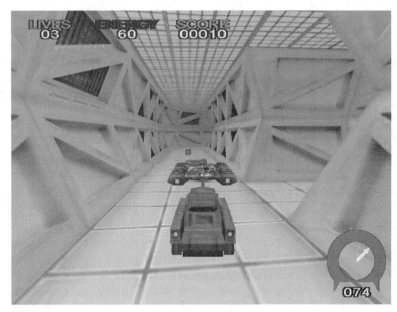

FIGURE 24.27   Encountering the first enemy.

Go ahead! Test the game. You'll see the enemies we placed into the level earlier. They are visible in Figure 24.27 and Figure 24.28.

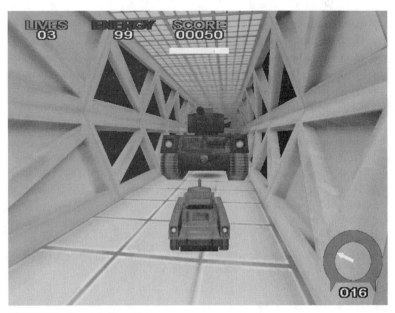

FIGURE 24.28   The end of level boss.

Chapter Review

In this chapter, we built a game using the Standard mode of the 3D Gamemaker. The built-in levels and models make it easy it is to build a complete project using the 3D Gamemaker. In the next chapter, we'll look at a new type of development: creating modifications for existing commercial games, using gmax.

INTRODUCTION TO GMAX

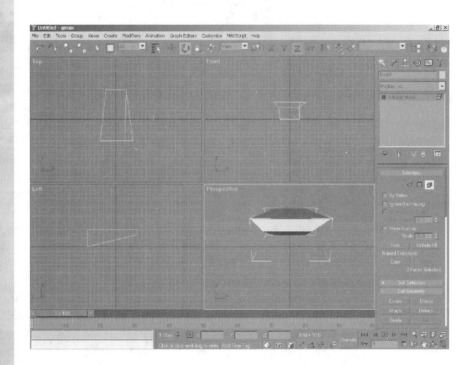

At this stage in the book, you have looked at a wide range of development tools, and in doing so; you have had the opportunity to walk through the development of several complete games, ranging from 2D action games to a 3D shooter. All of these were completed without a single line of code. Now, in the final section of the book, we're going to take a look at another opportunity for aspiring game developers. Rather than develop a game from start to finish, we're going to look at modifying existing commercial games using gmax, an excellent tool available freely from Discreet (www.discreet.com) the company that developed the industry standard 3D Studio Max.

OVERVIEW OF GMAX

Many avid gamers quickly tire of their games. Playing the same levels or flying the same ships over and over becomes boring. For these gamers, developing modifications has involved putting together online communities for the exchange of any information they could gather. While this did allow them to modify the games, the information was sketchy at best. Making the process even more difficult, the tools that have normally been available were put together without an end user in mind. Instead, they were created for the team working on the game or were put together by an individual (using the limited information) and released to the general public. Either way, the documentation is either lacking entirely or very sparse. Now, with gmax-supported games, gamers have a 3D modeling tool that is easy to use, comes with documentation, and includes a common framework that can be used for many games.

The gmax program incorporates a great deal of the functionality of 3D Studio Max and uses "game packs" that are released by the developers of a game. For example, suppose a company called "ABC" releases a game called "FPS." Company ABC would need to create a game pack for the game. These game packs allow you to modify the content of the game. For instance, you can create and edit in-game elements, including levels, materials, 3D objects, characters, and animations. In the next section, we'll walk through the installation of gmax and then look at the basic functionality it provides.

INSTALLING GMAX

The installation is a very simple process.

ON THE CD

1. In My Computer or Windows Explorer, locate the gmaxinst_1-1.exe file that is located in the gmax directory on the CD-ROM included with this book.

2. Double-click the file that you downloaded in the last step. It will probably be named something like *gmaxinst.exe*. You will be presented with a very simple screen (see Figure 25.1).

3. Click the Setup button. Files for the installation will be extracted. Figure 25.2 displays a sample of this.

4. After the files have finished extracting, the Installation Wizard will start up, as shown in Figure 25.3. This window will disappear after *gmaxinst.exe* has searched for previous installations. Wait for this window to disappear.

5. You'll see the main Installation Wizard screen, as shown in Figure 25.4. Click the Next button.

6. The gmax License Agreement is displayed. Read through the agreement, a portion of which can be seen in Figure 25.5. Then, click the "I accept" button.

7. The next window (see Figure 25.6), allows you to select the destination directory. Later steps that install the tutorials and help files will assume that you have installed to the default directory of *C:\gmax*. If you choose to install to another directory, write down its name and use it as needed later in the chapter. After you have selected the directory, click the Next button.

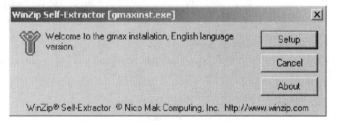

FIGURE 25.1   The first installation screen.

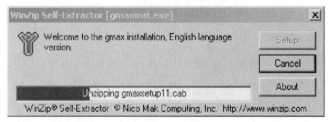

FIGURE 25.2   Files being extracted for the setup.

FIGURE 25.3   Checking for previous installations.

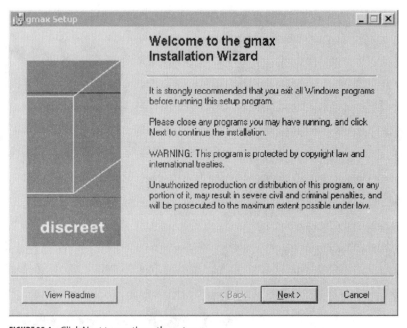

FIGURE 25.4   Click Next to continue the setup.

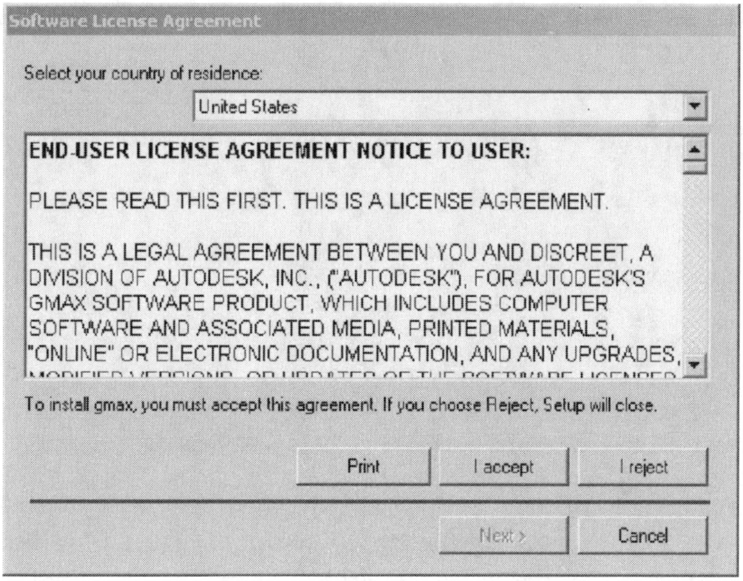

FIGURE 25.5   The gmax License Agreement.

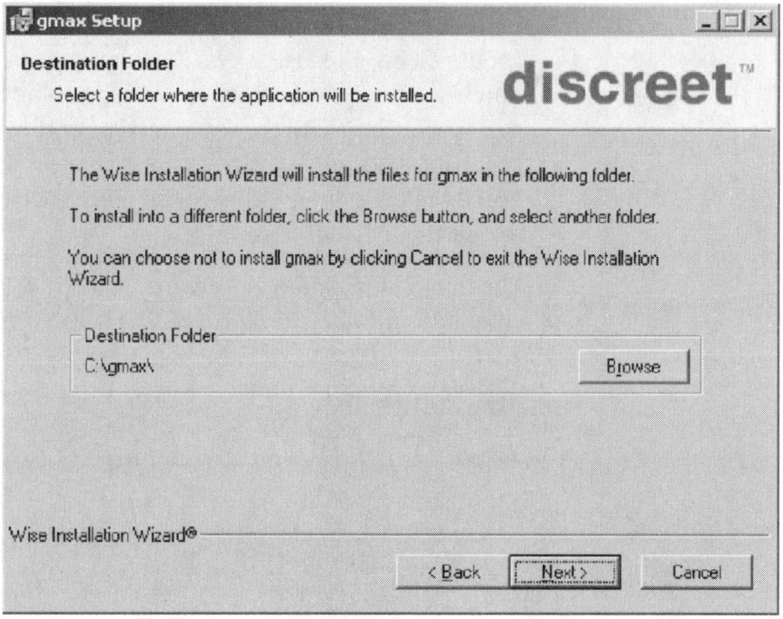

FIGURE 25.6   You should use the default installation directory if possible.

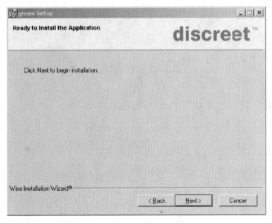 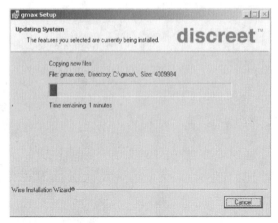

FIGURE 25.7 Click next to begin copying files.   **FIGURE 25.8** The files are being installed.

8. Now, a window similar to Figure 25.7 is displayed. Click Next to begin installing the files. Figure 25.8 shows the progress indiacator that displays during this step.

9. After the files have been copied, the installation process prompts you to install Flash 5. If you do not have Flash 5 installed, choose Yes to install it. If you already have Flash 5, choose No. If you aren't sure, just choose to install Flash, since it is required to see materials in gmax.

10. You'll see a window informing you that you need to reboot (see Figure 25.9). Choose No to this question at this time (you'll restart your computer later in the installation process).

11. You'll see the window shown in Figure 25.10. Click the Finish button to end the installation.

The gmax application is now installed. You will still need to add the help files and tutorials. We'll cover this below.

Installing the Help Files

The help files are quick and easy to install. Here's how.

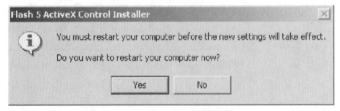

FIGURE 25.9 Choose No to the restart question.

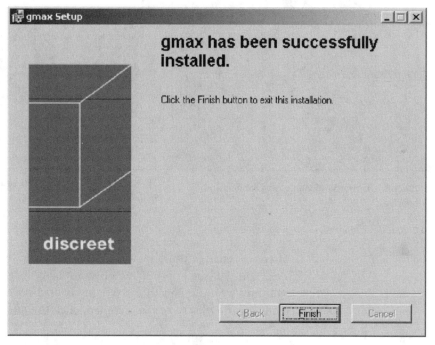

FIGURE 25.10   The final window in the gmax installation.

1. You can visit the Discreet Web site to download additional help files for gmax at *www.discreet.com*. Click on Products and then choose gmax. (The following URL takes you right to it *http://www.discreet.com/products/ gmax/*.) Next, click on the consumer or free version of gmax. The name of the help file is gmax_help.exe. Follow the directions on the gmax site to download this file to your computer.

 The installation of the help and tutorials aren't necessary to use gmax but they can be a big help. If you would prefer to skip over these steps, you can proceed to page 443.

2. Double-click *gmax_help.exe* to begin the extraction of the help files. This displays a window like Figure 25.11.
3. Make sure that the directory listed in the "Unzip to folder" box is the same one you used when you installed gmax itself. If you previously accepted the default installation directory, change *"gmax"* to *"c:\gmax"* here. If you changed the installation directory to anything else, type its drive and name here, or locate it with the Browse button. Figure 25.12 shows the change if you previously chose the default directory.

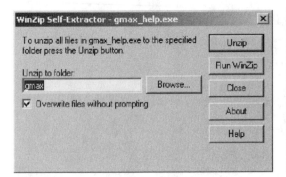

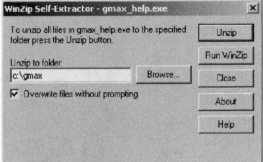

FIGURE 25.11 This window for unzipping the help and tutorial files.

FIGURE 25.12 Before continuing, you need to change the extraction directory.

4. After you change the directory, click the Unzip button to extract the files. You will see another window displayed (see Figure 25.13) that will show you the files that are being copied.
5. When all the files have been copied, click the OK button.

Installing the Tutorials

To install the tutorials:

1. Repeat the same steps you used for the help files (you will be installing *gmax_tutorials.exe*). Figures 25.14, 25.15, and 25.16 display the steps in order.
2. When all files have been installed, you'll see the message in Figure 25.16. Click OK to end the installation.
3. Now that everything is installed, reboot your PC to finalize the installation.

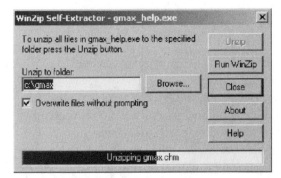

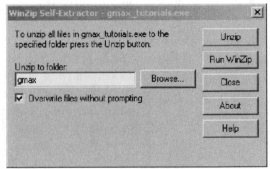

FIGURE 25.13 The files are being copied to the folder.

FIGURE 25.14 The first step for installing the tutorials.

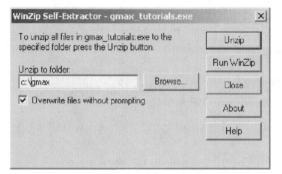
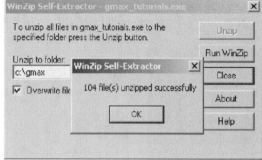

FIGURE 25.15   Choosing the tutorial installation directory.

FIGURE 25.16   Click OK to end the installation.

THE GMAX USER INTERFACE

When you run gmax for the first time, you will be required to register on the Internet. You can install the software on multiple computers, but every computer you use will need to follow the registration process. This is a simple process, and Discreet walks you through the necessary steps. After registration, gmax will open. You will see the gmax interface, shown in Figure 25.17.

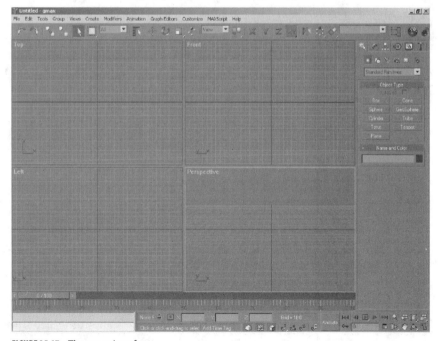

FIGURE 25.17   The gmax interface.

To quickly maximize a viewport, press the W key on your keyboard. To return it to its regular size, hit the W key again. Another common shortcut is the V key, which allows you to move the camera around your object. This makes it easier to see fine details.

This screen contains several important areas:

- Along the top, it has a variety of menus, with some icons under the menus.
- Along the right side are tool icons and option buttons.
- Under the menus are four "Viewports" that are used for positioning, displaying, and otherwise altering models. You can think of these as the views from four individual cameras, which look at objects from the Top, Front, Left, and Perspective. If you have used other modeling tools, you are probably accustomed to this already.

Let's review some of the basic components that make up any 3D model. If you remember, we looked at a 3D workspace in Chapter 2. With 2D graphics, you have the X and Y axis. For 3D, we add a third axis, the Z axis. It is this axis that gives an object depth. If you need to brush up on the topic, refer back to Chapter 2.

If you are planning to build models in gmax, you will need to learn about vertices, edges, and faces.

- A *vertex* is a point where two lines meet. Figure 25.18 shows six vertices.
- An *edge* is a line drawn between two vertices. Edges are straight lines and have vertices on each end. Figure 25.19 shows seven edges. Three are on the top of the cube, three are on the front of the cube, and one is shared between the top and the front.
- A *face* is a flat surface composed of edges and vertices. Figure 25.20 shows the visible top and front faces of the cube, with lines to suggest the four other unseen faces.

Creating a 3D Object

Now that we have a basic understanding of the interface, let's get to the fun stuff. There is a menu box on the right side of the screen (see Figure 25.21) that we can use to make basic objects called *primitives*.

Let's use the primitives to build a box.

1. Click the Box button.
2. Click in the Top viewport drag the mouse as you hold down the left mouse button. When the box is about the size shown in Figure 25.22, let go of the mouse button.

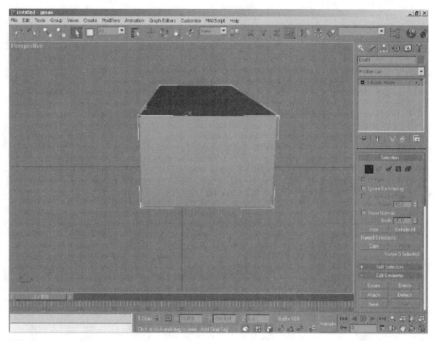

FIGURE 25.18   Vertices in gmax.

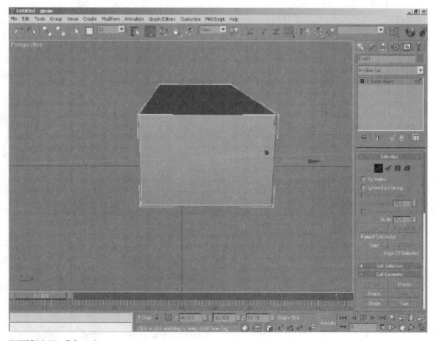

FIGURE 25.19   Edges in gmax.

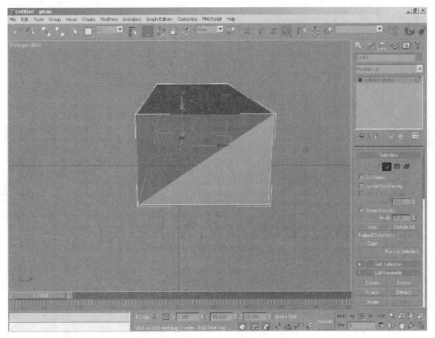

FIGURE 25.20 Faces are made up of vertices and edges.

FIGURE 25.21 Primitives are used to create basic objects in gmax.

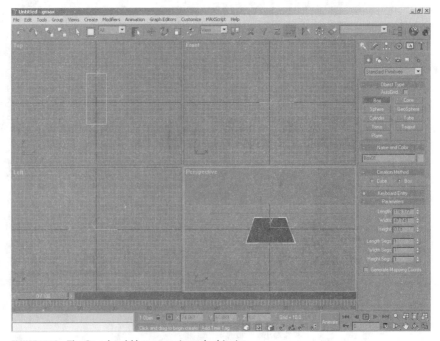

FIGURE 25.22 The Box should be approximately this size.

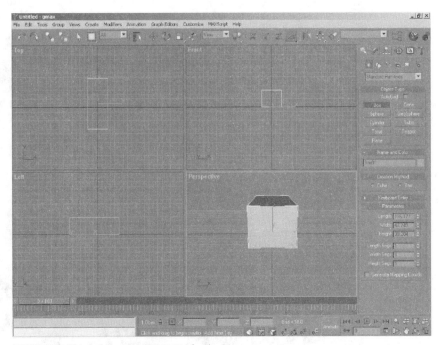

FIGURE 25.23 This is the approximate size for the Box.

If you look carefully, you can see that the box is visible in all of the viewports, although it is still a flat 2D object.

3. Next, slowly move your mouse up and you will begin to see some depth added to the box. Try to make it look approximately like Figure 25.23. When you have it at the correct size, click the left button.

If you make a mistake, you can press CTRL+Z to undo it.

Editing the Object

Now that we have a box, let's edit it. But before we do so, we need to set a property for the Perspective view. Although it isn't a completely necessary step, it makes it much easier for you to see what you are doing.

1. Right click on the text that says "Perspective View." This will display a pop-up menu.
2. On the menu, select the Configure option. It will display a window similar to Figure 25.24.

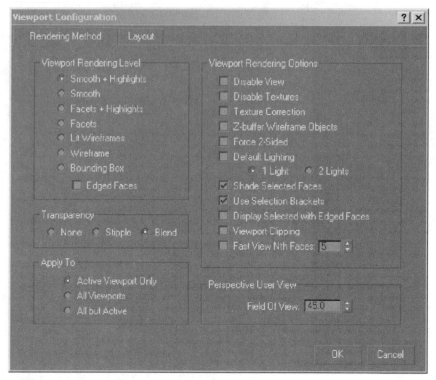

FIGURE 25.24 The Viewport Configuration for the Perspective view.

3. In the Viewpoint Rendering Options box of this window, click the option that says "Shade Selected Faces" and then click the OK button.
4. To alter the box, we need to convert it to an Editable Mesh. Right click on the box in the Perspective view and then choose Convert To from the pop-up menu.
5. In the sub-menu that displays, select Convert To Editable Mesh.

Now that we have an object we can edit, let's do it.

Click the Modify icon (looks like a bent piece of blue tubing) at the upper right of the main window, as shown in Figure 25.23. You will see a set of tools that allow you to select a vertex, edge, face, polygon, or entire object (see Figure 25.25). You are in object mode until you select one of the other options.

You should try to play around with all of these tools. For instance, suppose that you want to move an individual vertex in the Box. Select the Ver-

FIGURE 25.25 Various Sub-Objects available in gmax.

tex button (farthest to left of the sub-objects), or press the "V" key shortcut. This will display all of the vertices in blue. Next, click a vertex and move your mouse around the viewport. This will move the vertex you selected, and will deform the object. Try to duplicate the example in Figure 25.26 and Figure 25.27!

A gizmo is available to help you with your modeling. When you select a vertex, it will display a series of three arrows that point to the X, Y, and Z axes. To limit the movement to any one of the axes, click on that specific axis.

ON THE CD

You can find this example on the CD-ROM that accompanies this book, in the Examples\gmax *folder.*

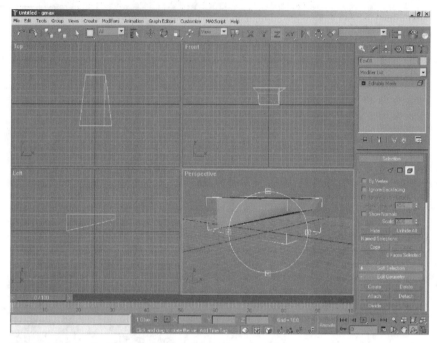

FIGURE 25.26   A simple example in gmax, rotated in the Perspective view by using the V key shortcut.

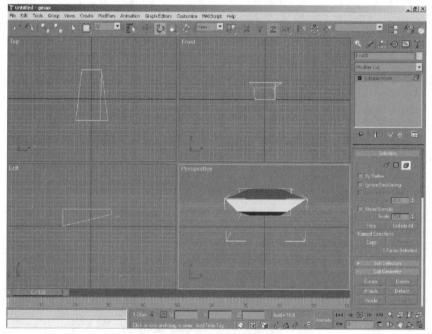

FIGURE 25.27   The same sample from the standard view we have been using.

CHAPTER REVIEW

That's all we're going to cover in the first chapter on gmax. We have lightly touched on the interface and modeling tools in this chapter, so it's important that you take some time to get used to them. You can also browse the terrific help files and tutorials that we installed with gmax. In the next chapter, we're going to focus our attention on creating some simple objects and scenery that can be used in Flight Simulator 2002, one of the first games supported by gmax with a game pack.

26 USING GMAX FOR FLIGHT SIMULATOR 2002 PROFESSIONAL

In the previous chapter, we installed the basic components that make up gmax and also looked at various aspects of the application, including its user interface. In doing so, you acquired some basic knowledge of the functionality it offers, but we have obviously just scratched the surface of this powerful application. In this chapter, we'll learn how gmax has been incorporated into Microsoft's Flight Simulator 2002 Professional and how you can use the two of them to create new planes, design scenery, or create nearly any type of 3D object you can imagine.

 We'll use the terms Flight Simulator, Flight Simulator 2002, and Flight Simulator 2002 Professional interchangeably here. Please keep in mind that the only version of Flight Simulator that supports the game pack is Flight Simulator 2002 Professional.

FLIGHT SIMULATOR INSTALLATION

When you read the topic of this section, you probably thought we were going to walk through the installation of Flight Simulator 2002 Professional. Instead, this section is going to detail how we get the game packs and supporting files from the Flight Simulator CD into the proper location, allowing gmax to export files in the Flight Simulator file format. Ideally, you will have installed Flight Simulator 2002 Professional on your PC, but you can follow along without it.

 The installation of these files requires that you have gmax closed. If you have not done so, you should close it now.

1. Put CD #2 from Flight Simulator 2002 Professional into your CD-ROM drive.
2. Double-click on My Computer and then right-click on your CD-ROM drive letter. Figure 26.1 shows an example of this, with Drive D as the CD-ROM drive. From the pop-up menu, choose Explore. This opens Windows Explorer set to Drive D.
3. As you can see in Figure 26.2, the CD-ROM includes a file called *gmax.CAB*. It is this file that we are interested in. If you are using Windows Me, 2000, or XP, CAB file support is built in. Skip directly to step 5, below.
4. If you are using Windows 95 OSR2 (if you have OSR1, you should update it to OSR2) , you must download and install a tool from Microsoft's Web site. To do this, go to: http://www.microsoft.com/windows95/downloads/contents/wutoys/w95pwrtoysset/default.asp.

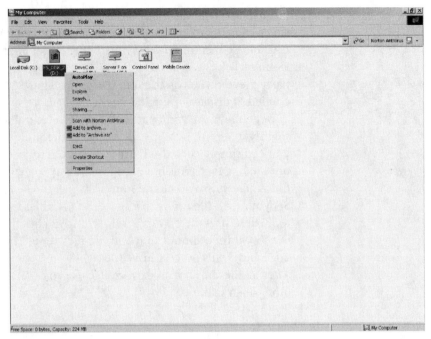

FIGURE 26.1   Choose Explore from the pop-up menu.

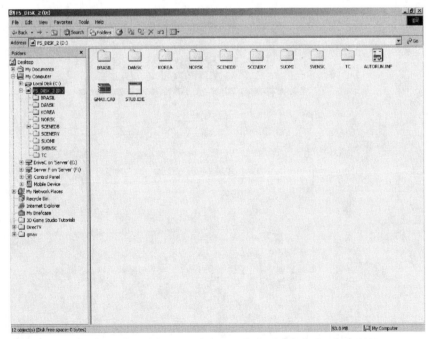

FIGURE 26.2   gmax.CAB is located in the root directory of CD #2 of Flight Simulator 2002 Professional.

From that Web site, follow the directions for downloading and installing the necessary files. We'll assume from here that you now have CAB file extraction/viewing capabilities either built in or downloaded.

5. Double-click the *gmax.CAB* file. This will open up a built-in or third party viewer, such as the one shown in Figure 26.3. When the file is opened, it displays a single folder called *gmax*.

   Depending on your particular system, extracting the file will be slightly different. In WinRAR, which is the utility used in the figures, you can simply click the Extract To button at the upper left (see Figure 26.4). Other tools have a different way to extract the files, but the ultimate results will be the same.

6. Set your CAB file utility to extract the CAB files to the Windows desktop. Then, start the extraction (in WinRAR click the OK button). Your CD-ROM drive should spin and the files should be extracted. (Figure 26.5 shows this process in WinRAR).

7. After all files have been extracted, close your CAB file utility and any other open windows.

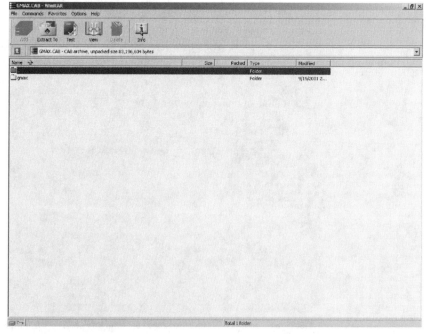

FIGURE 26.3 The CAB file after being opened.

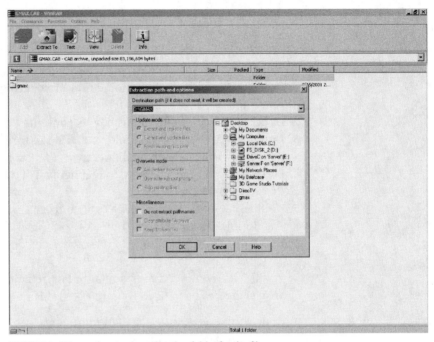

FIGURE 26.4   We need to set the extraction folder for the files.

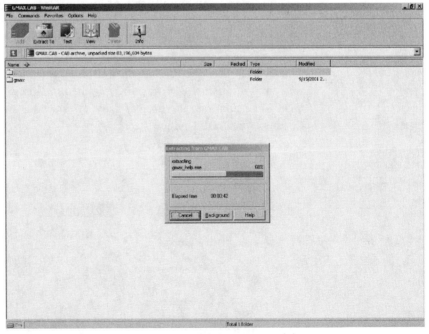

FIGURE 26.5   Files being copied to the desktop in WinRAR.

Installing the Downloaded Files

It's time to install the downloaded files. Here's how.

1. If any applications are currently running, minimize them, so that you can see your desktop. You should find a folder that is (not surprisingly) called *gmax*.
2. Double-click the folder to display its contents.
3. Double-click the *FlightSim* folder. You'll see three files that you need to copy to your gmax install directory (*C:\gmax* by default).
4. Press Ctrl+A on the keyboard to highlight all of the files, and then press Ctrl+C to copy them.
5. Double-click My Computer. Navigate to your gmax install directory and double-click it.
6. In the install directory (again, it is *C:\gmax* by default), press Ctrl+V to paste the files.
7. You'll see a window that is similar to Figure 26.6. Click Yes. Continue answering Yes each time you are asked this question.

Congratulations. Your installation of gmax can now export files into the Flight Simulator format.

There are a few additional items available in the gmax folder that we copied to the desktop. The *samples* folder contains several Flight Simulator 2002 plane and building models we can look at. We are going to leave them in their current positions at this time, although you can move the folder to another location on your hard drive.

 Warning! *Don't move the folder to any place where it would clobber the files in your gmax installation directory. In a normal installation, this means NOT to move the folder to the root directory of drive C, because it would copy the files into* C:\gmax, *the default gmax directory.*

FIGURE 26.6 The Confirm Folder Replace dialog box.

CREATING SCENERY

Now that we have everything installed, we will begin creating a simple building for Flight Simulator.

1. Run gmax and create a box that has a length of 20, width of 30 and height of 40. You can either use your mouse to manipulate the image, or if you would prefer, you can enter the figures in the box at the lower right, in the Keyboard Entry area (see Figure 26.7) and then click the Create button. Both methods will work for this tutorial. However,entering the values gives you the exact sizes, which could be important for more exact models.

2. Open the Material Editor. To do this, click the "Red Ball" in the upper right hand portion of the gmax interface. Your screen should now look something like Figure 26.8.

3. You need to create a new material and import a texture from a bitmap file. Start by minimizing gmax to the task bar. We'll be using materials from the Flight Simulator *samples* directory. Although they are in Photoshop® PSD format, you can still use them, as outlined below.

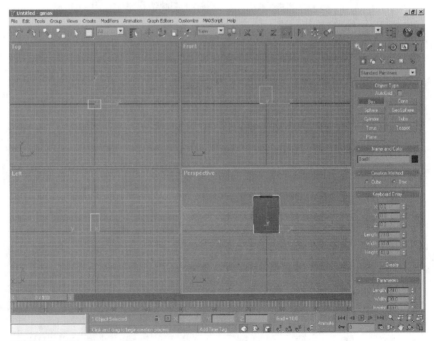

FIGURE 26.7   A box in gmax.

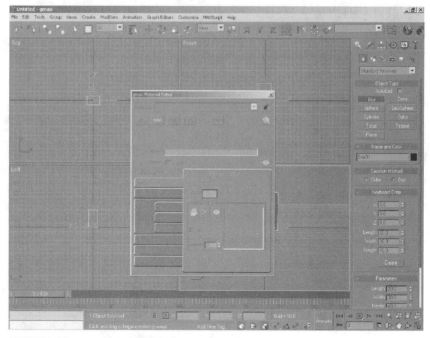

FIGURE 26.8 The gmax Material Editor.

4. Double-click My Computer and open up your gmax directory (by default, *C:\gmax*).

5. Double-click the *Gampacks* folder, then double-click the *flightsim* folder.

6. You should see a file called *Imagetool.exe*. Double-click this file to run it.

7. In Imagetool, select Open from the File menu. Navigate to the *gmax* directory you left on your desktop in an earlier step.

8. Open the *Samples* directory You should see several files inside it, but the one we are interested in is called *nv13a_lm.psd*. Open up this file.

If you don't see any files in the directory, make sure that the drop-down "type" selector is set to Photoshop PSD.

9. After you open *nv13a_lm.psd*, select the Edit menu and then choose Format | 8-bit. (The 32-bit file cannot be opened in gmax.)

10. If everything looks OK, choose Create MipMaps from the Image menu.

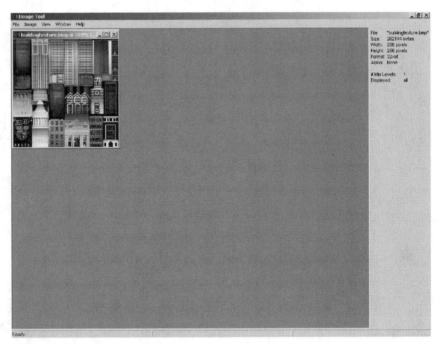

FIGURE 26.9   The texture saved as a BMP.

11. Select Save As from the File menu. Choose the *BMP* file format, and give the file a name something like "Buildingtextures" (see Figure 26.9). Click the save button.

12. Close Imagetool.

We're now ready to use the image in gmax. Here's what to do.

1. Restore gmax to its original size. When it is open again, you should see the material editor where we left it.

2. Click the New button. You'll see that Material #1 has been created.

3. In the Diffuse Factor tab, click the Assign Texture—Pick Map File button. This will allow you to browse to the *buildingtexure.bmp* file we just created.

4. Open *buildingtexture.bmp*. Your screen should look like Figure 26.10.

5. Click the Apply button at the top of the window to apply the texture to the box.

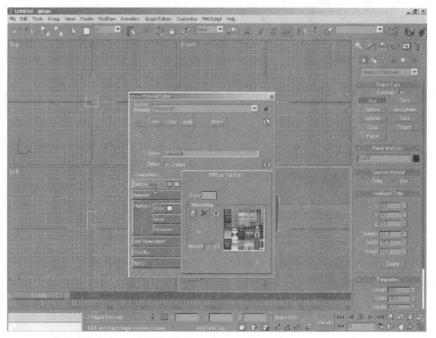

FIGURE 26.10 The material open in the editor.

As you can see in Figure 26.11, this will apply the entire texture to the face. This is obviously not what we need. We need to have a way to assign *part of the texture* to *only a single face* of the object.

To do this, the object must have mapping coordinates. These coordinates specify how the image is mapped onto the object (for example, is it tiled, or mirrored). Mapping coordinates are also known as *UV coordinates* or *UVW coordinates*. These letters refer to the coordinates in the object's space, as opposed to the XYZ coordinates that describe the scene as a whole.

First, select all the visible faces.

1. Because the box is still selected, start by clicking the Modify icon that is located to the right of the Perspective viewport. It is the second icon from the left and looks like a blue piece of tubing that is bent.
2. In the Modifier List at the far right of the screen, go to the UV Coordinate Modifiers section and select Unwrap UVW (see Figure 26.12). This will unwrap the object into individual faces that can each have their own portion of the texture.
3. Expand Unwrap UVW in the stack above the buttons. The Select Face function will become visible.

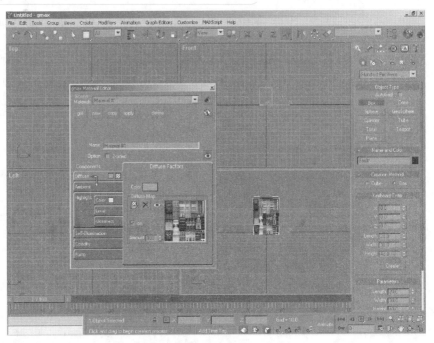

FIGURE 26.11   The material has been applied.

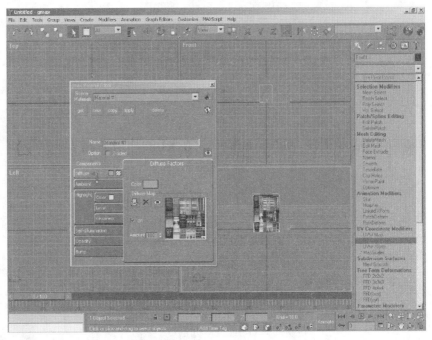

FIGURE 26.12   The Unwrap UVW modifier.

4. Click on Select Face, and then Click the Planar button.

You need to repeat this process for all of the visible faces. You can skip the bottom if you'd like, because it's not visible.

You may have a difficult time selecting certain faces. For example, the left side is easy, but the right side is probably difficult. You can just use the Perspective viewport and rotate the object to select the faces one at a time.

Now that you have selected all five visible faces, you need to go back through them one at a time to position the map appropriately. To do this:

1. Click the first face and then click the Edit button in the Parameters box. A new window will appear, like the one shown in Figure 26.13.
2. At the bottom center of the Edit UVWs window, click the triangle that is located directly to the left of the "All IDs" drop-down list. This will make only the the selected face visible in the editor.
3. Click on one of the square red handles and drag it around the texture (see Figure 26.14). Drag all four handles so that they are positioned in the area you would like to assign to the face.
4. Click the Update Map button and then close the window. The texture is now applied properly, as shown in Figure 26.15.

FIGURE 26.13 We can align the texture in this window.

FIGURE 26.14   You can move the handles around the editor.

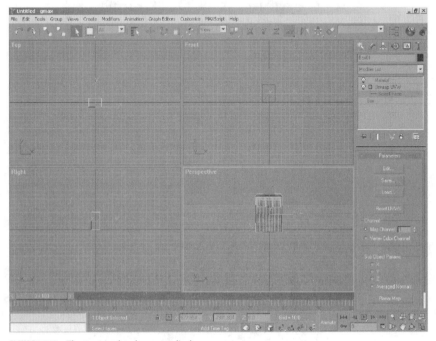

FIGURE 26.15   The texture has been applied.

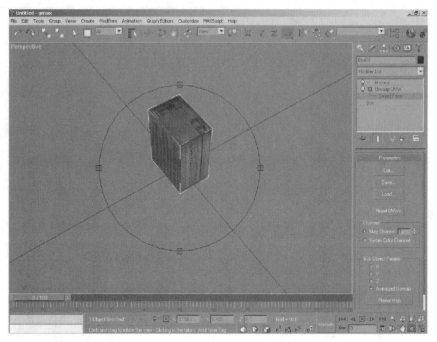

FIGURE 26.16 The final view.

5. Repeat steps 1-4 for all five of the visible faces. Figure 26.16 displays the final view of the building.
6. Choose Save As from the file menu and save the file as a gmax scene. This allows you to go back and edit it later if you need to.

EXPORTING THE FILE TO FLIGHT SIMULATOR

The next step is to export the file in Flight Simulator format. This is required before you can view it in the game.

1. Create a folder within the Flight Simulator install directory (*C:\Program Files\Microsoft Games\FS2002* by default) and name the folder something like *MyScenery*.
2. Inside the folder, create two additional folders, called *Scenery* and *Textures*.
3. In gmax, select Export from the File menu.

 If you are presented with a warning about Flight Simulator files being specified in Meters, you can ignore it for now. To change future models to the correct measurements, choose Units Setup from the Customize menu. Select Metric—Meters and click OK. Next, choose Preferences from the Customize Menu and set 1 unit equal to 1 meter.

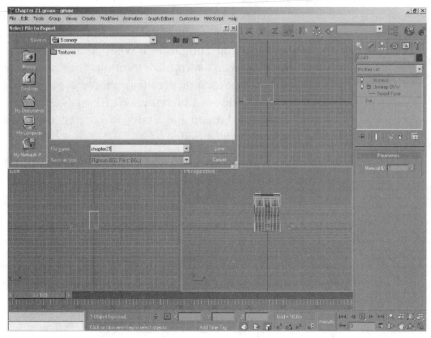

FIGURE 26.17 Choose a file name to continue.

4. When you choose Export, you are first asked for a name and format (see Figure 26.17). Choose any name you like and then click the Save button. A window appears, similar to Figure 26.18.

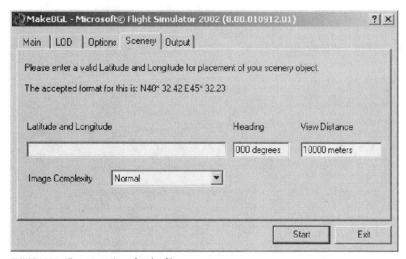

FIGURE 26.18 Export options for the file.

5. There are many settings that you could change, but for the most part, leave them set to their defaults. Here, change the coordinates (in the Latitude and Longitude box) so that Flight Simulator places your building in an appropriate location. There are many ways to find these values, but for practice, you choose N36* 00.07 W083* 55.45 (the northern side of Knoxville, TN). Then click start to create the scenery.

6. Copy the bitmap file that you created earlier to the ...*MyScenery\ Scenery\Textures* folder.

Now, you are ready to test the files. But you must first load the scenery into Flight Simulator. To do this:

1. Run Flight Simulator and choose Settings from the opening screen.
2. Choose Add Area from the Scenery Library.
3. Choose the directory you created for your scenery and then give it a name (such as *knoxvillebuilding*).

Now that the file has been added, run Flight Simulator and check it out!

Chapter Review

In this chapter, we continued looking at gmax and the possibilities it offers to people who like to modify games. Specifically, we created scenery for Flight Simulator 2002. We built a simple building, textured it, and exported it into Flight Simulator. In the next chapter, we'll walk through the steps necessary to build a simple airplane with gmax.

27 MODELING AN AIRPLANE WITH GMAX

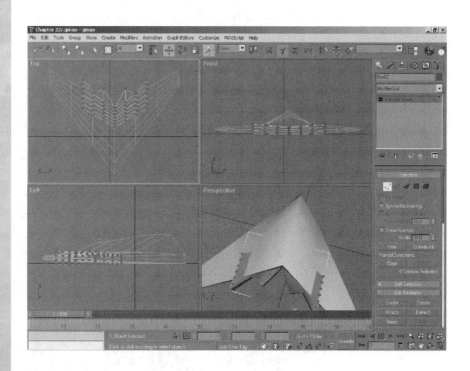

n the previous chapter, we looked at gmax in a little more detail and used it to create a building that we added to the scenery of Flight Simulator 2002 Professional. In this chapter, we'll construct a 3D model of a stealth airplane for Flight Simulator.

CREATING THE MODEL

1. To start, open gmax and create a Box, as described in the last chapter (see Figure 27.1).
2. Next, set the box's properties as follows, using the text boxes at the lower right of the window:

Parameters:

Length 35

Width 70

Height 5

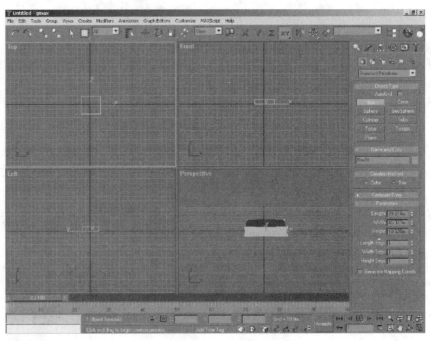

FIGURE 27.1 A box in gmax.

Segments:

Length Segs: 6

Width Segs: 6

Height Segs: 3

Figure 27.2 displays the box with the correct properties.

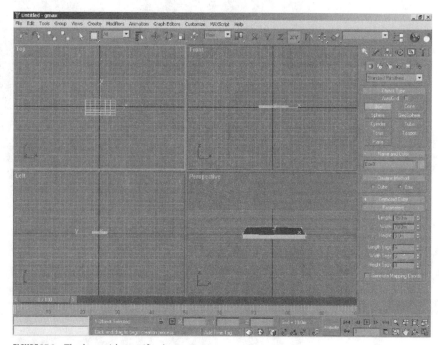

FIGURE 27.2   The box with specific changes.

3. Convert the box to an Editable Mesh, as covered in the last chapter. Set the following Parameters (see Figure 27.3):

Modifier Taper:

Symmetry: X

X Axis: X

Taper: −1.5

4. In Top View, use Center of taper to create "wings." Figure 27.4 and Figure 27.5 are a "before" and "after" for this operation.

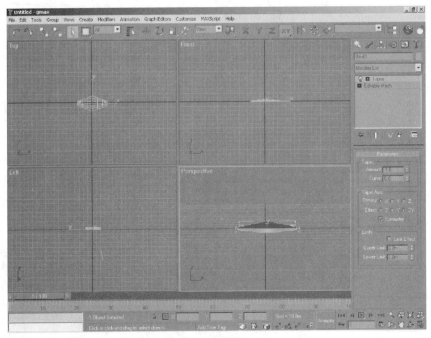

FIGURE 27.3   The box is taking a new shape.

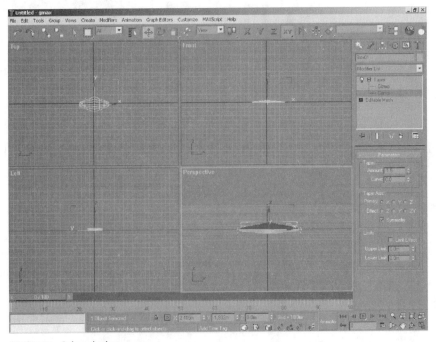

FIGURE 27.4   Select the box.

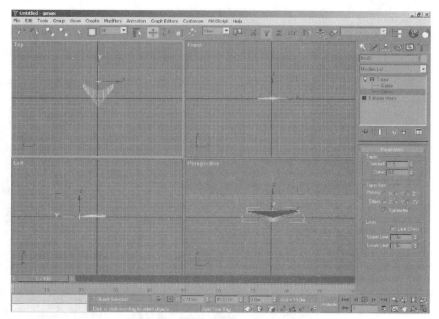

FIGURE 27.5 Move in the Y direction to change the shape.

5. The wings are beginning to take shape. Next, slightly adjust the front and left view to center of object (see Figure 27.6).

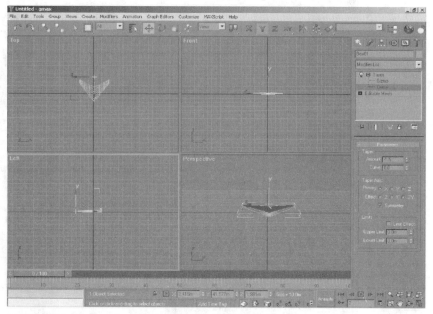

FIGURE 27.6 Your image should look something like this.

6. Convert the box to an Editable Poly, as seen in Figure 27.7.
7. Select Vertices from the menu at the right (you can hold your mouse above the options to display a popup menu, as shown in Figure 27.8).

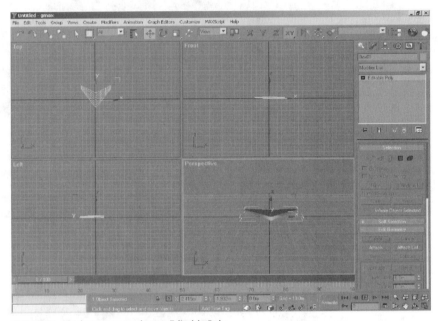

FIGURE 27.7 The box converted to an Editable Poly.

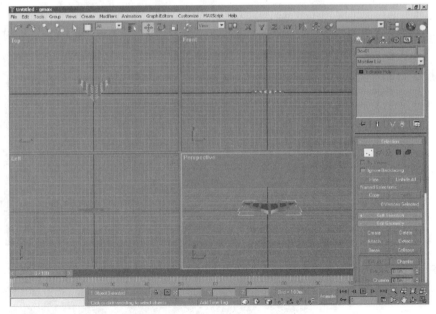

FIGURE 27.8 Vertices are selected.

8. Using the Front view, draw a box around the center vertices to select them (see Figure 27.9 and Figure 27.10).

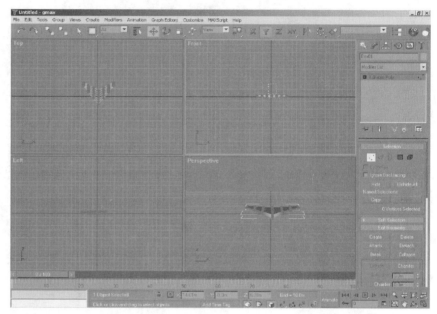

FIGURE 27.9 Beginning to draw a box.

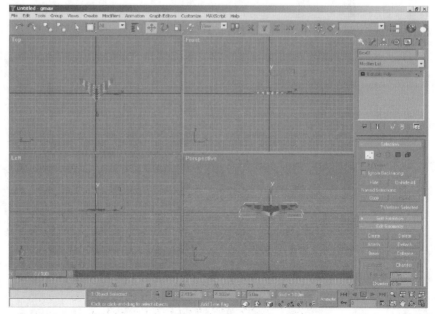

FIGURE 27.10 The final selection.

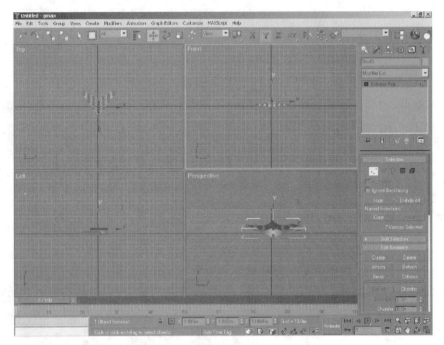

FIGURE 27.11 The middle is raised.

9. Click on Move and move the center vertices up by using the Front view. As you can see in Figure 27.11, this creates a taller mid-section for the model.

10. Click in one of the views to deselect the Vertices.

11. Zoom all views to their full extent. Figure 27.12 displays how gmax should look after you have zoomed the views and rotated the perspective view.

12. Select the single vertex on the front and top of model and move it down to create a pointed front (see Figure 27.13).

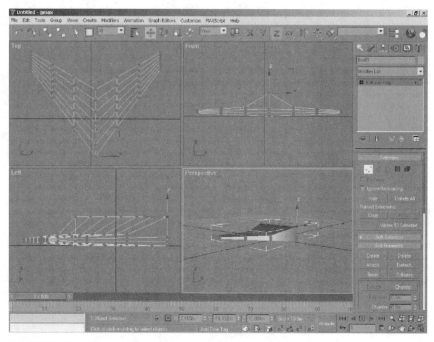

FIGURE 27.12   The views are all zoomed.

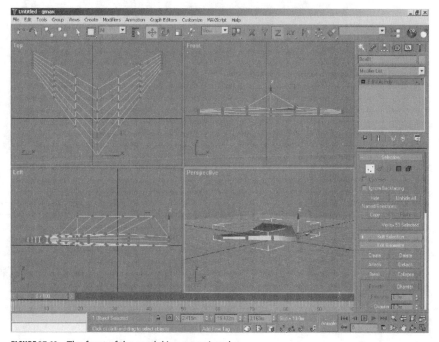

FIGURE 27.13   The front of the model is now pointed.

Adding Another Box

1. Press Shift+Z to turn the perspective view back to its original state and Deselect Vertices.
2. Add a box with the following properties:

Parameters:

Length 10

Width 35

Height 3

Segments

Length Segs: 6

Width Segs: 6

Height Segs: 3

The changes can be seen in Figure 27.14.

3. Position the box roughly in center (see Figure 27.15).
4. Convert the box to an Editable Mesh.

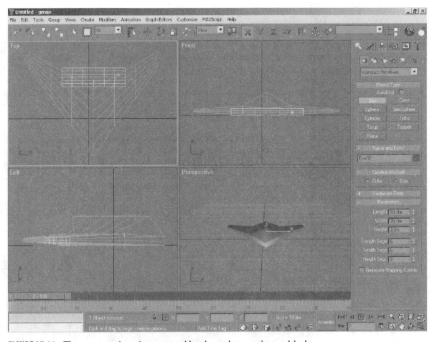

FIGURE 27.14 The perspective view moved back, and a new box added.

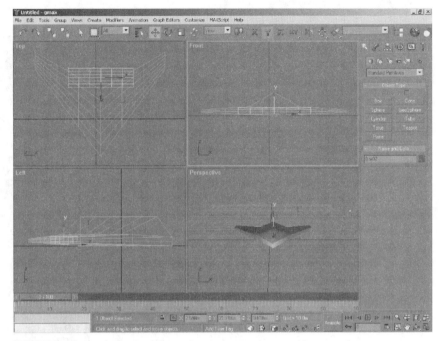

FIGURE 27.15   Center the box near the center.

5. Set the Parameters as follows (see Figure 27.16):

   Modifier Taper:

   X Axis: X

   Symmetry: X

   Taper Amount: 1

6. Move the center so that it roughly matches the earlier "bend," as can be seen in Figure 27.17.

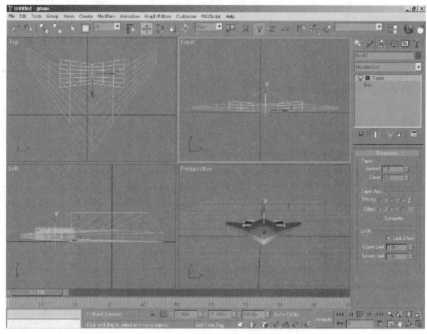

FIGURE 27.16 The box is converted to an Editable Mesh.

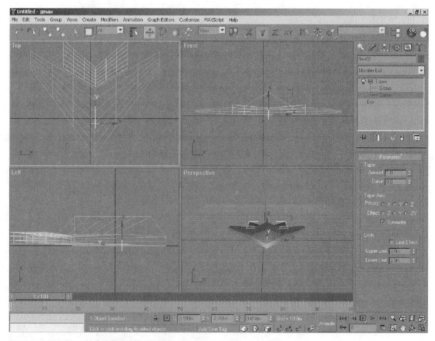

FIGURE 27.17 Match the "bend" of both parts.

7. After creating a bend, position it like Figure 27.18.
8. Deselect the modifier and position the Perspective viewport so you can see better. Rotate and zoom the Perspective view, as shown in Figure 27.19.

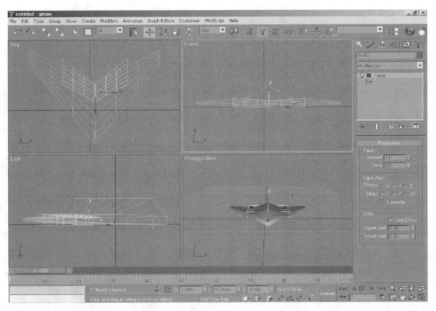

FIGURE 27.18   Position the part so that it overlaps.

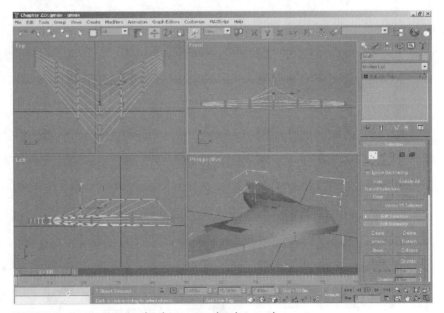

FIGURE 27.19   Perspective view has been rotated and zoomed.

9. Individually select each vertex from the top of the model.

10. Taper the model so that it looks like Figure 27.20 and Figure 27.21.

11. Convert the object to Editable Mesh and select Vertices Selection.

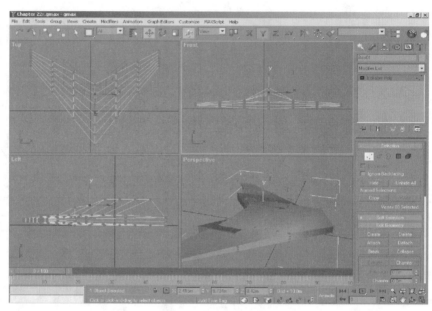

FIGURE 27.20 Select each vertex on top of model.

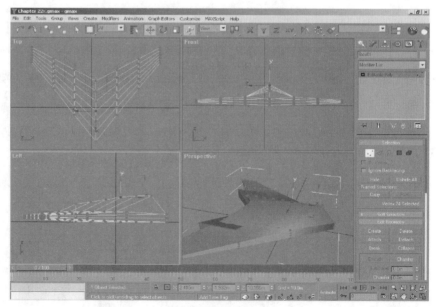

FIGURE 27.21 Move the vertices on top side to create taper.

Then, rotate the Perspective view so that you can see the back side of the model. It should look like Figure 27.22.

12. Using the Top view, select vertices from the back of the model with the selection box. Then move them, as shown in Figure 27.23.

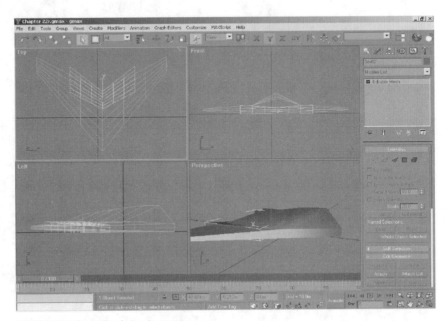

FIGURE 27.22   The rotated view in gmax.

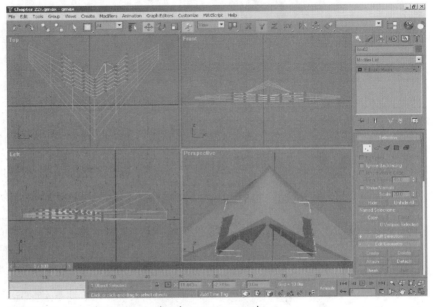

FIGURE 27.23   Move the vertices so that they create an angle.

13. After you move the first set of vertices, mirror them on the remaining side (see Figures 27.24 and 27.25).

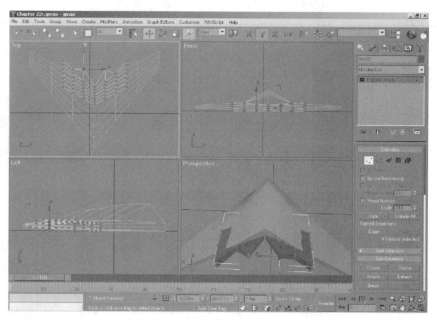

FIGURE 27.24 Moving the side to mirror the other.

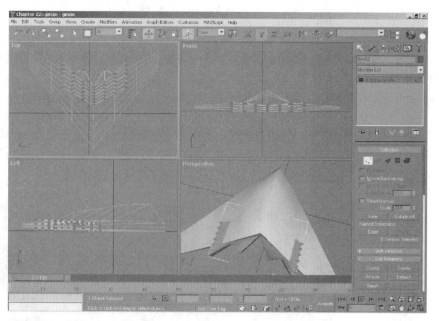

FIGURE 27.25 The final step.

CHAPTER REVIEW

In this chapter, we used gmax to build a type of stealth airplane. Using some of the features we used in the previous chapter, and adding some new ones, we were able to quickly construct it using two boxes. You can see that gmax is a very powerful application, which you can use to modify many commercial games. Visit the Discreet Web site for a complete list of currently supported games.

28

INTRODUCTION TO MILKSHAPE 3D

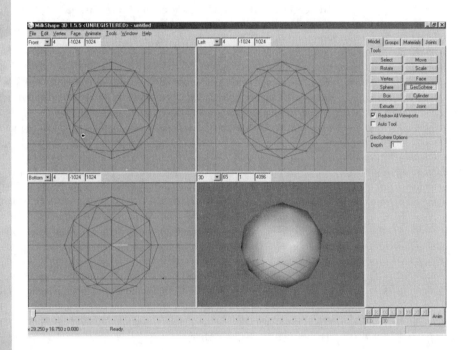

There are many good 3D modelers on the market today but you would be hard pressed to find an application that is as inexpensive as MilkShape 3D. Obviously, price isn't the only factor in choosing tools and fortunately, MilkShape offers everything you would need for the type of low-polygon modeling necessary for real time game development.

We'll use the term MilkShape, MS3D and MilkShape 3D interchangeably throughout the text although they are in fact the same product.

INTRODUCTION TO MILKSHAPE 3D

MilkShape 3D is a low-polygon modeler, which was initially designed for the creation of Half-Life models by Mete Ciragan. During the development of the product, Mete has added many file formats to the package including most common game formats.

MilkShape 3D offers a full set of basic modeling operations such as select, move, rotate, scale, extrude and turn edge to name a few and allows low-level editing with the vertex and face tool. MilkShape also includes a set of primitives like spheres, boxes and cylinders.

The most important feature that MilkShape provides is the ability to do skeletal animation. This allows you to export to morph target animations like those offered by the Quake model formats or to export to skeletal animations like Half-Life or Genesis3D. For our gaming project, we'll use the Half-Life model format as it offers one of the easiest and most powerful game formats.

Installation

Before we can begin using MilkShape, we first need to install it.

ON THE CD

It's located on the CD-ROM that shipped with the book in the Applications\ MS3D1510 Directory. Otherwise, you can download the most up to date version from http://www.swissquake.ch/chumbalum-soft/.

Once you have acquired the software, the next step is to run the setup.exe file. It will begin the installation process where you will be presented with a screen that looks similar to Figure 28.1.

Click the next button to continue the installation. From the next window, which appears in Figure 28.2, you should enter an installation directory or use the default value of C:\Program Files\MilkShape 3D 1.5.10.

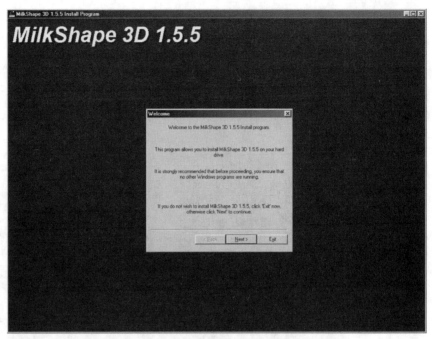

FIGURE 28.1 The installation program begins with this screen.

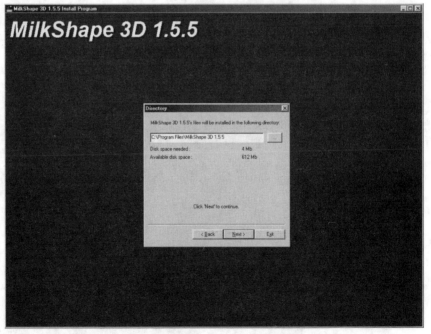

FIGURE 28.2 You should set the appropriate installation directory for MilkShape.

The default installation directory contains version information. As a result, it may be different depending on the version you have.

You need to click the Start button from a window that looks similar to Figure 28.3 to copy the files to the hard drive.

The last step in the process is to click the Exit button in the window, which is displayed in Figure 28.4.

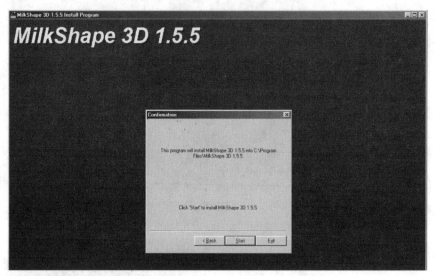

FIGURE 28.3   Clicking Start copies files to the hard drive.

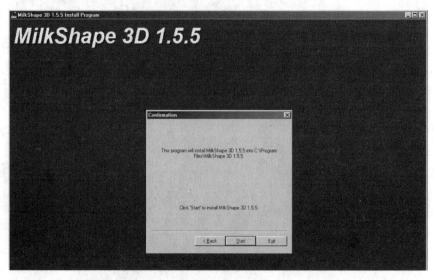

FIGURE 28.4   This is the final step in the installation process.

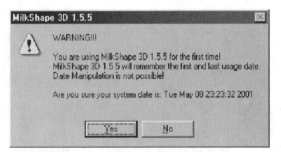

FIGURE 28.5   Make sure the system date and time are accurate before you click Yes.

Once you have finished the installation, you can run MilkShape by clicking the shortcut that was created in the installation. When you open MilkShape for the first time, a window will open which appears similar to Figure 28.5. This window will be displayed only when it is executed the first time and is very important. As you will notice, it displays you current system date and time.

You need to make sure the information is accurate as MilkShape allows you to use their software for only 30 days without registering it. If the information is incorrect, you need to correct it before you click Yes. Otherwise, if you attempt to correct it at a later time, the software will not function unless you register it. You should take the 30 days to try MilkShape and if you like it, you should consider registering it. It's currently only $20, a small price for a modeler with so many features.

Once you have determined the date is correct, you can click the Yes button, which will display the standard MilkShape interface that appears in Figure 28.6.

MILKSHAPE 3D INTERFACE

Before we begin looking at the modeling features of MilkShape, you first need to understand some of the basics of the MilkShape interface. Like the vast majority of modeling tools, you have the ability to alter the view windows. First, you can customize any individual window by right clicking on it and selecting from the available options. You can see the commands that are available in Figure 28.7.

Along with options for changing the individual viewports, you can also display the viewports in several types of sets. To change the viewports, you can click on the Window | Viewports menu option which is displayed in Figure 28.8.

Depending on your personal preference, the viewports can be displayed in several ways. First, you can display 4 viewports, which is the standard view and displayed in Figure 28.9. Otherwise, you can display the

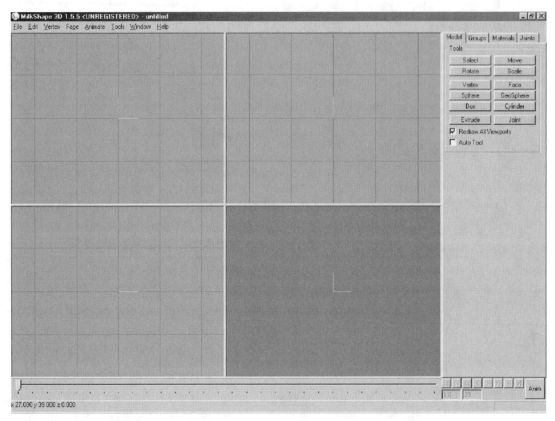

FIGURE 28.6 The standard MilkShape 3D interface.

FIGURE 28.7 You have many options available for the individual view windows.

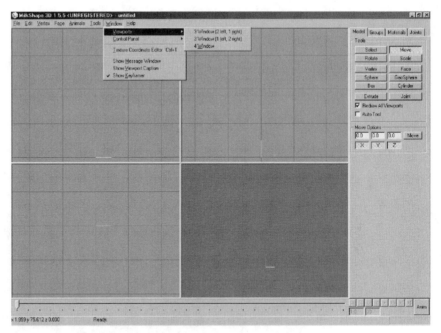

FIGURE 28.8   The viewports can be changed to your liking.

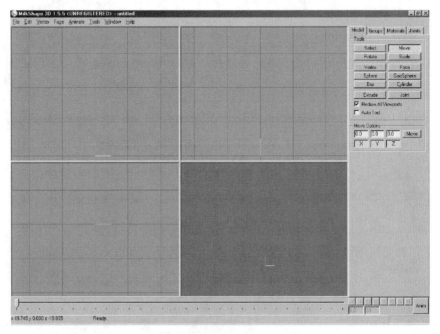

FIGURE 28.9   Viewports in standard 4-window setup.

viewpoints in 3 window views with 2 windows on the left (Figure 28.10) or 2 windows on the right (Figure 28.11).

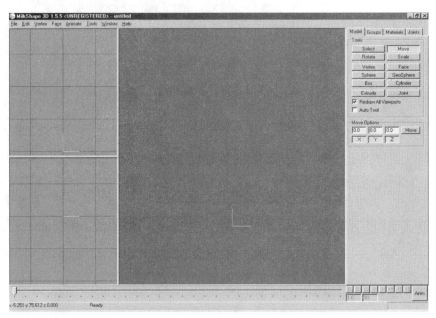

FIGURE 28.10   The viewports with 3 windows, 2 on the left and 1 on the right.

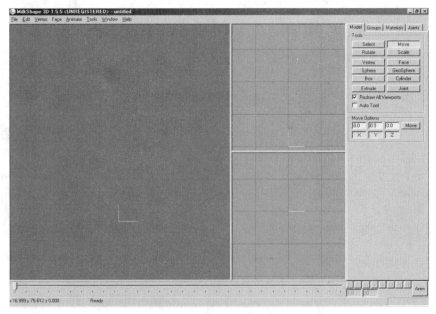

FIGURE 28.11   The viewports with 3 windows, 1 on the left and 2 on the right.

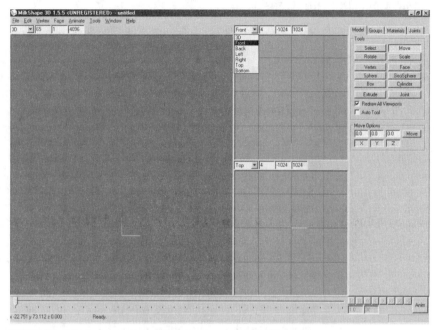

FIGURE 28.12   Displaying captions in the viewports can be a big time saver.

You can further customize the individual viewports by displaying captions in them. This allows you to not only enter parameters, but also to change the viewports from a drop down list. You can see these options in Figure 28.12.

VIEWPORT CONTROLS

Now that you have a basic understanding of the user interface, we'll move on to the basic functions of the viewports. A viewport can be zoomed by holding down the Shift key and the left mouse button and dragging the mouse vertically. It is important to note that zooming will not work if the Select button under the Model tab is selected. If the viewport is 3D, holding down the Shift key and the left mouse button will rotate it in a 360-degree arc. The viewport can also be panned by holding down the CTRL key when the left mouse button is selected and dragged.

BASIC MODELING FUNCTIONS

In Chapter 30, we'll use MilkShape 3D to construct models for the project we are creating in this book, but first, you need to be accustomed to many of the basic features that MilkShape offers.

Primitive Objects

To create models in MilkShape, you use the built in primitive objects that MilkShape offers. They are located in the upper right corner of the interface under the Model tab and can be seen in Figure 28.13. The vast majority of 3D programs provide geometric primitives such as spheres, boxes, and cones to use as building blocks.

Sphere

To draw a sphere, you need to place the pointer on the screen where you want the sphere's center point and then click and hold down the left mouse button while dragging the pointer to create the radius of the sphere. You'll see the sphere drawn as you drag the mouse. Once finished, simply release the button and the sphere will be placed in the available views. A sample sphere can be seen in Figure 28.14.

FIGURE 28.13 The primitives are used to construct models.

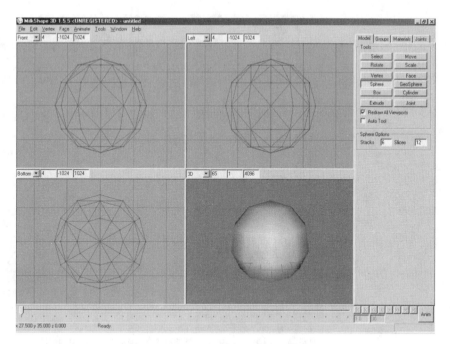

FIGURE 28.14   A sample sphere displayed in a 4 window viewport.

Geo-Sphere

Another form of sphere, but this is very smooth compared to the standard sphere. Creating the sphere is similar to the standard version as you click and hold the left mouse button at the desired center point of the geo-sphere and then drag the mouse to the desired radius of the sphere. The geo-sphere, a sample of which can be seen in Figure 28.15, will be displayed as you drag the mouse.

Box

Just like it sounds, a box is a six-sided cube. You draw it in much the same was as a sphere. Instead of placing the mouse where you'd like the center to be placed, you place it where you want the initial corner. Next, you click and hold the left mouse button while dragging the mouse until you reach the point where you would like the opposite corner placed. You'll see the box being drawn as you move the mouse. A sample box can be seen in Figure 28.16.

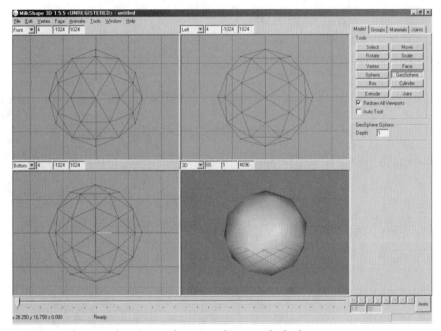

FIGURE 28.15 The geo-sphere is smooth compared to a standard sphere.

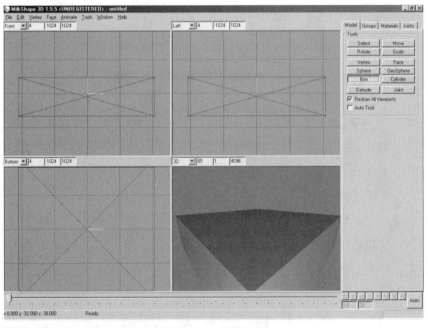

FIGURE 28.16 Boxes are drawn in a similar manner as the spheres.

Cylinder

A cylinder is created like the other primitives, but will always be drawn with the ends facing up and down. For instance, in the vertical views (which are front, back, left, right) you position the pointer where you want the cylinder to begin and then hold down the left mouse button and drag the pointer. The cylinder will be drawn as you drag the mouse. The diameter of the cylinder is scaled uniformly as you drag left or right and the height is set by the distance you drag vertically. In the vertical views, it appears that you are drawing a rectangle but you can verify that you are drawing a cylinder in the 3D view.

If you draw a cylinder in the top or bottom view, you click and drag the mouse similarly to the vertical views. However, you will notice that when you drag the mouse, you'll actually see a circle being drawn that scales uniformly. Again, you can verify you are actually drawing a cylinder by looking at the 3D view. You can view a sample cylinder in Figure 28.17.

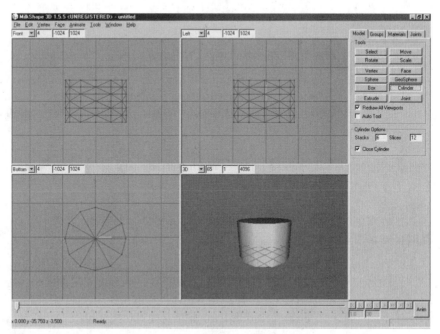

FIGURE 28.17   Depending on the viewport, a cylinder may look like a circle or a rectangle.

FIGURE 28.18 Mesh editing tools are available in the model tab.

Mesh Editing Tools

Along with the modeling tools, MilkShape provides several tools for moving, scaling, extruding and rotating your selected vertexes or faces. Like the modeling tools, the mesh tools are located in the Model tab, which is visible in Figure 28.18.

The mesh editing tools that follow only work on a selected vertex or face and will not work in a 3D view.

VERTICES AND FACES

Before we look at the mesh editing tools, we'll look at two of the basic components of MilkShape and 3D modeling in general: vertices and faces. A vertex (or vertices for more than one vertex) is simply a point in 3D space. You can combine them to form faces, which are a series of vertices that define a plane in 3D space.

You create a vertex by selecting the vertex button and clicking inside a viewport. Once you have placed the vertex, you will see a red dot that represents it. To create a face, you need to have a minimum of three vertices, which are then clicked on in a counterclockwise manner to create a face. Don't spend too much time worrying about this right now. We'll cover it in more depth when we create some actual models.

Select Tool

Now that you understand vertices and faces, we'll look at the mesh editing tools. The select tool is used to select a vertex, vertices, or faces. This is the first step before you move on to the other tools, which only work if a vertex or face is selected. You use select them in several ways but one of the easiest is by drawing a selection box around the vertices or faces that you want to select.

Drawing the selection box in MilkShape, which can be seen in Figure 28.19, works like most other graphics applications. You click in a viewport to set your initial corner and while holding the left mouse button, you drag the mouse. You will see the box being resized as you move the mouse and when you release the button, you'll notice that the selected vertices or faces will turn red to show that they are selected. The selected faces can be seen in Figure 28.20.

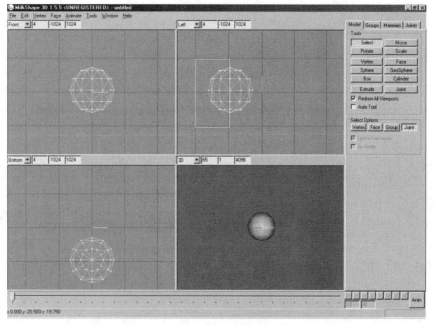

FIGURE 28.19   The selection box allows you to select multiple faces or vertices at a single time.

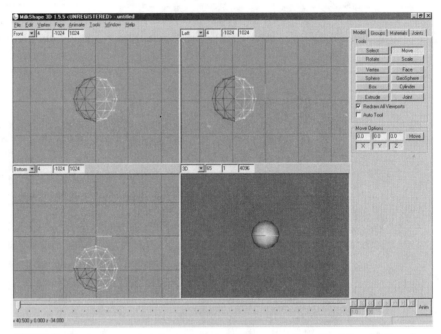

FIGURE 28.20   The faces or vertices that are selected will be colored in red to distinguish them from the others.

You may have already noticed the additional options available for the selection tool. Using these options and clicking on vertices or faces, you can select faces individually.

Depending on your accuracy when using either selection option, you will probably select unwanted faces or vertices. In this case, you should hold down the left mouse button and deselect any face or vertex that you do not want selected. They will return to their normal white color when you deselect them, which allow you to determine the remaining selected items. The last two selection options allow you to select an entire mesh group or a joint although we will not cover them at this time.

The next step is to look over the mesh editing tools move, scale, and rotate.

MOVE

The move tools works as you would expect. When you click on selected vertices or faces and drag them while the move tool is selected, they will move in the direction you are dragging. There are several options avail-

FIGURE 28.21   The faces have been moved –3 in all directions using the input boxes.

able when the move tool is selected. First, you can restrict movement of the faces or vertices by deactivating any of the X, Y, or Z buttons.

 X, Y, and Z coordinates refer to the directions in 3D space. X is the horizontal dimension (left to right). Y is the vertical direction (up and down). Z is the 3D dimension (back and forth).

Besides having the ability to move the vertices and faces by dragging the mouse, you can also enter exact amounts in the boxes, which are displayed in Figure 28.21.

SCALE

Scale is used to resize the selected faces by dragging the mouse or using the input boxes. It works ver similarly to the move tool in this respect. You can also restrict the movement as you can with the move tool.

There are a few additional options for the scale tool that originates with three radio boxes called Center of Mass, Origin and User Point. Center of mass means that the faces will be scaled from the center point of the se-

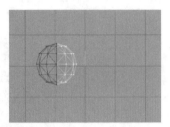

FIGURE 28.22 The origin of MilkShape.

lected faces. The origin of MilkShape 3D can be seen at the center of a viewport. It is the two lines that are displayed in Figure 28.22. If you select the origin button and then scale a face, the scale will be based on the origin point. The final option, user point, makes the scale radiate from the original position of the mouse when you click the button.

ROTATE

Rotate works similarly to the others with a click and drag operation being used to rotate the selected vertices or faces. The direction of rotation depends on the view you are in. As with the other tools, you can restrict the direction of rotation and you can manually input rotations into input boxes. It also has the same type of center point options that scale offers including Center of Mass, Origin, and User Point.

Extrude

The extrusion tool obviously allows you to extrude a face in a certain direction. You cannot extrude vertices and if you attempt to do so, some very strange things will happen. It becomes very unpredictable so you shouldn't even attempt to do it. The extrude tool has similar options that the other mesh editing tools offer including the ability to enter exact values into X, Y, and Z input boxes. Figure 28.23 displays a face that has been extruded.

ANIMATION TOOLS

Joints

You can create joints for models with the joint tool. You use it very similarly to the many of the MilkShape tools with one exception. Instead of

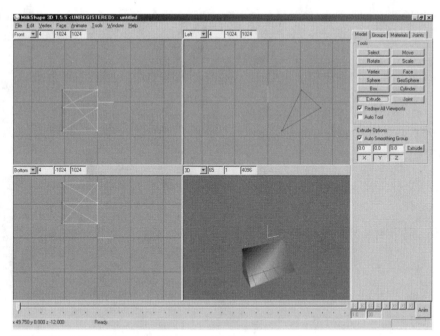

FIGURE 28.23   A triangular face that has been extruded.

clicking and dragging to create bones, you first click a single time, which creates the first part of a bone, and then move your mouse and click again to create the second part. A sample bone can be seen in Figure 28.24.

MilkShape uses keyframes to create animation sequences. We'll look at this further when we do a step by step tutorial later in the book.

MENU

File

The last thing we'll look at in this introduction to MilkShape is the file menu, which can be seen in Figure 28.25. There really isn't much to discuss with this menu. It contains all of the standard file operations such as open, close, and save. Most of the items in the File menu are self-explanatory with the exception of Merge, which does just what its name implies. It merges two 3D files together.

Lastly, the import and export options offer a great deal of functionality for game developers. Perhaps the most important aspect of any modeler is the file formats they offer. MilkShape excels in this area. Depending

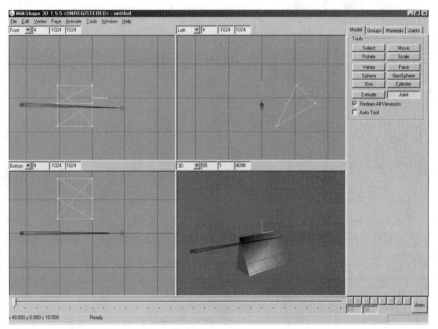

FIGURE 28.24 Creating joints and bones in MilkShape is a very easy process.

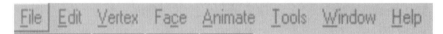

FIGURE 28.25 MilkShape has a standard Windows menu.

on your needs, MilkShape can export models to many popular game formats including the following list:

- Half-Life SMD
- Quake I MDL
- Quake II MD2
- Quake III Arena MD3
- Vampire t:MR NOD
- Lithtech ABC v11, v12
- Genesis3D BDY 1.0
- Genesis3D MOT 1.0
- Unreal/UT 3D
- Nebula Engine
- Wavefront OBJ
- 3dstudio ASC
- LightWave LWO

- AutoCAD DXF
- POV-Ray INC
- VRML1 WRL
- Autodesk 3DS
- MilkShape 3D
- ASCII RAW
- Renderman RIB

Edit

The edit menu is missing several of the normal features you might expect in a Windows application. It does not offer the standard cut, copy, and paste commands. Instead, you can use duplicate selection which will copy any faces you currently have selected. It will not copy vertices. Also, the duplicated section will be placed in the exact location as the original so you may not see it at first glance.

Vertex

The vertex menu offers several options all related to vertices. First, you can snap two vertices together with Snap Together. You can also snap a vertex to the grid or weld them together which you always do after you snap them together. Flatten allows you to flatten all of the vertices to a particular plane. Lastly, the mirror commands are particularly useful when you have duplicated an object.

Faces

This menu offers option for faces in MilkShape. The first menu option, Reverse Vertex Order, will make a visible face invisible or an invisible face visible. It does this because a face only has one visible side. You can just think of it as a type of toggle, which allows a face to be on or off. Subdivide 3 and 4 both subdivide a face into 3 or 4 parts respectively.

In Figure 28.26, you can see a square with 2 faces selected. If you click on Faces | Turn Edge, you will notice that the edge will turn and will now appear like Figure 28.27. The last command we'll look at is Face to Front which works opposite of Reverse Vertex Order.

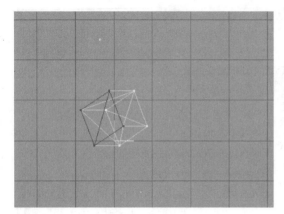

FIGURE 28.26 A square with two faces selected.

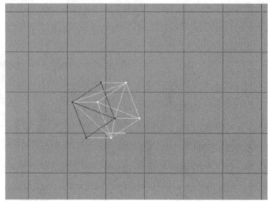

FIGURE 28.27 The edge has been turned between two faces have been turned.

Others

The remaining menus can be covered very quickly. The animate menu contains everything related to animation. We will look at it in greater detail in a later chapter. The tools menu contains information specific to individual model formats like Half-Life and Quake III Arena. If you are planning to use MilkShape for a specific type of file format, you may want to invest a little time to work through this menu. The last menu, Window, was already looked at earlier in the chapter. It gave us the option to arrange our viewpoints in specific ways.

CHAPTER REVIEW

While there are several great 3D modelers on the market that cost in the thousands, MilkShape provides some of their functionality at only $20. It would be difficult to find such a bargain in another software package. Not only is the program inexpensive, it also offers everything you need for the type of low-polygon modeling necessary for real time game development. With the basic information you have gained in this chapter, it will be possible to move on to creating simple game models with MilkShape and ultimately creating animated characters.

INTRODUCTION TO
PAINT SHOP PRO

INTRODUCTION TO PAINT SHOP PRO

Paint Shop Pro is an excellent graphics editor and is a great choice for game developers. Currently in its 7th release, Paint Shop Pro offers a tremendous number of features in a very low cost product. It supports both bitmap and vector objects which allows you to have the access to both types of graphics without purchasing another tool. For game designs and texture creation, Paint Shop Pro offers everything you need in one easy to use package.

INSTALLATION

Before we begin discussing specifics of Paint Shop Pro, we need to install it.

It's located on the CD-ROM that shipped with the book in the Applications Directory and is called PSP702ev.exe. If you would prefer, you could download the most up to date version from http://www.jasc.com.

The first step in the installation process is running the executable file. It will begin the installation process where you will be presented with a screen that looks similar to Figure 29.1. You can leave the directory as it is listed. It's only a temporary directory for the installation files.

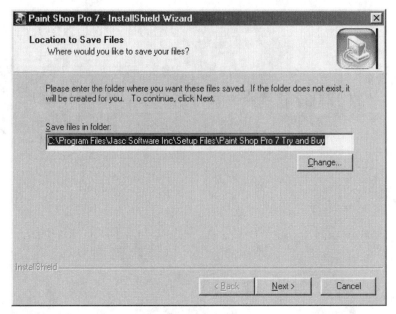

FIGURE 29.1 The installation program begins with this screen.

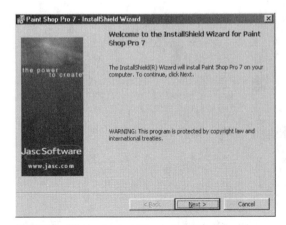

FIGURE 29.2   Clicking next at this window to continue the installation.

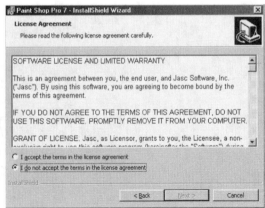

FIGURE 29.3   You need to accept the license agreement before you can continue.

Click the next button to continue the installation. The next step will take a few moments before another window will finally appear. It should look similar to Figure 29.2. You need to click the next button at this window.

The next window that is displayed is a license window, which can be seen in Figure 29.3. It displays the Paint Shop Pro license agreement you should read. In order to continue the installation, you need to accept the terms of the license.

After you select the agreement, click the next button. Next, a window, which is displayed in Figure 29.4, is displayed that allows you to select a complete installation or a custom installation. Leave the installation set at complete and click next.

The last step is to select the install button from the window that looks similar to Figure 29.5.

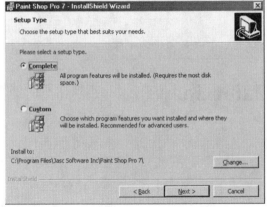

FIGURE 29.4   Choose a complete installation from this window.

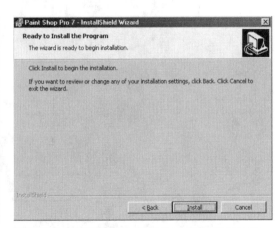

FIGURE 29.5   This is the final step in the installation process.

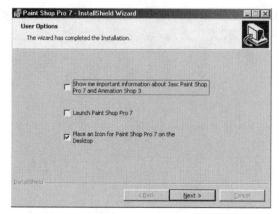

FIGURE 29.6 Clicking finish ends the entire installation process.

Once you have finished the installation, the InstallShield Wizard will display a window that looks something like Figure 29.6. You should choose to create a shortcut on the desktop from this window and click next. From the last window, you should click finish.

Once the installation has been completely finished, you will find a shortcut to Paint Shop Pro on your desktop. Double-click the shortcut Paint Shop Pro. When it is first started, a window will be displayed that looks like Figure 29.7. If you would like to purchase Paint Shop Pro, you can

FIGURE 29.7 This window allows you to purchase Paint Shop Pro or use it in trial mode for 30 days.

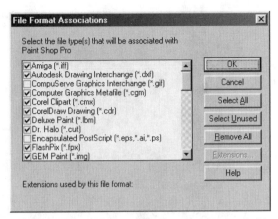

FIGURE 29.8   You can select certain files to be associated with Paint Shop Pro.

do so by clicking on the order button. It will give you details on how to - purchase Paint Shop Pro. If you do not choose to purchase it, you can use Paint Shop Pro freely for 30 days by clicking the start button to move on.

 Paint Shop Pro will function correctly for only 30 days unless you purchase it.

Another window will be displayed that asks you to pick your file associations. If you are unfamiliar with file associations, they allow a program like Paint Shop Pro to be opened simply by double clicking a file it is associated with. Unless you have some specific files in mind, you should leave the standard files selected, some of which are displayed in Figure 29.8.

Once you have determined the correct files, you can click the OK button to display the standard Paint Shop Pro user interface.

USER INTERFACE

One the software has been installed, we'll look at the basics of the user interface and a few of the most important tools that are available in Paint Shop Pro. In this chapter, we'll use Paint Shop Pro for designing textures and a user interface for the first person shooter we are going to create.

The Paint Shop Pro user interface can be seen in Figure 29.9. It's a very good design for a user interface as it provides excellent functionality but is very easy to learn.

Figure 29.10 includes basic descriptions for all of the user interface elements.

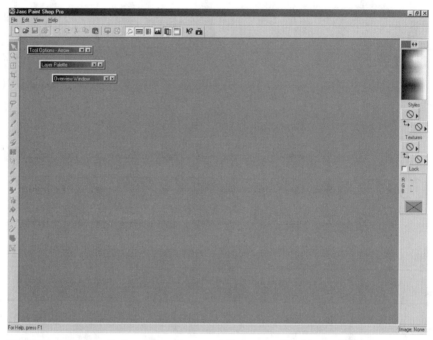

FIGURE 29.9 Paint Shop Pro has an interface very similar to most Windows applications.

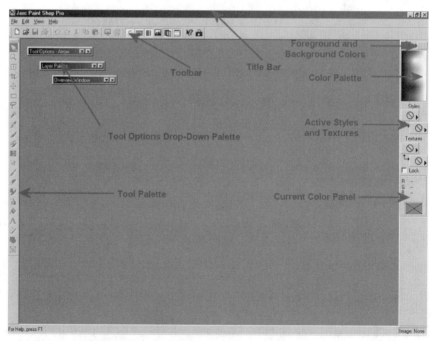

FIGURE 29.10 The Paint Shop Pro interface with everything labeled.

In the next step, we'll look at several of the labeled entries in more detail.

The Toolbar

The toolbar contains options for doing many routine tasks like opening, closing, saving and copying or pasting. The toolbar displays buttons corresponding to the menu commands. It's much easier to click the toolbar button instead of looking through the menu for the corresponding option. If a command is available, you can click on it. Otherwise, it will appear to be "grayed out" and will be unavailable for selection.

Tool Palette

The tool palette contains the painting, drawing, and retouching tools. You can see the tools in Figure 29.11.

FIGURE 29.11   The tool palette contains a variety of drawing, painting, and retouching tools.

Tool Options Palette

When you click a tool palette button, the Tool Options palette displays the options associated with the tool, and the Status bar displays a short description of its use. Depending on the current tool, you can select from a single tab of options to multiple tabs. The palette has a permanent tab that allows you to modify the appearance of the cursor and the settings for a pressure sensitive tablet.

Color Palette

You use the color palette to select the colors, gradients, patterns, and textures that you want to apply to an image. When you move the cursor over the available colors panel, it changes to the dropper tool. A single click will change the foreground color and a right click will change the background color. Directly above the available colors, you will see the currently selected foreground and background colors.

Style and Texture

The style and texture tools are useful for determining if you want to paint with a solid color, a texture, or a pattern. The upper boxes display the foreground and stroke styles while the lower boxes display fill and background styles.

Painting Tools

Paint Shop Pro provides several tools that you can use for painting. The painting tools, which are available on the tool palette, can only be used on raster layers while the drawing tools, which are also available on the tool palette, can be used on either raster or vector layers. We'll look at several of the most important features of the tools.

Paintbrush

The paintbrush is useful for painting freehand much like you would with a regular paintbrush. You simply select the paintbrush tool and click and drag the cursor while holding a mouse button. If you want to apply the current foreground and stroke style, you can use the left mouse button. The right button applies the background and fill style. Releasing either button ends your current painting. If you would like to create straight lines, you should hold down the Shift key and click the beginning point. Then,

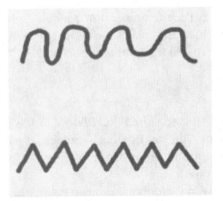

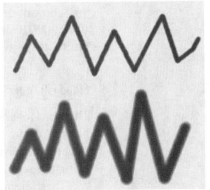

FIGURE 29.12 Painting freehand with the mouse.

FIGURE 29.13 The airbrush works similarly to the standard paintbrush.

move to where you would like the line to end and click again. Figure 29.12 displays the differences between freehand drawing and holding with a mouse and holding down the shift key to drawn straight lines.

Eraser

You can use the eraser to remove colors from an image, replacing them with the background color or transparency. Although you should be careful when using the eraser, you can easily restore a mistake by pressing CTRL-Z or selecting Undo from the Edit menu.

Airbrush

The airbrush works in much the same was as the standard paintbrush tool but instead of a solid color, it simulates an airbrush or spray can. You can use it to draw freehand or by holding the Shift key, you can force it to draw straight lines. Figure 29.13 displays a sample of painting comparing the standard paintbrush and the airbrush.

Picture Tube

Paint Shop Pro's picture tubes, some of which can be seen in Figure 29.14, are one of its best features as it allows you to paint with a variety of pre-existing objects. You can add everything from raindrops to flowers to an image very quickly. There are hundreds of picture tubes available on the Internet, or you can use the ones that come with the program. You can even design your own with Paint Shop Pro.

You can quickly see the power of the picture tubes by looking at Figure 29.15. Every object in it was added with the picture tube tool and the entire image was created in less than 30 seconds.

Flood Fill Tool

The last tool we'll look at is the flood fill tool. It fills an area with a color, pattern, or gradient. You can use this to quickly at patterns or solid colors to the entire background of an image. You can also fill only a selection using the selection tool.

There are many more tools available in Paint Shop Pro and you are encouraged to spend time going through its help file. This chapter is here to introduce you to some of the concepts of Paint Shop Pro. When we later use it for creating graphics and textures, we'll do everything in a step by step manner.

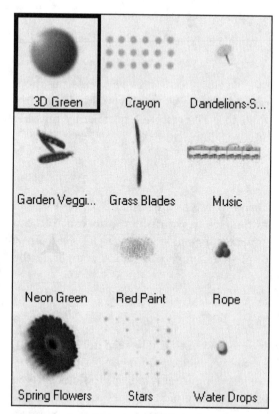

FIGURE 29.14 Picture tubes are available freely on the Internet.

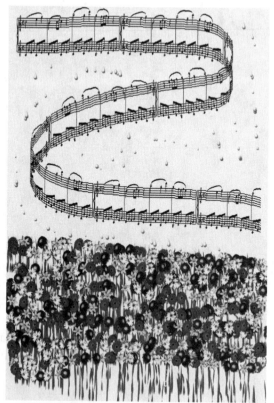

FIGURE 29.15 You can quickly create entire scenes with picture tubes.

Vector Drawing Tools

One of the newest trends in raster editing tools such as Paint Shop Pro is to add vector drawing and editing tools. Paint Shop Pro has added several tools that allow you to use raster and vector graphics in a single application, which makes your job much easier.

Vector Vs. Raster

Before we move on to look at the vector drawing tools, it's important that you have a basic understanding of the difference between vector and raster formats. A raster file is composed of units of light that are each called a pixel. By grouping these pixels, a raster image can be created. The pixels can be blended to create smooth transitions for objects, which makes it good for gaming. Raster images are resolution dependent. That is, you specify the resolution and pixel dimensions when you create the image and if you later decide to increase or decrease the image it can have a negative impact on its quality.

Vector images are not made up of pixels. Instead, they are composed of mathematical instructions that draw an image. This has several advantages over pixel based images. First, every object is stored as a separate item in an image. This information stores data such as position, width, height and color to name a few. Vector based images are resolution independent. That is, the can be freely resized without losing image quality. You may wonder how a monitor, which uses pixels, can display these mathematical computations in a manner we understand. The vector images go through a process so that the monitor can see them. The rasterized images can then be displayed on the screen.

Layers

Default Paint Shop Pro images consist of a single layer, the background layer which is comparable to a canvas you would paint on in the real world. You can create additional layers, stacking them upon one another. Paint Shop Pro supports up to 100 layers per image although the number might be smaller depending on your computer memory.

The layer palette allows you to switch between the various layers in an image with a single mouse click. As you can see in Figure 29.16, it lists details about each layer. By clicking on the layer visibility toggle (looks like glasses), you can display or hide any layer in the image. If you save your image to the internal Paint Shop Pro file format (psp), the layers will be saved with the image. Otherwise, the image will be flattened when the image is saved in another format.

You can create three types of layers in Paint Shop Pro: raster layers, vector layers, and adjustment layers. Raster layers, like raster graphics, contain pixel-based information. Vector layers mathematical instructions for drawing vector lines, shapes, and text. Lastly, adjustment layers contain color correction information that is used to alter layers placed beneath them. It's easy to distinguish between vector and raster layers in the layer palette. The layer palette displays the vector icon and when the layer contains vector objects, a plus sign appears next to the icon. You can see an example of this in Figure 29.17. If you click the plus sign, the individual objects that are on the vector layer can be seen.

 You cannot place vector objects on raster layers. Likewise, you cannot place raster objects on vector layers.

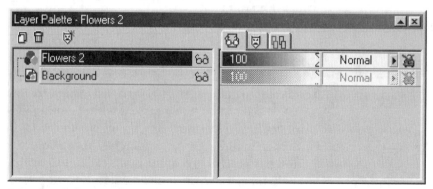

FIGURE 29.16 The layer palette allows you to quickly view layer information.

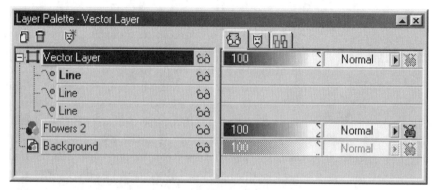

FIGURE 29.17 Vector and raster layers are distinguishable in the layer palette.

Draw Tool

The draw tool may be the most powerful tool available in Paint Shop Pro. You can use the draw tool for both raster and vector drawing depending on the type of layer you are working on. It can draw straight lines, freehand lines, or even Bezier curves. Vector drawn objects can be moved, deformed, and edited after they are created without affecting anything else in the image.

CHAPTER REVIEW

As you have seen throughout this chapter, Paint Shop Pro offers a tremendous number of features and is easy for beginners to learn as the user interface can be mastered with relatively little effort. We have just touched on the absolute basics of this software and will later use it to create textures and 2D graphics for our game project.

30

CREATING LOW POLYGON MODELS WITH MILKSHAPE 3D

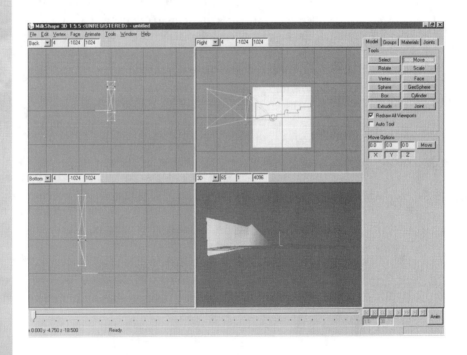

Now that we have learned some of Paint Shop Pro's basic functions, we'll begin working on using it along with MilkShape 3D. In this chapter, we'll design a gun that could potentially be used for our game. There are several ways we could begin this process, but starting out with some type of very basic sketch seems like it would be a good idea.

BEGINNING THE PROCESS

2D Sketch

We'll begin our model by creating a basic sketch in Paint Shop Pro. The sketch will serve as a basic outline for our model. Once it has been complete, we'll import it into MilkShape as a background and then remove it once we are done. You need to open Paint Shop Pro if you haven't already done so and select new from the File menu. A window will open and prompt you for several items. For a width and height you can use 144. The resolution can remain at default while the background color should be set to white.

The next step is to create a new vector layer by selecting New Vector Layer from within the layer menu. Now, using the drawing tool, we'll sketch a gun similar in appearance to figure 30.1.

Once you have created something similar, the next step is to save the image as a Paint Shop Pro file so that you can edit the file later. After it has been saved, you should also save it as a BMP format. MilkShape 3D needs it in BMP so that it can be imported as a background picture.

MilkShape 3D

We can import the image into MilkShape 3D once it is in BMP format. First, open MilkShape and right click on the Right viewport. If you don't have

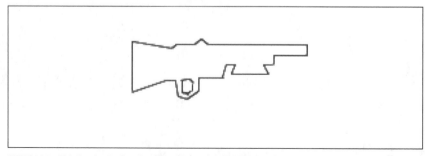

FIGURE 30.1 This is a basic sketch of the 3D model we'll be creating.

a Right viewport, change the upper right viewport to Right with the drop down box. Next, select Choose Background Image from the pop-up menu. It will then prompt you for the location of the file. You should choose the filename and location you saved the sketch in.

Gun Stock

Once you have imported it, you should draw a square in the same viewport. Your screen should appear similar to Figure 30.2.

You'll notice that the square model has been resized in the previous step. The width is much smaller than the default size. If you cannot remember, you do this by selecting Scale from the Model tab and then clicking and dragging your mouse in the appropriate viewport.

This square will serve as the stock for our gun so we need to shape it accordingly. You need to choose Select from the Model tab and then vertex from Select Options. Next, draw a line around the vertices that are on the far right of the model. They should then appear to be red. Choose scale and then click and drag the mouse down in the right viewport. You'll see the object being resized. Continue to resize it until it appears something like Figure 30.3.

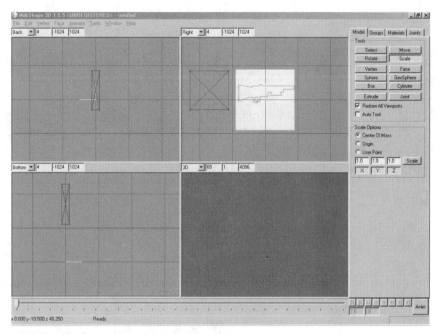

FIGURE 30.2   The first step in creating the 3D model.

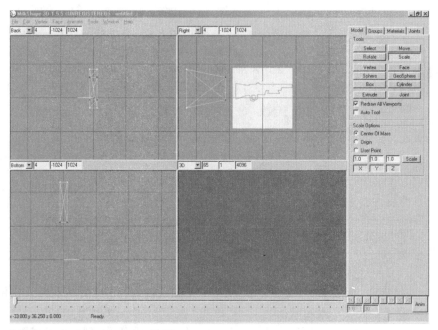

FIGURE 30.3 Resizing the stock in MilkShape.

Once you have it in place, we need to choose extrude from the Model tab. This will allow you to create an extrusion with the already selected vertices. Click and drag your mouse in the right viewport to the right until it has reached a size similar to Figure 30.4.

The next step is to select only the upper two vertices on the right side of the newly extruded piece. Once you have selected them, you can move the vertices until they reach a point similar to Figure 30.5.

Remember the undo feature in the edit menu if you make a mistake. It will allow you to recover from most mistakes you make along the way.

Once it is in position, you need to select the entire face that was extruded. You can see this in Figure 30.6. You'll also notice that the 3D view is constantly being changed. It allows you to see details you otherwise wouldn't have seen.

The face is then extruded again to look like Figure 30.7. As you follow along, notice that we'll basically keep an eye on the rough design offered to use by our drawing.

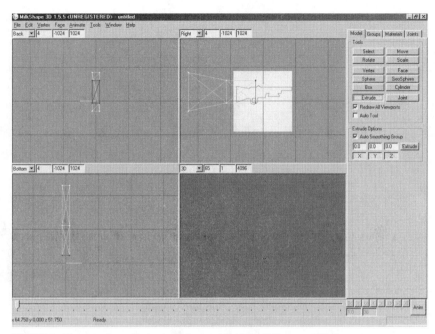

FIGURE 30.4   The extrusion will eventually be used for the middle parts of the gun.

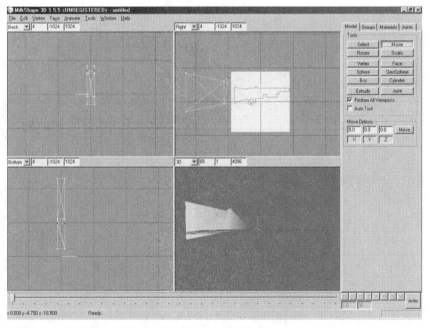

FIGURE 30.5   The vertices are being moved to create the angle.

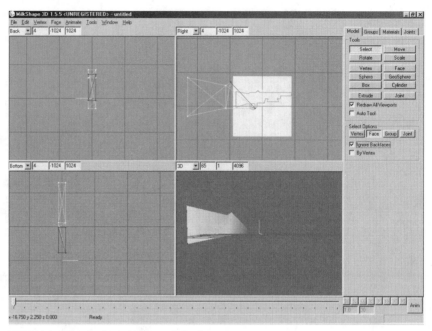

FIGURE 30.6 The extrusion with faces selected.

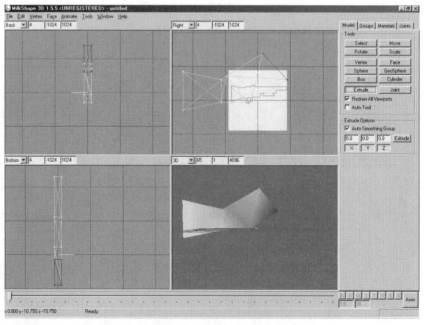

FIGURE 30.7 The extrusion tool is used several times in this tutorial.

You can then use the Selection tool to individually move sets of vertices so that the new extrusion now looks like Figure 30.8.

The next step will be for you to create another box like the one visible in Figure 30.9.

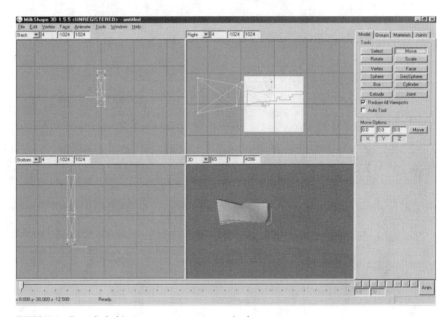

FIGURE 30.8   Extruded objects are very easy to manipulate.

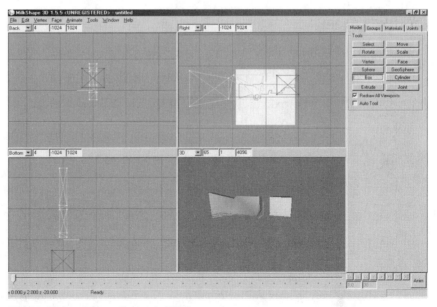

FIGURE 30.9   Creating another box in MilkShape.

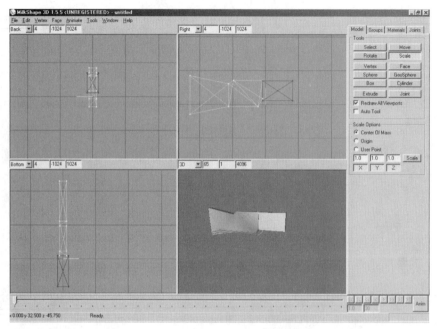

FIGURE 30.10 After we create them, the objects need to be sized and positioned appropriately.

You can resize the box and position it in a manner consistent with Figure 30.10.

CREATING A BARREL

In order to create a barrel for our gun, we must first decide what primitive object to use. The only one that makes a great deal of sense for a barrel is a cylinder, so our next step is the creation of a cylinder that is approximately the size of the one shown in Figure 30.11.

While the cylinder is still selected, click on rotate in the Right viewport and click and drag the mouse to the left or right to rotate it. You can rotate it so that the back view appears to be similar to Figure 30.12.

The last step in the creation of the barrel is to position it with the rest of the pieces of the gun so that it appears on top of the gun stock. It's useful to use the 3D viewport when attempting to align the barrel as you can look at the gun from several different directions. Your gun should now look similar to Figure 30.13.

If you need to zoom in or out of a viewport, simply hold down the shift button and click and drag with the left mouse button. You can also pan the viewport by using the Ctrl key in place of the Shift key.

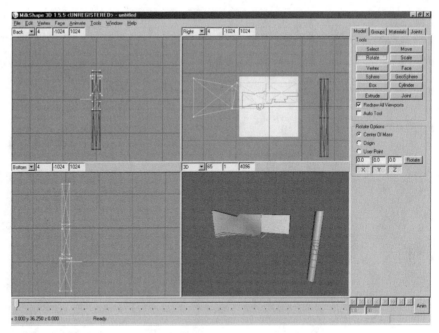

FIGURE 30.11 The first step in creating a barrel.

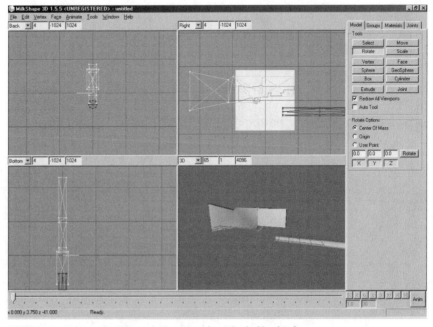

FIGURE 30.12 You need to rotate the barrel so that it looks like this figure.

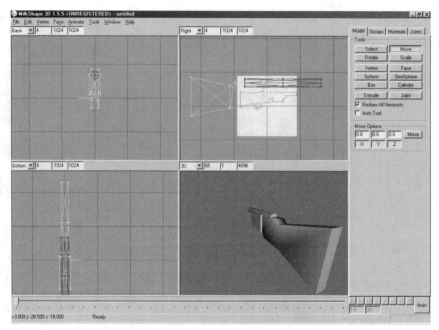

FIGURE 30.13 The barrel is now finished and in its final place.

The Clip

If you look at our hand drawing, you'll notice that we have to create another box to use as the gun clip. Like most of this project, we'll use a box as the basis for this part of the model. First, create the box similar to Figure 30.14.

Next, we need to select the vertices at the top of the box on both corners, which means that we'll have 4 of them selected. Now we can use the scale button to move the corners so that they are angled like our drawing. We also need to resize the width of the box so that it is smaller than the rest of the gun. Lastly, we need to move the box so that it rests in a location similar to Figure 30.15 which shows all the changes made to the box.

A Trigger

For a project like this, there are countless ways you could go about designing the entire gun. This is true of everything including a trigger. With most guns, in both the virtual and real worlds, there is an opening for your hand with the trigger inside of it. This gun will contain the opening but we'll skip creating an actual trigger although we'll actually call the entire assembly a trigger.

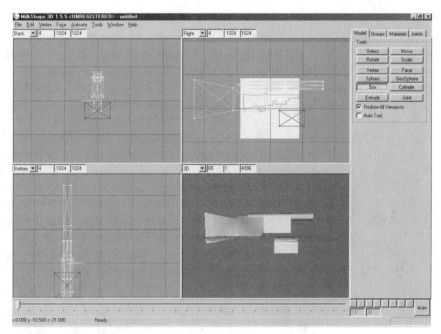

FIGURE 30.14   There are several steps needed to create the clip.

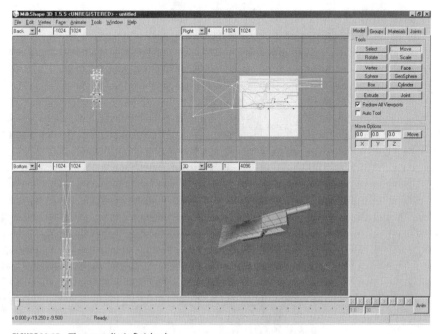

FIGURE 30.15   The gun clip is finished.

To create the opening we begin with a box that is sized similar to Figure 30.16.

Next, we need to resize the width making it smaller than the rest of the gun and also rotate it so that it looks something like Figure 30.17.

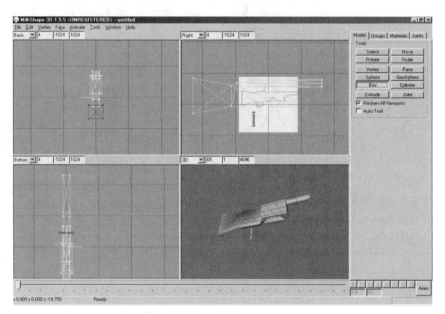

FIGURE 30.16   This is our first step for the trigger opening.

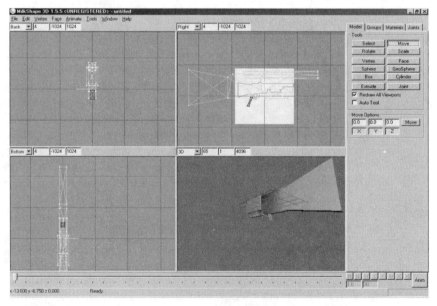

FIGURE 30.17   Rotating and resizing the box makes our opening begin to take form.

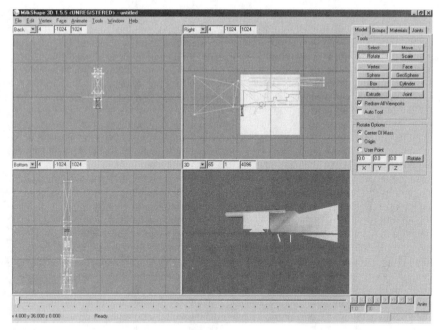

FIGURE 30.18   Duplicating objects can be a big time saver over creating completely new ones.

We could create another entirely new box and continue working on the opening, but it is easier to use Duplicate Object from the Edit menu. Once you have duplicated it, the new object will appear exactly over the old one. You need to move it before you'll actually see it. Position it similar to Figure 30.18. You'll also notice that it is rotated so that it is perpendicular to the stock while the old one remains angled.

With two parts of the trigger completed, we need to add a third one that will connect the other two. We'll again duplicate and rotate one of the other pieces so that the width remains constant. When it has been rotated correctly, it should like Figure 30.19.

The last step for creating the trigger is to zoom in and pan the 3D view so that the trigger appears very close. It allows us to resize the third piece of the trigger so that it fits perfectly. Figures 30.20 and 30.21 contain an example of this.

Congratulations, we now have a complete gun! In the next steps, we'll make slight changes to the overall shape of the model so that you see how quick and easy it is to fine-tune a MilkShape model.

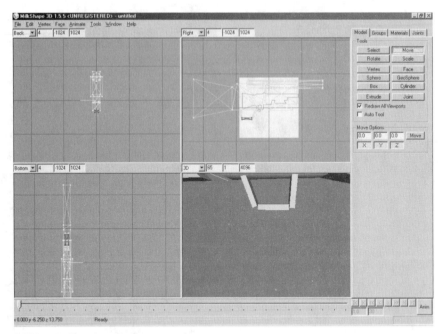

FIGURE 30.19 The trigger is almost complete.

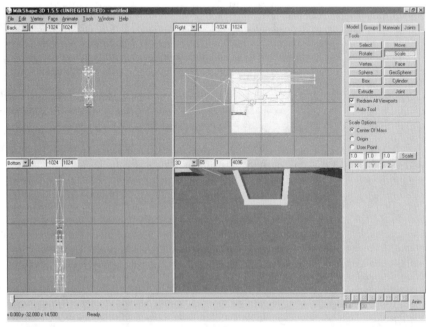

FIGURE 30.20 The 3D view is perfect for finely positioning and resizing of objects.

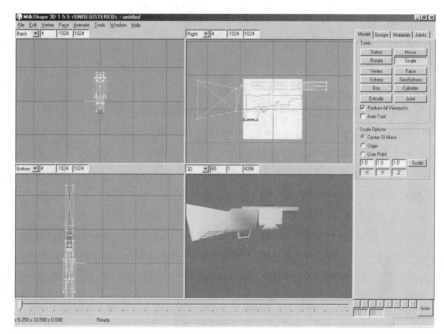

FIGURE 30.21   Our trigger opening is completed.

ADJUSTING THE MODEL

The model is finished and could probably be left alone and the texturing process could begin. However, it's very easy to make small or large adjustments to the model, which we'll do in the following steps that will hopefully make changes to benefit the model. It is probably a good idea to save the model at this time so that if you make changes that you don't like, you can always revert back to the old one.

The Stock

The first area that could use some attention is the stock. Like any form of artwork, modeling is often very objective, and often you simply go by how you feel. The angle on the stock, which can be seen clearly in Figure 30.22, is a little drastic. We can change this by moving the vertices at the end of the angle to form a larger angle like the one in Figure 30.23.

With the changes we made to the stock, it seems that the end of the stock could also use some changes. We can lengthen the stock slightly and also reduce the angles. Figures 30.24 and 30.25 show the before and after views.

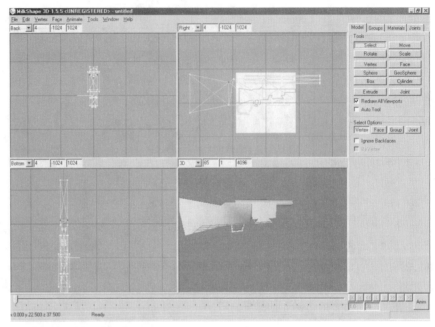

FIGURE 30.22 The short angle could be a source of concern.

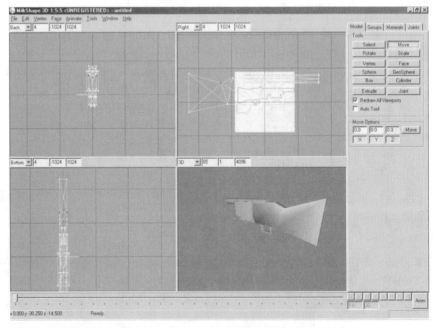

FIGURE 30.23 This looks much better after lengthening the angle.

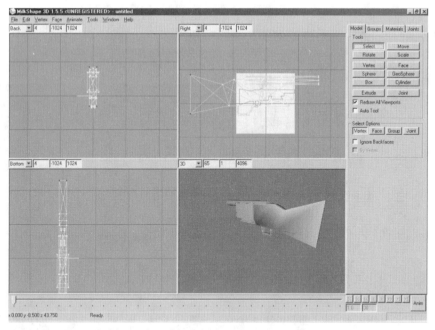

FIGURE 30.24   The end of the stock could need some adjustment made.

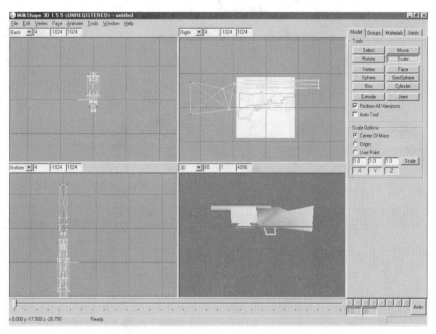

FIGURE 30.25   Reducing the angles on stock and lengthening it give it a much better look.

After we made the previous changes, it is apparent that the bottom vertices also need to be moved in order to make the end of the stock a straight edge. Figure 30.26 shows the necessary change.

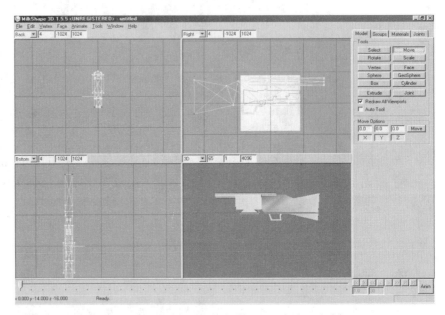

FIGURE 30.26   The stock is now at a 90-degree angle relative to the barrel of the gun.

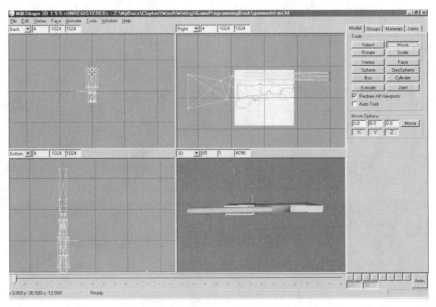

FIGURE 30.27   The barrel is now resized and is now in a better size relation to the stock.

Barrel

With the stock being elongated, it now appears that the barrel could use a little lengthening as well. We can select the vertices at the end of the barrel and simply move them in a manner consistent with Figure 30.27.

Smoothing

The final step in this chapter is to use the Groups tab to select every part of the model. We'll then assign a smoothing group to all of the items that will make them appear much better after the refinements we've made.

The first step is the select the models in the Group tab. Regardless of the names of your objects, you should begin this by clicking on the top group, which in Figure 30.28 is Box 01. When it is highlighted, you should click the select button that is located in this same tab directly beneath the highlighted groups. The individual box should now be colored red in the viewports. Continue doing this for all items until everything has been selected like Figure 30.28.

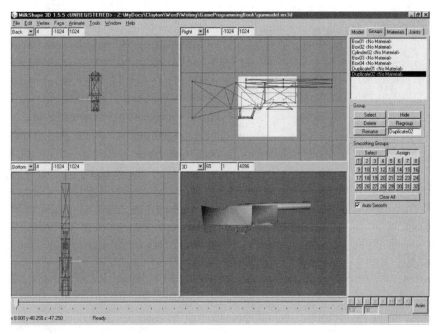

FIGURE 30.28   Every group has been selected.

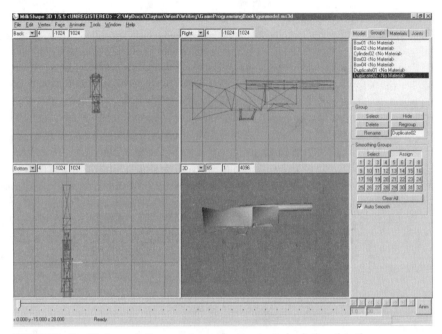

FIGURE 30.29   The 3D viewport allows you to see changes more clearly than the others.

There is one final step to smooth all of the objects. Click the Assign button followed by number 1. The object will appear much smoother and is particularly evident in Figure 30.29 in the 3D viewport.

CHAPTER REVIEW

In this chapter we modeled a complete 3D gun in MilkShape. You used many of the tools that it offers including several different primitive objects and moving, rotating, and scaling. The next step is the creation of textures for the model, which can be done in Paint Shop Pro and then imported into MilkShape. The next chapter details this aspect of modeling.

31

HALF-LIFE MODEL

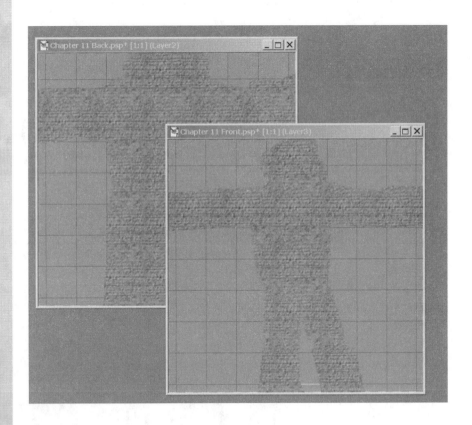

n this chapter we'll expand on our previous knowledge of MilkShape 3D in the creation of a Half-Life humanoid model. Although we could use DirectX, Quake, or any number of model formats, we'll utilize the Half-Life format for a number of reasons. The system allows us to create or customize an animation in a relatively easy manner. Additionally, Milk-Shape 3D supports the Half-Life model format and includes the ability to compile the animations.

ON THE CD

The creation of a model is a very involved process. If you would prefer, you can use one of the ready made models that are included on the CD-ROM instead of creating your own.

GETTING STARTED

Because this chapter involves the creation of a 3D humanoid model, it will contain a large number of steps. To aid you in the process, this chapter will include figures for many of the steps. The benefits are twofold: it will be easier to follow along and will allow you to check your progress regularly.

The first step is to open MilkShape at which time we are presented with a screen similar to Figure 31.1.

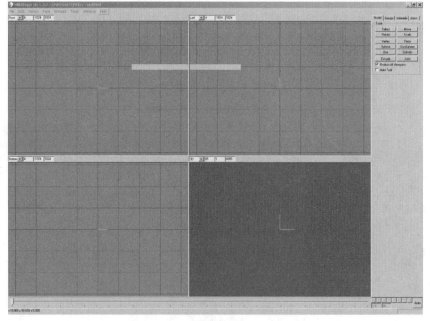

FIGURE 31.1 The MilkShape interface as displayed on startup.

FIGURE 31.2 The Open dialog is used to open the Valve skeleton.

Because we are creating a humanoid Half-Life MDL, we are going to utilize a Valve created skeleton for our animations. Fortunately, MilkShape ships with the skeleton which can be opened by choosing File | Open. From the Open dialog box, which can be seen in Figure 31.2, choose "valve_skeleton.ms3d". We are going to display the skeleton early in the project to give us a sort of template to use when we model our human.

After the file opens, MilkShape should look something like Figure 31.3.

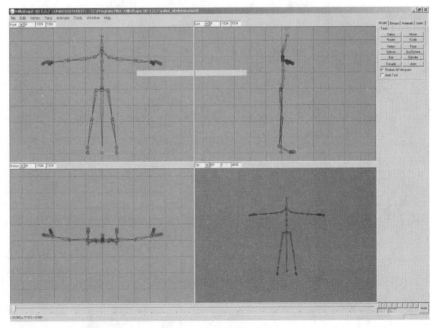

FIGURE 31.3 We'll use the Valve skeleton as a template.

Creating the Upper Body

We'll begin the modeling process by adding a Box to the scene. You should resize it so that it is similar to Figure 31.4.

 If you cannot remember the steps in basic modeling, you can refer to Chapter 6.

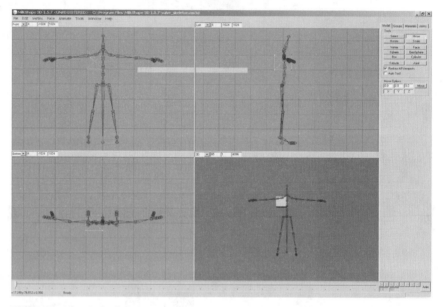

FIGURE 31.4 A box is the first step in our model.

FIGURE 31.5 Selecting the appropriate options.

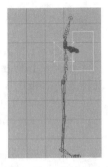

FIGURE 31.6   The selection tool is
used to select these vertices.

The next step is to resize the model so that from front to back it is
smaller. We can accomplish this by choosing Select from the Tools menu
and Vertex from the Options menu. Figure 31.5 displays the menu.

With the selection tool, draw a box around the 4 vertices that are at
the front of the model. You can see the selection tool being drawn around
the appropriate areas in Figure 31.6.

Once you have selected the vertices, the next step is to select Moves
from the Tools menu. You can then move the selected vertices closer to
the front of the skeleton. You can see an approximation of this in Figure
31.7.

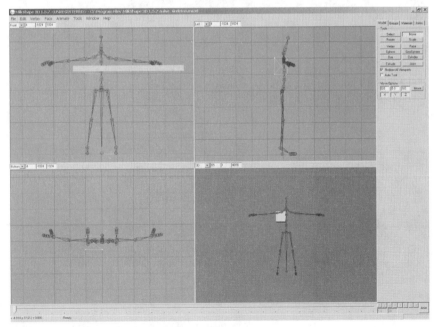

FIGURE 31.7   The width of the box should be similar to this.

You need to repeat the previous steps for the 4 vertices on the backside of the model as well. This will alter the width of the box which can be seen in Figure 31.8. As you resize the elements that will make up this model, please keep in mind that the skeleton itself will not be visible when the model is compiled. We are using it at this time for a reference. With that in mind, you don't necessarily have to cover every part of the skeleton with a piece of the model.

 It would be a good idea to save this model at this time making sure to save it to a name other than valve_skeleton.ms3d.

Our next step will be to use the extrude tool to add to our box. First change the upper right Viewport to Right. You can see this change in Figure 31.8.

Choose Select and Face from the Tools and Select Options menus respectively. You also need to make sure that Ignore Backface has been checked. Next, we draw a selection box around the shoulder area of the skeleton. You can see this selection being made in Figure 31.9.

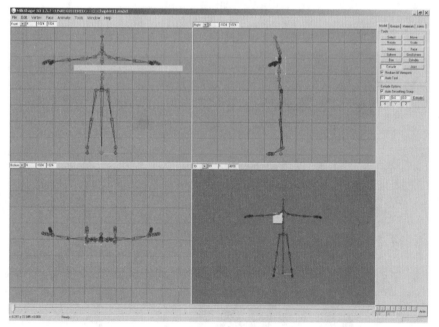

FIGURE 31.8 The upper right Viewport has been changed to Right.

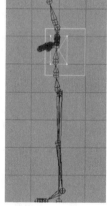

FIGURE 31.9 The selection tool is being used to select the entire face.

Make sure that you are selecting a face because we plan to use the extrude tool in later steps. MilkShape will do some strange things to your model if you try to extrude selected vertices.

Once you have selected the face (it should be highlighted in red), the next step is to use the Extrude tool to extend the box. Using the front Viewport, create an extrusion so that it is similar to Figure 31.10.

In Figure 31.10, you will notice that the "shoulder" area of our model appears to be lying too low on the skeleton. We can use the select tool (make sure Ignore Backfaces is unchecked) to select all vertices and then the move tool to move the selection up on the model in a manner similar to Figure 31.31.

The next step is to extrude the bottom edge of the area we have created. Choose Select and Face from their respective menus. Next, check the Ignore Backfaces option and draw a selection box around the bottom Viewport which can be seen in Figure 31.12.

You can now use the extrude tool to create the extrusion so that the model now appears like Figure 31.13.

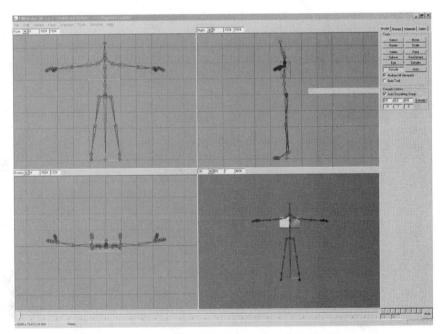

FIGURE 31.10   The face should be extruded so that it looks something like this.

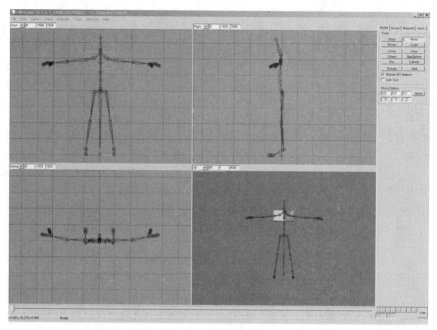

FIGURE 31.11 We need to move the selection to this area.

FIGURE 31.12 The faces we are selecting will be extruded.

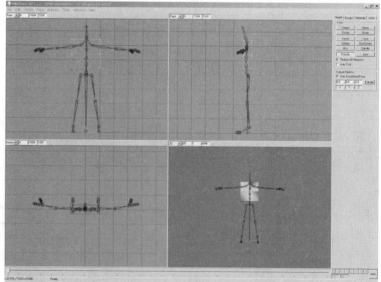

FIGURE 31.13 After extrusion, our model looks something like this.

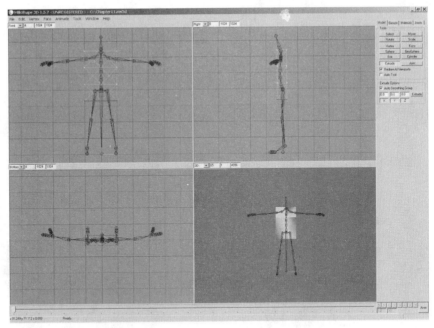

FIGURE 31.14   The extrusion is repeated.

Repeat the extrusion to create a "third row" of boxes. Figure 31.14 displays this step.

We'll finish this part of the model by moving several vertices to take away the "square" look. We are not going to spend a great deal of time with this but it is important that you understand how this can be accomplished. First, choose Select and Vertex from their menus, making sure that Ignore Backfaces is not selected.

Using the front Viewport, draw a selection rectangle around the lower right portion of the model. The selection can be seen in Figure 31.15.

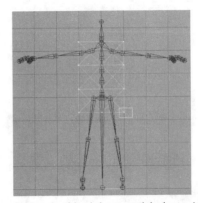

FIGURE 31.15   The selection should only be around the lower right portion of the model.

Once the vertices are selected, the next step is to choose Move. Again using the front Viewport, move the vertices so that the model looks like Figure 31.16.

Repeat the step for the opposite site to match Figure 31.17.

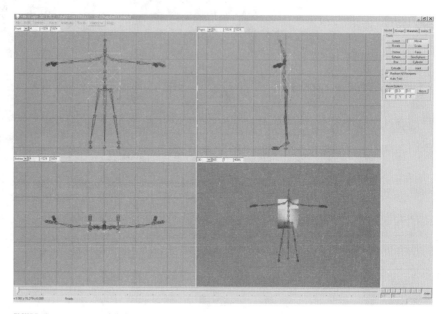

FIGURE 31.16 Your model should now look like this.

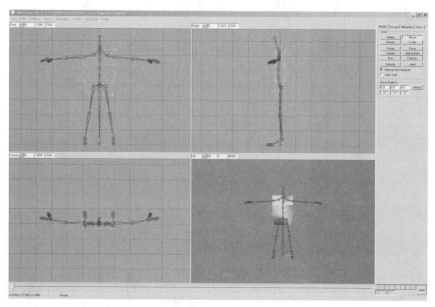

FIGURE 31.17 Moving the other side makes it symmetrical.

Creating Legs

The next step in the creation of our model is to create the legs. Begin this step by choosing Select and Face from their menus. Ignore Backfaces should be checked. Using the bottom Viewport (lower left of the MilkShape screen by default), hold down the Shift key and click the faces that are directly left of the center of the model. Figure 31.18 shows the areas highlighted in red.

Next, choose the Extrude tool and then create an extrusion like Figure 31.19.

Leaving the face selected, choose the Scale tool and then rescale it to create a large upper leg area. You can see the change in Figure 31.20.

Using the same ideas, extrude and scale another portion of the leg down to where the knee would approximately be. Figure 31.21 displays the scaling and extrusion.

We'll use the same steps to create two sections in the lower leg as well that will represent the increased size of the calf muscle and then the tapering down to the ankle. Figure 31.22 displays the model as it should appear after the step.

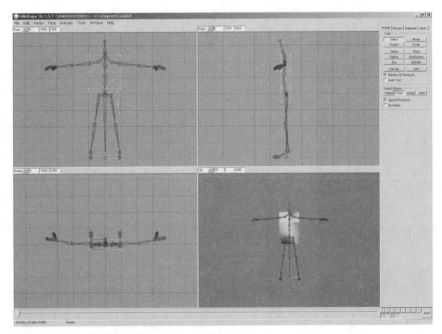

FIGURE 31.18   The highlighted area has been selected.

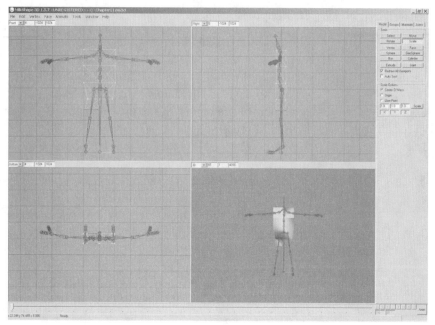

FIGURE 31.19   The beginning of our leg.

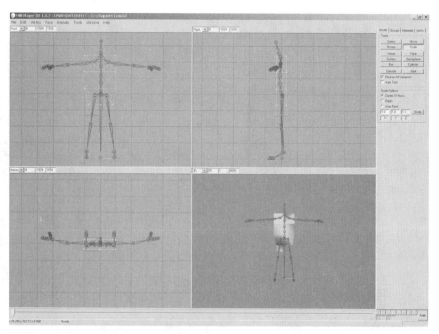

FIGURE 31.20   The upper leg has been scaled.

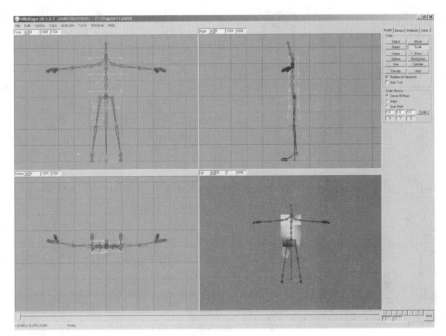

FIGURE 31.21   Scale and extrude were used again.

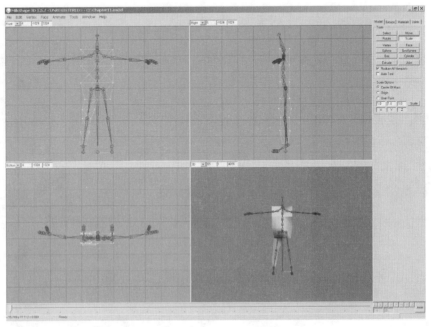

FIGURE 31.22   The model now has a lower leg.

The Foot

With the lower leg out of the way, our next step will be to create a foot. Continuing where we left off, we'll use the extrude tool to create the beginning area of a foot. Begin by extruding a straight segment down from the ankle. This can be seen in Figure 31.23.

Next, we choose the Select and Face tools and check the Ignore Backface option. Using the front Viewport, we need to select the face that will be extruded to create a foot. Hold down the Shift key and click to select the two faces seen highlighted in Figure 31.24.

Our next step is to use the extrude tool to create a length for the foot. You can see this in Figure 31.25.

Once the foot has been extruded, we need to choose Select and vertex. You should uncheck the Ignore Backface option and then draw a selection box around the upper front area of the foot. This can be seen in Figure 31.26.

The final step in the creation of the foot is to choose Move and then move the vertices slightly downward to create a slight angle for the foot. This can be seen in Figure 31.27.

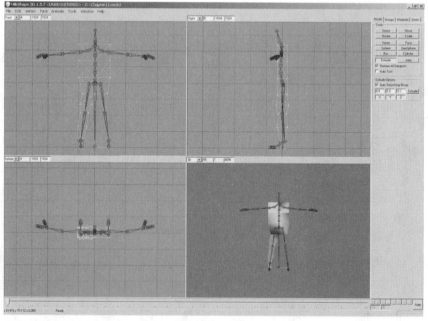

FIGURE 31.23   A foot begins to take shape.

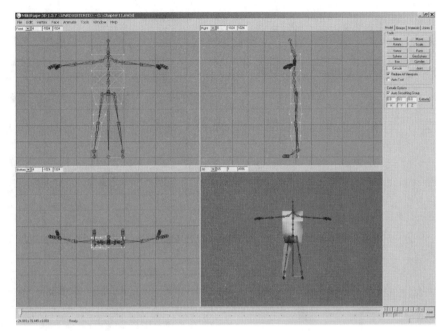

FIGURE 31.24   The face is selected.

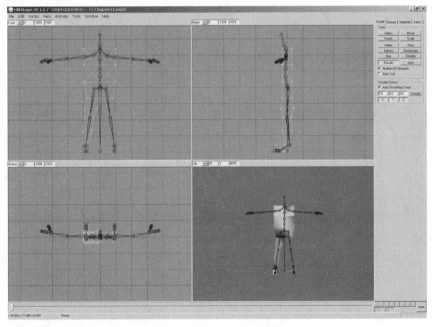

FIGURE 31.25   The foot has been extruded.

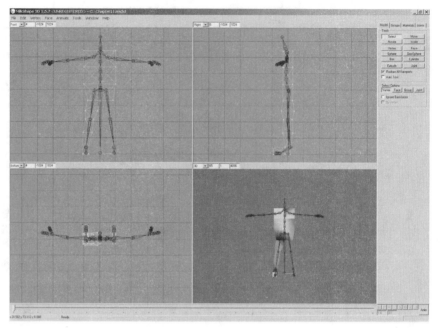

FIGURE 31.26 The vertices have been selected.

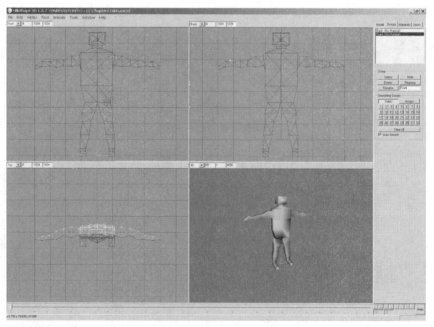

FIGURE 31.27 The foot is now finished.

Mirroring the Leg and Foot

We could repeat the steps to create another leg and foot but because we are at approximately the center of the skeleton, we can use another option mirroring. First, choose Select and Face from their respective menus. After making sure that the Ignore Backface option has been unchecked, you can draw a box around the leg to highlight it. The highlighted leg can be seen in Figure 31.28.

From the Edit menu, select Duplicate Selection. This menu can be seen in Figure 31.29.

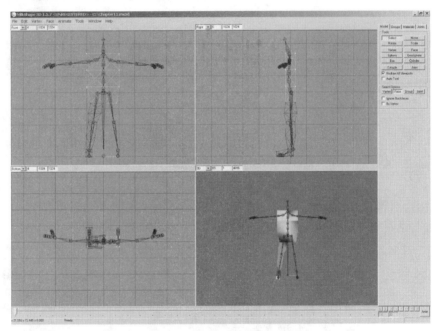

FIGURE 31.28 Selecting the entire leg is the first step towards mirroring it.

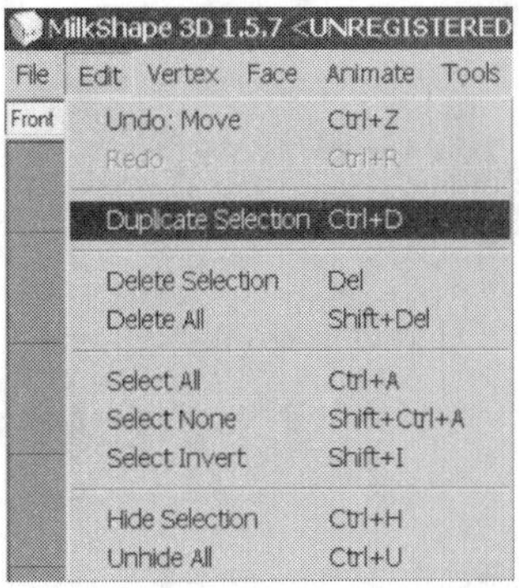

FIGURE 31.29 Choose Edit | Duplicate Selection.

FIGURE 31.30 The mirror option is located in the Vertex menu.

Strangely, nothing appears to have happened. However, if you now choose Mirror Left <——> Right from the Vertex menu, it will create an exact mirror. You can see the menu option in Figure 31.30

The mirrored leg, which can be seen in Figure 31.31, will appear at which time you can use the Move tool to move it left or right if necessary. This will only happen if you are slightly off center and should only be for a very small distance.

You can move the 3D Viewport at this time to see how the model is progressing. This can be seen in Figure 31.32.

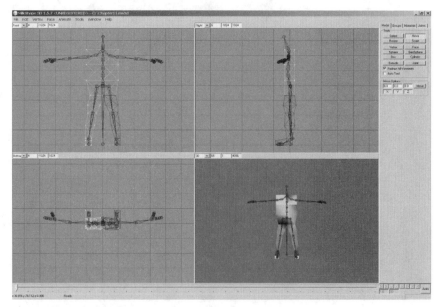

FIGURE 31.31 The leg appears as a perfect match.

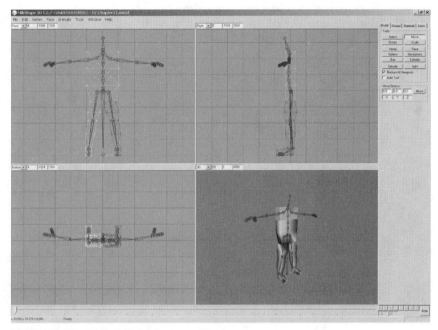

FIGURE 31.32   The 3D model is beginning to take shape.

Creating Arms

Now that the legs have been created, our next objective will be to create a neck, arms and shoulders for the model. We'll use the same basic approach that we used in the previous steps. That is, we'll use the Extrude, Scale and Move tools.

We'll begin this by changing the bottom View (in the lower left hand corner) to a Top View. You can see this in Figure 31.33.

Choose the Select tool and Face for the Select Option. You should also select Ignore Backfaces. Select the faces at the upper side of the model using the Top Viewport. You can see this in Figure 31.34.

After selecting the faces, you need to use the extrude tool so that you create a small area such as in Figure 31.35.

Use the Scale tool to resize the upper area so that the neck area has been scaled as can be seen in Figure 31.36.

We'll now create the left arm and then mirror it like the leg we did earlier. Select the left shoulder faces and then extrude them so that you create a very small area like in Figure 31.37.

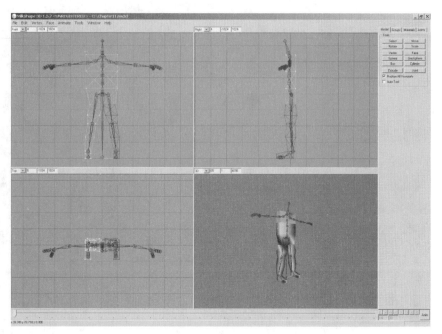

FIGURE 31.33   The lower left Viewport has been changed.

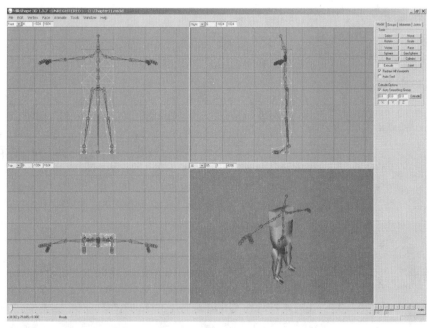

FIGURE 31.34   Select these faces.

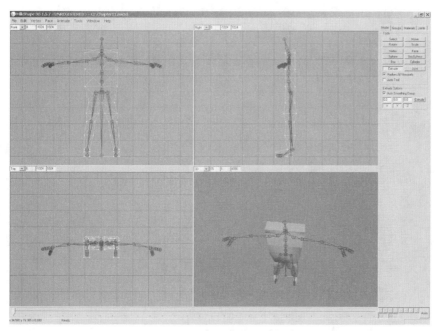

FIGURE 31.35   Extrusion is the next step.

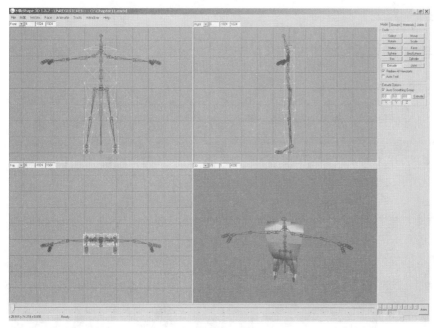

FIGURE 31.36   This very simple neck is now finished.

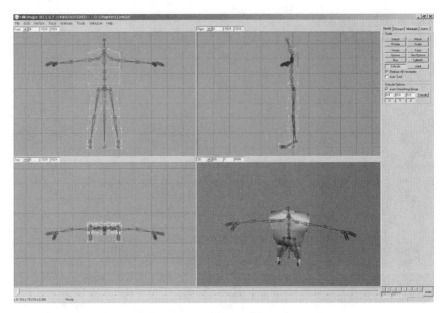

FIGURE 31.37   We create a small shoulder area in this step.

Next, use the scale tool and then create another extrusion. After the extrusion, which ends at the middle of the upper arm, use the scale tool again to enlarge the area. These steps should appear similarly to Figure 31.38.

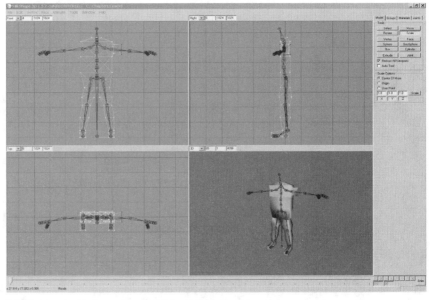

FIGURE 31.38   At this time, your model should look like this.

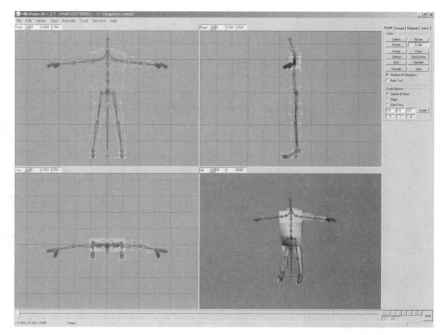

FIGURE 31.39 The arm should look like this.

Now that you have an idea of how the arm is going to take shape, we'll create the rest of it down to the wrist by continuing to extrude and scale the areas. Figure 31.39 displays the arm as it will look when you have finished it to the wrist.

Although you have probably tired of the same routines by this time, the creation of the hand will involve the same tasks. Extrude a section and the scale as necessary. We won't create fingers for this model so two sections for a hand is all that we'll need. You can see the finished hand in Figure 31.40.

You can now use the Select tool and draw a selection box around the entire arm. You can then duplicate and mirror like we did the leg. Figures 31.41 and 31.42 display these steps.

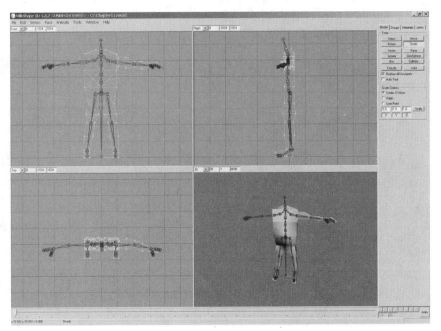

FIGURE 31.40 The arm is now finished.

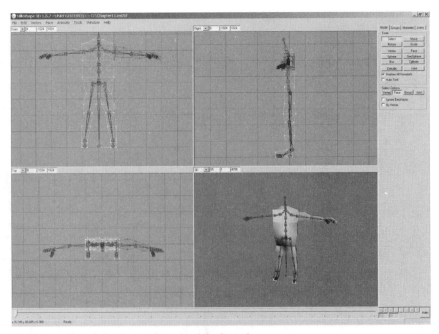

FIGURE 31.41 The arm has been selected and duplicated.

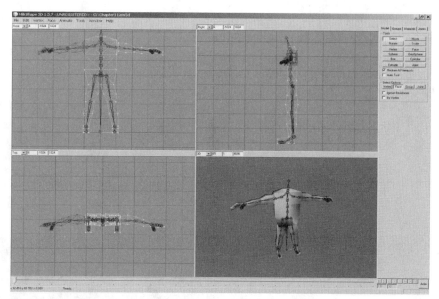

FIGURE 31.42   Mirroring the arm is completed.

Creating the Head

While we could approach the creation of the head several ways it is probably the easiest to continue using the same extrusion / resize methods. We'll begin by selecting the faces at the top of neck. This can be seen in Figure 31.43.

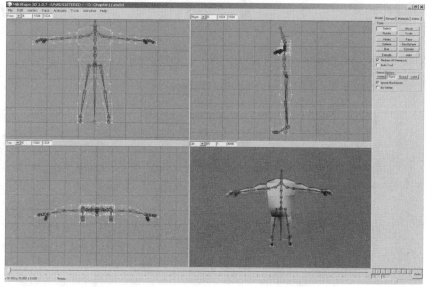

FIGURE 31.43   The neck has been selected.

Extrude the selected faces so that the neck appears like Figure 31.44. Create another extrusion about the same size and then scale it so that it looks like Figure 31.45.

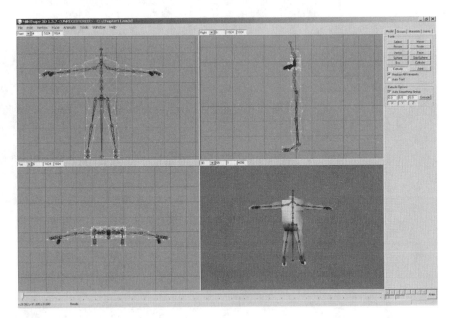

FIGURE 31.44   Extrude the faces.

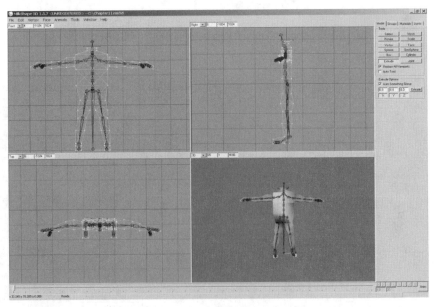

FIGURE 31.45   The neck and lower part of the face are completed in this step.

Next, extrude the neck to create a square head for the humanoid. Select the front face of the head so that we can extrude a small section. Figure 31.46 displays the figure after the two extrusions.

Scale the newest extrusion so that it creates a more rounded appearance like Figure 31.47.

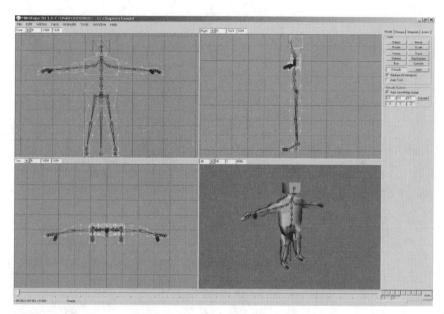

FIGURE 31.46   The two extrusions make up the majority of the face and head.

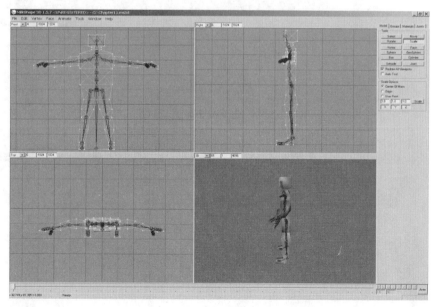

FIGURE 31.47   Creating a more rounded appearance for the face.

Our next step is to create another extrusion and then scale it so that we can create something similar to a nose. It can be seen in Figure 31.48.

The last step for our head is to create a more rounded appearance for the rest of the head using the same procedures. The final version can be seen in Figure 31.49.

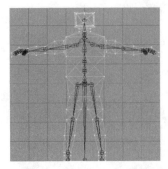

FIGURE 31.48 The face is now finished.

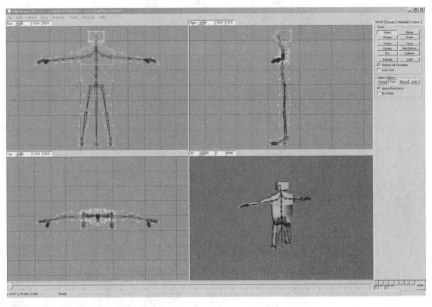

FIGURE 31.49 The head in its final state.

Texturing the Model

The next step is to create a texture for the model. This isn't too difficult to accomplish as we will simply divide the model into two groups, a front and a back. The first step is to hide the skeleton so that it is easier to see the model. Select the Joints tab and then deselect the Show Skeleton option. Next, select the Group tab in MilkShape. You may have several names displayed as groups but don't concern yourself with them.

It would probably be a good idea to save your model at this time with a new name so that if you make a mistake, you can simply revert back to the old model.

Now, select Edit | Select All to select every face on the model and click the Regroup button. Your screen should look something like Figure 31.50.

The previously visible groups will be replaced with a single group. In the upper left Viewport, make sure that it is set to Front. Next, hold down Shift key and the right mouse button and then draw a selection box around the front view of the model. This will deselect the front faces. You can see this in Figure 31.51.

Click the Regroup button. This will create a new group name. Select Edit | Select Invert. This will invert the selection allowing you to group only

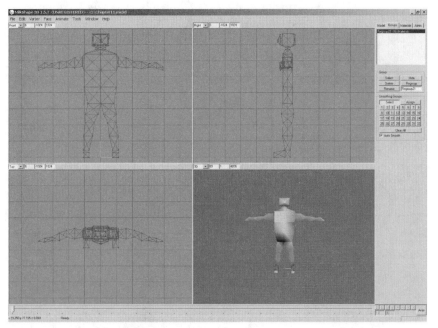

FIGURE 31.50   The model has everything selected.

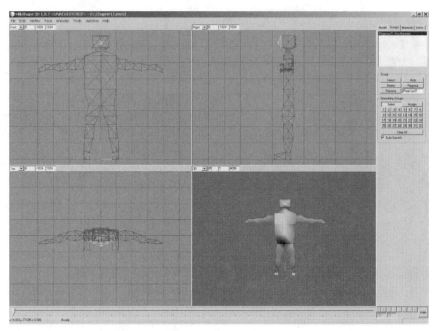

FIGURE 31.51 The front faces have been deselected.

the front faces. Click the regroup button which will now bring you to two distinct groups, a front and a back. You can rename the groups so that they are named appropriately.

CREATING A TEMPLATE

The next step is to create a template we can use to draw our texture. Change the upper right Viewport to back and then click the Print Screen button. This will take a screen shot of the current image which can be seen in Figure 31.52.

Open Paint Shop Pro and then select Edit | Paste as New Image. Your image will be displayed in Paint Shop Pro similarly to Figure 31.53.

Select Edit | Copy in Paint Shop Pro to copy the selection to the Clipboard. Next, choose Edit | Paste as New Image. You will see the image, an example of which can be seen in Figure 31.54, in Paint Shop Pro. It is this image that will eventually become the template for the first half of our model. Repeat the process for the back view.

Both sides of the template are virtually identical, so we could have used the same image for both sides.

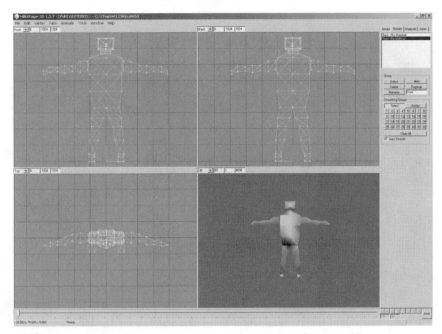

FIGURE 31.52   The upper left and upper right Viewports will be used for our template.

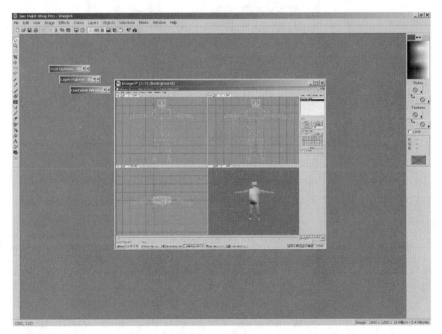

FIGURE 31.53   You can paste the image into Paint Shop Pro.

FIGURE 31.54   The first template has been created.

Before moving on, we'll resize both images. Choose Image | Resize and then type 256 into the Width. The Height will automatically be resized accordingly. Do the same for the other image and then save both of them.

Choose Layer | New Raster Layer to create a new layer on the front and back templates. This will allow us to draw over them without actually editing the template. We now will begin to paint our skin.

Painting the Template

To begin painting, choose the Paintbrush from the toolbar. Next, choose a style such as Cement and then a brown color that is a shade of gray. Paint the image so that you cover most of the areas. Figure 31.55 displays the way the figures should look at this time.

Like the model, this is a very simple texture. You can add as little or as much detail to it as you'd like. For our purposes, we'll simply add some green "eyes" and a different style to the hands and shoes.

To create the eyes, we'll set the paintbrush to a width of 30, a hardness of 100 and the style to "Green Emerald." Position the brush where you think the eyes would approximately be and single click in each position. The next step is to change the style to Light Streaks and paint the

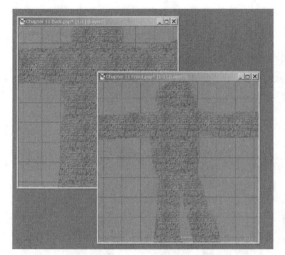

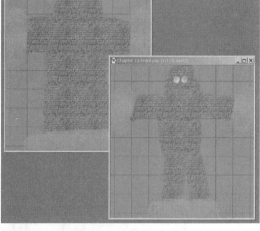

FIGURE 31.55   The template begins to turn into a skin.

FIGURE 31.56   The skins are nearly finished.

hands and feet area of both images. Your templates should now look something similar to Figure 31.56.

Once you have the skins where you'd like, you can save them to a format MilkShape can use such as JPG. This will convert the images to a single layer at the same time. Although it will not affect your final skin, you can remove the bottom layers before saving them to give a cleaner final skin.

 The Half-Life MDL format requires the skins to be saved in 8-bit format. You can change the number of colors in Paint Shop Pro by choosing Color | Decrease Color Depth.

Importing Into MilkShape

Once the skins have been saved in JPG format, we can move back to Milk-Shape and import them onto the model. We begin by selecting the Groups tab. You should make sure the Front group is highlighted and then click the Select button. Your model should appear like Figure 31.57.

Next, click the Materials tab. Click the New button and a material will automatically be created. Rename the material to Front and then click the top of the two buttons that says <None>. From the Open Image box, select the Front JPG image we created. Right-click the lower right hand Viewport and make sure that it is set to Textured. Click the Assign button. You should see your imported skin appear very small inside the model, something like Figure 31.58.

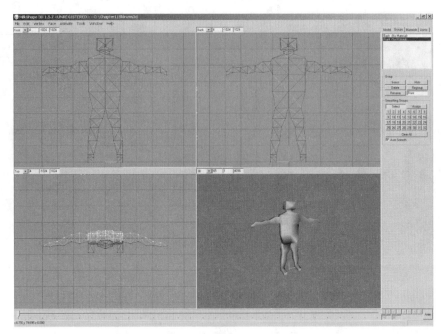

FIGURE 31.57   Your model should look like this when you click Select.

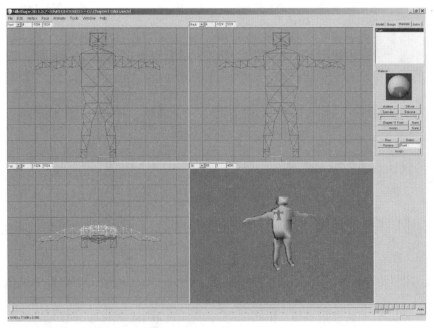

FIGURE 31.58   The material needs to be resized.

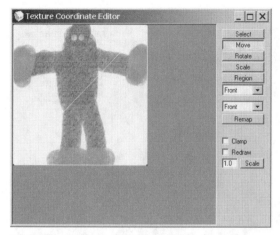

FIGURE 31.59 The Texture Coordinate Editor allows you to position the texture.

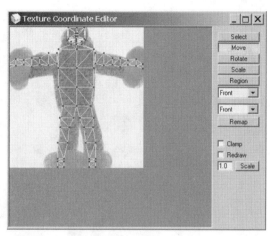

FIGURE 31.60 Position your model so that the texture aligns properly.

Select Window | Texture Coordinate Editor. From both drop down boxes, choose Front. Your window should look something like Figure 31.59.

Next, click the Remap button. The Texture Coordinate Editor should now display the outline of your model as can be seen in Figure 31.60. From here, you can accurately position the texture.

When you are finished, close the window. Your model should now look like Figure 31.61.

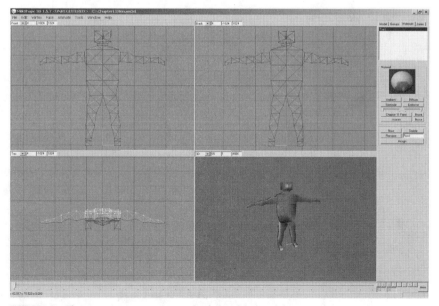

FIGURE 31.61 The texture now appears on the front of the model.

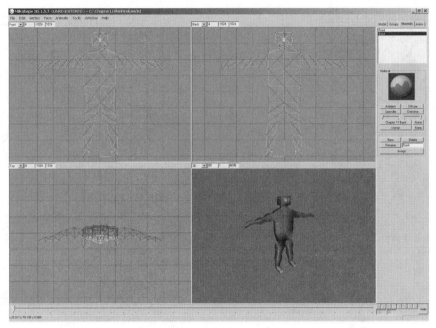

FIGURE 31.62   The finished texture on the model.

Repeat the entire process for the back of your model. When finished, the model will look like Figure 31.62.

 If the texture didn't line up properly or needs some adjusting, you can alter it an then repeat the steps as necessary.

BASICS OF ANIMATION

In order to animate a model in MilkShape we must first assign the bones to areas of the mesh model that we have created. For example, we need to assign the right calf area to the bone called Bip01 R Calf. We'll assign each of the bones in the skeleton to areas of the mesh and then use a series of animated files that have already been created to compile the model into a final MDL file.

To begin, let's click the Joints tab and display the skeleton that we had previously hidden. Once inside the Joints tab, click the Show Skeleton option which will display the entire skeleton. You'll also notice that the tab displays a list of each of the bones contained in the skeleton. If you click one of the bones, it will select it so that we can assign it to the mesh. You

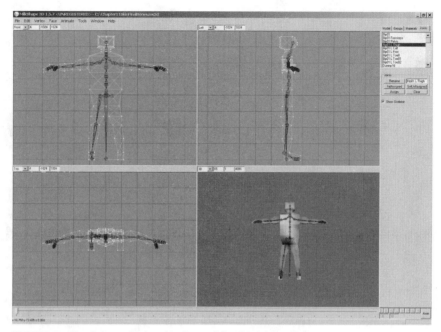

FIGURE 31.63   The skeleton displayed in the model with a selected bone.

will see the bone that has been selected as it will change color from blue to green as you can see in Figure 31.63.

You'll remember that our model is basically a bunch of simple blocks. Although we could have added a great deal of detail to it, we instead built it with simplicity in mind. Therefore, we have not added individual toes and fingers. With that in mind, we'll begin the assignment of our bones by selecting the bone named Bip 01 L Foot. This should select the left foot and all bones in it. Next, click the Model tab. You need to click the Select tool and the face option making sure that Ignore Backfaces is not selected. Using the Front Viewport, you need to draw a selection box around the left foot. After selecting the correct faces, go back to the Joints tab and then click Assign. This will assign the selected faces to the bone.

We'll now repeat the process moving up the leg to the Bip 01 L Calf bone. You should draw your selection this time around the calf area but not including the areas you previously selected. Your model should look like Figure 31.64 after the assignment.

You need to repeat this process for the rest of the model, assigning every bone to the appropriate areas. It's an involved process, and once you have finished, you should save it to a new filename thus protecting your previous and current work. This will allow you to return to the model with unassigned bones if you need to.

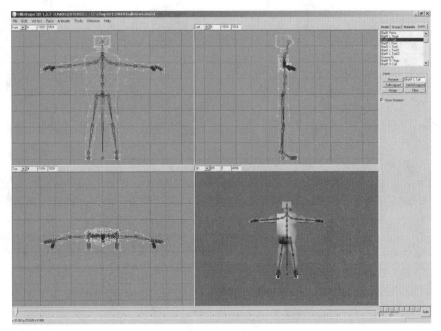

FIGURE 31.64 The bones have been assigned to the model.

Compiling the Model

After you have assigned the various bones to the model, the next step is to save the model as an SMD file. Before doing so, you should save it in the MilkShape format to protect your work. The saving of the SMD file is accomplished by choosing File | Export Half-Life SMD.

The CD-ROM contains a directory called PlayerMDL that contains a list of animations in SMD format and a .QC file. Copy all of these files and the SMD file you exported form MilkShape into the C\PlayerMDL directory. The next step is to compile the files into an MDL by choosing Tools | Half-Life | Compile .QC File. The QC file is located in the PlayerMDL directory and is named Player.QC. If everything has been created correctly, you will find the final model in the PlayerMDL directory. It will be named Player.MDL.

 If you're really interested in model creation, you should take the time to download the Half-Life SDK from www.valve.com. *It contains reference files and information about a wide range of models. Additionally, Appendix B in the book contains some information and sample .qc scripts for Half-Life models.*

CONCLUSION

In this chapter, we learned how to build and skin a model using MilkShape and Paint Shop Pro. We also discovered some basic information about the Half-Life model format and how to animate it using already built SMD files.

A

DESIGN DOCUMENT: FIRST PERSON SHOOTER

Document written by John Doe
Version # 1.20
September 25, 2001
Copyright 2001 by ABC Gaming. All Rights Reserved.

Design History

This is Version 1.20 of the document which began on January 15, 2001.

Version 1.10

For example, you can use Version 1.10, 1.20, etc.

1. Changed platforms for game. Added Mac OSX.
2. Graphics are now 32 bit.

Version 1.20

The story has now been rewritten.

1. Details of story now changed.
2. Enemy character is now a humanoid model.

Game Overview

Type of Game

This game is a 3D shooter with . . . .

Game Ideas

This game has been in the process of creation for many years. The idea has been tossed around for the past 5 and has been revised many times. We felt that it was the proper time for such a release.

Location

The game takes place on an uninhabited island. You are surrounded by rocky ledges and water for as far as the eye can see.

Players

You will control the main character in the story from a first-person perspective. You will begin the game with a rifle and additional weapons are available throughout the level.

Main Objective

Your objective is to get off the island.

Game Overview

This game takes a slightly different approach to the development of First Person Shooters in that instead of blasting your way through a level destroying everything in sight, you must also figure out a way to get off the island.

Features

General Features

- Large terrains
- 3D graphics
- 32-bit color
- Several types of enemies

Multiplayer Features

- N/A
- Might implement in Version 2.0

Editor

- No world editor at this time but planned for Version 2.1.
- Free levels on the Net.

The Game World

Overview

An island that is uninhabited and without an obvious means of escape.

Key Locations

- There is a cave on the south side of the island that has health.
- The creek that runs throughout the island is the quickest way to travel.
- There is a boat at the bottom of the lagoon. A repair kit is also inside it.

Objects

- A boat for getting off the island.
- Food such as bananas that give you energy.
- Old health kits from a ship wreck.
- Weapons.

Graphics

Rendering / 3D Engine

The renderings will be 3D with polygonal models based on the Half-Life model format. It will be a FPS view without the ability to move the camera in any way. The game utilizes the TrueVision 3D engine which is based on DirectX 8.

Game Characters

Main Character

There is only a single main character in the game.

Enemies

There will be several enemies that you'll encounter:
- Mummy
- Dracula
- Etc.

Weapons

Types

There are several types of weapons on the island including a rifle, hand-gun, machine gun, and laser gun.

Musical and Sound Effects

Music

The game will use wav files created with ACID.

Sound PDesign

The sound effects include basic information about the weapons being fired and the foot steps when walking.

Appendix ABC

Any additional information. . . . Ideas include:

User Interface

The basic user interface will consist of 3 menus, …

Character Rendering and Animation

For characters, we plan to use MD2 files …

B THE KEY POSITIONS IN A DEVELOPMENT TEAM

A s was previously mentioned, a development project is made up several key positions. Without any of these, it would not be successful. That being said, depending on the size of your team, a single individual may be forced to wear many hats, or in the case of the lone developer, all of the hats. That is, although all of the positions are required, a single individual may fill one or all of them.

Because the game industry is still in its infancy, it's sometimes difficult to discuss the positions that make up a team. The type of game being produced definitely also has a profound effect on the required personnel. Every development project is arranged differently. As the industry matures, there will certainly bemore standard types of arrangements. But until that occurs, we are stuck trying to explain most of the potential positions.

Designer

Many development projects have a lead game designer who is responsible for the creation of the game script. However, this position is often one of the most misunderstood of any of the key positions and is often left completely off the team. This leaves room for everyone, from the producer to programmers, clamoring for the title.

It is the designer who makes many of the decisions related to the creation of important aspects such as puzzles, or the levels in a FPS. Like a screenwriter for a movie, the designer is responsible for the overall feel of the game. Communication is a very important aspect of this job, as designers work with the other team members throughout the duration of a project.

In the beginning stages of a game, designers spend most of their time focusing on writing short scripts and working on the beginning storyboard sketches. A typical storyboard displays the action of a game, in a very simple manner. Depending on the basic talents of the designer, the storyboard may even include stick figures and basic shapes to convey the action. Storyboards are a sort of rough draft that will later be transformed into the game itself.

After the decisions have been made on the game concepts, the designers begin working on a blueprint for the game, called a *design document*. Simply put, the document details every aspect of a game and will evolve as the game is being developed.

Programmer

Game programmers are software developers who take the ideas, art, and music and combine them into a software project. Programmers obviously write the code for the game, but they may also have several additional responsibilities. For instance, if an artist is designing graphics for the game, the lead programmer could be responsible for the development of a custom set of tools for creating the graphics. It is also the lead programmer's job to keep everything running smoothly and to somehow figure out a way to satisfy everyone, from the producer to the artists. Unlike the stereotype portrayed on many Web sites, books, or even movies, programmers usually don't stroll into work at noon, work for a few hours, and then leave. The truth is, they often arrive earlier and leave later than anyone else on the development team.

Programmers are responsible for taking the vast number of elements and combining them to form the executable program. They decide how fast characters can run, and how high they can jump. They are responsible for accounting for everything inside of the virtual world. While doing all of this, they often will attempt to create software that can be reusable for other projects, and spend a great deal of time optimizing the code to make it is as fast as possible.

Sometimes, a given project may have several programmers who specialize in one key area, such as graphics, sound, or artificial intelligence (AI). The following list details the various types of programmers and what they are primarily responsible for:

- **Engine or Graphics Programmers:** They create the software that controls how graphics and animations are stored and ultimately displayed on the screen.

- **AI Programmers:** They create a series of rules that determine how enemies or characters will react to game situations and attempt to make them act as realistically as possible.
- **Sound Programmers:** They work with the audio personnel to create a realistic-sounding environment.
- **Tool Programmers:** As previously mentioned, programmers often write software for artists, designers, and sound designers to use within the development studio.

Audio Related Positions

High quality music and sound effects are an integral part in any gaming project. This is also an area that many teams simply cannot afford to throw a great deal of money at. Having superb audio components like music, sound, and voice can greatly enhance the total experience for the consumer. The opposite is also true, however. Music that is done poorly can be keep people away from your product, regardless of its other qualities. The positions listed below are usually filled by key audio personnel, although sometimes a programmer or other team member will fill in, as needed.

Musician

When compared with the stress and long hours of the programmers, musicians are often at the other end of the workload. They often have the least amount of work of any of the positions on the team. That's not to imply that they don't work hard; it's just that there isn't as much for them to do. They usually are responsible only for the music for a game. While this is an important job, it doesn't typically take a great deal of time, compared with the other team members' jobs. Because of the relatively short production times, musicians often have secondary work outside of the gaming industry.

Sound Effects

Depending on the makeup of a team, a musician could be involved with the creation of the sound effects in a game. This can often make up for the lack of work that they have and help to keep the budgets down. Another route that many teams choose to follow is the purchase of pre-existing sound effects. There are many sound effects companies that distribute their work on CD-ROMs or the Internet. Many teams choose to purchase the sounds produced by these companies, and alter them to their liking.

Art Related Positions

Artist

The artists are responsible for creating the graphics elements that make up a project. They often specialize in one area within a project, such as 3D graphics, or 2D artwork such as textures. The artists usually work from a set of specifications given to them by the programmer. Unfortunately, artists and programmers often have many disagreements on these specifications. For instance, artists might want to increase the polygon counts on a 3D model so that their work will look better, while programmers may want to decrease these same counts, to make the program run more smoothly.

Game artists have a variety of technical constraints, imposed by the limitations of the hardware that they are creating for. Although hardware continues to increase in speed and go down in cost, there is never enough power to satisfy a development project. Therefore, it is often the artists who are given the responsibility to create objects that work within the constraints.

Depending on the development team, there are three basic types of artists: character artists (or animators, as some prefer to be called), 3D modelers, and texture artists.

Character Artist

Character artists have one of the most demanding jobs on the team. They create all of the moveable objects in a game, such as the main character, a space ship or a vehicle. It is their job to turn the preliminary sketches that are often discussed by the entire team into a believable object on a computer screen.

Using 3D modeling tools like 3D Studio Max™, TrueSpace®, Maya®, or LightWave™, character artists use basic shapes and combine them to form characters. If you have never used a 3D-modeling program, you can think of it as a type of digital clay. Once created, characters are fleshed out with a 2D graphic image that is made in another program.

The character artists are also responsible for the animation of the objects. They may be required to animate a horse, a human being, or a creature that previously existed only in someone's mind. Character artists often look at real world examples to get their ideas on how a character should move. Depending on the type of game, they may have to create facial expressions, or emotions, as well.

It's often the responsibility of a character artist to implement cut scenes in a game, as well. Many artists enjoy creating cut screens even more than creating the characters in the game. They have much greater freedom and are not restricted as to the number of polygons a certain object can have, or the size of the object.

3D Modeler

The 3D modeler usually works on the settings in which a game takes place, such as a basketball arena or a Wild West wasteland. They work hand in hand with the designer to create believable environments that work within the constraints of a game. Like character artists, they use a wide range of tools for their jobs, including both 2D and 3D graphics tools, although they usually only model static objects.

Texture Artist

Texture artists might be the best friend of the other artists. It is their job to take the work created by the modeler or character artist and add detail to it. For example, they could create a brick texture that when added to a 3D box created by the modeler, creates the illusion of a pile of bricks. On the other hand, they could create a texture that looks like cheese, turning this same box into a block of cheese.

Producer

A producer oversees the entire project and attempts to keep everything moving along as smoothly as possible. A producer often acts as an arbitrator to help patch up any problems between team members. For instance, if an artist wants to increase the color palette and a programmer wants to decrease it, the producer often makes the final decision on these types of key issues.

Secondary Positions

There are several secondary positions that can be important to the development cycle, as well. Depending on the budget, these positions may or may not exist at all or could be filled by other members of the team.

Beta Tester

Beta testers test the playability of a game and look for bugs that may occur when the game is executed. This is one of the most undervalued of the positions and should never be done by the person responsible for programming the game. In reality, because of tight budgets and deadlines, beta testing is one of the steps that is often cut before it is completed, as due dates will unfortunately take precedence over most decisions. If adequate beta testing is performed, a development team can save a tremendous amount of time and resources without having to produce unnecessary patches at a later date.

Play Testers

The play testers are often confused with beta testers. The difference is that play testers only test the *playability* of a game. They often critique areas such as movement or graphic elements. Again, these positions are often filled by people who perform other tasks on the team. Unlike beta testers, play testers do not attempt to find or report bugs. Their purpose is to judge if a game is fun to play.

C

LINKS TO GAME PROGRAMMING WEB SITES AND NEWSGROUPS

LINKS TO WEB SITES

Snok Game Project
http://tihlde.org/~torbjorv/snok/
A 3D snake game, complete with source code.

Java Game Development Center
http://www.electricfunstuff.com/jgdc/
Java game development.

GameInstitute
http://www.gameinstitute.com/
Online game development courses!

Delphi Gamer / Development
http://www.savagesoftware.com.au/DelphiGamer/indexf.php
A site dedicated to Delphi game development.

Filipe's Page of Game Programming
http://www.mindlick.com/programming/
Various tutorials.

2D Game Programming
http://www.2dgame.nl/
Good 2D Site.

Damberg.de Game Programming

http://www.damberg.de/
A VB game programming site.

Lucky's VB Gaming Site

http://rookscape.com/vbgaming/
One of the best!

The Nexus

http://www.thenexus.bc.ca/
Another excellent VB site.

Amit's Game Programming Site

http://www-cs-students.stanford.edu/~amitp/gameprog.html
Information on path-finding—more.

Game Developer's Conference

http://www.gdconf.com/
Home of the GDC—not much else to say.

Darwin3D GD Section

http://www.darwin3d.com/gamedev.htm
A collection of useful articles from *Game Developer Magazine*.

Java Game Development Center

http://www.electricfunstuff.com/jgdc/
Source code, theory, and other resources related to Java development.

Game Design Web Sites

http://www.cs.queensu.ca/~dalamb/Games/design/gameDesignSites.
This is simply a collection of game development resources on the
Internet.

Mr-GameMaker.Com

http://www.mr-gamemaker.co.uk/
Mr-GameMaker.Com features tutorials on topics related to game
development, including some fairly hard to find D3D information.

CFXWeb

http://cfxweb.planet-d.net/
CFXWeb is a game programming and demo news site. It's updated quite
often and features some good tutorials, links, and other related features.
Definitely worth a look.

Golgotha Source Code

http://www.jitit.com/golgotha/

When Crack.Com went under, they released the source code to their project, Golgotha. The entire game engine, art, and so on is available for download.

Gamasutra

http://www.gamasutra.com/

Gamasutra is *Game Developer Magazine's* Web site.

Mad Monkey

http://www.madmonkey.net

Mad Monkey focuses on the independent gaming scene. There you'll find information on projects currently in the works, programming tutorials, message forums, and plenty more.

Game Programming Megasite

http://www.perplexed.com/GPMega/index.htm

Tutorials and information.

Pawn's Game Programming Pages

http://www.aros.net/~npawn/

Rex Sound Programming Engine.

The New Game Programmer's Guild

http://pages.vossnet.de/mgricken/newgpg/

Large Web ring for development sites.

GameProgrammer.Com

http://www.gameprogrammer.com/

Mostly old information.

GameDev.Net

http://www.gamedev.net

Articles, news, links, and more.

Game Development Search Engine

http://www.game-developer.com/

Search engine for game developers.

Linux Game Development Center

http://sunsite.auc.dk/linuxgames/

As the name says—mostly Linux materials.

flipCode

http://www.flipcode.com

Another highly recommended site!

LINKS TO NEWSGROUPS

Language Groups

comp.lang.asm.x86
x86 assembly language.

comp.lang.c
The C programming language.

comp.lang.c.moderated
Not much traffic, but good.

microsoft.public.vb
VB language.

microsoft.public.vb
VB language and DirectX.

microsoft.public.vb.winapi.graphics
Graphics and VB.

borland.public.delphi
Delphi Language.

borland.public.delphi.graphics
Delphi graphics.

macromedia.director.lingo
Director information.

Graphics Groups

comp.graphics.algorithms
BSP trees to texture mapping.

AI Groups

comp.ai.games
This newsgroup has useful info.

Game Groups

rec.games.programmer
Probably the most popular general newsgroup.

rec.games.design
Designing games.

D WHAT'S ON THE CD-ROM

The **Awesome Game Creation's** companion CD-ROM is packed with everything you need to make all of the fully interactive games in this book—and more! Each of the folders includes useful tools for you to learn game creation!

General Minimum System Requirements: You will need a computer that can run Windows 95 with a CD-ROM drive, sound card, and mouse to complete *all* of the tutorials and play all of the games in this book.

Included applications are contained in the Applications directory. The following descriptions detail which folder they are in and give some basic information about each application:

- **Game Maker 4** (http://www.cs.ruu.nl/people/markov/gmaker/) Full Version
  This application is included in the Gamemaker folder. You can get additional graphics freely for this program from the Web site.

- **The 3D Gamemaker** (www.the3dgamemaker.com) Demo Version
  It is contained in the 3DGamemaker folder. Everything is included in the installation file.

- **The Games Factory by Clickteam** (www.clickteam.com) Trial
  There are two folders on the ROM (TGF FINAL 16 and TGF FINAL 32) and each includes either the 16 Bit (Win 3.1 and NT) or the 32 Bit (Windows 95/98/2000) install files for the respective version of *The Games Factory*. The proper file will install everything you need to run *The Games Factory*. As long as you can run Windows or Windows NT, you can run *The Games Factory*.

- **The PIE 3D Game Creation System by Pie in the Sky Software** (www.pieskysoft.com) Full Version (1.13b) and Trial Version (3.0) With The PIECGS you can make your own stand alone 3D games with no programming. The (the 'PieGCS' folder on the ROM). Simply run the installer and you are in business. This application was designed to run on a 386 or better computer with a VGA graphics card. The best part of the PIEGCS is that it is free! The only limit being that there is no technical support, but on the Web site (www.pieskysoft.com) there is technical support files and information. You can also join the mailing list at www.gcsgames.com and get all the help you need.

- **Cool Edit 200 (www.syntrillium.com) Trial Version** Trial version of the popular audio editing application.

- **MilkShape 3D (http://www.swissquake.ch/chumbalum-soft/) Trial Version 1.510** A great and easy to use 3D modeler.

- **Paint Shop Pro 7 (www.jasc.com) Trial** Useful for creating 2D artwork for your games.

- **gmax (www.discreet.com) Full** A level building application that allows you to modify commercially available games. Depending on the available game packs, you can create new levels, characters or almost any imaginable object using gmax, which is based on the industry standard 3D Studio Max.

- **Sample Game Files** In the 'Examples' folder of the ROM are all the files and assets used in the exercises in the book in part 2. Please note that all needed assets are within the respective files.

- **Example Games folder**

1. Defiler
   spacedel2.gam
2. Dragon
   dragon.gam
3. Ghost Hunter
   GhostHunter.gam
4. tgflibs
   Dragon.gam
   GhostHunter.gam
   Spacedel2.gam

INDEX